DIVIDED WE STAND

Also by Roger Thompson

Mobility and Migration:
East Anglian Founders of New England,
1629–1640

Sex in Middlesex:
Popular Mores in a Massachusetts County,
1649–1699

Divided We Stand

Watertown, Massachusetts, 1630–1680

ROGER THOMPSON

University of Massachusetts Press
AMHERST

Copyright © 2001 by Roger Thompson
All rights reserved
Printed in the United States of America
LC 2001017154
ISBN 1-55849-304-2

Designed by Jack Harrison
Set in Adobe Garamond with Goudy display by Graphic Composition, Inc.
Printed and bound by Sheridan Books, Inc.

Library of Congress Cataloging-in-Publication Data

Thompson, Roger, 1933–
   Divided we stand : Watertown, Massachusetts, 1630–1680 / Roger Thompson.
   p. cm.
   Includes bibliographical references and index.
   ISBN 1-55849-304-2 (alk. paper)
   1. Watertown (Mass.)—History—17th century.
   2. Watertown (Mass.)—Politics and government—17th century.
   3. Watertown (Mass.)—Social conditions—17th century.
   4. Frontier and pioneer life—Massachusetts—Watertown. I. Title.

F74.W33 T48 2001
974.4'4—dc21

2001017154

British Library Cataloguing in Publication data are available.

For
David, Norman, and Winnie
with deep affection and gratitude

CONTENTS

MAPS ix
ACKNOWLEDGMENTS xi
INTRODUCTION xiii

PART I · NEW WORLD FROM OLD
1. *The Lie of the Land* 3
2. *The Peopling of Early Watertown, 1630–1640* 11
3. *The View from the Stour* 20

PART II · FOUNDATIONS
4. *Government* 37
5. *Land* 51
6. *Religion* 64

PART III · ECONOMY
7. *Living with Livestock* 83
8. *Livelihood: The Town's Economy* 92

PART IV · CARE IN THE COMMUNITY
9. *Welfare* 107
10. *The Rising Generation* 116
11. *The Family* 126

PART V · REINFORCING CONSENSUS

12. *Invisible Indians* 143
13. *"Foreigners" and Community* 156

CONCLUSION
Continuity and Change, Decline and Discord 164

APPENDIX A: *Case Studies* 177
APPENDIX B: *Lists of Residents* 199
ABBREVIATIONS 203
NOTES 207
INDEX 259

MAPS

1. *Early Watertown*   4

2. *The Original Watertown Grant*   6

3. *English Origins*   13

4. *Essex and Suffolk Border*   16

5. *Watertown Land Grants, 1630–42*   52

ACKNOWLEDGMENTS

I wish to thank the following individuals for their help: Julia Albert, Bob Anderson, Jerry Anderson, Elizabeth Bouvier, Frank Bremer, Ann Cook, David Dearborn, Peter Drummey, David Hall, Barbara MacAllan, Simon Middleton, Norman Pettit, Pamela Ross, Winnie Rothenberg, Melinde Sanborn, Kenneth Stuckey, David Thackeray, Oriel Thompson, David Waddington, Conrad Wright, and Laetitia Yeandle.

I am grateful for the assistance given by the staff of the following institutions: Charles River Museum Library, Waltham; Harvard University's Houghton, Law School, Loeb, Tozzer, and Widener Libraries; Massachusetts Archives; Massachusetts Historical Society; Middlesex County Probate Registry and Registry of Deeds; Newberry Library; Society for the Preservation of New England Antiquities; University of East Anglia Library; Waltham Public Library; Watertown Free Public Library; and Watertown Public Works Department.

Finally, I record my gratitude to the British Academy for an Exchange Fellowship at the Newberry Library in Chicago in 1994, to the Massachusetts Historical Society for a Benjamin F. Stevens Fellowship in 1997, to the Research Grants Committee of the School of English and American Studies for travel grants in 1996, 1997, and 1998, and to the University of East Anglia for sabbatical leaves in 1994, 1997, and 1998.

A shorter version of chapter 4 was published as "Enough of Thorough" in *The New England Quarterly* 73 (2000); "Whittaker" and "Page v. Page" in Appendix A appear in altered form as "Life on the Margin" in *The New England Quarterly* 74 (2001).

R. T.

INTRODUCTION

Henry Kitson's 1930 Tercentenary Watertown Founders' Memorial celebrates the most famous event of the town's history, which occurred less than two years after its white settlement. A bronze bas-relief represents the town's resistance to attempts by the Massachusetts authorities in February 1632 to raise taxes without popular consent. A defiant group of men, women, and children, gathered by the river's edge, support the assertion of their pastor and elder that "it was not safe to pay moneys after that sort for fear of bringing themselves and posterity into bondage." The minister is dressed in the conventional bands of an English seventeenth-century divine, his supporters in puritan costume, but behind them stand a frontiersman's log cabin and a landscape of heavily forested "wilderness." The scene encapsulates the two major themes of this book. The first springs from my previous work on East Anglian emigration to early New England[1] and asks: To what extent could English people preserve their ways of thinking and doing in a new-world environment, and to what extent must they innovate and embrace change? One of the best documented of the "companies" that left the eastern counties during the 1630s was that led by Rev. George Phillips, vicar of Boxted, Essex, in the Stour Valley. "Mr. Phillips's Company" settled in Watertown. The town over its first fifty years would be a testing ground for gauging continuity and change, as symbolized in the traditional old-world apparel set in the strange new world of Kitson's tableau.

The second theme impressed itself upon me more gradually. The town's refusal to pay unvoted taxes was the most notorious example, but not the first and by no means the last, of its questioning of authority, its penchant for debate, dispute, disagreement, and division, its all too frequent atmosphere of tension and contention. This theme reminded me of Bernard Bailyn's review of my last book. He took me to task (with some justification) for claiming that among East Anglian immigrants in New England "social harmony was the norm," that "order and social consensus" prevailed. He cataloged examples of dissidence, fragmentation, and bitterness: Winthrop's Boston, the antinomian crisis, the Pynchons' Springfield, the Connecticut River towns aptly encapsulated in the book title *Valley of Discord,* Sudbury, scene of bitter recriminations leading to a mass exodus, or Rhode Island, which he described as "a snake pit of contentious dissidents." The divisions of Watertown were plainly not unique, but they raised the critical question of how any such community could be sustained and what countervailing forces prevented anarchy.[2]

Despite (or because of) this leitmotif of contention, the 1632 protest turned out to be Watertown's great moment of colonial glory.[3] Thereafter a settlement begun with high hopes and wide horizons gradually lapsed into a rustic farming community. With discord went decline, a decline in ambitions that in many ways mirrored "the puritan ordeal" of Massachusetts.[4]

Studies of Watertown have gone through a series of stages that reflect a more general evolution of town histories: the antiquarian, the genealogical, the documentary, the "memorial," the "sociological." Convers Francis, a Congregational minister, produced a bicentennial account in 1830 that was essentially antiquarian annals. The great 1855 genealogical history of Watertown was the work of Philadelphian doctor Henry Bond, descendant of founder William Bond. Bond's own contribution has stood the test of time. His brief historical appendix also has much invaluable information, as do his maps. The Watertown Historical Society, organized in 1888, published the first of an excellent eight-volume transcription of the manuscript town records in 1894. This series forms a major documentary basis of my work. The society brought out a tercentennial memorial celebration, *Great Little Watertown,* written by G. F. and R. R. Wheeler. The town's 350th anniversary was marked by Maud de Leigh Hodges's lavishly illustrated *Crossroads on the Charles.*[5]

During the 1970s' heyday of "community studies," several scholars analyzed aspects of early Watertown using social science techniques, models, and theories. Kenneth A. Lockridge devised demographic tables and graphs based on the seventeenth-century vital records and, with Alan Kreider, computed statistics on the boards of selectmen elected over the first fifty years. William Boyd MacPhail investigated the town's land policy with a wealth of tables and carefully ordered data, and Robert Emmett Wall examined the extent of Watertown church membership and the franchise in comparison with other early Massachusetts foundations. Watertown was one of six towns chosen by David Grayson Allan in his tracing of "English Ways" to the new world. Yet no full early town history using modern techniques has been attempted.[6]

Introduction

Microhistory is currently enjoying an exciting revival. The view from the low-flying helicopter is reasserting its attractiveness as compared with the dehumanized panorama seen from the stratospheric jet. Recovering the intimate details of the lives and ideas of ordinary people, history "from the bottom up," reanimates the reality perceived by simple farmers, artisans, their wives, and children. "Working with these sources to the depth that is required to write convincing history of this kind is almost impossible unless the historian is prepared to write local history." The grand but rather arid generalizations about formative social, political, or religious movements and economic models tend to crumble when confronted with the revelations of sharper focused microanalysis. In-depth findings challenge the idealized existence of "economic man" or "the typical peasant" or "the working class." "Real experience" refuses to coincide with "average experience." Microhistory demonstrates that "it is impossible to understand society and culture without examining local contexts . . . the local is central to the nature of the historical process." Moreover, "the versatility of communities" was an essential, if untidy, element of early-modern society and culture.[7] In *Divided We Stand* I aim to recapture the details, textures, physical contexts, intimacies, aspirations, and tensions of individuals' lives in one such community.

Microhistorians must satisfy three requirements for effective local studies. Their analyses require rigorous computation as well as sensitive and informed re-creation of the lives of individuals, families, and communities from written records. Second, the obsession with recovering past "being" must combine with an equal awareness of "becoming." Change over time and its sources are as important as the recovery of the structure of times lost. Third, small-scale research must ask big questions. These queries may arise from relating local issues to broader trends, like the effects in Watertown of English parliamentary resistance to royal authority or changes in the Atlantic economy or the outbreak of international war. They may also be prompted by local revelations that challenge received truths, such as Watertown's assertive electorate hobbling the "oligarchy," vocal dissenter antagonism against the church, the questioning of patriarchy, economic conflicts and the divisiveness of "consumerism," or the pervasiveness of racialism and ethnic suspicion. The apparently idiosyncratic and individualistic may prove to have much wider relevance. Successful microhistory avoids the tunnel vision and the quaintness of antiquarianism. It alerts us to rippling circles of contexts and connections around the local and tests and reshapes broad generalizations on its laboratory bench.[8]

"To glean and glean again our small fields": this was Darrett Rutman's description of doing local history. Margaret Spufford, another leading microhistorian, describes it thus: "We are the resurrectors: we seek to make the past live, as accurately as we can. But the dry bones that are given us, unlike Ezekiel, only come in small splinters."[9]

I have been fortunate in my gleanings, my splinters. My central source has been the excellently edited first volume of *Watertown Town Records*. These include the first two Books of Proceedings, minutes of town and selectmen's meetings, yearly elections of town officers, and the town's annual accounts. The Book of Possessions lists five sets of early land grants and three inventories of individual holdings during the 1640s. Volume 1 concludes with the vital records of births, marriages, and deaths. Other invaluable peepholes into town life were afforded by the two docket books and ninety-two folios, or files of loose court papers, in the Middlesex County Court Records, especially the depositions by scores of residents in criminal and civil cases. The Middlesex Probate Records contain seven relevant registers with individual wills, which reveal attitudes and relationships, as well as inventories differentiating individuals' callings, lands, livestock, household possessions, and disposition of rooms. The earliest wills and inventories are summarized in the first book of *Suffolk Wills*. Similarly the first two decades of land transactions, mortgages, and other covenants are entered in the first book of *Suffolk Deeds*. The first seven Registers of Middlesex Deeds cover the period from 1649 to the early 1680s. A few letters detailing events in early Watertown add further color, as do entries in diaries, narratives, and promotional accounts. The early colony records have some invaluable entries during the 1630s on Watertown affairs, and several townspeople appeared in the Court of Assistants or used the services (carefully minuted) of local notaries. The archives of the General Court proved enlightening, especially its series of incoming petitions and its documents on appealed cases. Sadly, no Watertown church records for the period 1630–80 have survived, and none of the three early ministers was a copious publisher of sermons preached to their flock.

Apart from the enormous assistance I have derived from Bond, I have relied heavily for family history research in the subsequent 130 years on the publications of three leading contemporary genealogists. Robert Charles Anderson's authoritative three-volume, 2,386-page work, *The Great Migration Begins*, includes articles on the founders of Watertown down to the end of 1633. Dean Crawford Smith and Melinde Lutz Sanborn's *Ancestry of Eva Belle Kempton* contains invaluable material on many of the core families of early Watertown.[10]

Despite the herculean efforts of companies of predecessors and despite six years of steady personal research, I still have only gleanings and splinters to work with. The harvest and the body are gone forever. We must remind ourselves of the honest appraisal of one of the greatest community historians of our generation: we are engaged upon "reconstructing on the basis of always dubious evidence what we think happened and why."[11]

The examination of change and continuity, decline and discord—the major themes of *Divided We Stand*—is arranged under five major headings. In the first, I explore the raw materials for Watertown: the physical setting, the immigrants, and the cultural experiences they brought with them. Chapter 3, "The View from the Stour," is the benchmark for the measurement of subsequent change or continuity. In Part II I explore three foundations of life in Watertown: its government, its land, and its church. All three of these fundamentals were rocked with persistent conflict. Next, I turn to the creation and development of the town's economy, the problems of mixed farming, the tensions between ideals of self-sufficiency and engagement in the market, and the specialisms that succeeded and those that failed. The last two sections are concerned with community. Part IV, "Care in the Community," first investigates communal ways of looking after Watertown's vulnerable and isolated inhabitants. The "rising" of "The Rising Generation" incorporates three meanings: rising as in population rise; rising as in next, the heirs to the town; and rising as in rebellious—or, at least, restless, frustrated, or subversive. The central unit of the community was the household. The stresses and strains involved in its formation, relationships, and life cycle are the subject of chapter 11, "The Family," along with the changes in material life and rivalries they provoked. I had intended to include a chapter on women's roles, relationships, and status, but the source material proved too scanty. In the last part of the book, I look at two counterbalances that reinforced Watertown's sense of "usness": the Native Americans, and relationships with neighboring settlements and settlers. What forces helped bind this fractious group of households together?

Two appended features deserve notice. Appendix A contains ten reconstructions of particularly vivid cases or character studies from the Middlesex County Court Records. They are freestanding but topically linked to chapter subjects. Inclusion of these "thick descriptions" would unbalance the chapters, but as postscripts these social dramas encapsulate major issues that have gone before.[12] Appendix B has names in seven lists that give as full a roster as I can of the first two generations of Watertown people. Six are arranged according to residence—long- or short- or very-short-term—and first or second generation. The seventh is a catalog of office-holding between 1630 and 1680.

To the existing demographic and quantitative analyses of Watertown, I have added some more very basic computations and further raw material for cliometricians. I have tried to make this study both comprehensible and attractive to general readers, including citizens of Watertown interested in their early town history.

Present-day residents will, I hope, excuse me for amending some of the legends embedded in earlier accounts and for questioning some of the sentimentality surrounding modern ideas of community. I would give my eyeteeth for a chance to go back to early Watertown. I have thousands of questions I would like to ask its inhabitants; if only I could see what they looked like. I would love to walk over their fields, look out over their domain from Meetinghouse or Whitney Hills or Mount Feake, canoe on their Charles, visit their homes and their meetings, and witness their discussions and relationships. I could spend weeks or months following up my gleanings and splinters. Yet, like most modern anthropologists, I suspect I would want to return to my own world. To overstimulated modern senses, "the whole of life framed in a circle of loved, familiar faces, known and fondled objects" might seem appealingly simple and rich, but it would soon come to seem dreary and drab, dull and deadening. This verdict does not refer simply to Watertown. The conclusion of my argument urges that Watertown was in many key ways typical of most of the farming communities in early New England.

Note: The spelling of all quotations has been modernized. All dates start the year on January 1.

I
NEW WORLD FROM OLD

1

The Lie of the Land

Modern Watertown is a suburb of Boston, west of Cambridge on the north bank of the Charles River. It is about four miles east to west and one and a half miles north to south; its shape is roughly triangular, with the Charles as its base (see map 1). Its center today is Watertown Square, just north of the Galen Street Bridge leading to Newton. Here its main bisecting road from Cambridge to the northeast, Mount Auburn Street, meets Main Street, which heads westward to Waltham. The Charles River, two hundred yards across in places just downstream, narrows dramatically at Watertown Bridge and at the adjacent shallows and dam upstream.

A good panoramic view of contemporary Watertown is from the Summit Tower in the center of Mount Auburn Cemetery, at the eastern extremity of the town. From there can be seen the meanders of the Charles, the ponds at the foot of Mount Auburn's eastern slope, and the hills that dot the townscape westward: Meetinghouse Hill, three-quarters of a mile away; Whitney Hill, a mile beyond that and due north of Galen Street Bridge; and the east-west ridge near the Waltham line to the west. A mile or so eastward from this vantage point, the spires and cupolas of Harvard push up through the trees. Four or five miles beyond them rear the skyscrapers of downtown Boston, founded in the same year as Watertown but now a giant in comparison.[1]

There are few signs nowadays that Watertown is one of the oldest towns in New England. Even the observant wanderer could be excused for missing the surviving clues and for assuming that Watertown was founded in the late nineteenth or early twentieth century, with its late Victorian churches, public buildings, and office blocks and its solid, well-established family homes.

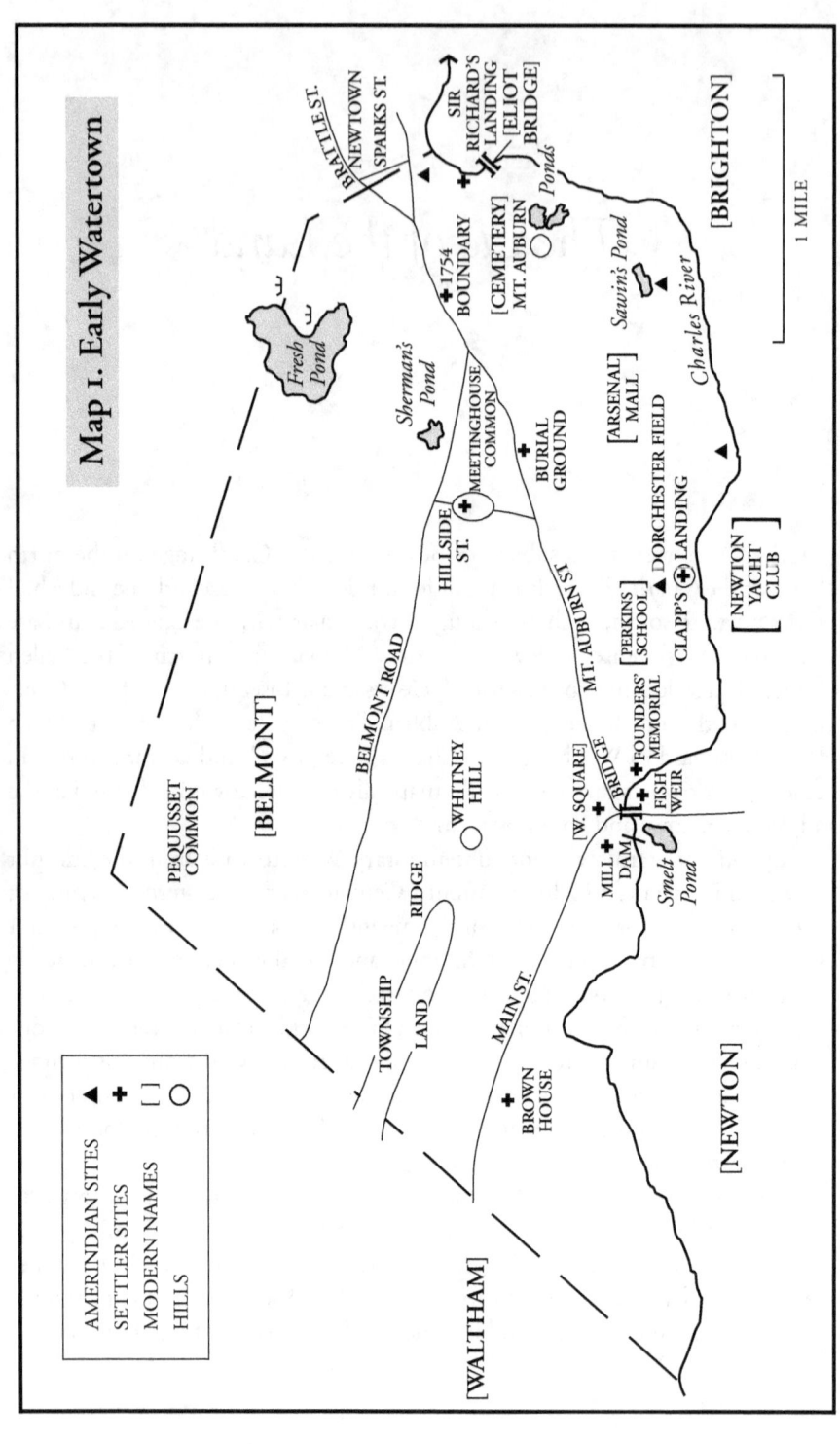

The Lie of the Land   5

We pick up some early visual hints in neighboring Cambridge. At the eastern entrance to Cambridge Common (across Massachusetts Avenue from Harvard Yard) a notice and plaque identify the route east to Kirkland Street and west across the greensward as the early trail from Charlestown to Watertown. Mason Street, heading west from the common, has "Watertown Path 1630" as its original name, as do its continuations, Brattle and Mount Auburn Streets. By the Charles River, just below the Eliot Bridge and well within contemporary Cambridge bounds, is a stone memorial erected by the Watertown Historical Society in 1948. It designates the spot as Sir Richard's Landing, conjecturing that it was here the first white permanent settlers stepped ashore. It also indicates that this land, eastward up to Sparks Street, was originally part of Watertown.[2]

In Watertown itself, the most obvious sign of seventeenth-century occupation is the Old Burial Ground on the corner of Mount Auburn and Arlington Streets, with its late-seventeenth-, eighteenth-, and nineteenth-century gravestones and its twentieth-century founders' memorials erected by family associations. At the other end of town near the Waltham line on Main Street is the almost hidden Brown House, begun about 1694, looking out over the southward slope toward the river and Newton beyond from its sheltered position under the east-west ridge. In a slight dip between two crests in the residential side street of Hillside, a stone marker by a driveway identifies the site of the 1635 meetinghouse, on what is still called Meetinghouse Hill.[3]

There is a standard cast-iron historic marker in Watertown Square, but two hundred yards east along bankside Charles River Road (near a stone marker indicating Thomas Mayhew's homestall, or house lot) is the grander marble and bronze tercentenary memorial. A half mile east, as Charles River Road crests a steep rise, a stone plinth in a grove of trees identifies "Clapp's Landing" in early June 1630.

The most obscure, but chastening, evidence of early occupation is on Beacon Street, just before it crosses the river, opposite the southern entry to the U.S. Arsenal grounds. A faded notice records the site where an extensive collection of stonecutting tools was discovered. Some are dated to 1600 B.C., while the majority come from the period 1100–600 B.C. In the long view of the Charles River Valley, the so-called founders were very recent arrivals indeed.[4]

The early English intruders left one other major mark on modern Watertown: their family names. Not only do several public buildings bear white planters' names—George Phillips Church, Phillips School, Coolidge School, and Brown (recently renamed Atrium) School—but twenty streets are named after their fellow settlers.[5] Some topographical features have also retained early English surnames, including Sawin's Pond and Whitney Hill.

It is easy to miss these few reminders of Watertown's heritage. Many local

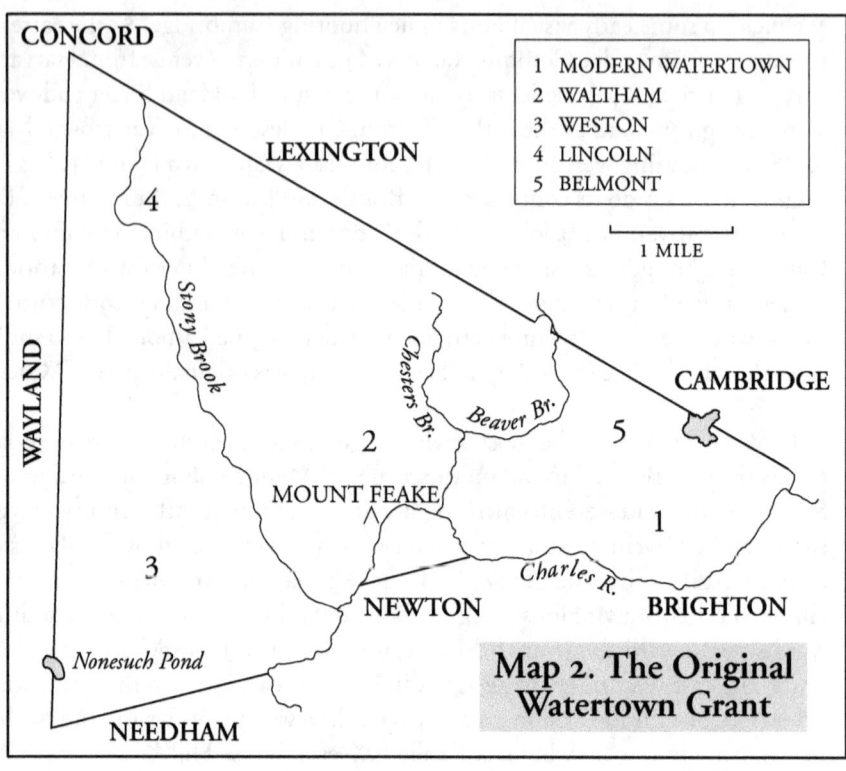

Map 2. The Original Watertown Grant

people are unaware of the evidence of three and a half centuries of settlement.[6] They would certainly not recognize their town as it was 350 years ago during the first two generations of white settlement.

The first unrecognizable feature would be the town's size in the seventeenth century. Dwarfing the present town's 2,624 acres, the original grant was 23,456 acres, almost nine times greater.[7] Early Watertown included what are now the separate towns of Waltham, Belmont, and Weston, as well as parts of Lexington, Concord, Lincoln, Cambridge, and Wayland (see map 2). Present-day Watertown is merely the bottom right-hand corner of an eight-mile-sided triangle whose apex is in Concord and whose western corner lies along the Needham line.

In this western area of the original grant, in what is now Waltham, several more features recall early settlement. Beaver Brook, for instance, still flows southward into the Charles at the lower end of Waltham Plain, originally called the Further Plain. The mill pond on Beaver Brook dates back to the second Watertown grist mill of the 1670s. Its tributary, Chester's Brook, was named for Leonard Chester, in Watertown during the early 1630s. The prominence at the great southward bend of the Charles, above Waltham's mills, is still called Mount Feake after a Watertown resident and is now the central feature of a cemetery.[8] Upstream from this magnificent vantage point, Stony Brook, so called in the 1630s, enters the Charles from the north but no longer as a rushing stream. Now it is a reservoir. Beyond Waltham lies Weston, originally called the Farms. At its southern end is a pond still known by its seventeenth-century name, Nonesuch.

A second surprise for modern Watertowners would be the site of the town center. The original settlement in 1630 was near the river on the eastern side of Mount Auburn. Early Watertown was in what is now Cambridge (which did not exist until its 1632 founding as Newtown). One of the anomalies of Watertown's history is the way that its center has moved three miles westward to its nineteenth-century focus at Watertown Square. The first site was probably replaced in the mid-1630s because it was so close to the line of the new neighbor. Proximity to the ponds east of Mount Auburn—now Halcyon and Auburn Lakes—and to Fresh Pond and riverine marshes would also make summer life unhealthy and would delay spring sowing. The new focus of settlement was Meetinghouse Common, about a mile westward, the triangular green formed by the modern roads Belmont, Mount Auburn, and Hillside, three-quarters of a mile by half a mile at its widest points. The common was dominated by Meetinghouse Hill at its western side. At the same time, the first foundations of the present town center were being laid with the building of the mill and the fish weir "three miles above the town" at the ford just below the falls, where Watertown Bridge and Square now stand.[9]

The settlement pattern and the first fifty-year human impact on this large land grant are in stark contrast to the modern suburban townscape. Even as early as the 1640s, the founders had begun to scatter, a dispersal that worried the authorities. It meant that in bad weather many people missed Sabbath services. It could mean families split up around widely distant plots during the busy times of the farming year. Some feared that living "not so compact for situation" would dilute the community.[10]

What the town looked like by the end of our period is hard to assess. The first surviving rough sketch map dates from 1720, but since frontier expansion was all but frozen after King Phillip's War (1675–76), Watertown's appearance may not have changed radically from the 1670s. On the 1720 map the eastern half of the grant—roughly modern Watertown—has 107 houses, compared with 79 in the western half. The southwestern quarter is very thinly settled, except for the road to Sudbury. The one and one-half mile northwestward track beyond the upper reach of Beaver Brook, along the line of the modern Trapelo Road, has a house every 260 yards on its northern side and every quarter mile on its southern. Even in the east, average farm holdings per farmhouse would have been about 100 acres. The thickest settlement in this section has eight houses to the mile along Mount Auburn, Orchard, and School Streets, one house about every 200 yards. There is also a marked concentration of dwellings in the area known as the Town Plot, bounded by Main, Lexington, and Belmont and by the Waltham line. This area is about 240 acres and contained 15 houses, each with average plots of about 16 acres. All the houses on the 1720 sketch map are drawn facing on to a "highway." Away from these tracks, there were no habitations, just fields, meadows, common land, waste, marsh, and forest.[11]

Another change from modern Watertown would be one of ethnicity. Then the inhabitants were almost without exception English, and many came from the eastern-counties region known as East Anglia. Though Londoners, Yorkshiremen, and West Countrymen would diversify the local dialects, almost everyone's mother tongue would be English, their religion Protestant, and their basic traditions Anglo-Saxon. Nowadays, Watertown has a large and influential Armenian population, as well as many Italians. It is not unusual to see statues of the Virgin Mary in suburban backyards, something that would make the early settlers gyrate in their graves.

The Charles River would also have been very different. For the founding generations of settlers, much of its bank was marshy and liable to flooding, which would explain why the first reconnaissance party clambered ashore at the steep bluff of Clapp's Landing. The water was tidal and salty up to the Watertown Falls, making its currents, flow, and level changeable. In spring it teemed with fish; in summer it swarmed with mosquitoes. At low tide its extensive mud- and mollusk-banks stood exposed. It was a far cry from the carefully controlled and channeled waterpark of today.[12]

Though the white settlers' trackways followed Indian paths and presaged modern roads, the comparative emptiness even of the present town area made them country cart-tracks and trails. Now 34,000 people inhabit Watertown; the first generation numbered about 500 in the far greater land grant. The landscape during the seventeenth century was overwhelmingly rural and agrarian, with small pockets of cultivation cut out of surrounding woodland and waste. The natural topography would be far more obvious without the modern clutter of buildings, roads, and other modifications of the terrain. The rolling landscape of the eastern part of the grant gives way to a broad alluvial plain on the north bank of the Charles River in what is now Waltham. The central ridge starting with Whitney Hill undulates westward through Ives Hill and Cedar Hill to Jericho in central Waltham. To the west and northwest, hills such as Mackerel Hill, Mount Enoch, Trapelo Hill, Stearns Hill, and Huckleberry Hill on the present border between Weston and Waltham hemmed in the town's domain. The height—up to 350 feet—and the steepness of tree-clad hills like Mount Auburn or Mount Feake would stand out far more imposingly in such untamed terrain. Between these uplands were dotted rich meadows—Rock Meadow, Beaver Brook Meadow, Chester Meadow, Pond Meadow, and Thatcher's Meadow—watered by streams and ponds. The abundance of surface water would also be far more evident, both as an asset for mixed farming and household needs and as a barrier, before drainage, bridging, piping, and channeling were undertaken. The soils near the river and streams were loamy with deposits of peat; the uplands were covered with glacial outwash with well-drained, light, sandy, or gravelly soils, easy to work, but needing organic feeding. Much upland was covered by trees, mostly hardwoods like chestnut and oak. It gave to the invaders a sense both of enormous potential and of "empty wilderness." In fact, this land had been peopled for centuries; it had not been in the interests of the Amerindians to "tame" it.[13]

The estuary of the Charles River was an ideal environment for Native American hunter-gatherers for at least 4,500 years before the arrival of the *Arbella* fleet, bringing the first permanent English settlers. They called the river the Big Eel. Thanks to long-term changes in climate and resultant rises in sea level, the intertidal gathering grounds gradually moved upstream, so that the bands who harvested shellfish at low tide and fished when the river was fuller moved their camps, over the centuries, farther inland along the banks. The people who constructed the Boylston Street Fish Weir in the lagoon that was Boston's Back Bay flourished around 4,800 years ago, whereas the descendants of the people who left archaeological remains in what would become Watertown visited their sites even after white settlement had begun.[14]

Four sites have been excavated in the area of early Watertown. All have certain features in common. They are on knolls or ridges well above the river; they are beside brooks or springs. None has any evidence of agriculture, though two have shards of vessels.[15] The easternmost site, and probably the earliest, was Simon's Hill, where Mount Auburn Hospital now stands, close to Watertown's eastern bounds in the seventeenth century and where initial white settlement took place in 1630. These early people had pots and shaped steatite but probably did not occupy this hill after 2,600 years ago. The Amerindians who camped or lived at the next site, by Sawin's Brook, below Sawin's Pond, left two ceremonial pits containing stone axes, adzes, hammerstones, and net sinkers. These tools were probably used for hollowing out punts and dugout canoes used in fishing and shell-gathering. At the third site, south of the Arsenal, drills and steatite shards were found as well as axheads. Its most recent artefacts date from about 2,600 years ago. The last known campground is on and behind the knoll known as Clapp's Landing. This site adjoined the spring-fed Perkins Pond and was about fifty or sixty feet above the river. First signs of occupation go back 3,000 years, but it was also visited in the Late Woodland period (ca. A.D. 1000–1600).

The teeth of the few human burials that have been recovered suggest that the prehistoric inhabitants had a diverse diet, but since the intertidal environment was so fruitful, and since they hunted for deer and turkey in the woodland and could gather berries and edible tubers, they may not have needed to cultivate for much of this time. European documentary evidence suggests, however, that by the arrival of the English intruders in the 1630s, the Indians did have stocks of corn.[16] The archaeological evidence is so fragmentary that it is impossible to be sure of the lie and the use of the land before white settlers arrived. Unfortunately, none of the newcomers had time to describe the Watertown landscape or Native American lifestyle. However, because population density was so low—and falling catastrophically after 1615—and because a healthy living could be made without plant cultivation, it is possible that the intruders who arrived in 1630 did indeed find a relatively untouched place, which they quickly set about "improving."[17]

2

The Peopling of Early Watertown, 1630–1640

The Watertown Founders' Memorial has a second bas-relief, which shows the initial encounter in early June 1630 between English newcomers and Native American residents and their exchange of gifts.[1] These white visitors were not the founders of Watertown, however. They were a reconnaissance party from the *Mary and John,* and within a few days they were recalled to Mattapan, later Dorchester. Had they settled on the Charles, Watertown might have developed very differently—as a predominantly west-country, rather than an East Anglian, town. It was only later that summer that one of the main *Arbella* fleet leaders, Sir Richard Saltonstall, led a party "two leagues [six miles] up the Charles" and established a bridgehead near what later became Sir Richard's Landing, two miles below Dorchester Plain, as the original brief encampment came to be known.[2] Saltonstall, whose likeness towers over the memorial, was only a very brief resident. Apart from insisting on a large entitlement of land, his interest quickly turned to the Connecticut Valley after his return to England in the spring of 1631.[3]

Completing the memorial on Charles River Road are lists of founders carved on either wing. From Thomas Arnold at top left to Richard Woodward at bottom right, these men, with their families and servants, are the subject of this chapter.[4] They were among the thirteen to twenty thousand people who migrated to New England during the 1630s. By the end of the first decade over thirty towns had been established. The central questions of this chapter are why the founders who joined Sir Richard and Rev. George Phillips in the summer of 1630 decided on Watertown rather than one of the other bridgeheads like Boston, Salem, Roxbury, Charlestown, or Dorchester, and why some dozens of later families among the thousands who followed in the Great Migration chose this town rather than the growing number of options elsewhere in New England. What were the magnetic forces behind the peopling of early Watertown? What were the future implications of this particular mix?

The early planting of New England during the 1630s was not a steady, year-by-year accumulative process. People came in a series of surges. Then, quite suddenly in the early 1640s, the surges stopped. Thereafter the population grew—and it *did* grow with unprecedented vigor as the century progressed—by natural increase.[5]

So it was with early Watertown. We can identify three surges that bore people to the town: one in 1630, a second from 1634 to 1636, and a third and final wavelet in 1637. These three influxes were dominated numerically by people from three counties of eastern England—Essex, Suffolk, and Norfolk—which together form a geographic region immediately northeast of London often called East Anglia or the eastern counties. This regional prevalence is somewhat surprising, since their lay leader, Saltonstall, was a Yorkshireman from Halifax in the north of England. His family, however, did have influential relatives in London and Essex (see map 3).

It is unusual to be able to recover individual motives for emigration. We know from English church records that some Watertown settlers had been involved in religious protests prior to embarkation. One of three surviving early letters from Watertown is deeply pious in tone, emphasizing as the primary purpose "to advance the glory of God in planting the gospel here." The other two are far more materialistic, however, suggesting that the beaver trade with the Indians or the breeding of cattle were top priorities in the decision to go to New England. One correspondent had gone bankrupt in 1630; the other apologizes for having been "an undutiful son" before he left Suffolk.[6]

Even if it is impossible to uncover individual motivation for most who made the journey to Watertown, we can at least demonstrate one factor that would encourage and channel their emigration. Closer examination of the personnel who founded the town reveals an intricate web of kinship, confraternity, and familiarity that not only connected those who traveled together in the same surge but also linked one surge to the next in a classic pattern of chain migration that covered the whole decade.

In a general study of East Anglian transferral to New England, *Mobility and Migration,* I described a large number of connected groups, often called companies, that were a common and communal means of planting the new world.[7] Three such Watertown companies can be traced in the first *Arbella*-fleet surge of 1630. The ties that bound companies were threefold: clientage to a gentry leader, membership of an inner puritan church group under a religious mentor, or kinship with an extended family clan. These ties frequently overlapped. Many members of "wandering congregations" were interrelated; individual gentlemen were often devotees of leading puritan clergy.

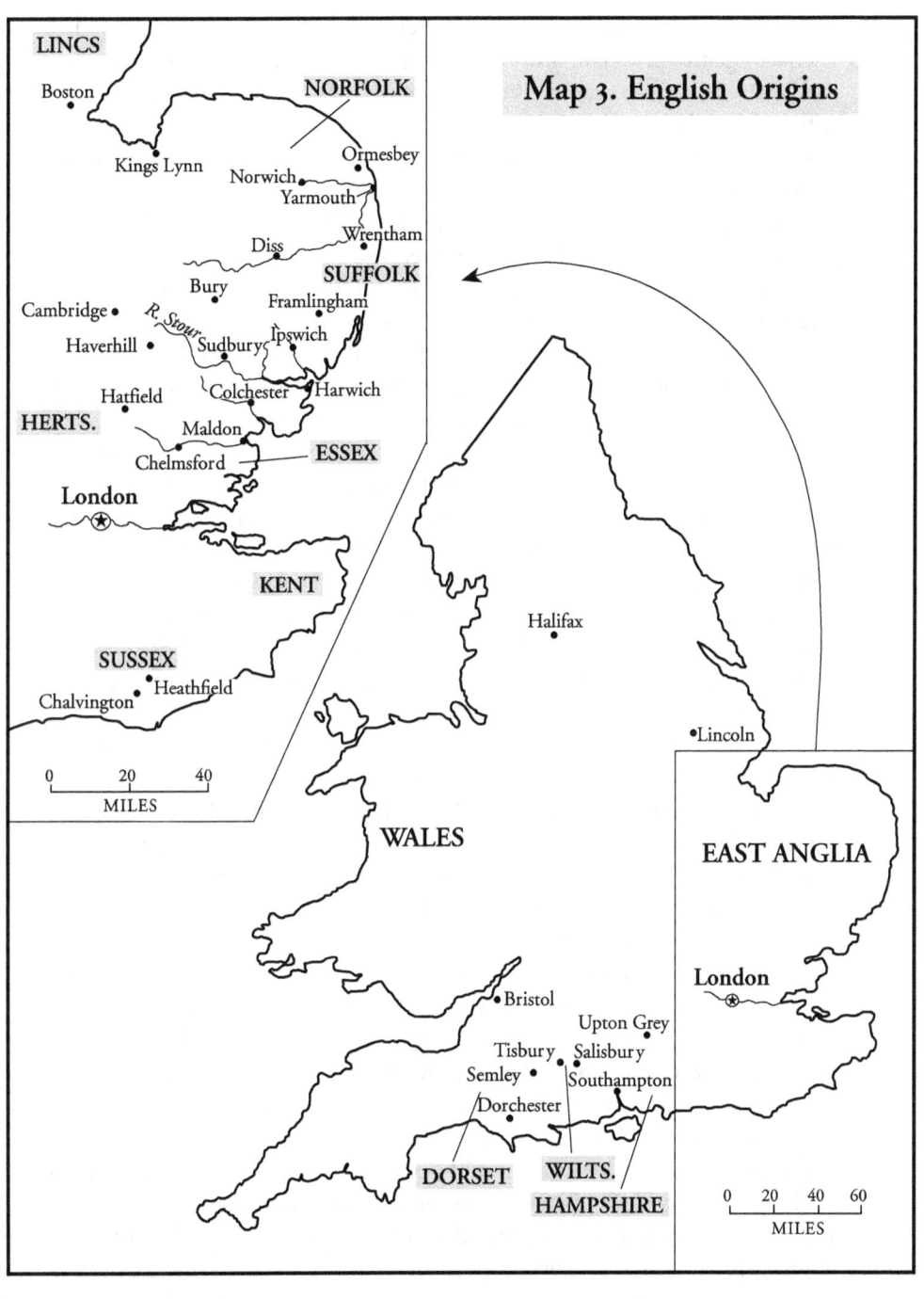

Two sets of the first Watertown planters from East Anglia were linked as clients of gentlemen. The third 1630 company was a richly interrelated puritan "conventicle" that rapidly became the nucleus of the Watertown church gathered in July 1630.

Our first 1630 company is, hardly surprisingly, a group of clients of the widower Sir Richard Saltonstall. He brought his own large family group with him: four sons, Richard, Robert, Samuel, and Henry, and two daughters, Rosamond and Grace. Richard and Robert soon became associated with Ipswich; Samuel seems to have stayed in Watertown, though his presence was rarely felt there. Henry, Rosamond, and Grace returned to England in 1631 with their father. An important figure within this household was John Masters, the steward, whose main function after Saltonstall's return to England was to "oversee Sir Richard's great family with his worthy son [Richard Jr.]." His financial, surveying, and engineering experience was much in demand in Watertown, neighboring Newtown, and the colony at large. Both he and his wife, Jane, died in 1639, probably in their early sixties, leaving a son and four married daughters, one of whom was the wife of Edmund Lockwood. Many of his kin, classic chain migrants, later settled in Watertown.[8]

A young gentleman traveling under Sir Richard's protection was William Pelham, whose family had links with Sussex, Lincolnshire, and the town of Bures in the Stour Valley. From there also came a large clan of woodworkers, the Knapps, whose fares were subsidized by Saltonstall.[9]

Servants formed an important if troublesome part of these early gentlemen's companies. Thomas Bartlett, later Watertown militia officer and town selectman, arrived in 1630 as "servant to Mr. Pelham." Saltonstall sent cattle and servants ahead of him in 1629, and some of his people's names occur in the records: Richard Diffy, an East Anglian, as we can surmise from his surname, and James Woodward, probably a Suffolk man related to later settlers.[10]

Gentry companies often relied on money to buttress loyalty in holding them together. Saltonstall's 1631 departure, quickly followed by that of his eldest son and William Pelham, no doubt deprived this group of twenty-seven of much cohesion. Its most important contribution to the peopling of Watertown occurred in the future: the chain migration, like Lockwood's or Woodward's kin, which increased the town's population later in the decade.

The second identifiable company in the first surge of the East Anglian contingent to Watertown came from mid-Suffolk. The most prominent member of this group was Henry Bright.[11] He came from a mercantile background in the puritan stronghold of Bury St. Edmunds and was distantly related to John Winthrop. Two other family groups made up this company—the Onges and the Hammonds—who both came from Lavenham, twelve miles south of Bury. The latter would become one of Watertown's leading families.

A nonemigrant eminence linked this group: Sir Simonds D'Ewes. This wealthy puritan investor in the Massachusetts Bay Company and friend and correspondent of Winthrop's owned land in Bury and Lavenham. He seriously considered emigrating in the mid-1630s. He was also a patron of Edmund Brown, briefly in Watertown in the late 1630s and first minister of neighboring Sudbury.[12]

By far the tightest knit of the three 1630s East Anglian companies that helped found Watertown was the interrelated group of eleven households who were followers of Rev. George Phillips. Phillips had been vicar of the Stour Valley parish of Boxted, Essex, for a decade by 1630, when he was recommended by the local squire to John Winthrop. The Phillips Company, which became the core of long-term settlement in Watertown, came from Boxted itself (like the households of John Eddy, John Page, Edward Howe, and Simon Stone), from Dedham (Thomas Rogers, John Coolidge, the Sherman cousins), or from Stour villages such as Nayland (Isaac Stearns, Ephraim Child, John Warren, John Firmin, and Lawrence Waters) or the Boxford area (John Doggett and John Pond). Bures, from which members of the Saltonstall company came, was the next town upstream from Nayland. Geography linked one company to another.[13]

Commitment to religious reformation was a powerful bond. Phillips was a radical puritan minister of considerable charisma. His patron in Boxted averred that "his excellency in matters of divinity is such as he is inferior to few if any . . . [according] to the judgment of all the eminentest christians that have ever exercised familiarity with him, of whom many are encouraged to go [to New England] for his sake and others to follow so soon as god shall so dispose." His followers shared his zeal. At the 1629 Archdeacon's Visitation, future migrants were presented, or brought to court, for refusing to kneel to receive Communion, a sure sign of commitment to hard-line puritanism. Howe was second ruling elder of Watertown church, and Ephraim Child became a deacon. One of the Shermans was the town's third minister, Eddy was the son of a puritan minister, and Firmin's son became a minister. This was "a wandering congregation of godly professors."[14]

Kinship and familiarity were also vital bonds for the Phillips company. It had a total of forty-eight members and was like an Israelite tribe, a giant extended family on the move. Twenty-two clan or neighborly linkages have been identified.[15]

Most households in Phillips's Company belonged to "the middling sort"— yeomen, craftsmen, literate, reasonably endowed. They provided a cadre of leaders who steered the affairs of town and church: Howe, Child, Eddy, Sherman, Coolidge, Stearns, and Stone. Unusually so among the original towns, Watertown lacked a resident magistrate after 1631. From the time of its found-

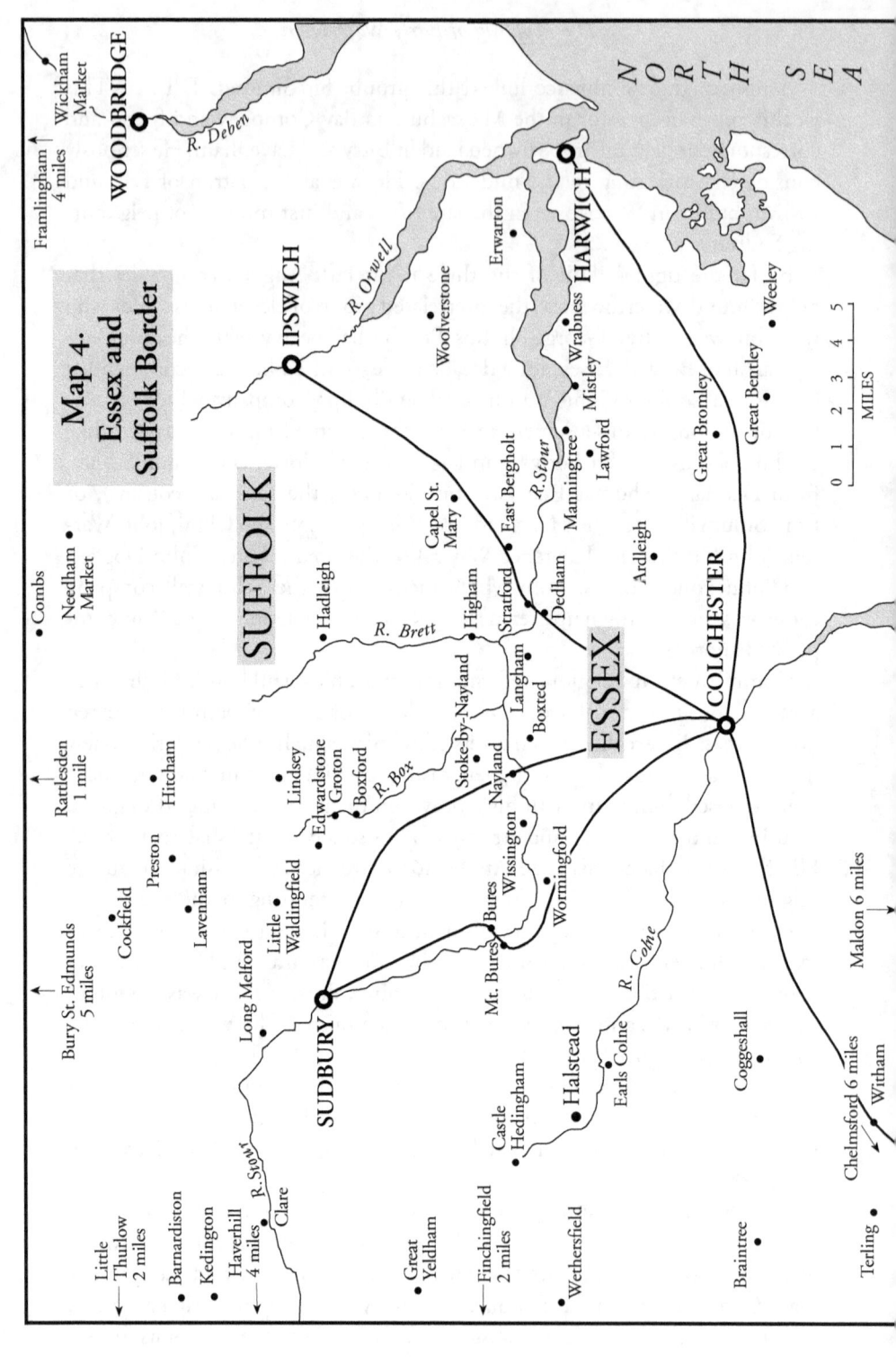

ing, however, it did not lack a large group of close-knit and long-lived East Anglians who were able to take up the reins of power and provide stability and continuity into the 1670s.[16]

Kinship and neighborly attachments may have been responsible for other early emigrant families choosing Watertown. Hosier and the Jennisons had Colchester connections, which would have brought them into the Phillips orbit. Abraham Brown would have been an English neighbor of John Masters of the Saltonstall party. Richard Brown may have been Abraham's relative, but his adult life had been associated with the south London borough of Southwark. He seems to have been linked with George Phillips, however, through his collaboration with a group of separatists from Colchester. Both Richard and Abraham Brown swelled the leadership group in the early years of settlement.[17]

A second surge in the peopling of Massachusetts occurred in 1634. After relatively few arrivals following the initial influx of 1630, the mid-1630s had immigrants again pouring in. For July 1634 Winthrop wrote in his journal:

> The last month arrived here [Boston] fourteen great ships, and one at Salem . . . Divers of the ships lost many cattle; but the two which came from Ipswich, of more than one hundred and twenty, lost but seven [cattle]. None of the ships lost any passengers, but the *Elizabeth Dorcas*, which . . . lost sixty . . .
> *August 4.* At the court, the new town of Agawam was named *Ipswich*, in acknowledgement of the great honour and kindness done to our people which took shipping there &c.; and a day of thanksgiving appointed a fortnight after the prosperous arrival of them there &c.[18]

The two ships from Ipswich, Suffolk, were the *Elizabeth,* William Andrews master, and the *Francis,* John Cutting master.[19] Again, our question is: Why did the families on board these two vessels travel together and then choose to settle in Watertown, especially as, by 1634, other plantations like Ipswich were opening up? The answers are somewhat more complex than in 1630, when options were so much more limited.

The formation of these new traveling companies had three main sources. Two men, John Firmin on the *Elizabeth* and William Hammond on the *Francis,* were making their second outward crossings. Firmin may have been fetching his wife. He may also have been actively recruiting emigrants for Massachusetts Bay, as others are known to have done. Hammond was definitely collecting members of his family from Lavenham, notably his wife of twenty-nine years, Elizabeth (Payne). He visited his patron, Sir Simonds D'Ewes, and carried back letters and £30 worth of vinegar donated to the colony.[20]

As with the Stour Valley Phillips Company in 1630, many 1634 emigrants were related to each other, like the Kemballs or the large clan from Dedham.[21]

Neighborliness was another factor causing these people to travel together. Groups of shipmates came from the areas of Colchester, Bury St. Edmunds, and Framlingham, as well as from villages in the Upper Stour Valley. These neighborhoods were notorious for their puritanism.[22]

All these linkages would help to explain why these families shipped together across the Atlantic, but not necessarily why they chose Watertown. The presence on each ship of townsmen, Firmin or Hammond, may have inclined some toward the upriver town. Much more telling, though, was the magnetic factor of chain migration. These members of the second surge were all too often joining pioneer kinsmen of the first. Furthermore, the Colchester contingent would all be familiar with Watertown's minister and his reputation as a pastor and preacher of "the congregational way."[23]

The succeeding two years of the second surge, 1635 and 1636, saw even more marked chain linkage. For 7 June 1635 Winthrop recorded: "The Lord's Day, there came seven other ships, and one to Salem, and four more to the mouth of the Bay with store of passengers and cattle. They all came within six weeks."[24] One of this armada was the *Increase* out of London, Robert Lea master. Among his passengers were further Watertown relatives from the Stour Valley: Paynes, Eyres, Stones, and Thomas Parish.[25]

Many 1634–36 second-wave settlers not recorded on shipping lists were linked by kinship or neighborhood to the 1630 founders: Eddies, Filbricks, Arnolds, Bigelows, Wincolls, Lawrences, and Fiskes, families from Essex and Suffolk whose names would acquire luster in the future.[26]

Up to the end of 1636, when Watertown had grown to some one hundred households, the East Anglian contingent of townsmen was predominantly from a band across the central part of the region, from northern Essex to northern Suffolk, a width of about thirty-five miles only. There were a few latecomers from this belt, including hounded minister John Knowles and Nathaniel Treadway; both fled from Colchester in 1639. By and large, though, the Essex-Suffolk immigration had virtually ceased by the end of 1636.[27]

There was, however, one final ripple of three East Anglian families into Watertown during 1637. These were all Norfolk people and somewhat older than usual. They came from puritan parishes in Norwich and its port, Great Yarmouth. It is no coincidence that Archbishop Laud's appointee Matthew Wren had become bishop there in 1635. The heat was now on dissent. Two Norwich emigrants, John Pearce and Nicholas Busby, were weavers. The 1630s depression in the cloth trade was taking its toll. Thomas Fleg, a servant in this party, would rise to prominence in his new home on the Charles.[28]

By the end of the Great Migration in 1640, the founders of Watertown had shipped across the Atlantic from a small area of eastern England a simplified but potent group of networks, bound together by kinship, religious confraternity, or neighborhood. There were four Payne and four Eddy siblings and their families in or near the town. The Stone-Cutting-Kemball-Scott-Lockwood-Rayner-Allen clan numbered forty-eight members. Old neighbors settled beside each other in the new world. Young settlers married sweethearts from England; older settlers sometimes followed their example.[29]

The peopling of Watertown was, then, a far less random process than has sometimes been suggested. The settlement of this New England town (and others) did not involve the creation of a totally new community from scratch. The heart of the town was a transplant. The centrality of the Phillips congregation meant that religious zeal was undoubtedly important, but this factor does not rule out material betterment. The ultrascrupulous could yearn for rich meadow.[30]

Watertown was not an exclusively eastern counties' plantation, however. People like Thomas Mayhew, Brian Pendleton, Michael Bairstow, and Richard Beers arrived with their families each year from other parts of England, including the West Country, London, and Yorkshire. As individuals, they were an important element in town life. However, they seem to have been no more than that: individuals.

I have been unable to find any extended patterns of prior connectedness among them. For instance, the considerable London contingent had all lived in different parishes in that already teeming city, and there is no evidence that they had known each other before they met in Watertown.[31] Lack of English contact is also true of the West Countrymen. Yorkshireman Bairstow did not reach Watertown until a decade after Saltonstall had left, and then marriage rather than prior neighborhood drew him to Watertown.[32]

This process of the peopling of Watertown during the 1630s was both a force for cultural, religious, and social continuities and a potent recipe for divisions. Some 242 East Anglians, centered on Phillips's Company (which numbered 85 by 1640), formed a communal core with shared regional experience and familiarity. Many Stour ways would become Watertown ways of doing things. However, the presence of people from a variety of other backgrounds (including craftsmen brought over for their skills)[33] with different agendas, different experience, and different values was bound to create misunderstandings, disagreements, and discord. Some outsiders would depart in disgust, but other discordant elements would stay and make the 1640s as confrontational as the 1630s. Not only were there innumerable disputes about how to proceed in their "wilderness work," but the very nature of the immigrants' beliefs and recent English experiences predisposed them to obduracy, provocation, scrupulosity, and opposition. These aggravating people were not for nothing nicknamed "puritans" and "precisians" by their opponents back in London, Yorkshire, the West Country, and East Anglia.

3

The View from the Stour

George Phillips's parish of Boxted lay in the Vale of Dedham, which John Constable loved to paint. In the 1620s his church, St. Peter's, recently illuminated by new dormer windows, formed the focus for the dispersed farms and cottages of the village. Half a mile across the fields of rich, light loam lived the squire, John Maidstone, at Pond House, hidden in a sheltered dip. In the opposite direction, a mile past Langham and Stratford and over meadows that were the most valuable in all Essex, rose the great tower of Dedham church, surrounded by inns, timber-framed clothiers' and weavers' houses, and the new school building. Linking Boxted and Dedham and enriching the meadows was the meandering River Stour. On its north bank, Babergh Hundred in Suffolk began, but its broad green valley united its inhabitants with the North Essex folk of Lexden and Hinckford Hundreds. Below Boxted and Dedham the river flowed past Flatford Mill to the great estuary starting at Manningtree and Henry Kemball's Mistley and ending at the fortified seaport of Harwich, just after joining the Orwell estuary winding down from Ipswich. The Stour-Orwell estuary provided a water route for barges or hoys (some laden with fullers' earth from Kent, others with "cheese and butter bound for London") and for people on the Wrabness Peninsula, like the Stone brothers, to travel inland.[1] (See map 4.)

Upstream from Boxted the bank was dotted with nucleated villages with their mills and fine churches and woolhalls of cloth merchants' guilds: Nayland, Wissington, Mount Bures (Essex side), Bures (Suffolk), then the market and textile towns of Sudbury, Long Melford (Hammond country), and Clare, before turning northwest to Kedington. Overlooking the busy valley were other small towns, including Stoke-by-Nayland, with its church tower on the bluff visible for miles, and Wormingford (where William Knapp found his bride.) Its tributaries had yet more settlements: Boxford, Groton, Edwardstone, and the Waldingfields on the River Box; Higham, Hadleigh, and Lindsey on the Brett.

The parallel river valley three miles to the south was the Colne, supplier of many leading settlers to Newtown, Massachusetts. Near its mouth stood Colchester, the only major town in the whole of Essex. By 1603 it had paved streets and a population around ten thousand, which contained a significant minority of Low Countries origin. The major trunk road linking the deepwater port of Ipswich with Colchester and thence to Witham, Chelmsford, and London crossed the Stour at Stratford (Suffolk) and Dedham (Essex). Down this road trundled two-ton, six-wheeled wagons drawn by teams of six or more horses. The Sudbury to Colchester road went over Nayland Bridge a mile upstream from Boxted, and another route between the two towns passed through Bures.[2]

The Stour Valley was the heartland of East Anglian emigration to Watertown. This chapter explores the cultural background of these Essex and Suffolk people who went with Phillips to the Charles Valley. The emigrants did not compartmentalize their lives into economic, political, and religious aspects. To them, all happenings were a working out of God's providences. For us, though, such divisions are helpful in disentangling the causes of the crisis of the 1620s and 1630s and the decisions to emigrate.

Economically, North Essex and South Suffolk were among the most populous, diversified, and well-endowed areas of England. This amplitude was demonstrated in the region's magnificent churches, the flourishing industrial and commercial centers like Sudbury, Long Melford, Hadleigh, Lavenham, Braintree, and Coggeshall, and the ports of Maldon and Harwich. Most of these smaller centers had populations between one and two thousand, like Dedham, with two hundred households in 1597. Much building and renovation had been done both in towns and in rural areas over the last half century. Essex was nicknamed the English Goshen (land of milk and honey), and Suffolk's fat beasts and rich dairies were widely celebrated.[3]

The region provided "many good feedings" for cattle and sheep on pasture and such bankside fodder and grazing lands as Sudbury's ancient flood meadows. The dairy produce of Stour, Colne, and tributary valleys and of "High Suffolk" to the north was such that "yearly from London at all seasons cheesemongers flock hither to buy." Sheep and cattle grazed all along these valleys, but large flocks were commoner in the upper part of the valleys to the west, near the chalk downs bordering Cambridgeshire. Colchester also had extensive common pasture for sheep. Most farming was mixed farming; cereal crops, vegetables, and fruits were commonly grown for subsistence. Much of the arable land was long-since enclosed, though there was still common grazing land. In the west the common-field system of cooperative farming continued.[4]

The Stour Valley was famous throughout England and northern Europe for its "wool towns" and clothing industry. Six out of the eleven main towns in Essex were textile centers. Colchester's primacy was based on the cloth industry; its Low Country citizens had arrived as refugee Flemish weavers. Sudbury, Long Melford, and nearby Lavenham were similarly full of weavers' cottages, with their larger windows for good light, wool- and guild halls, and clothiers' houses. The villages in the valley were also weaving centers. Dedham had had a fulling mill since the thirteenth century. The town's quadrangular building Southfields was the textile store, dye-room, administrative center, and dwelling of a prosperous clothier. Of its 200 households, 120 were dependent on clothiers in 1597.[5]

Heavy broadcloths were still being produced in Dedham and its neighbors in the 1620s and 1630s, but the Flemings had brought with them the mystery of weaving "bays and says," much lighter textiles that sold well in the Mediterranean, even India, and boosted exports. These "New Draperies" had "transformed Colchester during the second half of the sixteenth century." The early years of the seventeenth century had seen more than a decade of prosperity after the general European pacification of 1604, which was shared by many inhabitants of the region, though the "Old Draperies" were in long-term decline after 1600.[6]

Although a few clothiers became extremely wealthy, most of the organizers of the industry were men like the Shermans of Dedham or the Morses of Stratford, local yeomen clothiers who masterminded cottage production from distributing wool to selling finished cloth. Thanks to the many processes involved, one loom would "set on work forty people."[7] By 1610 around twenty thousand people in the Stour Valley were supported by the industry. Some farm families saw spinning and weaving as by-employments during the quieter winter months. For a disturbingly growing proportion, however, textiles had become their main money-earner. The reviving fortunes of the industry forced clothiers to reach out deep into the countryside for labor.[8]

Much more worrying was the inexorable rise in the number of landless families caused by general population increase and price inflation. Between 1586 and 1612 annual leasehold rents in Boxted had soared from four shillings to twenty-six shillings per acre, a 650 percent increase. In Suffolk the rise was between 300 and 500 percent between 1590 and 1650. Even where rents were controlled by custom, entry fines for new tenants were similarly soaring. Winthrop judged that fifty acres would provide economic well-being for a family. Yeomen with more than this "half-plowland" (only 6 to 10 percent in most parishes) could afford extra labor and market their surplus produce, profiting from dearth and resultant price rises. Husbandmen with less than twenty acres, however, were in danger. They could just about make ends meet in good years, but bad harvests, illness, or domestic tragedies could drive them to the wall. All up and down the valley, family subsistence farms were being "cannibalized," and villages were "filling up from the bottom."[9]

As landless laborers multiplied in the countryside, many headed for industrial centers in search of work. Urbanization was already under way. Colchester's corporation complained that "incomers" were "the principal cause of the great poverty within this town." Suffolk squire Robert Ryece concurred: "The greatest number of poor [occur] where clothiers do dwell."[10]

Though the economic view from the Stour might be reasonably bright in the years 1603–18, when many of the founders of Watertown were growing up and learning their ABCs,[11] prosperity was uneven and fragile. Divisions between classes had been widening for a century; pauperism was destabilizing the growing population of landless cottagers. Vagrancy had become a major problem. North Essex and South Suffolk might be insulated by the employment offered by the clothing industry, but if its overseas markets were dislocated, thousands of wage earners and subcontractors faced the abyss. Their sufferings permeated the whole social system: rents and debts went unpaid, poor rates rose, clothiers went bankrupt, theft and violence exploded. Though few emigrants to Watertown, except some servants, came from the new underclass, many supplemented their incomes by spinning. Their well-being would be undermined if the bubble of Jacobean prosperity were to burst.[12]

The cloth regions had long been identified with radicalism since the 1381 Peasants' Revolt. Boxted had seen conflict in 1584 over the villagers' timber rights. The parliamentary boroughs of the region usually returned "country" rather than "court" members of Parliament, as did the shires of Essex and Suffolk. The Maidstones of Boxted refused to subscribe to Charles I's extraparliamentary Forced Loan. Maldon's response was described by the Privy Council as "particularly obstinate," as was Dedham's with thirty-four defaulters, including its well-endowed preacher, John Rogers. One-third of those "invited" in Hinckford Hundred and one-fifth in Lexden Hundred declined to "lend" the king what he asked. Before the 1628 election (the last for twelve years) Nathaniel Ward, later minister in Ipswich, Massachusetts, preached at Maldon against absolutism. References to Magna Carta, no liberty without property, and no taxation without consent were commonplaces of political opposition. After Charles I's dissolution of Parliament in 1629, Sir Simonds D'Ewes, patron of Watertown emigrants, wrote: "Infinite almost was the sadness of each man's heart, and the dejection of his countenance that truly loved church and commonwealth." The date 2 March would live as "the most gloomy, sad and dismal day for England that happened in five hundred years last past."[13]

Ordinary people asserted their rights and liberties. The corporations of both Colchester and Maldon felt the effective ire of the boroughs' freemen when they attempted to increase their powers. When judges from London infringed Colchester's privileges, however, corporation and freemen united to see them off: "What care we for the order of the judges? They have nothing to do within our corporation and we have the power to do whatever we please." When military draftees were ill treated and neglected at Harwich in 1627, they mutinied and took hostage their commanders (one of whom was a kinsman of Sir Richard Saltonstall). An official appointed by London wrote of "strident" Colchester, "Their Diana is their liberty." In 1634 another agent described Ipswich as factious. In April 1635 Dedham resisted royal demands for Ship Money ("they had not signed away the liberties of the realm"), and Samuel Sherman, one of their collectors, was imprisoned for negligence. The Essex magnate Lord Maynard was outraged at the elections of 1640 to be "challenged by fellows without shirts." Long Melford, Stoke-by-Nayland, and Colchester all witnessed antiroyalist (and anti-Catholic) riots in 1642. "This fury was not only in the rabble," wrote one alarmed observer, "but many of the better sort behaved themselves as if there had been a dissolution of all government." The fury was fed in part by thirteen years of royal trespass on customary liberties. The founders of Watertown treasured "the rights of Englishmen" and were just as determined as their kinsmen back home to defend them.[14]

The 1642 Stour Riots were fueled too by anti-Catholicism. Fear and hatred of that Antichrist, the pope, and all his followers, secret or open, plotting and exploiting, in league with Irish assassins and bloodthirsty foreign powers, infecting the court through the French queen, and poisoning the church through fellow-traveling archbishops and bishops—this whole paranoid mind-set lay at the core of puritan thinking. The Essex-Suffolk borderlands held enough terrors to sustain these fears: resident Catholics like the Mannocks, patrons at Stoke-by-Nayland, and the wealthy Riverses at Colchester and Long Melford. Irish soldiers were billeted in Maldon and Witham in 1627, two years after the panic about a Catholic invasion through Ipswich or Harwich. For most of the 1620s Dunkirk pirates ravaged shipping up and down the east coast. There was the long history of Jacobean kowtowing to Spain and, from 1618 to 1630, the pathetic inability of English arms or diplomacy to aid the puritans' beloved "Winter Queen" of Bohemia or the Huguenots of La Rochelle.[15]

Underlying all these fears was the folk memory of Bloody Mary Tudor, kept fresh in parish churches by Foxe's Book of Martyrs (many of them East Anglians), the dastardly plots against the life of Queen Elizabeth ("of blessed memory"), and the 1605 Gunpowder Plot. Rumors fueled hatred. Reports arose in 1625 of a "very dangerous and secret conference of recusants and popish-affected persons in multitudes together . . . in Suffolk"; in Essex in the same year, intelligence revealed "a great concourse to the papists' houses, and of their preparations [to rebel]."[16]

This virulent hatred spread in the reign of Charles and his Catholic queen to the rising flock of anti-Calvinist Arminians led by William Laud. Battle was joined over specific symbolic issues: bowing at the name of Jesus, use of the Book of Common Prayer, the surplice, the cross at baptism, Sunday recreation, and the placing of the Communion table altarwise and railed at the east end of the church.[17]

Boxted had long been divided in the conflict between Anglican conformity and resistance. Patrons, ministers, and some laypeople were avid Calvinists, but conservatives and Arminians in the parish were equally avid about conforming with orders from above. They accused a predecessor of Phillips with nonconformity, brawling, and defamation. In 1618 and 1633 John Maidstone was "detected for [sexual] incontinency." In 1628 and 1632 they complained about the nonconformity of Phillips and his successor, and in 1637 they had a set-to with John Maidstone Jr. about obeying the Laudian injunction to set up rails round the altar. The patron "doth threaten all men that come into his chancel to set [the rail] up, to sue them." Discord was deep-rooted in the parish.[18]

Anti-Catholicism was strongest among those people who called themselves the godly, professors, the elect, or even the saints, while their opponents scorned them as puritans, precisians, or zealants. Puritans were not just good haters of Antichrist, though. They had a positive, century-old program of reform, their Great Cultural Revolution. It involved incorporating the Reformed doctrine and "primitive" practices of John Calvin's Genevan church into the Church of England, imposing a "culture of discipline" on superstitious, fun-loving, indolent, incontinent, and irresponsible neighbors and generally purifying, through preaching, punishment, and example, a nation that God had chosen but whose negligence and waywardness were sorely testing His mercy. They saw themselves as an elite cadre predestined for God's purposes. Despite private agonies of doubt, deflation, and self-castigation, they appeared to critics, victims, and the authorities to be interfering, self-righteous, directive, strident, neurotic, arrogant, excluding, aggressive, uncompromising, humorless, somber; a swarm of busybodies, bores, prigs, and interminable nasal droners. One of their happiest hunting grounds was the Stour Valley and its environs.[19]

Reformist dissent was not new in the Suffolk-Essex borders in the 1620s. There had been Lollards in Colchester in 1402 and for decades during the subsequent century in several North Essex villages. Boxted had been one of the distribution points of Tyndale's subversive translation of the Bible in 1526. Suffolk and Essex had many Marian martyrs in the 1550s. Colchester prefigured Winthrop's ideal for Massachusetts in 1630: "This town, for the earnest profession of the gospel, became like unto a city upon a hill." This "provincial capital of heresy" boasted an influential lectureship whose incumbents included Watertown's second minister, John Knowles. George Gifford of Maldon was another magnet for puritans.[20]

Closer to Boxted, the focus of reform was Dedham. In 1578 a wealthy puritan clothier, William Cardinal, endowed a lectureship; four years later the Dedham Classis was founded, a group of twenty-odd local ministers and one or two pious laymen. In Dedham they sometimes met in Edmund Sherman's house. Their fourth meeting, on 4 March 1583, was at Boxted, where, after prayer, Mr. Morse (ancestor of emigrants to Watertown) agitated the issue of remarriage after divorce. Meeting in secret, they discussed knotty points of theology, practical issues, and disciplinary problems. The Dedham secretary corresponded with the saints of Maldon, with the far more radical classis in London, and with "our [sixty-four] Brethren in Suffolk," who met at Cambridge, Lavenham, and Ipswich. They were a puritan activist group seeking reform *within* the church. The monthly meetings continued until 1589, when the bishop of London suppressed the classis. Their zeal persisted, however, in Boxted and along the valley, though by the end of Elizabeth's reign, their campaign for a Genevan church organization had made little headway.[21]

Under the early Stuarts, the Stour Valley was Rogers country. Not only was the great preacher John Rogers holding forth at Dedham from 1605 to his death in 1637, but his uncle Richard was lecturer at Wethersfield, and his son Nathaniel (later minister of Ipswich, Mass.) was incumbent of Assington. Richard Rogers's stepsons were equally sharp thorns of dissent: Samuel Ward, lecturer at Ipswich, and Nathaniel Ward, attacker of Arminians in Parliament before emigrating to Ipswich. This was a formidable puritan clan, a model of that "tribalism" among ministerial families in New England.[22]

The puritan minister was trained to strive with his flock in three particular areas: preaching, the saving of souls, and instilling the culture of discipline. John Rogers was the greatest preacher of his generation. People came from as far as Cambridge to hear his weekly lectures. Robert Ryece wrote to Winthrop in early 1637 that "whilst the Bishop [of Norwich, Laudian Matthew Wren] was at Ipswich, one day, having occasion to ride forth, [he] commanded his servants to hire post horses, who brought him word that all the horses were taken up by such as went to the sermon at Dedham." At his funeral, there were, according to Emmanuel Downing, "more people than three churches could hold." Dedham is a very big church![23]

Rogers was a "hot" preacher. He put the fear of God in his hearers. He denounced sin with fury. He brought not peace but the sword. He was a thunderer. He attracted and influenced a generation of young acolytes like John Sherman and Thomas Hooker, who studied under him at Dedham after Cambridge.[24]

"Roaring" Rogers embodied the puritan conviction that the pulpit rather than the altar should be the focus of any church. Where preaching lectureships were endowed by corporations, as they were at Ipswich, Colchester, and Maldon, preachers could be elected, or called, by the citizens. The Bishop of London's Commissary described Colchester's "factious multitude, who will allow no minister but of their own calling," and his master described the petition for a revival of the East Bergholt lecture in 1636 as "a popular course of hands."[25]

North Essex and South Suffolk rang with puritan sermons. Samuel Ward was the scourge of Laudian innovations at St. Mary-le-Tower, Ipswich (1605–38). He was accused in 1635 of advocating that "all that bear office in church or commonwealth ought to be elected by the people." Many emigrants to Watertown would have heard Ward's revolutionary agenda as they waited to sail in 1634 and 1635.[26]

The Stour Valley boasted other famous sermonizers: Richard Blackerby at Ashen, Samuel Fairclough at Sudbury and Hadleigh, and Stephen Marshall at Finchingfield, as well as town lecturers like Lewis, Northey, Ames, Bridge, Maddon, and Knowles at Colchester. Several of the forty-one puritan lecturers preached during the 1620s in emigrant towns like Mount Bures or Sudbury, home of John Wilson, first minister of Boston. They also "abounded in Suffolk. Not a bowling-green or an ordinary [inn] would stand without one . . . [they were] set up by private gents at their pleasure."[27]

Many churches had visiting preachers. Winthrop's father, Adam, recorded hearing twenty-five different divines in Groton church in the one year of 1620. The formidable Thomas Hooker preached "The Faithful Covenanter" in Dedham about November 1629, before his flight to the Netherlands. A rising star of the Colne Valley, Thomas Shepard, was also in demand during the 1620s in other Essex and Suffolk pulpits. John Winthrop's "insatiable thirst after the word of God . . . though it were many miles off, especially of such as did search deep into conscience" was typical of "professors." Godly gentlemen like Winthrop were reported to punctuate powerful passages with a chorus of "Amens" and would vie with each other to take the preacher to dinner. This spiritual thirst spanned the social scale. When four gossips in Ipswich in September 1637 "fell to speak concerning preaching [silenced by the bishop], one [the wife of John Dixon, a ships' caulker] wished she were in New England," where exhortation was unconfined.[28]

Sermons might terrorize souls and manipulate tender consciences, but the puritan minister was also expected to catechize and give counsel in preparation for gracious rebirth. In such ways they were the means toward salvation. Richard Rogers's *Seven Treatises* was a handbook for daily conduct and devotion, rivaling Arthur Dent's *Plain Man's Pathway* in popularity. His nephew John's *Treatise of Love,* for whose third edition Hooker wrote a foreword in 1629, was an inspiration for Winthrop's "Model of Christian Charity," a Massachusetts manifesto delivered during the 1630 crossing.[29]

"Cases of conscience" were the puritan minister's most pressing private priority. Hooker saved the life of a suicidal gentlewoman racked with fears of damnation. When another lady at Dedham confided "long and sad stories of her bad heart, sad state, God's wrath, danger of dropping into hell &c.," John Rogers leaped from his chair and "fetched a few frisks on the floor," saying "God be thanked! God be thanked!" He had seen the vital signs of conviction of sin, which must precede conversion to sainthood.[30] Inducing and then treating such cases of conscience was the "saving work" of ministerial therapists. Their converts formed around them an inner church of the elect, the God-favored gathering of the saved.[31]

Instituting what has been called a culture of discipline or a reformation of manners was a third aim of this great purifying crusade. The intention was revolutionary: to undo folk customs, superstitions, and behaviors going back into the mists of time and to remake conduct and attitudes on a new, godly, scriptural, "rational" model. The passion and urgency of this campaign for social transformation was heightened by the demographic and economic problems threatening England between the 1540s and the 1640s and by the sense that condoning misconduct invited divine wrath.[32]

The reforming focus on the parish or the town reflected the decay of manorial government and Tudor emphasis on the parish as the crucial unit of local government. Dedham was an early and influential initiator of purifying reforms. In 1585 the home of the classis adopted orders imposing strict Sabbatarianism, full attendance, and patriarchal control of families in church and for catechizing of youth, orderly seated Communion every fourth Sunday with preparation in church on the previous days, collections for the deserving poor, and monthly meetings of ministers and elders "concerning the good government of the town." The new system excluded from the Lord's Supper townspeople in dispute and required ministerial and neighborly arbitration before resort to law. All householders and as many servants as possible must attend two lectures each week, and all children were to learn to read in a schoolhouse, the poorer being subsidized by Communion collections. Nonreaders were ineligible for apprenticeships. The town authorities would "warn out" (or renounce responsibility for) the nonresident and the masterless and regularly inspect "the poor and chiefly the suspected places." The orders finished by requiring ostracism of the weddings of "any [who] have known one another carnally before marriage." Public declaration of their "filthiness" would precede baptism of their children "to the humbling of the parties and the terrifying of others." Nine ancients, including two Shermans, formally agreed to maintain all Christian order "on the whole body of the town."[33]

All the elements of the new culture were foreshadowed here: godly, patriarchal family government, education and training, the work ethic, relentless puritan propagandizing, control of town government by clergy and established townsmen, social shunning, ruthless clampdowns on illicit sex, drinking, gambling, dancing, or wenching in "suspected places" catering for "the naughty disposition of disordered persons," and on the Sabbath "travelling to fairs, markets, marriage dinners and dinners abroad or in the town." Instead of the boozy "ales" to raise money for church or poor, regular collections were instituted. The poor were divided between "the better minded," deserving of neighborly gifts, loans, or charity ("Help them ere it is too late," exhorted John Rogers), and the "rude, idle and profane." Rogers had a short answer for them: "For those that can work and will not, let them starve." "Alehouse merriment," "festive sociability," and easygoing "good fellowship" that condoned immiserating vice must give way to directed, disciplined order. "In a town where the chief men hold together," Rogers asked, "what evil can stand against them? What good may they not effect?"[34]

Such successes were repeated elsewhere in North Essex and South Suffolk: at Castle Hedingham, Maldon, All Saints Sudbury, Bury St. Edmunds, Terling, Braintree, and Finchingfield. Sometimes the reformers, as at Dedham, were self-perpetuating "closed vestries." Braintree's Company of Four-and-Twenty protested against the "admittance of all sort of persons into their vestries and meetings for the public good because of the disquietness and hindrance by the dissension of some evil-disposed and others of the inferior and meanest sort of parishioners and inhabitants being greater in number and thereby more ready to cross the good proceedings for the benefit of their church and parish."[35]

Other parish governments remained "open." In Finchingfield, though the seven to eleven "townsmen" performed many executive functions, "the parish" met at the church to approve taxes and expenditures, to express "the mind of the town," and, in policy matters, "the consent of the town." Boxted appears to have adopted this open form of parish government through minister, townsmen, and inclusive vestry.[36]

The revolutionary campaign to impose the culture of discipline was bound to create conflict. Its puritan exponents took no prisoners. To ignore sin condemned them as accessories. They savaged hallowed customs, Sunday sports, May Day, Christmas hospitality and carnival, wedding feasts, and well-oiled beatings of the parish bounds. They scorned traditional institutions and attitudes, like undiscriminating "good neighborhood" (i.e., communal sociability and welfare), entertainments like plays, dances, and help-, bride-, or church-ales. Settling arguments over a "drink together in the alehouse" was treating sickness with poison. Alehouses were the headquarters of the "dark parish," fostering riot, drunkenness, gambling, pauperism, promiscuity, and sedition.[37]

The Dedham Classis noted two reported confrontations with folk culture: "A man's wife beating her husband, there was hereupon a man in woman's attire and a woman in man's attire carried on a cowl staff with a drum and caliver and morris pikes on men's shoulders." The narrator "had vehemently inveighed against it, and told them his credit was greatly touched in it." An apostle of the new discipline thus denounced the outrage of the old folk-shaming of uppity wives by charivari.[38] When another member asked "how he might know a witch, [when] some said she might be found out by search of her body, some [others] thought that to be [a] fancy in the people easily [gullibly] conceiving such a thing and to be reproved in them," the meeting recommended him "to give it over to some justice to examine it." Rather rely on law and rationality than popular superstition.[39]

John Rogers taught that "our saviour comes not to such [good] fellowship, but debate," and puritans were popularly seen as troublemakers, agents provocateurs, and antagonists. The puritan zealot expected "storm and fret . . . stir and hurly-burly" from "the world." Antipuritans remembered "a merry world when there was less preaching"; "profane persons" loved the saints much "as a dog loves a pitchfork." In power the godly could be intolerably high-handed, in opposition stiff-necked. In 1629, for instance, seven parishioners of Nayland, including Watertown emigrants John Warren, John Firmin, and Simon Stone's brother, were presented for refusing to kneel at Communion. Boxted puritans adamantly resisted "Romish innovations." As the earl of Strafford confided to Archbishop Laud what both knew from bitter experience: "The very genius of that nation of people [puritans] leads them always to oppose as well civilly as ecclesiastically all that ever authority ordains for them."[40]

East Anglians had considerable contacts with London, a second source of migrants to Watertown, through trade in cloths, supply of food, and the spiritual brotherhood of puritan ministers often begun at Cambridge and nurtured by correspondence, mutual suffering, and visits. There was concerting of plans between the classes during the 1580s, and some of their correspondence has survived. Richard Rogers in remote Wethersfield soon heard of the silencing of London ministers by Archbishop Whitgift in 1604. In the late 1620s London lecturers and Cambridge fellows joined fasts, sermons, and conferences held in Essex and Suffolk. Since Essex was in the Diocese of London, there were many administrative contacts beween the city and the county. There was contact too between separatist or voluntary groups in Colchester and Southwark. Thomas Cotton in Colchester heard the latest news from London regularly via a "peevish intelligencer" and spread it among "zealants" on market days. East Anglian familiarity with London nonconformity might help to reduce friction in their new-world cohabitation.[41]

The villagers of the Jacobean Stour Valley lived in the heart of a remarkably fruitful, advanced, and radical region. Economically, it had mixed agriculture stimulated by the insatiable market of London, and the cloth trade exported textiles all over Europe. Politically, it was highly resistant to royal pretensions and to any show of authoritarianism. Puritan reformism prospered in many of its parishes; charismatic ministers were aided and abetted by lay patrons and zealous vestries in an atmosphere of economic expansion and international peace.

This favorable situation proved extremely fragile, however. Between 1614 and 1637, when the emigration to Watertown from the region effectively ended, a series of disasters devastated the Stour Valley:

1614–17	Cockayne's project to stop export of unfinished cloth cuts Old Drapery exports.
1618	Start of Thirty Years' War. Cloth sales further disrupted. Dunkirk pirates prey on east coast shipping. James I issues *Book of Sports* for Sunday recreations.
1619	London clothier fails. A total of 180 Essex and Suffolk clothiers face losses of £20,000.
1621–23	Disastrous harvests.
1624	England enters Thirty Years' War. Cloth worth £39,000 goes unsold in Suffolk.
1625	Fears of Catholic invasion of east coast.
1626	Plague in Sudbury and Colchester. Charles I's Forced Loan.
1628	Laud appointed bishop of London.
1629–30	Further disastrous harvests. Complete stop on cloth exports. The depression of the 1630s begins.
1629	Nadir of Protestant cause in Europe. Charles I dissolves Parliament and begins eleven-year Personal Rule.
1630–32	Campaign against Essex puritans peaks.
1633	Laud becomes archbishop of Canterbury. *Book of Sports* reissued.
1635–36	Bitter winter.
1635–39	Ship money demanded from the whole country.

1635	Laudian Matthew Wren appointed bishop of Norwich (Norfolk and Suffolk).
1636–37	Plague returns.
1637	Harvest failure.

Other measures of suffering are the statistics for cloth exports and food prices: as the former plummeted, the latter soared. The vulnerable economy might have withstood the bad harvests if cloth had been selling well, if taxation had been low, and disease dormant. The combination of negative factors was lethal.[42]

The first to suffer in the Stour were the poor and those dependent on wages.[43] In September 1622 the justices of the peace of Suffolk had to admonish the churchwardens of Groton, Boxford, and Edwardstone "for failure to support the impotent poor or provide employment for the able bodied." This warning was soon extended to all the parishes in Babergh Hundred. The bench informed the privy council that "times are so exceeding hard." Essex, meanwhile, swarmed with "vagabonds, beggars and gypsies." Riots of unemployed clothworkers broke out in both counties in December 1622. By 1624, as the "decay of cloth" worsened, parishes had to raise their poor taxes. Weavers were reduced to spinning, stone-picking, poaching, pilfering, and begging— "unlawful and disorderly courses to get relief," which alarmed the Essex authorities.[44]

After a brief respite in the mid-1620s, distress redoubled in 1629. Three thousand unsold cloths piled up in Dedham and Langham; "fewer than a hundred had been sold in the preceding eighteen months." A menacing group of two hundred unemployed weavers dogged the Essex justices "from place to place complaining of extreme necessity and disability to maintain . . . themselves and their families." Much disorder was reported from Lavenham. The news of food riots in Maldon and the plundering of a grain ship bound for Hull in May 1629 quickly spread. Another grain riot erupted in Colchester in July.[45]

Hunger threatened to turn into starvation. Winthrop "trembled" at meeting "so many wandering ghosts in the shape of men, so many spectacles of misery in all our streets, our entries [full] of hunger-starved Christians . . . and under our stalls lie our own flesh in nakedness." In 1629 a lecture by John Rogers was suppressed. That summer Thomas Motte, the minister of Stoke-by-Nayland, made inquiries about emigration to New England. He supposed "many will go." Joan Lady Barrington heard from Ipswich in December 1629 of "many poor Christians who are in want, much pinched in these hard times with penury and famine." Destitution affected creditors and landlords. Winthrop complained, "I have no money and I am so far in debt already." His wife reported in May 1631 that she had "been constrained to send to the tenants for rent, wanting money, but have received little yet . . . They complain of the hardness of the times."[46]

Smaller clothiers in Colchester and the Stour were going to the wall. The business of Watertown emigrant William Hammond of Lavenham "broke" in early 1630, at the same time as Thomas Hooker was silenced by Laud. In February 1631 the inhabitants of Nayland reported that "their distressed state for want of corn is so great that most of the inhabitants are ready to perish." The spinners, weavers, and combers of Sudbury were forced to sell their beds, spinning wheels, and working tools for bread. Hadleigh clothiers told the same story. By early 1635 the clothiers of Essex and Suffolk had £100,000 worth of cloths "lacking vent." The famous staple of the Stour, the broadcloth, was in terminal collapse.[47]

The Suffolk justices informed London that "the poor come in great troops to the writers telling them they are like to starve." The local authorities warned that the "impatience of the poor" would lead to "licentious fury and desperation." Two hundred textile families were thrown out of work in Hadleigh alone by the arrival of the plague in 1636. Reflecting on "these so evil and declining times," Winthrop wrote that "this land grows weary of her inhabitants . . . children, neighbours and friends (especially if they be poor) are rated the greatest burdens." This pervasive "scourge and judgement" on the land was "the hand of God." The saints ignored such providences at their peril. Alarm was spreading up and down the Stour Valley, sounded in pulpits in Boxted and Dedham, Sudbury and Stoke, Colchester and Maldon, wherever groups of professors gathered to bewail the times and seek the will of the Lord. In such a mood of despair and desperation, some came to understand that they were to transfer their godly companies to the new world. The "immoderate rains" of the winter of 1629–30 confirmed them in their belief. From a waterlogged Stour Valley they came to Watertown.[48]

II
FOUNDATIONS

4

Government

English parish government had been expanding its range of duties over the past two generations. The establishment of towns in the wilderness added yet more weight to the inherited rock of local administration—no wonder contemporaries in New England likened "the toil of a new plantation" to the "labors of Hercules." In these founding years, all kinds of new responsibilities had to be organized: land allocations, public buildings, education, infrastructure. But who should be the organizers? The new settlement on the Charles had mixed administrative precedents from its East Anglian background. Some Stourland parishes had consulted all householders for "the mind of the town" on major issues. In 1606, for instance, Ashdon in northwest Essex had started keeping parish accounts because "a great suspicion was grown among some parishioners of the honest and just business of such officers as were chosen." Others had developed oligarchic leaderships, self-perpetuating, nonaccountable, "closed" or "select" vestries, often intent on imposing the "culture of discipline" on the "inferior and meaner sort of parishioners." This was the rationale for oligarchy by "the people who know best," not only for Elizabethan Dedham or Jacobean Braintree but down through the ages.[1]

Analysts of town government in early Massachusetts have almost invariably argued that towns were run by their elites, with or without the added authority of a resident magistrate. Town meetings, so celebrated by nineteenth-century commentators on American democracy, were, they claim, mere rubber stamps; old-world oligarchic institutions were rerooted in New England soil and grew lustily during the seventeenth century. Men of wealth and standing in the community could expect membership on the selectmen's board as a right (if they wanted it). Annual elections by "a crew of rustics" were a convenient means of satisfying the "broadly diffused desire for consensual communalism," but the outcome was never in doubt, and the leadership thereafter behaved as though their authority was God-given. In such an authoritarian environment, serious political conflict would be unimaginable. Watertown is often cited as a typical case. Elaborate statistics are presented to demonstrate the length of tenure, regularity of reelection, age/wealth profiles, and decision-making clout of a small band of perennial town leaders.[2]

Building on recent studies of concepts of liberty and the influence of public opinion in early modern England, I would like to advance a different interpretation. While no one would deny the contention that only a limited number of townsmen were considered suitable for town office, there is ample room to doubt that they exercised virtually unchecked elite rule. All *major* decisions were taken by the town meeting. Officials were held accountable by their constituents. If they failed to keep the voters' trust, they were unceremoniously dumped. Long service was not just a sign of voter indifference or plebeian deference. It was, rather, a reward for public-spirited commitment. Furthermore, the ordinary people of Watertown had a highly developed sense of their rights and freedoms, with well-schooled suspicions of authority. They had seen enough of "Thorough," or nonaccountable autocracy, in the England of Charles I and Archbishop Laud to be ever alert to the signs of executive tyranny.[3]

Running a New England town was a highly complex business. By the 1650s the administrative year had settled into a regular rhythm of activities. In seasonal terms, there were far more meetings in the winter than during the busy farming months of summer and early fall. The administrative year 1657–58 was reasonably typical of the routine of local government.[4] On 16 December, at a public town meeting, various elections for the following year took place. The seven selectmen were chosen, along with the town clerk, "whose work is to keep all the town's accounts and to receive such debts [owed to the town] as are brought to him, and to pay all instant debts [owed by the town]," with the selectmen's approval. He also kept the minutes of meetings, lists of births as well as of marriages and deaths, and records of possessions. Other posts filled at this meeting were the surveyors of highways, who joined the already elected constables as town officials for 1658. A second meeting of "the whole town" on 22 January agreed the town tax rate of £50 and ordered that the verger and schoolmaster should be paid their usual salaries. There was not another town meeting until the following fall.

Meanwhile, the selectmen had held six meetings in each other's houses. On 11 January they "reckoned" with the schoolmaster for the second half of his salary for 1657. Two weeks later the town clerk was authorized to let out the land and cows of an elderly resident; two selectmen were to check on his provisions, and three others "to make the town rate," that is, to appraise each household's share for local taxes. Accounts of debts due to be paid by the town were presented: refunding of payments made by townsmen on behalf of poor neighbors; wages owed to three town boundary walkers (townsmen who walked along town boundaries with neighboring towns' boundsmen to mark and agree on the exact location of each border), the verger (meetinghouse janitor), and the schoolmaster; bounties for people who had killed foxes; and taxation due to the county. Except for the county levy, these monies were to be paid out of the £50 voted by the town. On 12 February, however, the town clerk noted that the three town raters (tax assessors) had made an appraisal totaling £67. The increased taxes for each household were handed to the two constables to collect. The next selectmen's meeting was on 13 April. They made a contract with the town herdsman, let out some land of an aged neighbour to help finance his care, arranged for the town measures to be checked for accuracy in Boston, tightened up arrangements for the nightly watch, and made an order about herding of sheep and cattle for the summer months.

There was then a typical four-month gap during the busiest farming season before the next two board meetings in August. On the 9th two men were chosen hogreeves/fence viewers by the selectmen, since the town had for some reason neglected to do so back in January. The champion fox trapper was paid three shillings. On 30 August the appraiser reported the town estate (all the private and communal real estate) to be worth £7,298 among 153 polls.[5] The "country" rate apportioned by the colony treasurer to be paid by Watertown for 1658 was £43. On 20 September the selectmen supervised contracts of apprenticeship with two foster parents for two young children of a demented townswoman.

The first town meeting in ten months convened on 1 October, agreed on the pastor's salary at £120, appointed rate-makers, and approved an agreement with the town herdsman. On 25 October the town met again, chose two constables, and appointed the three deacons to regulate the seating in the meetinghouse.

Two more selectmen's meetings, the seventh and eighth, filled out the year. On 2 November the raters delivered their list of house-by-house charges to be collected by the two constables, who handed in the county treasurer's receipt to prove that they had duly collected and delivered the £10 county tax to Cambridge. The pastor's tax to be paid proportionately by each household was presented and approved. At their last meeting, on 3 January 1659, they "warned out" two couples who had recently started lodging with relatives in the town; they could expect no welfare, since they were thus formally declared non-residents. The board received the constables' accounts for the previous year, arranged for some disputed land to be surveyed, and, finally, entered recent expenditures due on the town account.

At the town meeting a week later, after election of a moderator, the accounts were presented listing debts to the schoolmaster, verger, wolf and fox trappers, caregivers for the poor, witnesses for town business at court, town representatives at the general court, the town invoice-taker, the militia quartermaster for ammunition, and wages for the hogreeves/fence viewers. They approved the deacons' seating plan, reappointed the schoolmaster, and set a town tax rate. They reelected the town clerk and five of the 1658 selectmen, choosing two other experienced neighbors to rejoin the board. The choice of surveyors of highways and hogreeves closed the business. So a new administrative year began.

Officials, timing, ad hoc business, and financial needs would vary, but 1658 incorporated in its town minutes all the routine annual local business: finance, welfare, education, policing, and relations with neighboring towns. Most significantly, all the major decisions and appointments were made by the town meeting. The one exception was the board's raising of the approved town tax rate from £50 to £67. This extremely unusual move was provoked by unanticipated town debts. It is impossible to tell whether there was any consultation with the town at large over this exceptional rate increase. The fact that very detailed accounts were presented the following year may indicate that the seven men had been put on notice to get their sums right in future. Such an executive rate increase never occurred again.

The precise dynamics of the relationship between town meeting and selectmen cannot be recovered from laconic entries in the town records. Townsmen may have nodded through everything put to them for form's sake by their betters on the board, or they may have asserted their constitutional sovereignty within the town by holding their elected officers to strict account. How power changed hands over time and how the town dealt with crises may help to illuminate the relationship further.

During the first fifty years, 1630–80, the government of Watertown went through three stages. During the first four years, the church formed the main institution for collective action and decision making within the town. The decade after 1634 saw a group of leaders annually reelected to the town's board of selectmen as local government became more institutionalized and regulated throughout the colony. Third, from the mid-1640s a second group of laymen took over as selectmen. Except for the late 1640s and a period in the 1660s, they were frequently reelected until the 1680s.

From 1630 to 1634, when the population of the whole colony was probably under a thousand, two established authorities dealt with urgent business. The governor and assistants of the Massachusetts Bay Company were the only legally constituted lay authority at this stage, and they held regular "courts" handling not only disciplinary cases but also colonial and local administration.

There were only six or seven towns in these first years, and central control was thus practicable. So, on 19 October 1630, it was the court that *appointed* Watertown's first constable, John Page, and, on 9 May 1632, his successor, William Clark. The following year it made William Jennison "ancient," or ensign, to Captain Daniel Patrick, their military commander north of the Charles River.[6]

Since assistants were given the same powers as justices of the peace in England, it is probable that the town's resident magistrate, Sir Richard Saltonstall, ordered much minor business in the town during his brief sojourn. Indeed, he seems to have been rather too autocratic, as he was fined £5 for whipping two people without the presence of another magistrate as the law required. In March 1631 the court actually met in Watertown, perhaps at Sir Richard's invitation before his departure for England. This central control of the tiny bridgehead was inevitable during the critical months after arrival.[7]

Equally inevitable, from such stiff-necked planters who had ample reason to distrust any imposed authority, was the questioning of the powers of the court and its officials. Early in 1632, according to Winthrop, "Mr. [William] Clark [constable] of Watertown had complained to the governor, that Captain Patrick, being removed out of their town to Newtown [Cambridge], did command them to watch [patrol at night] near Newtown, and [Clark] desired the governor, that they might have the ordering within their own town." An almighty row with the "rash" commander followed, but thereafter Watertown constables set their own watches where the town required.[8]

This assertion of local control was part of a much more famous constitutional dispute. In 1632 the magistrates who made up the General Court ordered a levy from the various settlements to pay for the fortification of the proposed capital, Newtown, later Cambridge. In February the minister, George Phillips, and the ruling elder, Richard Brown, called the people together in the new meetinghouse and delivered their opinions that this demand was illegal. This is the first evidence of the church as a de facto institution of local government, but it had probably fulfilled that role from the beginning. As the only town institution (and at that early stage relatively inclusive), it was very similar to a parish, the equivalent unit of English local government. The founders of Watertown would have been entirely familiar with parish procedures. They would have sat in their parish churches in England while village business was conducted.[9] The new church, then, was the natural forum both for protest and for decision making, and during subsequent months it continued as the focus for other conflicts with central authority. Although the town's stand against the Newtown levy proved "after much debate" to be faulty, which their leaders publicly acknowledged "and made retraction and submission," nonetheless, their objections—along with the growth of population and settlements due to the second surge of immigration—did have long-term constitutional effects.

In May 1632 an invitation arrived, and "Mr. Oldham and Mr. Masters [were chosen] two [representatives] for Watertown to confer with the Court concerning raising a public stock." By 1634 the freemen, or male church members, of established towns could elect deputies to represent them at general court meetings, and local business was devolved to the individual towns. As lay institutions developed, the church withdrew from local government, though town meetings took place in the same all-purpose building, the aptly named meetinghouse.[10]

In 1634, the start of the second stage of town government, the Watertown records begin, and recapturing the running of town business becomes easier. In that year the town had three selectmen: Ensign William Jennison; Mr. Brian Pendleton, a merchant from London; and John Eddy, one of the Boxted congregation who had accompanied Phillips's Company to the new world. Richard Brown was first representative to the General Court, with Jennison and Lt. Robert Feake.[11] When responsibility for land allocation was localized in 1636, the board of selectmen was expanded to eleven. It stayed at this level until 1639, when it rose to twelve, dropping back to nine in 1642. By the time the interrupted minutes restart in book 2 (1647), the board had steadied at seven. With few exceptions, it held to that number for the rest of the century.

The fourfold expansion of the board in 1636 may have been a move toward opening up leadership to a wider group. There certainly seems to have been a conscious attempt to involve new men in the board each year.[12] For the year 1636 eight of the eleven "prudential men" were inevitably new, but next year six other new names appear, and the following year seven. After the elections for 1639, when four new men were chosen (including two subsequent record-breaking selectmen Hugh Mason and Thomas Hastings), experimentation tailed off. Twenty-eight householders had served on the town executive by the end of 1640; suitable candidates were probably running out.

Another factor, however, was behind changes of personnel after 1638. In that year the members of the eleven-man board had provoked popular outrage by granting themselves farms. Several were driven from office, and it took years to restore their reputations. The town had exerted its authority over its self-serving selectmen for the first, but not for the last, time.[13]

Despite the liberal appearance of this rolling cycle of town leaders, there was, even by 1640, an inner group who were reelected again and again: Jennison, Pendleton, Richard Brown, the town surveyor Abraham Brown, Thomas Mayhew (first elected in 1637), the surgeon Simon Eyre, Elder Edward Howe, and Lt. Robert Feake. What these men had in common was status. All were entitled to the honorific "Mr.," and two were commissioned officers. Several had mercantile backgrounds: Jennison, trading with the Chesapeake and

Bermuda (where he had previously lived); Pendleton and Feake, land speculators from London business families; and Mayhew, a Southampton trader and agent for London merchant Matthew Craddock, who had invested in Watertown mill and weir. Richard Brown had owned a wherry, or river barge, in London and lived in the commercial borough of Southwark on the south bank of the Thames. The merchants Mayhew, Feake, Pendleton, and Jennison were a decade younger than the remainder of the core group, who all were East Anglians aged over fifty.[14]

The missing records between 1634 and 1647 prevent precision, but at some point in the mid-1640s, all of the early core group disappeared. This complete turnover had several causes. Some established selectmen died. Some fell ill. A scandal blighted one volatile career. On 7 March 1643 "Mr. Richard Brown being questioned for unmeet and filthy dalliances with Sarah now wife of Thomas Boylston, for want of full evidence, they were dismissed with an admonition." Brown was never again elected to the Watertown board.[15]

The commonest reason for this wholesale change was that members of the first core group moved elsewhere. Eyre the surgeon moved to a larger clientele in Boston; merchants Busby, Clark, Payne, and Pendleton to growing ports and fisheries. Others sought fresh starts: Mayhew, near financial ruin, on Martha's Vineyard with its agricultural and fishing potential; and Patrick, discharged and sexually compromised in Watertown, to new settlement down the coast. The Feakes, already restless, went with him. Jennison, Biscoe, and Pastor Knowles joined the remigrators attracted by the exciting potential of the godly republic in England.[16]

Apart from such personal reasons for departure, what most leavers shared was outsider status in the predominantly East Anglian town. All except Eyre (who kept his Watertown holdings when he moved across the Charles) and possibly Jennison came from what is known in the eastern counties as "away."[17] They had not intermarried with the East Anglians. They might have had social status, wealth, broad horizons, and administrative experience, but they were strangers to the Suffolk-Essex core of Watertown residents.

The small core group who replaced them on the board were no strangers. The four men who were henceforward reelected time and again to town office were Suffolk men Thomas Hastings and Ephraim Child and Essex men Hugh Mason and John Sherman. All first entered office between 1639 and 1642, and after their executive apprenticeship, one or another of them was usually the first-named selectman, presumably the year's chairman. They were not just selectmen either but held multiple offices. Mason and Sherman were militia officers, Hastings and Child deacons. All brought specialist skills to the town's service.[18]

The "board revolution" was complete in 1644, when two other regulars, Richard Beers and Michael Bairstow, were first elected selectmen. Beers was a leading militiaman whose origins are unknown.[19] The Yorkshireman Bairstow had moved into Watertown in 1641 or 1642 as the new husband of the widow Carver, an East Anglian by affinity.

Several other men joined the six regulars as occasional recruits to the board: Sergeant (and later Deacon) Henry Bright, Ensign Thomas Bartlett, Deacon Simon Stone, Charles Chadwick, and Deacon Samuel Thatcher. The origins of the last two are unknown; the first three were East Anglians.[20]

The apparent continuities in government of the regulars between the 1640s and the 1670s and the pool of occasional recruits to the board have convinced several scholars that Watertown had come to be ruled by a tight and persistent East Anglian oligarchy. Setting aside the significant minority of selectmen not from East Anglia, this conclusion is still seriously misleading. Mason, Sherman, Child, and Hastings did not have things entirely their own way. Outrage against cronyism in 1638 had been a warning shot. The upsets of the 1640s and 1650s, discussed elsewhere, demonstrated voter rejection of unresponsive executives;[21] those of the 1660s left them in no doubt about who were the ultimate masters in the town.

In the early 1660s town government was become increasingly casual and incompetent. Elected officials were failing to do their jobs properly. The rot seems to have set in most seriously in 1662 and 1663. In January 1662 there was a routine town meeting at which officials were elected, including Ephraim Child as town clerk. One selectmen's meeting is recorded in March, then there is a blank page and another misordered page. In January 1663 only five, instead of the normal seven, selectmen were elected: the usual gang of Mason, Beers, and Hastings, joined by William Bond,[22] stepnephew of Ephraim Child, and Nathaniel Treadway. No town clerk was named, though Child was close to death; there were no town accounts included in the most perfunctory annual records. The selectmen met only three times and were insolently rebuffed by a young man behind in his rates to the pastor. In December the accounts of the constable Roger Wellington were so unsatisfactory that Beers and Bond were deputed to "deal with him," presenting him to the grand jury if necessary. Something was rotten in the state of Watertown.[23]

The town meeting of 4 February 1664 began the cleansing process. The choice of selectmen represented a virtual clean sweep. Mason, Beers, Hastings, and Bond were out, and nine men were elected in their place. Treadway alone was reelected. He was joined by Joseph Tainter. The two of them for the next three years were the shakers and movers of the town's executive. Their board colleagues were new or newly returned to favor. Tainter and Treadway were slightly younger than Mason and Hastings, but the average age of the new nine-man board was not a major factor of change.[24]

What was new was a determination that full records be kept—Ensign Sherman was elected town clerk—and that consistent procedures be followed. Accountability to the town as a whole was the new watchword. The first order after the choice of selectmen laid down that town meetings to elect officials and approve budgets should be held every year on the first Monday of November at 9 A.M. Henceforward, the most important gathering of householders would be predictable and regular—the same principle demanded by England's Parliament throughout the seventeenth century, but only permanently established three decades later.[25]

There were three more town meetings and eleven selectmen's meetings in the ten months before the new procedures went into force on the first Monday of November. Town meeting agendas were posted outside the meetinghouse, and the constable reminded the congregation the Sunday before. Tainter and Treadway were the terriers of the board, appraising, revaluing, seating the meetinghouse, and inspecting the town ammunition and gunpowder.[26]

The minutes kept by Sherman give a strong impression of selectmen reporting back conscientiously and holding people to account. Colony laws, such as the dress regulations, were enforced with a new rigor. Though meticulous in caring (and entering the outlays) for the unfortunate of Watertown, the new selectmen were careful to prevent unnecessary additions to the welfare rolls. The board issued a detailed order to control cattle herding. Similarly, they confronted the growing scandal of tax evasion, calling delinquents to long overdue account.[27]

Although Mason was back as first-named selectman in 1665 and the board reverted to seven selectmen, the four most active officials of 1664 remained in harness. Tainter and Treadway continued to undertake much of the most important town business. The old guard of Hastings and Beers did not return to prominence until the 1670s.

Why they had been so unceremoniously dumped is open to conjecture. Controversy over church membership and the Half-Way Covenant may have been a cause; four of the new board were nonfreemen. The Watertown land conflict was yet again a threatening issue. The new king's commissioners were apprehensively and disunitedly expected. War was in the air. All may have contributed to town dissatisfaction. The minutes of town proceedings, however, give the impression that the old guard had been in power too long and had grown casual, careless, and unaccountable. In 1663 there is an unmistakable sense of a wallowing ship being manned by a new crew, turned into the wind, and getting under way again.[28]

The new officers soon learned who were the masters. Despite a majority of artisans on the board, a 22 February 1664 town meeting laid down that "tradesmen's trades and incomes" were to be included in valuations alongside real property.[29] The townsmen of Watertown had in 1663 given notice to their elite—a captain of militia, his lieutenant, the senior deacon, and the rising son of another deacon—that they were no longer satisfied with their performance, and now in 1664 they underlined their authority.[30]

These shots across elite bows proved no isolated assertions of popular power. In 1667 money had to be raised by the town for a new bridge across the Charles. Rather than increasing the taxes, it was proposed that some common land be sold to help defray the cost.[31] Flogging the family silver seemed to some shortsighted. Robert Harrington led a campaign of opposition and "with some others went from house to house gaining a subscription to a writing, the purport whereof [according to the authorities] was to make division in town." Again the town was thrown into turmoil. A special town meeting had to be called and the whole issue debated and put to the vote again. The opposition was silenced only when a complaint against Harrington and his allies was filed with the county court.[32]

Two years later, local sovereignty of the inhabitants was asserted with devastating directness: "Whereas the selectmen affirm that they are the town and their orders shall stand, we humbly [submit] that according to law title Township 75, 76, that the power of making orders belongs to the inhabitants that are there allowed to act, and where selectmen [are] chosen by the town to act in prudential affairs yet they are to act according to instructions given them in writing by the inhabitants, but in this case it is not so and therefore their orders will not stand by law and these [orders] are not to be submitted to."[33]

Another snub was delivered in 1671 with the summoning of a special town meeting in December. The selectmen, including Mason, Tainter, and Treadway, by now elite figures themselves, had appointed a committee of leading figures—Mason, in the chair, Beers, Hastings (lately embroiled in a bruising and embarrassing paternity suit), Sherman, and Bond among them—to find a solution to the renewed problem of cattle herding. They drew up new regulations, but "these not agreeing to the satisfaction of the town," the meeting chose three *outside* arbiters instead.[34] On difficult and contentious questions, the "establishment" of the town could not rely on its prestige and authority to impose its solution.

The same lesson had to be learned eight years later. Retrenchment was in the air after the fearsome expense of King Phillip's War (1675–76). One controversial saving was attempted by reducing the schoolmaster's salary and closing down the school for part of the year, but hostilities grew to such a pitch that protest was carried to the county court. On 1 April 1679 they minuted:

In answer to the complaint submitted by sundry of the inhabitants of Watertown concerning the settling of a schoolmaster among them by the selectmen. The court approves and commends the care of the selectmen in taking care that an able schoolmaster may be settled and provided among them as the law directs. Yet considering that the law hath referred that matter to *the inhabitants in general* [emphasis added] who are concerned in payments to be made for the maintenance thereof, and they are at their choice whether they will maintain a schoolmaster among them or allow £10 to the next town that keeps a grammar school, [we] do advise the selectmen speedily to warn the inhabitants to come together and issue the controversy among themselves as the law directs.[35]

When necessary, higher authority could be brought to bear on the town's executive if they failed to satisfy their constituents.

The selectmen were also constrained by the legislation of the General Court. On many occasions the board took action on orders rather than by choice. Keeping a Book of Possessions, building a schoolhouse, rating procedures, policing youth in the meetinghouse and in rowdy gatherings, caring for the poor, preventing living alone and pretentious dressing, and overseeing families and educational standards were all responses to central authority.[36] If they failed in their responsibilities, they could be presented to the grand jury of the county, or the General Court could be petitioned. Under pressure from above as well as below, the selectmen were always liable to be called to account.[37]

During the 1670s the names of the men regularly chosen by the town for a generation to administer the day-to-day business of this farming community are seen less frequently in the records or disappear. Michael Bairstow died in 1674, Captain Richard Beers, ambushed by Indians, in 1675, and Hugh Mason in 1678. John Sherman, usually very active about town business in the late 1660s, may have been "deselected" by his constituents, he may have gone off to sulk in his tent, or he may have suffered ill-health or injury. Deacon Thomas Hastings similarly slips into the shadows for much of the 1670s, eclipsed by the joint tragedies that struck his family around the turn of the decade.[38] Nathaniel Treadway simply retired at the age of sixty-five in 1675, though his fellow terrier Joseph Tainter remained active up to 1680.[39] He could induct and guide the new generation that was taking over, sons of the founders or adolescent arrivals coming into their prime. The town gave them a taste of office, and if the householders approved their performance, they returned them regularly to the board.

What won that approval? What qualities made a regular selectman? Most regulars were church members and therefore freemen of the colony. From 1636 to 1647 freemanship was a prerequisite for town office; after the lifting of this restriction, church members usually predominated on the board (as the General Court required),[40] but they did not always have things their own way, as we have shown. Certain managerial, business, scribal, surveying, and arbitrational skills were necessary, as was a sense of public service and communal obligation. Selectmen needed energy and authority too. It can be no coincidence that so many regulars were either church or militia officers, or both. Indeed church and trained band may have provided their leaders with organized support.[41] Status and wealth were usually important qualifications, though wealth was not essential and did not of itself guarantee office.[42] Some regular choices were not that rich, and some rich townsmen were only rarely given responsibility. One of the richest, Thomas Hammond, never held any town office. He lacked that other vital prerequisite, age. He was a mere thirty-seven when he died, and his father was still alive.[43]

Most important of all, though, if our interpretation of the Watertown records is correct, was the ability and readiness to reflect the will of the town. Selectmen held office on sufferance. Provided they satisfied their neighbors' wishes, they could expect reelection, if they sought it. Woe betide them, however, if they dared presume upon their offices.

There is powerful evidence to support the case for accountability. In a 1639 letter to Winthrop requesting a boundary concession in Watertown's favor, Captain Daniel Patrick spoke forebodingly of serious trouble "from our too impatient spirits." As we shall discover, the young men of the town had a similar reputation of fierce independence and assertiveness four decades later.[44] In the same year as Patrick's letter, Winthrop also heard from Nathaniel Ward, minister of Ipswich, to which several Watertown founders had moved. "I see the spirits of people run high, and what they get they hold."[45] Thomas Hooker, sometime influential minister of Cambridge, articulated this popular aspiration in 1638: "The foundation of authority is laid in the free consent of the governed . . . Those who appoint to power can also set a limit to power."[46] Twelve years later another neighboring minister, the reactionary Peter Bulkeley of Concord, complained that "here where the heady or heedless multitude have gotten the power into their hands, there is insolency and confusion."[47]

The often-used phrase "the mind of the town" warned those in authority that the town had a mind of its own. The equally popular idea of "the good of the whole" presumed that those vested with power must not abuse it on behalf of themselves or of groups within the town.[48]

None of these claims and assertions presumed social or political equality. The men of Watertown recognized that only a few neighbors were gifted with the qualities needed for managing town affairs. They conceded eligibility to the elite and would have ridiculed youthful or lower-class pretensions. They had no sense of being "as good as the next man." What they did have, however, were high expectations of public service and a deep-seated awareness of their own rights and freedoms. This mind-set produced predictable constitutional consequences. Since, in old England, "long nurture as an outgroup had accustomed many [puritan] laymen to resent official power . . . they wanted in New England a political system that included strong checks on executive prerogative."[49] William Hubbard, a neighbor in Essex of many Watertown families, looked back on his youthful experiences of popular assertiveness among the founders: "In the beginning of times was occasioned much disadvantage to . . . the civil government, by too much contriving to advance the liberties of the people."[50]

The few known precedents suggest that parishioners and citizens of the Stour and Colne Valleys were used to regular communal meetings and to holding their elected officials to account.[51] Furthermore, higher authorities at county, diocesan, and even national level were vigilant for any local lapses. The Watertown electorate was moved to protest by a variety of perceived infractions. In the early years, when towns were centrally administered, their targets were external attempts to override local control of defense and central taxation without consent. After the 1634 assumption of local government, watchful eyes turned their focus on the local elite. Thereafter there were regular evictions of board members who displeased townsmen—granting themselves farms, discriminating against nonfreemen, becoming complacent and incompetent, assuming too much authority, claiming that the selectmen rather than the inhabitants were "the town." Suspicion of their executive led Watertown people to summon the countervailing power of outsiders, including the General Court and its commissioners over land allocations, the county court over financing education and land sales, and arbitrators from other towns over siting the meetinghouse and herding arrangements.

Amid these assertions of the power of the electorate were important constitutional issues traditionally considered the province of the elite—the Cokes, the Eliots, the Hampdens. The long confrontation in 1632 turned on the very fundamental nature of colonial government. If, as Watertown claimed, it was a mere corporation, then its freemen must approve every levy. Winthrop managed "after long debate" to persuade the town that the General Court had become a parliament and that the assistants annually elected or removed by the freemen had tax powers delegated to them as did members of Parliament. Despite eliciting public submission to his interpretation, Winthrop soon found himself ousted from the governorship, his and other officials' accounts scrutinized, and executive authoritarianism severely criticized. His colonial "parliament" was rapidly forced to call town representatives to discuss revenue and approve taxation. The new lower house of deputies immediately set about questioning magisterial "tyranny" and veto powers. With the Forced Loan and the Petition of Right fresh in people's minds, spokesmen for "divers of Watertown" were insistent "that it was unsafe to pay moneys after that sort, for fear of bringing themselves and posterity into bondage."[52]

The "neo-Roman" fear of slavery and defense of liberty against the faintest possibility of tyranny had percolated well down the social scale. Quite ordinary people were intent that the constitution of the unformed Massachusetts should safeguard "the rights and freedoms of Englishmen." The long conflict of the 1640s about the rights of nonfreemen arose from similar well-articulated revolt against potential bondage and actual discrimination, as we shall see. These townsmen were "tenacious of their liberties." Subsequent conflicts turned more on issues of accountability and local sovereignty. This was not just antiauthoritarianism. It reiterated the communitarian doctrine that "the town" was "the inhabitants in general," signing a petition taken door to door or signifying their displeasure with board proposals, and that "prudential men . . . are to act according to instructions given them." The householders of Watertown demonstrated decade by decade what John Davenport told the General Court in 1669: "The power of rulers of the commonwealth is derived from the people's free choice."[53]

It is unusual to encounter popular justification for constitutional resistance at this level of society. The first two generations of Watertown people were veritable "Village Hampdens" who knew that the "the price of liberty is eternal vigilance."[54] Town meetings were no rubber stamps. The selectmen and other officers of Watertown, held as accountable in the 1670s as the 1630s, jostled and jangled in conflicts and confrontations, might have echoed the frustrations of those mighty proponents of authoritarianism, Strafford and Laud, that "the very genius of that nation of people [puritans] leads them always to oppose . . . all that ever authority ordains for them."[55]

5

Land

Within twelve years of their first setting foot in Watertown, its inhabitants had allocated almost all of its 23,456-acre land grant. Most of this bonanza had occurred between 1636 and 1642. They had furthermore declared on 30 November 1635 that "there be too many inhabitants in the town and the town thereby [is] in danger of being ruinated." Proprietorship, the right to free shares in land allocations, was therefore closed. These grants raise two thematic problems: first, to what extent land policy in Watertown represented a continuity of East Anglian practice and economic philosophy, and second, the causes and divisive effects of growing proprietorial exclusivity and discrimination.[1]

Allotments of land had begun in 1630, when each household received a "homestall," smallholdings on which pioneers built the first shelters for their families and beasts and grew their first crops. These grants were located at the far eastern end of the town's domain, to the east, north, and south of Mount Auburn, near the Newtown line (see map 5). In this initial town center the first meetinghouse was built. Later arrivals received homestalls to the west of this area.[2] We know the size of individual homestalls only retrospectively from the Inventories of Grants and Possessions for every individual householder compiled in the early 1640s. What the *original* grants were is not recorded, though they may have been as small as an acre or two. The average by the time of the inventory is twelve acres, but this figure conceals distinctly uneven allotments. Hierarchies of land allocation conformed to the principles codified in 1641: "The number of persons in family, the number of beasts, by which a man is fit to occupy the land assigned to him and subdue it, and eminent respect (in this case may be given to men of eminent quality and descent) in assigning unto them more large and honourable accommodations in regard of their disburse-

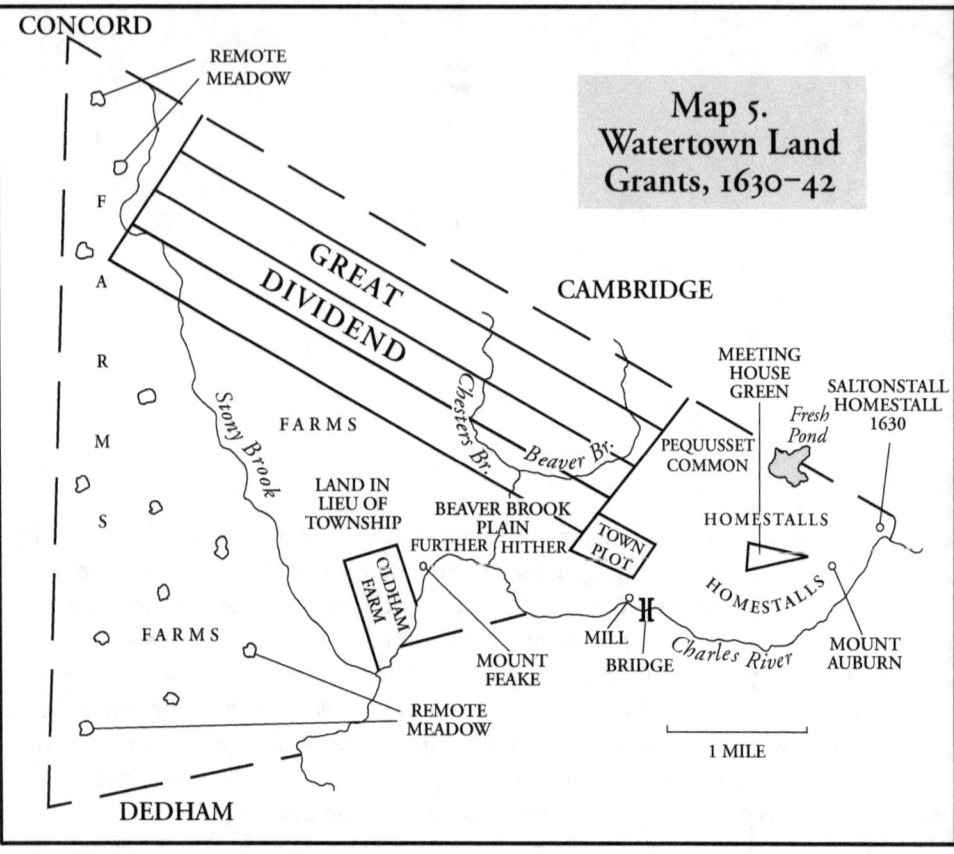

Map 5. Watertown Land Grants, 1630–42

ments to public charge." This factor might involve investment in the Massachusetts Bay Company or in the expenses of starting town settlement. Just over half the households got one to eight acres. These included young and unmarried settlers, some newly qualified craftsmen, and a considerable number of "poor men" who lacked the resources to cultivate more than a few acres. By the 1640s just under half had been allotted ten to twenty-four acres. They were usually older, longer-established families, with growing offspring, some servants, and more reserves. Finally, there was a small elite group, eight early leaders, who, by the time of the inventory, had homestalls of thirty-four to fifty acres.[3] In all, 1,327 acres were listed for homestalls, but given the gargantuan task of clearing the land of rocks, trees, and scrub, only a proportion of this total—especially of the larger allotments—could have been cultivable.

Between the summer of 1636 and the spring of 1642, Watertown's records list five further allocations of land. The first new land grants by the Watertown freemen on 25 July 1636, the "Great Dividends" of livestock pastureland "for them to inclose or feed in common," were divided into four "squadrons," each one-half mile wide with thirty lots in each, varying from Sir Richard Saltonstall's 100 acres down to 20 acres for young men like John Mason or Thomas Parish. The four huge divisions, each over 1,000 acres, totaled 4,595 acres and were "bounded with Cambridge line on the northeast," that is, to the northwest of the town center and Fresh Pond.[4]

The next two divisions were much smaller in size. On 28 February 1637 the freemen divided out potential plowlands—often called uplands to distinguish them from low-lying marsh or meadow—on Beaverbrook Plain (divided by the brook into Hither and Further Plains and situated north of the riverbank and southwest of the town center) to all "106 townsmen then inhabiting." A few leaders received sizable lots, but 86 of the 106 recipents got single-figure grants, some as little as one acre. Acreage continued to reflect status in the community, though much greater weight was given to household size. In 1637 Beaver Brook marked the western limits of any town settlement or cultivation.[5]

Four months later, on 27 June 1637, the "Remote or West Pine Meadows" on land beyond Beaverbrook Plain granted "by the freemen to 113 townsmen then inhabiting" were specifically linked to mouths, human and bovine. Most recipients again got single-figure acreages of these parcels of natural meadowland dotted among the heavily wooded western section of the town domain. Many householders got the same allotment of fodder land as for plowland.[6]

The fourth allotment, on 9 April 1638, saw forty proprietors granted relatively small lots, typically six acres, on land called the Town Plot, a reserved area of 238 acres northeast of the town mill and two and a half miles west of the meetinghouse. The object was that forty families should "build and dwell upon their lots at the town plot, and not to alienate them by selling or exchanging them to any foreigner, but [only] to the freemen of the congregation; it being our intent to sit down there close together, and, therefore, these lots were granted to those *freemen* [my emphasis] that inhabited most remote from the meetinghouse, and dwell most scattered."[7]

Three months later, on 17 July 1638, those who had not benefited on the Town Plot were given land in compensation "beyond Beaver Plain." This 800-odd acre consolation to sixty-seven inhabitants was known in the land inventory (and in subsequent complaints of injustice) as Land in lieu of Township.[8]

That autumn, on 14 October 1638, a committee was appointed to lay out individual farms in the western reaches of the town grant at a ratio of 20 acres of meadow for every 150 acres of upland. The first beneficiaries of this order were, as we saw, eleven members of the elite, who awarded themselves and took possession of rolling acres. Renewed allocation on 10 May 1642 was quite specific: "*All the townsmen* [my emphasis] that had not farms laid out formerly shall take them by ten in a division, and to cast lots for the several divisions allowing thirteen acres of upland to every head of persons and cattle." The attached list of nine divisions numbers ninety-three names, but the lot numbers go up to 104.[9]

By the end of the farm allocations in May 1642, fully 20,206 acres of the town's total grant of 23,456 acres had been lotted out. Only 3,250 acres, 13.9 percent of the total, remained town land. This last bonanza had offloaded 11,073 acres, nearly half the whole land grant.

Watertown was unique in its lavishness. Other early towns were far more abstemious. In 1634 Boston, for instance, "would rather leave a great part [of the town] at liberty for newcomers and for common fields." Of Ipswich's land, it was said: "A principal motive which led the court to grant them and other towns such vast bounds was that (when they should be increased by their children and servants growing up, etc.) they might have a place to erect villages, where they might be planted." New towns initiated similarly conservationist policies. Dedham, Watertown's southerly neighbor, distributed only about three thousand acres of its vast bounds in its first twenty years. Another neighbor, Sudbury, to the west, was equally cautious, likewise Andover and Hampton, some of whose founders had perched in Watertown in the late 1630s. So there was no need for Watertown men to feel that they had to keep up with the Joneses; the Joneses were keeping down.[10]

A reason often advanced for the helter-skelter share-out is cultural continuity. Suffolk and Essex were two English counties where enclosure was most advanced. It was a region where commercial farming was important, especially for the ever-demanding London market. In New England too the buying and selling of land had become commonplace. East Anglians, we are told, wanted their discrete farms, like the ones they had painstakingly glued together over decades and generations back home. They rejected nucleation and close, communal living. That was the way of the backward, pace-of-the-slowest, committee-run, common-field system, which deterred individual enterprise and innovation, expected everyone to live cheek by jowl, and wasted time, land, and labor. The dispersion attributed to the men of the eastern counties was graphically described in 1651 by the Kentish man Edward Johnson, from nearby Woburn: "Watertown is a fruitful plat and of large extent . . . which hath caused her inhabitants to scatter in such manner, that their sabbath assemblies prove very thin if the season favour not, and hath made this great town (consisting of 160 families) to show nothing delightful to the eye in any place." It was, he concluded, "a plantation of husbandmen principally . . . [with] very many and great farms."[11]

By distributing all their land so precipitately, it is further claimed, the proprietors of Watertown implicitly rejected a utopian vision. Certain leaders of the puritan exodus, notably John Winthrop and John Cotton, had expressed an idealized communal dream that perpetuated a God-given social hierarchy in which cooperation, personal restraint, and godliness would create a close, loving society—"A Model of Christian Charity," as Winthrop called it. Watertown, unsupervised by a magisterial ideologue and freed in 1636 from General Court control of land policy, was able to assert an alternative philosophy, more worldly, more realistic, a belief that God helped those who helped themselves.[12]

These explanations of regional and ideological motivation are unconvincing. The more we learn about the farming districts of East Anglia, the more difficult it becomes to generalize. Parts of the region, including areas producing many emigrants, remained unenclosed or partially enclosed. The leaders who articulated the model of godly love themselves came from the eastern counties—the Winthrops had been embedded in south Suffolk since the mists of time; Cotton had spent all his adult life in Cambridgeshire and Lincolnshire; most of the clergy were likewise from eastern England. Small land grants in the Town Plot restricted to church members seemed to be a conscious attempt to reverse dispersal by forming a nuclear settlement.[13]

The counterposing of religious idealism and commercial ambition also crumbles on closer examination. John Winthrop was one of many promoters who had emphasized the prospect of "many hundreds of acres of land each in America," compared with one or two acres available for expansion at home. England's lack of land, indicated by rising prices, signaled its glut of people and its "God-forsaken" exhaustion. Material inducement, as well as spiritual, had been advertised to encourage the awesome step of emigration. Anyway, people in the seventeenth century did not recognize such stark oppositions. They developed myths and belief systems that smoothed off grating edges and allowed them to reconcile self- or family-interest with the will of God. Men who eventually grew rich through land speculation, trade, or manufacture devoted large parts of their lives to the service of the public and the church. Some of the richest townsmen in Watertown were deacons responsible for nurturing the poor, elderly, weak, and disabled.[14]

Proponents of East Anglianism must furthermore confront the awkward fact that some very influential leaders of Watertown during the land bonanza were *not* East Anglians. Wiltshireman Thomas Mayhew was regularly chairman of the town board and representative at the General Court during the five allocations. Brian Pendleton from London was equally important up to his 1638 emigration to Sudbury and after his return in the mid-1640s. The reasons given by those Watertown men who petitioned for fresh colonial land grants so that they could found new towns was that they wanted more land, not less.

Other Massachusetts towns with a strong East Anglian presence, like Cambridge, Dedham, and Sudbury, did not indulge in rapid disposal of land. Regional explanations must falter in the face of such arguments.[15]

Finally, and most irritatingly for regional determinists, it is not at all certain how much of Watertown's land *was* enclosed. One problem with the records is the fact that the word "enclosed" in seventeenth-century New England parlance meant "surrounded by a fence." It did not necessarily mean an independent farm separate from other people's holdings and farmed without regard to others by an independent household. Such an agglomerated enterprise was described as "a particular enclosure" or land "taken orderly out" of common farming. One of the last entries of the Second Book of Proceedings minutes a 21 April 1680 complaint by the commoners of Howe's Field about defects in fencing around the outside of the field. At least four different fields farmed or grazed in common are named in the period 1666–80. The proprietors had written covenants, rules, and regulations about mutual obligations and special procedures if a member wanted to take his land out of the shared field and farm it independently. It was the town's expectation that the Hither and Further Plain allocated for plowland in 1637 would be cultivated in common. Cattle, sheep, and goats were likewise normally herded together during the summer months under town-appointed herdsmen and shepherds. Even the dispersion of homes might have been exaggerated. The earliest map of Watertown suggests that various nuclei of neighbors had developed, on the Town Plot, for instance, and round Meetinghouse Green. There were also strings of adjacent houses along Cambridge, Sudbury, and Orchard Streets.[16]

The case for English farming systems dictating land allocations and ideological conflict is not proved. We need not reject *some* regional influence on events in Watertown from 1636 to 1642, but to make cultural continuity the central causation flies in the face of too many objections.

Sharing out this king's ransom of land in a few years was a revolutionary change from the cautious and meager-minded scrimping and saving of the old world, adding an acre here, a close there. A few years before, back in Essex or Suffolk or Yorkshire, they would have thought this average acreage of two hundred acres per family a good estate for a country squire, and a fourth of it a fit share for a yeoman.[17]

Fear is a more plausible motivator for wholesale land distribution. By the end of 1635 one major source of apprehension was of the town losing land. Already in the five short years of its existence it had been raided by the genteel land filchers of the General Court three times. In 1634 some meadow went to Mr. Hooker's Company in neighboring Newtown; then a choice five-hundred-acre site had been granted to John Oldham, and Concord was allowed by the court to slice off a northwest tranche of Watertown's grant. Sir

Richard Saltonstall laid claim to certain valuable town meadowlands. A township at Dedham to the southwest had just been authorized. Perhaps Watertown might become a prototype of Poland, carved up by its greedy and powerful neighbors. Both Great Dividends and Farms were allocated to individuals at times when it seemed the town's borders were threatened. There was a fear too that town land not improved within three years might revert to the colony. Such reversions were written into grants to new towns after 1636. Who was to say that clawing back would not be retroactive? Distribution of title to individuals would be their best safeguard. The General Court would be most unlikely to try to claim back land already granted to a large group of individuals. There was safety in numbers.[18]

Another fear was of loss of valued members of the community. Watertown had early lost its civil leader, Sir Richard Saltonstall. His eldest son, Richard, had moved to the new foundation of Ipswich, which also lured away the wheelwright Richard Kemball with offers of land. The town miller Thomas Cakebread, another vital craftsman and militia officer, had similarly been tempted to move to Sudbury, along with wealthy Brian Pendleton. Oldham's "New Watertown" on the Connecticut River might inveigle other good citizens (like Edmund Sherman) with its broad acres of meadow. Other specialists were known to be restless. The town could ill afford to lose civic and economic pillars of the community. Lieutenant Feake and Mr. Payne were both richly endowed with plowland and meadow, a way of binding them to the town.[19]

Yet another anxiety after 1634 concerned rocketing land values. If the people of Watertown did not distribute this asset among themselves and limit the beneficiaries, they might be unable to afford to set up their offspring when the time came, or to profit from sale on a rising market. The 1637 exodus to Sudbury proved a warning. Despite Watertown protests, those leaving were allowed to retain title to all grants, unimproved as well as improved. This setback underlay the decision made in the Watertown town meeting of 16 February 1638 to distribute all remaining undivided land in the town.[20]

Amid a bundle of other anxieties affecting land was the fear of starvation. By November 1635 Watertown had just received the second year's installment of its second surge of immigration, 1634–35. It had taken in the better part of three shiploads of families, about 120 people, often chain migrants linked with the eighty-odd people who had founded the settlement in 1630. Food had to be found for hungry, malnourished kinsfolk. Furthermore, there were fifty-four families "perching" in Watertown over the winter of 1636–37 before moving on to new settlements. Meanwhile the town's settled population was burgeoning by natural increase. In the winter of 1636–37, twenty-eight barely established farming families had some four hundred mouths to feed.[21]

Early harvests had been disappointing as newcomers wrestled with growing alien corn and a climate of extremes. Maize, once its cultivation was mastered, proved a high-yield cereal, but it quickly consumed soil nutrients. As early as 1631 young Pond had learned the expensive truth that "if we set . . . eindey wheat . . . without fish [fertilizer] they shall have but a poor crop." In 1637 it was observed: "After five or six years [the soil] grows barren beyond belief, and puts on the face of winter in time of summer."[22] Given New England's latitude on a line with Rome or Barcelona, the founders had anticipated a generally warmer climate. Indeed the summers were a lot warmer, often enervatingly and sickeningly steamy. There was a severe drought in 1633, with harvest failure prevented only at the last moment by the Lord answering the prayers of the parched. Next year a hurricane in the wake of ferocious heat destroyed the maize crop. Winters were not warmer, however, and the 1630s saw some of the fiercest weather of the century. The bay often froze, cattle died, and fires consumed cord after cord of wood.[23]

Lack of hirable hands, or "servants in husbandry," exacerbated these challenges. The four ships bringing settlers to Watertown between 1634 and 1637 recorded only two servants on their lists. Sixteen out of twenty-nine mature men were artisans, rather than farmers. They brought many young children. The number of mouths to feed increased far faster than did the number of capable hands to till.[24]

Self-sufficiency was impossible in such circumstances. In this crisis, three townsmen were instrumental in procuring aid for the colony. John Oldham brought back five hundred bushels of corn from the sachem of the Narragansetts in 1634, and William Jennison returned the same year with five thousand bushels from Virginia. One hungry winter was thus prevented, but the immigrants brought news from England of spreading persecution, silenced ministers, and economic depression. More and more refugees could be expected. In 1635 and 1636 the swollen population could not begin to feed itself. Thomas Mayhew brought potatoes, corn, pork, and antiscorbutic oranges and lemons from Bermuda, but he could not find much replenishment when he sailed north to the Isles of Shoals early in 1636. Despite warnings that emigrants to New England should bring a year's or eighteen-months' supplies, famine continued a real threat. This was the "ruination" that terrified 1635 and 1636 town meetings into starting wholesale distribution of land and the closure of the proprietorship.[25]

Allocation of twenty thousand acres of land in six years and the closing of the privileged proprietorship would have created problems enough. A new ingredient was added, however, that transformed mere problems into fierce confrontations. Exclusion and discrimination in grants triggered conflicts that rumbled and roared like a hyperactive volcano for the next three decades.

At the simplest level, exclusion produced a sense of grievance and injustice. In early 1640 Winthrop received one such expression:

> Worshipful Sir—When I came in the country which was seven years since, upon taking an oath of an inhabitant here in this jurisdiction [oath of allegiance] I was promised that I should have all privileges of a free inhabitant and particularly in disposals of town lots with other men. Since which time I have twice been sent forth a soldier from Watertown in the country's service. I never had yet anything but bare wages for my reward. Neither hath the town of Watertown given me any lot but some of them say their town is full, and yet I know where ground lieth undisposed of wherein they may give me a portion, if it please them. I have a wife and child and reason to look for my subsistence and the maintenance of my family. And now upon my presenting my case unto you, I humbly desire your worship's counsel and best help to be afforded to me, resting your humble servant,
>
> John Stubbin.[26]

Exploitation and deprivation were individual slights, but between 1638 and 1640 a new, group-divisive element had crept into land distribution policy: a them-vs.-us discrimination between church-member freemen and nonmember inhabitants.[27] It took its cue from the General Court order of 2 September 1636 that only freemen could hold office or vote in town meetings. It took its teeth from the order of 3 March 1636 devolving to towns the distribution of their own land. Its first fruits in Watertown were instructions that "foreigners" should pay taxes on a par with freemen. At a stroke two types of outsider had been merged into one: strangers and the nonregenerate were now both dubbed foreigners. There followed decrees that "the Body of Freemen" empowered the selectmen "to divide all town land undivided" (16 February 1638) and that they could start with the Town Plot. Almost all the choice land there went to "freemen of the congregation." The two most blatant acts of discrimination affected the area called Land in Lieu of Township and the grazing commons.[28]

The favoritism in Town Plot grants must have created a furor. However, when compensatory land was allotted in the Land in Lieu of Township, freemen were given twelve acres, but mere "townsmen," nonmembers of the church, only got six. Common land was also reserved in a publicly discriminatory manner for the first time that summer. In May Pequusset Common, a relatively small area north of the Town Plot abutting the Cambridge line, was granted to the nonfreemen for their grazing. Two months later, however, the vast area so far unallotted in the western part of the town grant toward Sudbury, amounting to about sixteen thousand acres, was declared common land for the use of the freemen's, or church members', cattle. This huge range was reserved for the privileged half of the households of Watertown.[29]

The last straw was the self-enrichment of insiders with large farms. This plundering of communal land united the remaining freemen with the nonfreemen in a sense of outrage at "establishment" corruption. The 1639 town board bore a very different look, and a back-pedaling concession was enacted on 27 November: "If the land in view for farms shall not suffice to accommodate *the rest of the townsmen that are behind* [my emphasis], that then they shall have their lands out of the freemen's common." It was not enough for the colonial authorities, who must have been aroused by townsmen's protests. The Court of Assistants in Boston in 1640 issued a general order that freemanship should not be grounds for granting extra acreage in the colony. Then on 1 December 1640 it was recorded: "Watertown freemen, promising to yield to every townsman his proportion alike according to rule, *without respect to freedom or not freedom* [my emphasis], were dismissed." Further farm distribution was abruptly halted. Renewed allocation in 1642 was specifically for "All the townsmen."[30]

The blatant partiality of Watertown land policy between 1638 and 1640 polarized factions for a decade. In 1642 John Winthrop recorded continued "stir" across the Charles, and the following year there was news of further "disturbance" and "affront" between nonfreemen and freemen at public meetings.[31]

Nathaniel Biscoe emerged as the leader of resistance in the 1640s. In 1647 the General Court was moved (in the wake of the crisis provoked by the Child Petition) to reverse its policy limiting local government to freemen, thus doubling Watertown's electorate. Almost immediately Mr. Biscoe was elected selectman. His name is listed first in the records, implying that he topped the poll and chaired the board meetings. The 1647 board represented something of a clean sweep with five new members and one returning to office after ten years. The only links with past regimes were the ubiquitous Hugh Mason and John Sherman. Other responsible town offices were filled by known allies of Biscoe.[32]

The very first act of the town meeting that elected the new board was to require them to right the wrongs in the Remote Meadows, around which farms had subsequently been granted. Mason bowed out a week later, "burdened with the service of the town." He somehow contrived to bear heavier town burdens in more congenial and "select" company for most other years up to his death in 1678. He was replaced by Isaac Stearns, yet another new man to the board. Other land-grant and taxation wrongs figured large in subsequent town and selectmen's meetings. On 30 January 1648 came the first general redress: all nonfreemen who had been given only six acres of Land in lieu of Township a decade before were to have twelve, the same as freemen. Biscoe was reelected to the board in 1650 but left the following year for London and liberty of conscience.[33]

Biscoe's improbable replacement as leader of the nonfreemen was Christopher Grant.³⁴ In 1654 his name headed a list of Watertown petitioners about town land to the General Court; this and concurrent complaints from Mr. Jeremiah Norcross brought the town's internal differences into the wider public domain. The court appointed three commissioners, who visited Watertown in the fall of 1654 and the winter of 1655. The commissioners' report the following spring was damning. They decried the grievances unredressed "for sundry years past." They identified abuses in the various allocations of the late 1630s and laid down proportional compensation. They were especially scathing about the way the farm allotments had been "illegally and unequally done." They ordered a completely fresh start and majority approval by all townsmen. It had taken three leading surveyors from neighboring towns and the authority of the General Court to bring the festering dispute under control.³⁵

There were fifteen more years and endless meetings of the town, the selectmen, the proprietors of the farmlands with and without the rest of the inhabitants, orders about surveying, laying out land, and proving title, as well as court cases, confrontation, and anger. Immediately after the commissioners reported, eight owners of the farms laid out to the 1638 "insiders" protested that they had paid for surveys and the laying out of their farms, which some had "improved." Starting all over again would cause them to "lose that charge that we have been at." They got the brush-off from the House of Deputies. In 1659 outside commissioners were back to validate the boundaries of the plowland (allocated in 1637!). Even twenty years after this allocation there were still complaints that Beaverbrook Plain had not been correctly measured. In a general, common field, fencing was proportional to acreage, so accurate surveying was essential.³⁶

Accurate surveying revealed another potential hornet's nest during the 1660s. "When the farms were actually laid out, it was discovered that there was not enough land available, and everyone's farm as surveyed was reduced in size proportionally. These farms were laid out in the same area as the Remote Meadows, which had been surveyed much earlier, so the farms frequently had, as enclaves, parcels of Remote Meadow that belonged to somebody else."³⁷

Even for a saint, this task would have been thankless, but John Sherman, town surveyor since 1647,³⁸ seems to have been prickly, proud, and provocative. He disdained "new money" in the town. He had upset Norcross by denying his title to land and, during surveying, by going "too fast ahead so that Mr. Norcross was left behind and lost them despite his calling halloo, halloo."³⁹ The 1655 commissioners' report criticized his lack of expertise. By January 1667 he felt that he had accomplished a herculean feat in separating Remote Meadow from Farm land and lotting them out. He was to be paid by the town from any land remaining. According to Ephraim Curtis: "In January [1667]

Ensign Sherman said in assembly, 'I have done my work in laying out the Farms. There are now but two or three hundred acres left and that is very mean land hardly worth going over a threshold to look after.' Joseph Garfield said, 'I believe there is at least one thousand acres left.' Ensign Sherman turned about and answered him, 'If I had you before Master Danforth [Cambridge magistrate] I would make you pay ten shillings for so saying . . . If I had not been deceived in carrying of the chain [i.e., by my assistants] there had been no land left.'"

However, an independent survey of Nonesuch in March 1668 found that indeed 1,102 acres were left over, about 100 acres of pond and meadow, but the rest farmland. This corroboration of suspicions encouraged several objectors to charge that they had been "greatly damnified [by] lands laid out neither in the true place nor number of acres." After losing an expensive court action in 1669, Sherman got his discharge.[40]

Thereafter, peace did at last descend over the vexed issue of land grants, but the price was Ensign Sherman's virtual disappearance from public life. He held no elected office for the next seven years. He may well have served as the scapegoat for all the inequities, incompetence, and arrogance of the elite from 1638 to 1669.

A grant of nearly twenty-five thousand acres of land presented the founders of Watertown with revolutionary opportunities. Their frenzied grasping of these opportunities was prompted less by regional traditions and commercial greed than by apprehensions and anxieties: fears of loss to neighbors, loss of valuable citizens, loss of self-sufficiency, loss of life. More positively, there were ambitions: hopes for prosperity, for posterity, for elbowroom, for diversification. These ideals are reminiscent of those lauded in the "Essay for the laying out of Towns": "When the number of the inhabitants are rightly resolved upon, *then it may be necessary that the whole town be set out into portions by doles* [my emphasis]. For though there be none expectation of sudden [immediate] inclosing, yet it will be such a goad in the side of the industrious to draw on and make the speediest and best employment of his known proportion that others will of necessity be drawn on by his good example to their much benefit and comfort on every side."[41]

"Inclosing" was far from sudden in Watertown. Grants were often on paper only. By 1 January 1648, a decade after the town order, most of the Remote Meadows had not even been properly surveyed, let alone physically parceled out. The Great Dividends of 1636 and the 1638 Lands in lieu of Township remained mere lines on a plat until the 1660s; the Farms were similarly insubstantial for twenty years at least. When Edward Johnson described Watertown in 1651, he reported less than 1,800 acres in tillage—just over 10 acres per household on average. The great Watertown land bonanza from 1636 to 1642 was not, after all, a binge of instant gratification. It was a prudential "laying up for posterity." As such, it was not so alien to Winthrop's preference for delayed distribution. Where it did differ was in its earmarking of particular tracts to particular families, to members of the closed corporation of proprietors originated by the order of 30 November 1635.[42]

Unfortunately, this exclusiveness, exacerbated by discrimination, corruption, arrogance, insensitivity, and incompetence, created an atmosphere of grievance, injustice, and suspicion that poisoned town business for three decades.[43]

6

Religion

The core of Watertown's founding generation was the "Wandering Congregation" following Rev. George Phillips to a new "Canaan." They were joined by equally zealous puritans from centers of nonconformity in Suffolk and Essex, as well as London, Yorkshire, the West Country, and the Home Counties. Even among the Stour Valley company there were disagreements about important issues; other nonconformists brought different perspectives and interpretations. Once the English puritan alliance in opposition to Laudian innovations breathed the freer air of the new world, these repressed divisions would emerge.

Two problems would perplex the best minds in the colony for much of the first generation: first, what was the precise nature of the Bay's brand of congregationalism? and second, what was the precise measurement of purity required to qualify for church membership? Although the records of the church in Watertown in these formative years have not survived, other sources show that these two issues vexed the saints there too during the 1630s and 1640s.[1] These issues had been settled at considerable cost by the Cambridge Platform of 1648. Evidence conflicts about the persistence of zeal during Sherman's pastorate, which coincided with the rise of the second generation. There is less doubt about the persistence of disputes and divisions up to 1680 and beyond.

The Watertown church was founded on 30 July 1630 during a fast day at Charlestown. Some forty people subscribed to the church covenant. Church membership must have included almost all the households in the opening months of settlement. Twenty-five male church members of the town were subsequently granted freeman status in the first creation on 19 May 1631 and thus qualified to vote in colony elections.[2]

Although many people on board the *Arbella* fleet of 1630 had no personal experience of a congregational church organization, and although Dr. Samuel Fuller of the separatist Plymouth Plantation reported considerable disagreements among magistrates and clergy,[3] the two men who launched the religious experiment in Watertown were somewhat better prepared. Rev. George Phillips, a Norfolk man and Caius College, Cambridge graduate, had been the incumbent of Boxted church, in the heart of Stour Valley puritanism. Phillips had been a signatory of *The Humble Request* on the *Arbella* on 7 April 1630, which denied any intention of separating from their "dear mother," the Church of England. Nonetheless, he was, according to William Hubbard, "better acquainted with the true [congregational] church discipline than most of the ministers who came into [this] country." Indeed, he had affronted some of his more conservative parishioners in Boxted by a sermon that had favored nonconformity. John Rogers had had to reassure them that "Mr. Phillips would preach nothing without some good evidence from the word of God." During debates about ministerial ordination in the summer of 1630, he advocated the radical line that it was the congregation's call to a man that elected him to ministerial status. He thus completely rejected Bostonian John Wilson's claim that his membership of the clergy depended on ordination by an Anglican bishop. Phillips was reported as threatening that "if they will have him stand minister by that calling which he received from the prelates of England, he will leave them [and go elsewhere]." Later such assertions of individual congregational sovereignty led to congregationalists in England being aptly dubbed independents.[4]

Such independence would have been warmly seconded by Phillips's first lay lieutenant, Mr. Richard Brown, Watertown's ruling elder. Brown was "well-versed in the discipline of the separation, having been a ruler of one of their churches in London." As owner of a Thames barge, Brown had helped the hunted proponents of congregationalism, William Ames and Robert Parker, escape by sea from ecclesiastical pursuivants. He became a founder-member of Rev. Henry Jacobs's voluntary covenanted church in Southwark in 1616, which was swelled four years later by a dissenting group from Colchester. This connection may explain how Brown first became acquainted with Phillips.[5]

The elder seconded the minister as a powerful asserter of Watertown church's independence. When an authoritative delegation came to debate the currently agitated question of whether the Church of Rome was a true (though corrupt) church, they were accepted only as friendly counsel from neighboring churches. Any idea that they represented a higher, central authority was rejected. So was a motion from the Court of Assistants on 23 November 1631 that the argumentative and opinionated elder ought to be dismissed. That was a decision for the church alone. At Shepard's induction as the new minister of

Newtown in 1636, neighboring churches were invited "to send their elders and messengers [delegates] to assist"; all did so except for Watertown, where Master Phillips insisted that "every church was competent to act alone." In 1640, when John Knowles joined Phillips as co-minister, Watertown unconventionally declined to invite elders and representatives from other churches to give sanction, in effect, to their choice.[6]

Brown's "passion and distemper in speech" and stubborn "persisting in his opinion of the truth of the Romish church" opened up a serious rift among Watertown's godly. Some "could not communicate with the elder, being guilty of errors, both in judgment and conversation." This was separation within separation for purity's sake. Despite a temporary reconciliation, Brown was discharged by the church in the autumn of 1632. Although the church was better off without so perverse and divisive an elder, he had helped establish a vital principle of self-rule in early Watertown.[7]

Brown's successor was Edward Howe, who had been a devoted member of Phillips's congregation in Boxted, Essex. He too, along with the other members of Mr. Phillips's Company, may have brought experience of "the true church discipline" from England, where groups of the godly had sometimes formed themselves into purified cells, or "conventicles." In such groups they would hold special meetings for prayer, meditation, self-discipline, and extra sermons away from the "mixt multitude" who attended Anglican services. They were a true church within the inclusive Church of England, an "inner temple" of the pure. Members of his company had certainly resisted Laudian innovations, like the requirement to kneel at Communion. De facto separation may already have been a well-trodden path for many subscribers to the Watertown church covenant in 1630.[8]

At the same time as asserting congregational autonomy, the debate about purity, broached with Brown, burst into flame. In 1632 Mr. John Masters, Saltonstall's steward, led a group out of the church because someone they considered unfit had been admitted to membership. Masters had ostentatiously turned his back on the sacrament and separated from a church polluted and polluting. He had thereby touched a sore nerve that would continue to nag away at the New England churches for most of the seventeenth century. No wonder "divers ministers and others" labored with him to change his scrupulous mind. All in vain, though some of his followers submitted. It took two more solemn days of argument in the church and a brief excommunication before he came round.[9]

Cotton Mather printed the original covenant of Watertown church in *Magnalia Christi Americana*. The subscribers were required to undertake "to renounce all idolatry and superstition, will-worship, all human traditions and inventions whatsoever, in the worship of God; and forsaking all evil ways, [t]o give ourselves wholly unto the Lord Jesus, to do him faithful service, observing and keeping all his statutes, commands and ordinances in all matters concerning our reformation." This undertaking made no mention of the need to demonstrate a spiritual rebirth, a new beginning, a conversion experience. Its criteria for admission to church membership were external conduct and obedience to the "rule" of discipline.[10]

The withdrawal of Masters's ultrapuritan group signifies that Watertown's church officials—minister and elder—were including within the church covenant all adults except those few who were blatantly unqualified. Under this regime church and town were roughly the same, though some church members would be much more spiritually intense and committed than others who remained content with a reputation for formal respectability. The only outsiders would be families brought over for their skills, like the disreputable carpenter William Knapp, or Christopher Grant, boozer, bruiser, glazier.[11]

The year 1633 saw a marked change in the religious temperature of the colony at large with the arrival of such ministerial stars as Cotton and Hooker and many refugees from the nationwide campaign for Anglican uniformity waged by the newly appointed Archbishop Laud and his like-minded bishops. This "saving remnant in the wilderness" demanded far greater rigor in admitting to church membership only those who could demonstrate to all members a conversion experience, a covenant of grace. The new purism led to a widening gulf between those "who regarded the church as a means of grace or nurture to the many, and those who wanted it to resemble the coming kingdom in its purity." Zeal to "separate the precious from the vile" reached its apogee with Mrs. Hutchinson. After her expulsion from Massachusetts, some clergy, seeking to control overenthusiastic purification, preached insistently that the laity should obey and respect their spiritual betters. In certain churches in the late 1630s the officials assumed the role of a presbytery, with clergy, elders, and deacons preempting more and more decisions and symbolically sitting apart on raised seats. They also advocated involvement of neighboring churches in overseeing the formation of new churches and the ordination of their ministers. By the end of the 1630s the "gathering in of weak Christians" had become for many godly "gathering out" from polluting "scum," and the creation of Samuel Stone's "speaking aristocracy in the face of a silent democracy."[12]

We know frustratingly little about how these radical changes affected the church and people of Watertown. The unsupervised 1640 ordination of Rev. John Knowles, sometime fellow of that puritan seedbed, St. Catharine's College, Cambridge, suggests their spirited assertion of congregational independence in the face of the new policy of neighborly involvement. They may also have been emphasizing the rights of lay church members to ordain their own minister, the covenantal relationship, in the face of oligarchic demands for obedience and respect, the sacerdotal claims to special authority that preferred ordination by fellow clergy.[13]

Watertown was spared the civil war that traumatized Boston over antinomianism. George Phillips had been present when ministers confronted Anne Hutchinson in Boston in December 1636, and he had asked her opinion of his ministry. At her trial on 7 and 8 November 1637 his evidence underlined Watertown's remoteness from the conflict: "For my own part I have had little to do in these things, only at that time [December 1636] I was there but not privy to the ground" on which she was questioned.[14]

The only overt sign of opposition as the authorities wrought their vengeance on the antinomians was the refusal of Watertown's leading citizen, Mr. William Jennison, selectman, deputy, and captain of militia, to endorse the sentence of banishment passed on Mrs. Hutchinson in November of 1637. A fellow demurrer was Ensign Thomas Cakebread, Watertown's miller. In March 1638 they were summoned to appear, as "favourers of the familistic persons and opinions"; they satisfied the court and were discharged. Other leading townsmen may have been sympathetic to Mrs. Hutchinson. Lt. Robert Feake left Watertown and the colony in 1640 in company with Capt. Daniel Patrick, who was reported by Winthrop to have been infected with the heresy. The antinomian upheavals did not seriously divide Watertown.[15]

The town's response to heightened distinction between those in or out of church membership is harder to gauge. On the one hand, they were deemed less exclusive than elsewhere. Ann Fiske, awakened during her adolescence in England by the soul-melting preaching of John Rogers of Dedham, reported in 1644 as she applied to join the Salem church that "when at Watertown, she heard oft that the church [in Salem] was more strict regarding receiving members. Yet she is willing to come thither." In 1644 George Phillips appeared to have been in favor of the Half-Way Covenant, allowing baptism of the grandchildren of church members, even though the babies' parents had not been admitted to the elect. On the other hand, we have already encountered the freemen's adoption of a land policy in December 1638 that was highly prejudicial to nonfreemen. By 1647, out of 150 adult males in the town, only 62 (41 percent) were freemen, well below the percentage of neighboring towns.[16]

Ill feelings were exacerbated by the thorny issue of financial support of the church by the nonmembers, on which the General Court had insisted in 1638: the annual salaries of £80 each for Revs. Phillips and Knowles, plus other expenses, fell on nonmembers as well as members. This decision did not please the excluded, especially conscientious dissenters. In the late winter of 1643 John Sherman and Hugh Mason reported to the governor various outbursts of Nathaniel Biscoe.

At another town meeting about midsummer last, upon occasion of making a rate &c., Mr. Biscoe moved that such as were not freemen should have equal power with the rest, which being denied, as being against the order of the court, he replied that if the rest would be rated by him they should pay never a penny. At another meeting upon a Training Day this winter, some speech being used about those which were not freemen, Mr Biscoe said they were freemen in England, and they would be freemen here shortly, or he would know why they should not. It is a very common thing with the said Mr. Biscoe to affront the town in public meetings with high words and to much disturbance, and being privately admonished of these things, his answer was still, he would fain come to the court to answer there.

On 5 March 1643 Winthrop added that "amongst others, one Biscoe of Watertown who had his barn burnt [destroying £200 worth of goods] being grieved with that course [of taxation] in the town, the rather because himself and others, who were no [church] members were taxed [in the church tax], wrote a book against it wherein besides his arguments, which were naught [wrong], he cast reproach upon elders [here, ministers] and officers. This book he published underhand, which caused much stir in the town."

The governor was economical with the truth in his dismissive "one Biscoe of Watertown." Nathaniel Biscoe was in fact a wealthy tanner. His huge losses in the barn fire Winthrop had seen as providential punishment for refusing to barter leather for corn. Once the nonfreemen recovered the town vote in 1647, he was immediately elected chairman of the board.[17]

The pilloried George Phillips described Biscoe's underhand "book" (actually a hand-written and hand-copied pamphlet) as "fuller of teeth to bite and reproach the ministers of the country [New England] than arguments to convince the readers." He was too optimistic. Stephen Fosdick of Charlestown, kinsman of John Wetherall of Watertown, was fined the draconian sum of £20 and excommunicated for reading this sedition. Watertown's John Stowers "for reading two diverse offensive passages (before company) out of a book against the officers and the church of Watertown and for making disturbance there was fined forty shillings." Stowers was a church member and had been a selectman in 1638. The author was fined £10, later reduced to £2.10.0 after a pathetic petition rehearsing "so many and so great" losses in the colonial depression.[18]

Biscoe was voicing a wider resentment, expressed in proposals to the General Court in March 1644 and the 1646 Child Petition against the "perpetual slavery and bondage" of nonfreemen. In 1649 Samuel and Alice Stratton of Watertown were convicted of saying that the magistrates would do anything for bribes or for church members. Such suspicions could fuel the fires of dissent within colony and town.[19]

There was far more than mere resentment to this "stir in the town." Winthrop's account of Biscoe's book was disingenuous. George Phillips revealed that he had conferred "in my chamber with him [Biscoe] alone ... divers hours we spent in that discourse" about the validity of infant baptism as well as enforced support for the ministry. Biscoe "desired that I would pen down those arguments that had passed betwixt us on my [Phillips's] part ... and then [Biscoe] communicated it to some that were contrary to my apprehensions on these points, and either himself or some others by his means sent them to England."

Later in 1643 Biscoe wrote an answer in manuscript to Phillips's defense of infant baptism. Meanwhile, John Prescott, a young blacksmith recently arrived with his wife from Halifax in Yorkshire, had somehow acquired a book published in England: Thomas Lamb's *Confutation of Infant Baptism,* featuring this leader of the Colchester Baptists' point-by-point refutation of Phillips's arguments. "It put me in a kind of wonderment," wrote the buffeted minister, "to see my name set forth in print, and as the author of a treatise, who never writ any such treatise." In 1646 Mr. Biscoe, the perpetrator of the minister's literary debut, visited other theologians in the Bay to try to resolve his doubts over infant baptism.[20]

The presence of a cell of Baptists in Watertown was a serious threat to Massachusetts orthodoxy. These people objected to infant baptism, which was administered to the children of church members only, on the grounds that it had no biblical precedent. To Biscoe and his cell, baptism should take place only when a new saint entered the covenant. These Baptists were in fact objecting to the New England Way because it was insufficiently pure.[21]

More than purity and unity were at stake, however. The Baptists were deeply anti-intellectual. They attacked graduate clergymen with the weaponry of scriptural literalism. To the ministers, they were "illiterate exhorters," reminiscent of the wild and dangerous populistic ranters of early Protestantism. To the Baptists, reliance on "humane learning" from a "ninneversity" was a monstrous betrayal of the God-given word. Obligatory universal taxes for ministers, as opposed to voluntary contributions, reduced the clergy, in Baptist eyes, to mere hirelings. In 1644 the authorities began a campaign against them that culminated in the 1648 Cambridge Platform accentuating ministerial authority, orthodox intolerance, and centralized control of individual churches.[22]

Biscoe left for London in 1651; Stowers had headed west for Newport, Rhode Island, the previous year, and Prescott left to help found Lancaster in 1647. En route he lost his horse and lading in the Sudbury River, and the following week his wife and child were almost drowned. To Winthrop, these events were a sure providence of God. Once in London, Biscoe joined with the irrepressible Rhode Islander Dr. John Clark in rallying "our churches" amid the corrupt, hostile, and hypocritical sects jostling for precedence before the self-serving Rump of the Long Parliament. He concluded his September 1652 account: "If you in Massachusetts had liberty of conscience, I had rather be there."[23]

Other less affluent Baptists in Watertown had little option but "to be there," without the luxury of liberty of conscience. John Warren, persecuted in England and a founder of the Watertown church, became a freeman in the first creation of 1631. He was elected selectman in 1636 and 1640. Thereafter he is rarely seen in the town records. The court records tell a different story. His name appeared in 1651, 1654, and 1661, charged with dissent over the issue of infant baptism, and he was regularly fined for his refusal to attend weekly meetings—in 1654, for instance, £6.8.0 worth of peas and gunpowder. At his death at the age of eighty-two, he left his daughter "a book called *The Plain Man's Pathway,*" Dent's perennially popular guidebook to salvation.[24]

In October 1651 another church member, Thomas Arnold, was charged with uttering the seditious statement that "the churches in Watertown are no churches and no fit matter for churches . . . [and] children have no more right to baptism . . . than the heathens." Three years later he was stung for £5 for neglecting the rite of baptism and absence from public worship for twenty Sabbaths; the following year he had to pay twice as much. He sold out in 1661 and joined his fellow Baptists in Rhode Island, which now included his old Watertown neighbor John Stowers. That year Warren's house was searched in a McCarthyesque hunt for Quakers, those seventeenth-century Reds under the beds. In 1663 the people of Watertown witnessed their constable laying ten stripes of the whip on the naked back of Elizabeth Howton, Quaker, as she was escorted from Cambridge Prison toward Dedham. Such were the rewards for those who had come to New England for conscience' sake.[25]

"Ill News from New England" had induced Watertown's founder, Sir Richard Saltonstall, to write from London in 1652 to Boston's ministers: "It doth not a little grieve my spirit to hear what sad things are reported daily of your tyranny and persecutions in New England and that you fine, whip and imprison men for their consciences. First you compel such to come into your assemblies as will not join with you in your worship, and when they show their dislike thereof or witness against it, then you stir up the magistrates to punish them for such (as you conceive) their public affronts . . . These rigid ways have laid you very low in the hearts of the saints [here]."[26]

Biscoe's "underhand" publishing of George Phillips's private thoughts on infant baptism stung the minister into writing a reply, which appeared in 1645, with the typically electrifying title for such polemics of *A Reply to a Confutation of Some Grounds for Infant Baptism.* It involved detailed and wearying refutation of Lamb's arguments. *A Reply* proved both a debut and a swan song. In 1644 Watertown church sustained a double loss through the deaths of its pastor and of its ruling elder, Edward Howe. Although the magistrates were detained at court on 2 July 1644, Winthrop recorded "a great assembly of elders and people" at Phillips's funeral. He was, wrote the governor, "a godly man specially gifted and very painful in his place, much lamented of his people and others." To Thomas Shepard, Phillips was "well known in the gates of his people and among the churches of Christ in this western world for his learning, godliness and peaceableness of disposition." Phillips was only fifty-one when he died. He had lost his first wife within weeks of arrival in the Bay and had weathered violent controversy during the founding years before facing renewed confrontation in the 1640s.[27]

The career and character of Watertown's founding pastor contain an intriguing paradox. He is credited with spirited assertions about the nature of ordination, the independence of congregations, and the necessity for consent and representation in governmental decisions. Yet after this confident start, he seemed to lapse into obscurity. We see him occasionally engaged in colony affairs. In 1636 he wrote to the younger Winthrop in Connecticut requesting that he "would be pleased to set down with that plantation begun there by Watertown [Wethersfield, which was] a company without a head . . . subject to many errors, distractions, confusions and what not," the "what not" being a gloss for complete anarchy. The same letter conveys a candid admission of a loss or lack of confidence: "I had spoken unto you [when you were] here but was discouraged by the sense of mine own disabilities to perform anything that might be satisfactory on my part to such a favour if you should be pleased to yield it. Were I not conscious of my own weakness I should be exceedingly importunate if not impudent in pressing my request in this case, but mine own infirmity makes me (though litterae non erubescunt [letters do not make me blush]) ashamed."

The same tone pervades a letter of 1639 to the elder Winthrop. Phillips dismisses his own notes on "The Body of Laws Intended" for Massachusetts as "a little as good as nothing . . . not thinking them worthy the looking after (being so sudden and unpolished a transcript)." His account of his one encounter with Mrs. Hutchinson has him merely asking her opinion of his ministry. Otherwise he took no part in the critical events of the mid-1630s. Except as a beneficiary of lucrative land grants (£301 of his £553 estate was real estate), his name never appears in the town records during the increasingly turbulent years at the end of the decade, either as a leader or as a conciliator.[28]

The early firebrand had lost its fierce flame. The disabilities, weakness, and infirmity he cites may have been physical—Cotton Mather described him as a martyr to "the cholic, the extremity of one fit whereof was the wind which carried him afore it to the haven of eternal rest." The real heat of founding independence may have come from the ruling elder, the cranky Richard Brown. Phillips may have flourished as a big fish in a very small pond, one of only a handful of clergy during the first years. When pike of the caliber of Cotton and Hooker, Shepard and Peters arrived in mid-decade, along with a shoal of other distinguished divines, he may have felt himself reduced to minnow status. The knuckle-rapping he received in 1632 from the governor and the Court of Assistants may have shattered his nerve. It is possible that Phillips's humble origins played a part in his later inhibitions. His father, Christopher, a carpenter, was of only "moderate means," though he served as a churchwarden at South Raynham. This northwestern Norfolk parish was dominated by the Townshend family. Nearby Tittleshall, where George attended school, was similarly under the thumb of the Cokes. One or other of these families may have encouraged the boy's education. At Caius College, Cambridge, Phillips was older than most freshmen and was admitted as a sizar, the meanest rank of undergraduate, who had to work his way through university. When he decided to emigrate, his fare was paid by Winthrop. When Watertown was sited, Saltonstall agreed to build the minister's house. All of this reliance on sponsorship may have eventually undermined his confidence, especially when confronted with reproofs from his social superiors. Whatever the reason, Phillips's initial promise was not sustained, and he sank into the lower clerical ranks.[29]

Watertown still had a pastor in Rev. John Knowles, but he had so far spent little time in the town. Called in 1640, he had been sent to Virginia in 1642 but was back in 1643. Even for a puritan he seems to have been overscrupulous and hyperintense. He never forgave himself for being persuaded to vote for a Laudian candidate for a college fellowship at Cambridge. Although a brilliant scholar and beloved by his pupils, he was forced to leave the university. He was invited to lecture in Colchester in 1635. He was so fervent in the pulpit that he sometimes fainted away. According to Laud, writing to Charles I, "He had forborne to receive holy communion [alongside the unregenerate] for two years since he came to be lecturer and being enjoined [by the church authorities] to perform the duty within a month he was so zealous as that he forsook lecture and town and all rather than he would receive communion." His North Essex connections may have recommended him to the church in Watertown, but there is little evidence of his impact there, except that the church felt the need to appoint a young co-pastor in 1647. In 1651 Knowles left for England. Despite persecution after the Restoration, he refused the offer of the presidency of Harvard in 1672.[30]

Watertown's sole pastor after Knowles's departure was very much an insider. Born in Dedham, Essex, adjacent to Phillips's Boxted, the young John Sherman had sat at the feet of the charismatic John Rogers, the town lecturer. After graduating from Trinity College, Cambridge, Winthrop's alma mater, he emigrated with a gaggle of Shermans, Rogerses, and other Dedhamites and perched briefly in Watertown. There, in 1634, according to Cotton Mather, who knew him well, he delivered his first sermon, which proved a brilliant debut for that "honey-dropping and golden-mouthed preacher." After moves to the snakepit of Wethersfield, to New Haven, where he was elected a magistrate, and to Branford as the plantation's first preacher, he returned to Watertown in 1647, where he remained until his death in 1685.[31]

Sherman was a fitting successor to Phillips, unspectacular, well-read, and industrious. He acted as peacemaker, censor, defender of orthodoxy, and oracle. He was a fellow of Harvard, and his fortnightly lectures were popular with students for over thirty years. He was a distinguished amateur mathematician and astronomer. His second wife, Mary Launce, of wealthy and titled Cornish-Kentish extraction, bore him, according to Mather, twenty children to add to the four by his first wife. He was, indeed, "industrious."[32]

Sherman's call to Watertown in 1647 coincided with the close of the stormy founding years of congregationalism in the colony at large and in individual churches. The 1647 enfranchisement of nonfreemen and the 1648 Cambridge Platform emphasized a more oligarchic and centralized tone and no doubt assisted the patient Sherman in maintaining greater order. The departure of leading subversives also eased his path. Nonetheless, Cotton Mather exaggerated when he claimed that "peace . . . was preserved in his populous town as long as he lived, notwithstanding many temptations unto differences among the good people there."[33]

The sources of the "differences among the good people" of Watertown from 1647 to 1680 centered on two, more secular, issues: financing the ministry and locating the new meetinghouse. There were also spiritual confrontations involving witchcraft. These issues and growing testamentary and deposition evidence provide a window on the shadowy world of popular belief.

Mandatory support of the ministry had been contentious from the beginning of settlement. Protests were unavailing, however; all must attend; all must pay. Sherman and Knowles initially shared a stipend of £120, which rose to £160 in 1649. After Knowles's departure, Sherman was soon being paid £120 for his annual "wages," voted each autumn, not by the church, but by the town meeting. In 1651 a church tax of £100 represented "four pence farthing [four and a quarter pence] upon the pound" in the taxable value of property in the town, or roughly 2 percent.[34]

All townspeople were required to bring their church tax to the deacons at the pastor's house at the beginning of each January. The debts of nonpayers would be "forced in by distress." In 1657 the town meeting added £60 that year to the church tax to pay off Sherman's debt. By 1661 his stipend had reached £160 and then for the rest of our period settled at £140 in 1662. This was considerably higher than other ministers' salaries, partly due to the size of the congregation and partly to the size of Sherman's brood.[35]

During the 1660s more and more people were falling behind with church taxes. For instance, in 1663 the insolent Henry Mattack, 7/2d in arrears, was threatened with appropriate punishment by the selectmen. Yet, for someone like Mattack with a young wife and baby to support, with apparently very little in the way of provisions or possessions, and a nonchurch member to boot, the pastor's annual £140, including his cut and carted firewood, may well have seemed excessive. He would probably have to pay by so many days of work for Mr. Sherman, which he could ill spare from the constant demands of his own family.[36]

Reluctance to meet the church tax may have also arisen from dissatisfaction with the Half-Way Covenant of 1662, which allowed baptism of the infants of the baptized offspring of parents in the covenant of grace. This concession in the face of falling second-generation church membership incurred resentment both from lay saints who feared the pollution of half-way members and from nonmembers who saw this as yet another act of discrimination against them. The numbers of new Watertown freemen in the 1660s, however, showed only a slight increase and then plummeted in the 1670s.[37]

Support for Watertown ministry reached a crisis between 1669 and 1673. Various strategies were tried without success. In 1673, after the deacons had gone on strike, an amnesty was worked out that involved Sherman receiving some land in lieu of unpaid taxes. In 1674 the town agreed to approach Mr. Thomas Clarke to "be helpful to Mr. Sherman in the preaching of the word among us." The young minister went instead to Chelmsford. It is likely that salary proved a stumbling block in Watertown.[38]

In the critical years of the early 1670s, when the ministry was at a low ebb, people with Watertown connections played important roles in the crisis. In May 1670 the two houses of the General Court became embroiled in conflict over the clergy's responsibility for God's anger. Sherman had been a signatory to a clerical remonstrance against such calumnies. Watertown's deputy, Richard Beers, was one of seventeen members of the Lower House dissenting from a rather craven apology to the ministers.[39]

A second divisive town issue of Sherman's long pastorate was that of a new meetinghouse. Back in 1635 a sum of £80 had been appropriated for a meetinghouse. It was probably a relatively small building, and in 1649 and again in 1652 it needed repairing and enlarging. By the 1650s Watertown had grown to about 160 households, with many youngsters, who were crammed into the back of the meetinghouse. Their misbehavior in Watertown and elsewhere was causing alarm and outrage at the colony level.[40]

The minutes of the 14 October 1654 town meeting could not have been simpler: "Ordered by the inhabitants that there should be a new meetinghouse." Subsequent orders named a convenient site, the agreed pattern, the cost of £400, completion date of the end of September 1656, and the building contract. Within a month a row had erupted over the site. On 20 February 1655 three magistrates had to be called in to settle the conflict. By 3 November 1656 arrangements for final construction payments were concluded with "loving agreement." The new meetinghouse was square with a hipped roof crowned with a turret. It was modeled on Cambridge's 1650 building, and each side measured forty feet. It was high enough so that a gallery could be added if necessary.[41]

The three deacons then had to arrange a seating plan. This was a task of the utmost delicacy. Meetinghouse seating reflected "1. Office. 2. Age. 3. Estate. 4. Gifts." The seat allotted calibrated a person's status, seniority, reputation, and precedence within the community. Self-worth and diaconal valuation did not always coincide. Sure enough, on 10 January 1659, it had to be "ordered . . . that all, both men and women, do go into their first appointed seats and whoever refuse so to do after warning given . . . shall pay the fine appointed." How could they have preferred Goody Roe to me? Such outrages and injustices were grist to the gritty millstone of community living. Since deaths or departures led to slow movement up the order of precedence, a standing committee had to make frequent adjustments, not always with happy results.[42]

Ominously, one of the last entries in the Second Book of Town Proceedings, on 3 February 1680, minuted a meeting of selectmen and craftsmen agreeing on details of the enlarging of the meetinghouse by building a gallery. That would last the town for twelve years, after which there would explode a volcanic struggle about a new building that would not be settled until 1720.[43]

Pastor Sherman had one other accomplishment. In 1674, 1676, and 1677 he composed colony almanacs. His mathematical and astronomical interests made him an ideal compiler of tables of celestial motions of the sun and planets, and according to his hagiographer, he reclaimed the popular pocketbook "from that common abuse, of being an engine to convey silly impertinences or sinful superstitions into almost every cottage in the wilderness." Ordinary people bought almanacs to gain at least the illusion of foresight in their frighteningly capricious and uncontrollable world. Sherman's first almanac had a scientific essay on Kepler's theory of planetary motion; nonetheless, he could not resist the astrological temptation of warning his readers that "the too great predominancy" of Mercury and Mars portended "no small evil." How prescient he was![44]

The fact that Sherman's prediction of war would have entered "almost every cottage in the wilderness" suggests the pervasiveness of religious and supernatural issues in early Watertown. They might derive from the clerically compiled *Wonders of the Invisible World* or from the folk magic associated with cunning men and women, which was rife in the new world as it had been in the old, especially the north Essex–south Suffolk band from which so many early settlers had come.[45]

One of the earliest cases of witchcraft in Massachusetts occurred in Watertown. In the late 1640s one of the children of Robert and Grace Jennison in the care of a nurse unexpectedly sickened and died. The nurse claimed that the child had been bewitched by Elizabeth Kendall, a woman from neighboring Cambridge in her midforties, who "did make much of the child" just before its fatal illness. Though Goody Kendall protested her innocence, she was condemned and hanged. Belated investigations by Mr. Richard Brown argued that the nurse herself had been the cause of the child's death because she had kept it out in the cold when it had "the red gum." She was later charged with adultery but died in prison during childbirth while awaiting trial. The fact that she gave her life bringing a child into the world smacks of poetic justice.[46]

Some townspeople retained the skepticism aroused in the Kendall case. Samuel and Alice Stratton derided the superstition surrounding Margaret Jones's execution for witchcraft 1648: "she died wrongfully . . . and her blood would be required at the magistrates' hands." They were supported by Mr. Brian Pendleton. Similarly, in the witchcraft accusations by Charles Stearns's wife against Winifred and Mary Holman of Cambridge, the jury found Rebecca Stearns "deprived of her natural reason." Belief in the supernatural did not necessarily mean uncritical gullibility.[47]

Watertown vigorously enforced colony legislation ensuring religious education. Each year the town selectmen inspected literacy and knowledge of the catechism. In 1679, in the wake of God's dreadful wrath in the war, the pastor took over catechizing the town's youth aged from ten to twenty. The town took very seriously the expiatory invention of tithingmen (who oversaw discipline in ten families), in line with its sustained determination to encourage godliness throughout the first fifty years.[48]

Testamentary records for Watertown contain useful indicators of piety. The great majority of wills begin with a preamble about committing the soul to the mercy of God and hopes for salvation. The expressions are sufficiently varied to suggest that they are the sentiments of the decedent rather than a formula routinely entered by the scribe. They often sound deeply heartfelt: Nathaniel Bowman "daily looking for my change," Samuel Hosier ending "my wearisome pilgrimage," Deacon Henry Bright, hoping to "leave my soul in the arms of my redeemer." Charles Chadwick, eighty-five in 1681, though "being at present in health, yet not knowing how soon it may be the good pleasure of God to put an end to my pilgrimage here," sums up the prevailing providential tone, as does Captain Richard Beers, off to war: "Not knowing how it may please God to deal with me in the service I am now going out upon." Jeremiah Norcross arranged disposal of "such worldly estate as the Lord has lent me," including two ewes "unto the poor members of Jesus Christ in Watertown to breed for a stock" and £1 each to Pastor Sherman and five other ministers. Several other decedents made £1, £2, or £5 bequests to Sherman, and in 1674 Michael Bairstow left his "dear pastor" a hundred-acre farm.[49]

The surviving probate inventories provide information about family ownership of Bibles and other books. Eighteen list Bibles, ten of which are described as "great Bibles," and six estates owned two Bibles each. Even Old Knapp had a copy of the good book. Thirty-two inventories contain references to books, mostly unspecified. Thomas Underwood's, however, is a little more precise: "20 books of divinity"; similarly, Michael Bairstow's "several divine books" and Ellis Barron's "five books of divinity and physic." John Biscoe's "29 old books" may have contained a copy of George Phillips's *Reply*. Although John Warren's *Plain Man's Pathway* is the only named title, many of the undifferentiated books were probably also works of popular piety. Any townspeople wanting to refer to more advanced studies could borrow from George Phillips's extensive library. One book on his shelves was itself borrowed; in Bullinger's *One Hundred Sermons on the Apocalypse* (sometime owned by Adam Winthrop) is the note: "This is Mr. Feake his book, 1634, G. P."[50]

Ordinary people took their faith seriously, for good and ill. Ann Pearce, for instance, described herself in 1678 as executrix "of all that the good Lord our maker and preserver has given us." She compared her husband's provision for son Daniel to "Jacob giving extra to his son Joseph in the Land of Canaan and what he got from out of the hand of the Amorite by his sword and his bow." When the Stearnses and her parents reacted to Rebecca's terrifying fits, they were automatically "stirred up to seek the Lord that if [Widow Holman was] aworking of wickedness that the Lord would be pleased to prevent her." Rebecca "begged prayers of her neighbours and wished her husband to pray hard." Winifred Holman's supporters described her as "a diligent hearer of and attender to the word of God." Goody Stratton and Edward Sanders both turned to their Bibles when trouble threatened. There is every reason to believe that Nathaniel Biscoe's conscientious confusions over the doctrine of baptism were heartfelt.[51]

On 5 July 1632 Winthrop recorded: "At Watertown there was (in view of diverse witnesses) a great combat between a mouse and a snake; and, after a long fight, the mouse prevailed and killed the snake. The pastor of Boston, Mr. Wilson . . . gave this interpretation: That the snake was the devil; the mouse was a poor contemptible people, which God had brought hither, which should overcome Satan here and dispossess him of his kingdom."[52] Combat was certainly one of the early characteristics of the Watertown congregation, which in its assertive purism and doctrinal obstinacy comes across as anything but poor and contemptible. Conflict and controversy over arcane points of theology and church membership sorely tested the patience of the overworked Winthrop. "The strife in Watertown congregation continued still," reads a weary journal entry of the same year. Watertown's escape from general embroilment in the antinomian controversy suggests that this issue was confined to Boston and people in trade. The stressful confrontation over baptism in the 1640s mainly involved people from outside Phillips's Company. This dispute concerning issues of purity and biblicism led to early calls for toleration and liberty of conscience.[53]

The church's other major characteristic was its fierce independence: advice it might take, but not orders. This radical assertion of group freedom from central control persisted into the 1640s. Watertown church's virtual separation was a clear claim of subjective right based on its relationship to God. Though the doctrines and ecclesiology adopted in Watertown were often foreshadowed in covert practice back in the Stour Valley, their defense at the grassroots level represents revolutionary change, thanks to the new "experimental" environment, more innovative than their political challenges to colonial authority. The seamlessness of life in early Watertown is indicated by the interrelation of politics, economics, and religion in the confrontation between nonfreemen and freemen.[54]

All this lively libertarianism, debate about fundamentals, and congregational independence evaporated during Sherman's ministry, to be replaced by banal arguments about seating, rating, or siting. This change was due partly to the Cambridge Platform of 1648, partly to the 1647 defusing of nonfreemen's sense of outrage, and partly to the departure of troublemakers like Biscoe, Jennison, Arnold, Prescott, and Stowers. Yet "declension" also played a part. The number of new church members declined after 1650. Problems with nonpayment of church taxes escalated in the 1660s. Cases of sexual immorality increased in the 1670s, as we shall see. In the great debates in the 1660s and 1670s over the Half-Way Covenant, the town does not merit a mention. This absence coincides with a more general impression of Watertown lapsing into a sleepy farming backwater, rarely rippling the surface of colonial affairs, rarely providing, as before, leadership and service at the colonial level.

If the creative contentions of the founding years lost their energy, if standards slightly slipped, if valuable citizens were lost, ordinary people nonetheless retained a sense of piety and providentialism. They contributed £400 to their new meetinghouse, gave their children a Christian upbringing, and maintained their minister in considerable style. The first fifty years of Watertown suggests that such quiet steadfastness may have been more important for local residents than the antinomian or Half-Way Covenant controversies that have grabbed the historical headlines.

III
ECONOMY

7

Living with Livestock

Extreme efforts were required to establish a settlement. "Plantations in their beginning have work enough, and find difficulties sufficient to settle a comfortable way of subsistence, there being buildings, fencings, clearing and breaking of ground, lands to be attended, orchards to be planted, highways and bridges and fortifications to be made, and all things to do, as in the beginning of the world."[1] During the first decade of settlement, fears of failure, of starvation, of disease, of having to abandon plantations were very real, as we have seen. The precedents were hardly reassuring. Only recently the Dorchester Company had failed; Plymouth was dourly hanging on. Confronting these "first brunts," some founders came close to despair. Young Pond, already distressed by the poor yield of unfertilized "eindy wheat," complained to his father: "Provisions are here at a wonderful rate . . . and if this ship [the *Lyon*, William Pearce master] had not come when it did, we had been put to a wonderful strait . . . We do not know how long we may subsist, for we cannot live here without provisions from old England . . . we do not know how long this plantation will stand . . . there come back again [to England] four score and odd persons and as many more would have come if they had the wherewithall to bring them home . . . my provisions were almost all spent . . . I should and mine [family] have been half famished."[2]

As the first winter came on, many were still living in tents. At the end of September 1630, "one Finch of Watertown had his wigwam burnt and all his goods." Six weeks later, in the chill of November, "Firmin of Watertown had his wigwam burnt."[3] Two years later settlers were still making do with fragile huts: "Mr. Oldham had a small house near the weir at Watertown, made all of clapboards, burnt down by making a fire in it when it had no chimney."[4] The use of open fires and poorly insulated "catted" or "daubed" wooden chimneys made fire an ever-present danger. Several Watertown people suffered severe losses through house fires. When barns burned, like George Phillips's or Nathaniel Biscoe's, "cattle both hogs and other bigger cattle were much hurt for want of meat [food]."[5]

The untested and unimagined environment presented some daunting shocks. Winthrop reported "the people of Watertown falling very short of corn" in 1631. Early attempts to grow winter grain sown in the fall were, in that climate, disastrous. New pests preyed on them. William Hammond described the huge numbers of pigeons darkening the sky in a letter from Watertown in 1633: "So many pigeons as might have loaded two or three ships. For two hours we did behold them. They did fly for six miles of breadth, so thick that they covered the air that we did think the first flight was twenty miles afore the last came." Wolf packs threatened young cattle and swine. The weather was violent, extreme, unpredictable, un-English.[6]

In their battle for survival, shortage of tools, plus absence of infrastructure and haulage power, made life dauntingly laborious. All grain, much of it unfamiliar maize, had to be ground by hand until 1634. One of the first crimes in the town involved the theft of tools. The first mention of a plow did not occur until 1634, and then in a complaint that the borrowed ox-team pulling it had been removed.[7] These shortfalls represented insufficient initial capital investment in the town (exacerbated by Saltonstall's early withdrawal, D'Ewes's nonarrival, and subsequent outmigration of merchants), planter inexperience, and disappointing lack of Indian trade and assistance. A new-world baby boom and the unanticipated, unaccustomed dearth of servants and farmhands heightened the sense of apprehension and foreboding.

To meet this dizzying challenge, the founders of Watertown carried two weapons. The first was their English farming and craft experience. It needed adaptation to new-world conditions, but East Anglia was an enterprising, progressive, and experimenting region. The second resource was "the culture of discipline," the earnest work ethic and commitment to physical "improvement" that they had advocated with such zeal in the decadent old world. They also had a potentially "fruitfull plat," with considerable cleared land, the river for fish, fish-fertilizer, power, and transport, and an array of skills among their townspeople. They were predominantly "the middling sort," aware of their rights but not afraid of responsibility. The "poor," dependent elderly, and the halt and lame were burdens left behind in England, along with prevalent tenancy, postfeudal encumbrances, and high taxation.[8]

To "replenish the earth and subdue it" was these planters' prudential imperative as well as their providential duty. How they painfully and laboriously pushed back the threats of starvation and the "wilderness," their economic achievements and setbacks, are the subject of this and the next chapter.

Without animals, the people of early Watertown could not have survived. Pigs, "neat" (or beef) cattle, and sheep provided essential proteins through their fresh or cured meat and dairy products. Steers and horses were the major source of motive power for the multiplicity of heavy tasks involved in the founding and developing of a town and in cultivating the land. In 1661 a yoke of oxen were equated with five acres of plowland in an exchange deal. Horses were the main means of transportation. Animal hides were processed into all kinds of vital leather goods; sheep's wool was spun and woven into clothing, blankets, and other textile goods. Many other products derived from animals, like glue and brushes, vellum and parchment, hornware and fertilizer, tallow and mattress stuffing, and manure to hearten tired soil. Since the native Americans had no domesticated animals, at the outset all livestock had to be imported. During the 1630s inflation their prices soared. Every fresh cargo of farm beasts was a victory in the war for survival, not only for their dietary value, but also for the muscle power that could extend the farming area of the settlement.[9]

For all their benefits, livestock also brought conflict. Cattle needed to be fed, both on summer pasture and on fodder during the bitter winters. It was quickly realized that much of the local hay was of poor quality: "Our beasts grow lousy with feeding upon it, and are much out of heart and liking." Almost immediately the hunt was on for more meadow. This hunt led to problems with other towns, competitiveness within the town, and loss of important investors. Because Newtown complained of "want of accommodation for their cattle," Watertown was persuaded to "lend" meadowland in the east, which its inhabitants only ever recovered by expensive piecemeal purchase. "Straitness of accommodation and want of meadow" were cited for the 1635 migration to "New Watertown" (Wethersfield) in the lush Connecticut Valley and the 1637 exodus of townsmen to Sudbury. The remoteness of the West Pine meadows and their scattering among the lands assigned for farms produced a highly charged market for more convenient grassland in the short term, and in the long term decades of wrangling, as we have already seen.[10]

Besides these major sources of contention, living with livestock engendered endemic, workaday, occupational conflict, less spectacular than battles over land or government, but always liable to catch fire. Fencing crops and controlling animals, the inherent problems of mixed farming ingrained from English experience, dominated the first two Books of Proceedings of the town records. Each year two men were elected to a thankless task that combined both sides of the town's and the colony's policy on this literally vital issue: fence viewers and stock reeves.[11]

Fences were less essential in the early years when livestock was rare. Milk was supplied by goats rather than cows, and an early town order impounded untethered goats. By the mid-1630s, however, cattle and hogs were sufficiently numerous to require fencing regulations. The first order, on 7 October 1635, placed the obligation for preserving crops solely on the cultivators. A year later, however, the town meeting had to concede that "great cattle" might push over a sound fence, in which case the animals' owners would be liable. Thereafter the potential for conflict escalated.[12] Fields farmed in common created perennial vexations. Fencing around such fields, where each commoner had a block of land, was meant to be proportional. Someone with ten acres was responsible for twice the length of exterior fencing as someone with five. There were in actuality innumerable possibilities for friction and combat. Inaccurate surveying, common fields from which some individuals had "taken themselves orderly out" and enclosed their holdings, one or more commoners' substandard fencing, or the hiatus caused by land sale or a commoner's death just before fencing time—these and other problems sorely tested farmers' patience, sometimes to the breaking point. Board arbitrations and orders in specific cases underline the complexity of land usage and different owners' obligations. Without a mutual sense of equity and responsibility, "great contention" was inevitable.[13]

Conflict had become so pervasive that the 1653 General Court instructed towns to introduce comprehensive fencing regulations. The whole Watertown fencing ordinance, including a seven-month warning before opting out of general fields, majority rule in general fields, proportional fencing decided by 1 March each year, and clear fencing standards buttressed by draconian penalties, "was read at a public town meeting the 22 January 1654 and voted to be entered as the act of the whole town."[14] In the next eight years complaints about fencing derelictions and disagreements gradually diminished, though the possibility for outbursts of anger and violence was always present.[15]

As Robert Frost knew only too well, there was no substitute for good boundaries in sustaining good neighborliness. Boundaries must be mutually agreed. Disagreements about fence lines could run on for years.[16] Some disputes polarized neighbors, precipitated violence, and ended up in the courts. Fencing issues had the potential to rive a whole community. The phrase "mending one's fences" has powerful peacemaking connotations, with good reason. In 1672 Watertown's potter, John Livermore Sr., gave William Shattuck a triangle of valuable meadow "in consideration for a parcel of fence thirty-two rods in length being maintained for ever." Fences were high on any farmer's list of priorities from March to October.[17]

"Orderly" stock were as important as sound fences for survival and communal peace. During the first two decades of settlement, policies were gradually developed for the three main types of farm animals: hogs, cattle, and horses. Sheep became sufficiently numerous to require regulation only in the late 1650s, but thereafter their numbers increased rapidly.

Pigs were a vital element in Watertown's agrarian economy from the start. Well adapted to the climate and to the deciduous woodland with its rich fattening mast of acorns and chestnuts, large enough to fend off wolves, they could be left to forage for themselves; producing meat that the settlers were experienced in curing and preserving, swine were a virtually self-supporting asset. "The best cattle for profit" in the early days, the numbers of hogs doubled on average every eighteen months by natural increase.[18]

On the loose, pigs were also a potential menace, not only through their "ravenousness" attacking children and spreading infectious diseases among the elderly, but also as persistent uprooters and powerful infiltrators. Nothing was safe from them. They even tore to pieces one of John Sherman's feather pillows hung out to air. The earliest known convention in the colony was that any cultivator who found a hog in his crops could kill it. This draconian solution was replaced in late 1640 by the rule that regulated swine management for the rest of our period: that their snouts should be ringed all year round to prevent uprooting, and yokes fitted under their throats during the growing season to deter them from burrowing under or barging through fences. Neglect of ringing and yoking incurred fines and damages.[19]

Nonetheless, signs of neglect, of "irregular" hogs, are not hard to find. Three purges in 1657, 1663, and 1678 flushed out over three hundred infractions each year. Most of Watertown was represented on this roll of dishonor, from the minister and captain of militia, through the deacons and selectmen, down to the lowliest townsman. Despite these periodic drives and further regulations, as late as 1679 the disorderliness of swine, turned out to forage for themselves, was continuing to cause concern.[20]

Pigs could certainly raise emotional temperatures faster than any other livestock. Frustrated hogreeves could come near to violence with stiff-necked offenders. Anger against negligent neighbors is often tangible. Damage caused by swine sometimes led to tit-for-tat accusations about defective fencing. They could make the blood boil, but their ham boiled beautifully in midwinter.[21]

"Neat cattle"—bulls, steers, bullocks, cows, heifers, and calves—represented a far larger investment than the humble hog and were generally more carefully supervised by their owners. Common herding was labor saving in a labor-scarce community. Once out of winter stalls, they were divided into milch and dry herds. The milch herd was needed close to home for their daily milk, and in 1643 stints, or allotments, on the common were laid down depending on householders' acreage.[22] The milch herd would be summoned by the driver's horn to Meetinghouse Green after morning milking just after sunrise and then returned from their pasture for evening milking "a little before sunset."[23] Thanks to abundant fish for fertilizer, heifers and the cattle being fattened in the dry herd could be grazed at a safe distance from the town's arable fields throughout the summer while crops were growing. During the 1650s and the early 1660s, the herdsman lived out at Cowpen Farm near the Sudbury line. Besides controlling the dry cattle, he was contracted to supply an "able bull."[24]

The whole westward grazing of the dry herd was thrown into confusion by changes in land policy. At the end of 1663 the town proprietors finally decided to lay out on the ground the farms allotted on paper in 1642, thus ending the open range. For the future, cattle must be grazed in "particular enclosures" or else with one of the four herds on the reduced town land remaining. After several attempts by the selectmen to impose order, three outside arbitrators recommended that grazing arrangements should be left with the individual herdsmen.[25]

It is clear from all the time and energy expended on their control that neat cattle were highly important to the life of Watertown. The only clue we have to their numbers is in Edward Johnson's estimate of 450 head in 1651. The 1669–70 division into three, then four, herds argues that numbers had increased. Two factors make estimates difficult. We do not know how many farmers were grazing their cattle in "particular enclosures" on their own pastureland in the Great Dividend and elsewhere. Since the purchase of the town bull in 1660 signaled more selective stock rearing, farmers who could afford it would also want to control their cattle's fodder. A dry herd of only eighty head is mentioned in 1660; much fattening would have been transferred to the owners' pastureland.[26] Inventories provide information on stock-holding only at the time of death, when numbers were likely to be lower than in the prime of life, but every household appraised had at least one cow. The total of all neat cattle listed, including oxen, steers, heifers, and calves, is 381. Though it is impossible to calculate from this fraction the size of the whole town herd, it is nonetheless striking that a cow was considered as essential in seventeenth-century Watertown as a refrigerator would be now. Valued, on average, at £3 a head, the neat cattle in many estates outstripped the worth of household chattels.[27]

We may not know their numbers, but the crucial role of milch, beef, and working cattle in Watertown's economy cannot be doubted. The town's situation presented several ideal conditions. Its long bankside along the Charles provided not only meadow for haymaking but also rich bottomland pasture. Water was vital for cattle rearing; during summer, a working steer would drink fifteen gallons of water a day. As the town's name suggests, it was amply blessed. There were several brooks flowing into the Charles as well as Fresh Pond, Great

Pond (Waltham), and other smaller ponds.[28] Although the luxury of "ranging" in perhaps sixteen thousand acres of wood and grassland was curtailed by the 1660s land divisions into farms, there remained sufficient summer pasture up to 1680. By the end of the century, Watertown had become famous in New England as a cattle-raising town, arguably, the first cow town in British America.

The third element in animal husbandry with which immigrants from East Anglia and the West Country would have been all too familiar was sheep. But sheep were only occasionally mentioned in the town records for most of our period. On 27 November 1654, for instance, the selectmen were requested to arbitrate over disputed ownership of a lamb. The 5 May 1657 meeting of selectmen issued brief orders that sheep must be under a sufficient keeper in public places and that rams must be secluded from the flock from 1 July to 25 October, in order to optimize the time of lambing.[29]

In July 1670 came the first admission that the ovine population was growing rapidly. The selectmen were concerned about Watertown "commoners who have feed little enough to keep our own sheep." A crisis was signaled by "many complaints" at the town meeting on 3 November 1679 about "the multitude of sheep in the town." On 26 January 1680 the town meeting approved detailed orders drawn up by the selectmen and read twice to the meeting.[30]

The early rarity of sheep is easily explained. They were too vulnerable in the founding years. They proved poor sailors. They could not defend themselves or their lambs against predators. They did not thrive on native grasses. The first settlers did not have time for all the elaborate processes involved in domestic production of homespun cloth. Edward Johnson spoke for Watertown when he wrote: "Those that laid out their estate on sheep . . . sped worst of any at the beginning . . . for until the land be often fed with other cattle [i.e. manured and grassed] sheep cannot live."[31]

However, this situation changed—"some [sheep owners] have sped [prospered] the best of any now"—in the 1640s as demand for homespun increased. In the throes of economic depression and the commercial isolation caused by the English Civil War, the 1645 General Court issued an order to encourage the increase of colonial flocks. Woolen cloth was perceived as "a profitable merchandise . . . to transport to other parts." In 1654 butchering of immature rams or wethers (castrated rams) and the export of ewes or ewe lambs was prohibited. Three years later, "the selectmen of every town [were required] to make orders for the clearing of their commons for the better breeding of sheep." Selective breeding was also urged, since "experience doth show that the breed of sheep is much decayed by reason of not breeding suitable rams."[32]

Apart from the value of their fleeces and their meat, sheep were well-known "menders" of tired land by the spreading of their nitrogenous dung. Though the fierce winters prevented the sheep-cereal husbandry practiced in parts of East Anglia and the West Country, they could manure fields after harvest, as well as their owners' homestalls during milder winter days. Since they cost only a sixth of the price of a cow, bore offspring—often two, sometimes three—in five rather than ten months, and could reproduce within a year of birth, sheep were a very attractive stock proposition, especially for the less affluent. These factors help to explain why the Watertown flock had grown to more than five hundred by the 1670s. At this point, the warning bells began sounding. The ever-expanding ovine numbers might reproduce the English crisis where the voracious "sheep do eat up the men."[33]

The least noticed of the farm animals in the town records is the horse. Essential at the homestall and farmstead for haulage and transport, its major drawback was "the great damage done in corn fields, meadows and pastures by horses that go in commons and highways within the range of the houses and corn fields, some going without fetters, some with clogs, and some that will not be restrained though fettered." A series of orders about fines and damages was not wholly effective,[34] as shown by a steady trickle of civil and criminal cases in the Middlesex County Court records. Mistaken identity and the "stealing of horsekind and selling as their own" had become such a problem by 1668 that the General Court instituted a complex system of "toll books" of ownership to be kept in each town. Thanks to some horses ranging free in the woods or escaping, the court also forbade that any "stout horse above two years old shall be suffered to go in commons or woods at liberty unless he be of comely proportion and sufficient stature, no less than fourteen hands high on penalty of £1 fine, because the breed of horses is becoming utterly spoiled . . . [and] a useful creature is becoming a burden."[35]

The damage that horses could inflict on standing crops sometimes led to violent confrontations. In 1680 John Bigelow, aged sixty-three, reported to the county court how thirty-eight-year-old Jacob Bullard, as agent of his octogenarian father, "coming to the field where he [John] was at harvest, and swore three times by Him that made him he would knock John Bigelow in the head, and once by God's wounds he would knock his [straying] mare in the head, and called him old rogue and bade him kiss his breech and that he had none to bear witness but one of his young snip [James Bigelow, aged about thirteen]." In response, John Bigelow was, unsurprisingly, "displeased, and did threaten Bullard to do some displeasure to him . . . Bigelow continued to give [Bullard] bad speeches and said he [Bullard] was self-conceited and knew so much law, and if he [Bigelow] could not do it [get justice] by law, he would do it some other way and vowed he would do it." Bullard escaped with an admonition from the bench and payment of court costs. The court probably took the mutual nature of such slanging matches into consideration.[36]

Some townsmen became involved in the livestock trade. At the start of colonization, Thomas Wincoll was employed in caring for Matthew Craddock's cattle. Roger Wellington and his son Benjamin were involved in suits about cattle sales in 1661 and in 1677. We shall meet John Clary as another dealer in the case study of John Sawin. Sometimes these bargains caused bad blood between or even within families. In one such deal, when Thomas Fleg Jr. opined that "if she was his cow, he would not take her out of [brother-in-law John] Dix's hands till he could find a chapman that would give him the same price," his brother Gershom Fleg demurred from passing on his brother's loan (at 16 percent interest) to the seller. Livestock dealing demanded trust. If a party thought they were suffering "a shrewd turn," latent suspicions exploded.[37]

The first two generations at Watertown had to make many changes to adapt to a new environment for livestock. They had to replace or improve the fodder available. They could not practice sheep-cereal husbandry because of harsh winter conditions. Breeding seasons had to be postponed because of later springtimes. They had no hedges or drystone walls to seclude their beasts from their crops. They had to learn to cope with wolves as predators and with the impact on their animals of far greater temperature ranges. With these challenges came great benefits. Ample fish-based manure, along with ample land and water, meant that swine and much neat cattle and some horses could be turned out to range.

Despite these needs to innovate, other aspects of livestock husbandry were familiar continuities. The pounding and crying of strays, plus tollbooks of earmarks, were long-tested English procedures. So were the proportional stinting of grazing commons, communal herding, fencing regulations, and the office of hogreeve responsible for checking the yoking and ringing of swine. The commonest continuity was the endemic problem of damage to crops by unrestrained animals and the resultant intracommunity fury.[38]

Despite the problems of management and neighborly conflict that large numbers of animals and stock deals were bound to pose, especially in a constantly expanding arable farming area, it is beyond doubt that the benefits far outweighed them. Indeed, there would have been no neighbors but for the nutrition and muscle power of their varied stock. The people of Watertown had to learn, painfully and contentiously, how to live with animals in their new environment; there was no living without them.

8

Livelihood: The Town's Economy

All sorts of trades and crafts were represented in the founders of the town and their successors, but every householder received land in the allotments between 1630 and 1642. The fact that all early inhabitants had a variety of grants—homestalls, meadow, pasture, plowland, upland—emphasizes that they expected to *make their livings* through mixed farming. However skillful a person might be in some craft or "mystery," feeding must come first in these cliff-hanging years.[1]

Gradually the threats of the wilderness and of starvation were pushed back. As we saw, relief supplies sent from England or fetched by Watertown merchants tided the town over as they brought their homestalls under cultivation. The town's housewrights and carpenters replaced tents and shacks with framed houses, small but weatherproof and sturdy. The kinsfolk arriving in 1634 brought tools and 113 head of cattle with them, including oxen and bullocks, four-legged tractors.[2]

The town's infrastructure was painfully laid out. The first nonanimal labor-saving devices exploited the Charles River. In the early 1630s, "a little below this fall of waters, the inhabitants of Watertown have built a weir to catch fish, wherein they take great store of shads and alewives. In two tides they have gotten one hundred thousand of those fishes. This is no small benefit to the plantation." The catch at spring spawning time was used or sold for fertilizer.[3]

In 1634 Thomas Mayhew requested the loan of Governor Winthrop's ox team to haul lumber for the building of the town's first water mill, which also required a dam and water race. Thomas Cakebread, Watertown's first miller, oversaw the work. About 1639 he was replaced by Richard Woodward. Wheelwrights Henry Kemball, David Fiske, and Richard Cutting were responsible for the mill machinery and its maintenance.[4] By the end of our half-century, cultivation had expanded westward far enough to warrant the building of a second corn mill on Stony Brook.[5]

As new tracts of land were opened up, roads became essential. There already were rudimentary trails blazed by the Native Americans, both east to west along the north bank of the Charles, and from Fresh Pond southward to the shallow river crossing near the mill. These trails would form the pattern for the basic track system of Watertown, which would link it to Cambridge and Charlestown in the east and to Sudbury and Concord westward. There were two foci to the early town: the meetinghouse and the river crossing at the central southern point, from which all main tracks fanned out west, north, and east.[6]

The early town records are full of orders about "laying out of highways." In 1637 the town agreed that all able-bodied men—"all soldiers and watchmen"—must put in eight days of annual labor maintaining the tracks, bringing wheelbarrows or carts, mattocks, spades, or shovels. Each year the fall town meeting followed English precedent and appointed two surveyors of highways. Subject to the grueling wear from carts or two-wheeled tumbrels loaded with hay, grain, firewood, or maize, and subject also the heavy hooves of oxen and horses, these dirt trails became seas of mud in winter and rutted, pitted dust bowls in summer. Though "highway" flattered them, these tracks were nonetheless vital to a mixed-farming, arable-pastoral, community. Each household had different kinds of land scattered all over the vast land grant. Without cartways their multifarious activities would be impossible. As the town developed, its links with its neighbors and the world beyond would also grow.[7]

Besides the through trails from Cambridge to Concord or Sudbury, the other major route out of the town was across the river. Because of bends this route was the most direct way to Boston, via Muddy River (Brookline) and Roxbury. In the earliest days this journey involved the hazardous fording of the Charles at the shallows near the weir. In late 1633 former Thames wherryman Richard Brown was licensed to keep a ferry. The first mention of a bridge is in the colony records in 10 October 1641. It was a footbridge and was located near the mill and the ford. It was financed by Thomas Mayhew, who received three hundred acres in recompense.[8] On 26 May 1647 the General Court issued orders for the building of a "horse bridge," to be completed by 1 November 1647, an overoptimistic target that had to be extended by ten months. Deacon Child was reimbursed for his outlay for wine for the builders.[9]

With this bridge "a loaden horse carrying a sack of corn" or an animal on the hoof could cross to the south bank and the trail to Boston without risking the treacherous riverbed. This traffic inflicted heavy wear and tear on the bridge.[10] In the bitter winter of 1666–67, the increasingly rickety base was swept away by ice. Its replacement had a three-feet-wide walkway laid across a series of stone-filled baskets. With regular repairs, this novel form of construction maintained Watertown's contact with the outside world.[11]

That outside world of the colony experienced grave economic instability from 1634 to 1642, and Watertown was no exception. The wave of refugees between 1634 and 1637 changed the economic climate from dependent survival to inflationary boom. As money from liquidated English estates and businesses poured into the town, where goods were still desperately short, prices and wages rocketed.[12] The prospect of heady profits from sales of food and necessities to newcomers boosted production. This newfound bullishness (in two senses) is reflected in a 1639 letter of Edmund Brown, briefly in Watertown before heading west to Sudbury, to his (and other townsmen's) patron in Suffolk, Sir Simonds D'Ewes. Brown encouraged investing £20, £40, or even £60 in cattle and wrote of possible land grants of six hundred acres, which would yield £2 per acre annual profit.[13]

Watertown's Richard Brown was appointed on 12 March 1638 to a General Court committee charged with getting prices and wages under control. As towns like Watertown closed off access to proprietorship, a highly profitable market in land developed.[14] The land boom of the late 1630s was matched by a boom in food production. The busy series of land grants for extra pasture, plowland, and meadow reflected the ambition to clear and break in more and more land as immigration surged. In this new climate of economic expansion, Watertown gained the right to have two fairs each year on the first Fridays of June and September, to be "kept upon the Training Place" on the south side of Meetinghouse Common. Here could be followed "the common practice of those that had any store of cattle, to sell every year a cow or two, which clothed their backs, filled their bellies with more varieties [of victuals] than the country itself afforded, and put gold and silver in their purses beside."[15]

Then, suddenly, at the turn of the decade, the boom collapsed. The promise of "a general reformation of church and state . . . caused all men to stay in England in expectation of a new world." By 1641 the inrush of hungry mouths and heavy purses had declined to a dribble. The Massachusetts economy reacted accordingly. Winthrop wrote: "The scarcity of money made a great change in all commerce. Merchants would sell no wares but for ready money; men could not pay their debts . . . prices of lands and cattle fell soon to the one half and less, yea to a third and after one fourth part."[16] For a time corn was unsellable at any price. Numbers of people returned to England: "They concluded there would be no subsisting here, and accordingly they began to hasten away."[17]

The crash hit the people of Watertown hard. Provision for "the poor" was

Livelihood: The Town's Economy 95

entered for the first time in town expenditures in 1642. On this economic roller coaster some were derailed. John Page almost went to the wall, as we shall see. Fourteen families pulled out of Watertown in the early 1640s. Robert Jennison had to go to Robert Keayne for a loan to keep afloat. Ephraim Child also had to borrow heavily. Robert Saltonstall sold land at a loss that he had bought from Daniel Patrick. Thomas Dudley complained that his £560 share in the mill had plummeted to less than half its value by 1644. Mayhew's mill mortgage was foreclosed as he began selling what he could salvage. In October 1643 Biscoe complained that "much hath been my loss by very many of my debtors." The land market was very volatile, and indebtedness increased. The town authorities moved to stabilize the situation. The closing of the proprietorship to newcomers was reiterated at the end of 1640, and the distribution of farms was temporarily halted. New valuations were published in July for land and stock to conform with plummeting prices. All this volatility, exploitation, suffering, and fear helped to create a contentious atmosphere in the town that exploded in the series of land, religious, and governmental battles already described.[18]

For the town's economy to survive the loss of immigrant cash and markets, two options presented themselves. The first, attractive to those wishing to maintain distance from a corrupt mother country and corrupting commerce, was the possibility of greater self-sufficiency. The second, advocated by mercantile expansionists, was to develop staples and maximize exports, thereby paying for imports and engaging in the burgeoning Atlantic trade system. These choices represented the two ideological motives behind puritan colonization, namely, the cooperative commonwealth and the hope of economic betterment. As things turned out, both were tried simultaneously.[19]

In June 1641, as measures were announced to encourage servants to spin hemp for twine-, rope-, and sack-making,[20] a group of Watertown men were rewarded with over £4 between them for weaving 83 1/2 yards of cloth. A further, overdue bounty was paid in October 1643. Two of these beneficiaries were master weavers: Martin Underwood and Nicholas Busby. The others had no recorded weaving experience.[21]

Concern that "clothing was not likely to be so plentifully supplied from foreign parts as in time past" produced further exhortations to spin and weave in May 1656, with targets of three pounds of spun wool per week, penalties for nonperformance, and instructions for clearing common land for sheep. The idle or delinquent in houses of correction were to process flax and hemp.[22] In the following February (1657) two leading selectmen were nominated to visit the demented Elizabeth Ball, "and there to acquaint her that it is the mind of the selectmen that she set herself to the carding of two skeins of cotton or sheep's wool and her daughter to spin it, with other business of the family and this is to be her daily task, the which if she refuse she must expect to be sent to the house of correction." The community's aspirations for greater economic self-sufficiency extended to the most disadvantaged. By 1663 Watertown had its own fulling mill, and five probate inventories list looms. The fact that much cloth was being woven at home in Watertown is borne out by inclusion of homespun in eleven probate valuations, and of yarn, cotton, wool, and hemp in nineteen.[23]

Colonial home production could reduce reliance on expensive British textiles. The strict enforcement of sumptuary laws regulating dress could further safeguard the balance of payments, as well as preserving hierarchy and a proper puritan respect for austerity and modesty. On 12 April 1659 the Watertown selectmen reiterated the colonial law "that none of our inhabitants, except such as the law doth allow, do either wear silk goods or silk scarves, gold or silver lace or buttons, ribbons at knees or trossed handkerchiefs, upon the forfeiture of what penalty the law doth appoint, which is, that they shall be rated in the country [colony] rate after £200 in the same."[24] That this was not mere gesturing was discovered by an overdressed Watertown youth on 1 November 1664.[25]

Individual Watertown men invested in other projects of the 1640s and 1650s designed to ease the economic dependence of the colony. Onetime Watertown residents William Paine and his son John were major players in iron production at both Saugus and New Haven. Deacon Ephraim Child, related to other ironworks investors, negotiated a large loan while in London from 1647 to 1648. Thomas Parkhurst was involved in the plan for colonial salt production to try to decrease the one-thousand-ton annual import.[26]

Concurrently with these projects aimed at self-sufficiency, entrepreneurs eager to engage in international trade began exploiting the natural resources of New England in short supply elsewhere. Watertown's John Oldham was attracted by the fur trade, as were the younger men who left town for Lancaster and later for Groton. Others spent time on the Piscataqua preparing exports of worked timber, like shingles, clapboards, and pipestaves to the Atlantic wine islands—Malaga, Madeira, the Canaries, and the Azores. In the 1640s both Brian Pendleton, who had moved from Watertown to Maine, and the Mayhew group who settled Martha's Vineyard became involved in the international fisheries project that supplied dried, smoked, or salted fish to the wine islands, the Mediterranean, and the Caribbean. Watertown merchants William Jennison and William Hammond engaged in this export drive, neither very successfully. In 1645 Jennison was wrecked at Hellgate near the mouth of the East River, Manhattan, and Hammond's cargo succumbed to the currents off Long

Island. Hammond, who had measured the volume of the plaguey pigeons against that of ships' cargoes, continued to trade in Watertown, and his inventory of 21 November 1662 included woven and knitted goods, spices, wine, and money on loan. Other town traders, like Edward Dix, Thomas Boylston, and Richard Brown, engaged in retailing imported goods but, compared to the merchants of Boston, on a very small scale.[27]

As the town's economy recovered and matured by the 1650s, farming was clearly the one common and predominant activity. Official town business had to go into recess between April and August. The minister's swine were "disorderly" more than once; three of Phillips's cattle wandered off one summer to Cambridge, where the meadow grass really *was* greener. The schoolmaster was given two weeks vacation during haying season to gather his winter fodder. Depositions often allude to people engaged on the relentless round of farm work: young Sawin's midwinter "threshing corn at Henry Curtis's barn," for instance, or John Hammond in "the barn as he was giving the horses meat [food]." Depending on need and available labor, between eight and fifteen acres of arable land were cultivated, with Indian and English corn, rye, barley, and wheat the usual cereals. Watertown farmers rotated their crops, growing peas and turnips to restore soil nutrients. Hops and tobacco in leaf were not uncommon in probate inventories; pumpkins and mustard seed were also listed. Most homestalls included an orchard, and apples and cider were frequently stored in cellars. In 1674 the town provided cider at a burial, and in 1677 John Nevinson sold four barrels at eleven shillings each in Boston; two years later workmen mending the bridge were warmed with cider after they had "wrought in the water." Most farmers grew three or four acres of grain for sale, on average sixty to a hundred bushels worth £12 to £20 "in English goods."[28]

One crucial commodity in which Watertown is known to have specialized was cattle and its by-products. The town thereby fostered self-sufficiency but also contributed to colonial exports. By the 1640s beef was being sold for three purposes: the feeding of Boston; the export market, especially the West Indies, but also the Chesapeake and Newfoundland; and the provisioning of outgoing vessels, "the store of victual both for their own and foreigner ships who resort hither to that end."[29] When Watertown leader William Jennison sailed to Virginia in 1645, hometown grain, cured meat, and other foodstuffs would have been part of his cargo and his ship's stores.[30] In 1659 the Middlesex Grand Jury presented Watertown for "want of a sworn packer of beef, pork, &c.," an inspector to ensure sound quality of meat cured or packed in barrels of salt water. Inventories often list barrels of preserved meat and "powdering tubs," alongside the cheese and cider presses stored in cellars.[31]

Among the many artisans who founded the town, leatherworkers were among the most important.[32] Those who controlled the conversion process from hides to leather reaped the highest rewards. Two leading figures in town affairs were both tanners: Mr. Nathaniel Biscoe and Captain Hugh Mason. Both were active, enterprising, wealthy men, often in confrontation.[33]

Watertown was ideally situated for tanning. The craft required good grazing, oak trees, and "great store of running water," all of which the town had in abundance. As early as 20 December 1642 the town appointed Mason and George Munnings, a cordwainer, or shoemaker, as searchers and sealers of leather.[34] They were responsible, as had been similar officials in England for centuries, for inspecting finished leather and stamping the satisfactory with their seal of approval. The first reference to tanpits in Watertown is for 1657/58. On 14 August 1672 Deacon Henry Bright "fourteen or fifteen years agone . . . granted to Captain Hugh Mason half an acre bounded with a watercourse the head whereof is in said Bright's land . . . for the planting of a tanyard in the said land." In 1666 Nathaniel Bowman Jr. confessed that he had sold Mason two loads of tanning bark from illegally felled trees.[35] Biscoe had forty-seven acres of land just north of the Town Plot, on the western edge of early settlement.[36] After Nathaniel's departure for London in 1651, his son John took over the business. When he died in 1690, he was worth £680.[37]

Leatherworking had become such an important employer and money earner that the export of "band leather unwrought" (unworked leather) had been prohibited. After King Phillip's War, however, when trade was in a "dull and dying state," ready money was scarce; "the war hath cut off very many of that craft," Hugh Mason wrote to the colonial authorities, advocating the ban's repeal "for one year for an experiment." He argued that allowing the export of unworked leather would at least keep barkers, tanners, and producers of tallow, oil, and lime employed; earn money, "which is the life of trade"; and dissuade butchers from virtually giving away hides to exporters. It is, of course, a tanner's special pleading, but it reveals both economic sophistication and the wide reach of the leather industry.[38]

Watertown boasted a similar range of other craftsmen as the parishes and towns from which they had come: blacksmiths, woodworkers (such as coopers, housewrights, wheelwrights, and carpenters, who were granted felling rights by the town), shoemakers, tailors, masons, glaziers, a brickmaker, a maltster, and a potter. Town and court records give us occasional glimpses of these artisans' contributions to the town's economy and their craft needs.[39] Most of these tradesmen were involved in a "dual economy"; as in England, they would farm and provide for their families, practicing their specialist callings on a part-time basis. The one exception to this system of by-employment would have been the construction workers at the start of settlement.[40]

Whenever possible, continuity with ingrained methods was the rule of these initially English-trained artisans. This continuity is borne out in the one example of later carpenters' craft surviving in modern Watertown: the Brown House, begun about 1694. It was built for Captain Abraham Brown, grandson of founder Abraham Brown, one mile west of Watertown Bridge on a valley terrace overlooking Dirty Green and the Charles. It had a single-room plan and measured twenty-five by eighteen feet externally. The frame was oak, the outside walls clapboarded, and the inside walls finished with white pine boards. Its walls were about one foot thick, with bricks (some laid in herringbone pattern) set in clay as infill and insulation between the studs. The floorboards averaged fourteen inches wide; the summer beam was one foot square. The fireplace was nearly nine feet across. The window was two feet high by four feet and had leaded glass; only one of three sections opened. A narrow staircase beside the chimney led up to the chamber, whose walls were daubed with clay. There was a garret in the peak of the steep-pitched roof. The house had a cellar and lean-tos beyond the chimney and along the rear. Allowing for adaptations needed because of shortage of mortar, climatic necessity, and different kinds of timber, construction was plainly modeled on East Anglian methods. That it stood for over two hundred years before requiring rescue in 1919 is a tribute to the skill of its housewright and carpenters.[41]

The culture of discipline, thorough English training, and adaptability to the new environment combined to elicit from Watertown's farmers and farmer-artisans solid achievements. Within twenty years the town had broken nearly two thousand acres of tillage and raised a beef herd of 450 head, as well as constructing more than two hundred houses and barns, workshops, a mill, a bridge, miles of highways, and fences. In 1664 the appraisers' valuation was £7,572, down to £6,691 in 1678 after King Phillip's War. Similarly, the probate inventories of individuals show that many families had come to enjoy financial comfort and competency by the time of the waning of the first generation. I have been unable to find evidence of improved yields; given the size of family land grants, incentives for intensification of arable production would have been low. Much of this success was due to cooperation and joint planning, which included the creation of a rudimentary infrastructure, the borrowing and lending of tools, of money, and of parcels of land or labor, as well as the regulation of breeding and herding of livestock, common-field fencing, and public buildings. Much too was the result of individual striving in the family firms dispersed around the town.[42]

Without disparaging the "improvements" wrought by the first two generations of Watertown people, we should note that the town did gradually lag behind rivals like Boston and Charlestown. From the 1650s there is a sense of some stagnation in the town's economy, exacerbated by the wider recession from the late 1660s onward and by such natural disasters as the recurrent "blastings" of wheat by stem rust or mildew after 1660 and visitations of locusts.[43]

Four other specific areas combined to hold back the town's economy, and incidentally to provoke considerable conflict: the issues of specie and credit, attitudes toward land, labor supply, and quality control.

Hugh Mason's attempts to boost the economy of the Bay—and of Hugh Mason—pinpointed money as "the life of trade." After the crash of 1640 cash was a rare commodity in Watertown transactions, and during the 1670s it became rarer still. Payment in kind became the normal order of business, and following colonial practice, Watertown laid down values associated with goods used for "country pay."[44] Payment could also be made in labor. No doubt the major creditors of the town, the minister and the schoolmaster, were often reimbursed for their services by so many days' work on their land or on their houses.[45]

Exchange of goods and services might encourage a cooperative interdependency, but it required an agreement as to relative worth of "commodity money" and encouraged a haggling mentality that could stretch neighborly patience. It also assumed agreed need, but in 1642 Nathaniel Biscoe refused to accept worthless corn in exchange for his scarce leather. John Barnard only wanted land for what he was owed for damage caused by Jonathon Brown's stray horse. There *was* cash in Watertown—probate inventories show there was—but anyone who still had it hoarded it, at least until rate and tax discounts for specie were introduced. Some wealthy men left no cash at all. Absence of legal tender slowed trade, inhibited capital accumulation, and created problems, irritations, and arguments; it also wasted inordinate amounts of time.[46]

Credit was one way around these impasses, and borrowing and lending were well-nigh universal. Many inventories list numbers of small debts, one pound here, ten shillings there, like Charles Chadwick's in 1681. Some probate documents include debts for large amounts, often dowries. Seventy-four-year-old Michael Bairstow had many loans out, which he listed in his "book." Although older childless people and wealthy widows found lending a useful way to secure assets, such book debts formally receipted and witnessed could drag on for years. Three years was the limit set by the General Court in 1672, as a result of creditor pressure as trade stagnated. Bills of credit or exchange are also occasionally listed as assets. Certain specialists ran up large amounts of credit with their customers. In 1657 John Fleming, the town maltster, was owed £144. His widow, Anne, had collected or written off £120 of this by her death at the end of the year, but her executors had a hard time gathering in the rest. Retailer John Hammond was himself heavily overextended when he died aged only thirty-seven in 1657.[47]

For large loans land was often the only acceptable collateral, and some mortgages were entered in the registers of deeds. These were usually short-term, for a year or two at most. In 1647 Nathaniel Biscoe lent Angel Holland £7.6.0 for one month on the security of Holland's Boston house. Endorsements made debt instruments assignable, a type of currency. "Debts receivable" were part of a decedent's estate and might be bequeathed. Though puritan dogmatists condemned usury and Winthrop urged the rich to *give* to the less fortunate, interest *was* charged on loans, even by one brother to another. All of these stratagems helped instill life into a money-starved town economy, but they could also create ill feeling, frustration, and the polarized perceptions that have divided borrowers and lenders through time.[48]

Besides the eruptive issue of allocations of the town grant, land, the most vital town asset, could also be bought and sold, and this market posed another inciting challenge to values. Was the land to be treated by families and community as a sacred trust, a primitive symbol of identity, something upon which a man's or a family's name could be stamped, to remain (like the Brown House) in their possession over many generations or "for ever"? Or was land merely another commodity, like a bushel of wheat or a barrel of pork, to be bought or sold, an item for speculation and profit?[49]

Watertown land sales between 1635 and 1682 are recorded in 253 deeds. Since conveyances were written to a formula and payments were rarely specified, it is exceedingly difficult to uncover the motives behind many of these covenants. Certain categories are clear, however. Those leaving Watertown sold out, and the steady trickle of incomers from England or other towns bought, either directly from the leavers or from Watertown middlemen. On three occasions the middlemen made quick profits. These are the only deals by townspeople—wives, because of their dower rights, were almost always parties to sales—that look unequivocally speculative. With so much land on the market, some townsmen like Ephraim Child or John Page sought to increase their own holdings, dangerously assuming steadily rising land values. There was other speculation in town real estate, but the money came from wealthy outsiders. The only townsmen involved were Thomas Mayhew and Ephraim Child, both of whom were representing London investors during the land boom of the late 1630s. Thereafter the manic phase ended.[50]

The Watertown realty market soon came to be devoted to three main purposes: to rounding out or adding parcels to existing holdings, to increasing fodder, and to providing for the next generation. Sixty-one transactions consolidated family holdings by adding small pieces of abutting land. The piecemeal acquisition of meadow was similarly family oriented. It reflected growing human and grazing populations and the need to increase hay crops for winter feeding. Many Watertown families bought grassland at the extremities of the town grant, in the Remote Meadows to the far west and in the eastern Rocky Meadow, several even in western Cambridge. The high value of winter fodder was reflected in the prices paid—as much as £5 per acre. Sixty-nine transactions in the deeds involve familial meadow purchases. Like the consolidation purchases, there was a dip in activity from 1670 to 1678, but the next four years saw renewed buying in both markets.[51]

The buying of sets of proprietorial grants was hardly ever followed by sale for profit. The new upland, plowland, marsh, meadow, and pasture were investments in the next generation. For example, Robert Harrington had to provide for seven sons and three daughters; his purchases of 642 acres looked less grandiose once they came to be divided. There is, then, little evidence of speculative buying of town land among its citizens.[52]

This is not to deny elements of acquisitiveness in a community that came from a land-starved old world. William Page, for instance, was a steady buyer of land, though he died without issue. Nathaniel Coolidge managed to inflate the value of the town weir by threatening to sell it to the Indians. Laying up land for one's family was inevitably competitive, exciting rivalries, petty revenges, and point-scorings. However, the fact that land was not generally treated speculatively would have had a braking effect on enterprise and expansionism in the town economy. Attitudes toward land suggest a protocapitalist mind-set.[53]

After the first decade of immigration, when some servants were brought over by gentlemen or by artisans, labor outside the individual farming family became increasingly scarce. Indeed, as early as February 1632, shortage of hands in Watertown was already a problem: "Good sir, encourage men to come over, for here is land and means of . . . livelihood sufficient for men that bring bodies able and minds fitted to brave the first brunts, which the beginnings of such works necessarily put men upon. Without hands nothing can be done nor anything with any great profit until multitudes of people make labour cheap. It is strange the meaner sort of people should be so backward."[54]

The meaner sort, however, did not find it at all strange that they should want to exchange their cheap labor in familiar English surroundings in order to provide cheap labor in a howling wilderness. Few came to Watertown. The children of the poorest Watertown families might be apprenticed to wealthier neighbors, and young men were required to get themselves masters before they married.[55] Newlyweds might have to sell their labor part-time by day or by monthly contract or to rent land for a while before taking over family lots or acquiring sufficient capital to buy their own. By and large, though, the people of Watertown must have realized by the mid-1640s that their town would be a community of family farms reliant especially on the labor of their children and, despite the grandiose distribution of thousands of acres among them, that shortage of labor would be the determining factor in the town's, and the whole colony's, economy.[56] It was also a perpetual source of friction, both between the generations and between rich and poor. The "excessive dearness of labour" was an uninterrupted lament of would-be employers.[57]

High wages, however, did not prevent the people of Watertown from trying every stratagem to get help. The General Court closed one possibility in 1646 when it rejected perpetual slavery as a punishment. Watertown was too far up the Charles to be able to exploit the 1652 arrival of Scottish prisoners of war, though Samuel Stratton managed to get one on a six-year contract. A few wealthier townsmen could afford to buy slaves. Three inventories appraised unexpired servant's time. At harvest time, the annual crisis of survival, Indians from as far away as Martha's Vineyard had to be employed. Such a concession confirms the desperation of Watertown's farmers and the depressive effects of labor shortages on the town's economic potential.[58]

The few servants in the town not only emphasized the gulfs between rich and poor planters but also put strains on communal obligations by their running away, stealing from others, and having to be pursued by hue and cry (in which two or three deputed men, led by a constable, went after runaways). The servantless had to take time off their ever-pressing family concerns to recover those escaping from the served. Some servants were wild and violent, like Thomas Fanning's farmboy Thomas Browning. He fought in the meetinghouse, stole fifty-four shillings from Simon Stone, ran away just before harvest, and was then put in the house of correction, thus depriving his sick master of vital labor. The presence of a few, often exotic, servants and the disposing of hands from poor to rich created frictions within a community needy of help.[59]

Not to mention the frictions between masters and servants, that age-old problem! Servants sent or lured to New England under false pretenses found themselves exploited and short-changed. Stephen Maddock, arriving aged twelve in 1641, was forced to do fourteen years' labor. He seemed more like an unredeemed captive than a redemptioner. There were one or two cases of brutality by masters. Christopher Grant was fined £10 for cruel usage of Nicholas Gilberd on 2 March 1641. In contrast, some masters, like Thomas Fanning, were plainly at their wits' end with violent, refractory, dishonest, and runaway servants. It is often impossible to tell where the fault lay in these troubled relationships, but they were hardly conducive to harmony, productivity, or quality.[60]

Ineffective quality control in a labor-scarce society was a potential blight on the town's economy and a rich source of contention and distrust. Livestock sometimes failed to live up to overflattering descriptions. Several Watertown craftsmen's work was shoddy and unacceptable. Samuel Benjamin and Deacon Child fought over the quality of Samuel's fence-building; the selectmen were suspicious of William Knapp's workmanship, and Widow Smith was galled when her well, dug by Knapp's son John, twice ran dry (in Watertown, of all places).[61]

Established artisans also complained about defective ware. In 1648 shoemakers, coopers, and vintners separately petitioned the General Court to be able to expose and prevent unfair, shoddy competition by forming traditional companies with masters and wardens to control quality. George Munnings, Watertown's shoemaker, moved to Boston at this time in order to become an accredited member of the shoemakers' "guild." Some "country" craftsmen saw these groups as sinister attempts by Boston to monopolize the market, but there seems little doubt that poor quality was a recurrent problem. The butchers were targeted in 1672 for their careless flaying of hides and skins, and at the same time tanners and glovers were reprimanded for the excessive wages they were paying. As the case involving the malt produced by John Fleming demonstrates, poor workmanship could create widespread annoyance and commercial suspicion. The work ethic might be a prized outcome of the puritan culture of discipline, but an ethical attitude to workmanship was crucial to communal well-being.[62]

Discipline and tried-and-true working methods adapted to a new environment assured survival and the creation of a solidly based town economy. Watertown's progress was comparatively modest, however, and most of its households enjoyed a stable competency rather than increased standards of living. The estates of even the most successful townsmen were insignificant beside the fortunes of leading Boston merchants. Many techniques, institutions, and offices adopted in Watertown were based on medieval English traditions. The sources of much economic conflict were similarly time honored. Insofar as economic motivations can be inferred from land transactions, systems of exchange and credit, and, given the crippling labor shortage, the predominance of family-based enterprises, economic attitudes also seem to have harked backward. There is little evidence from Watertown's first fifty years that the Protestant ethic had set alight the spirit of capitalism.

IV

CARE IN THE COMMUNITY

9

Welfare

How communities and societies treat those unable to look after themselves is an acid test of their profoundest values. Immigrants to New England had left a nation confronting "the most terrible years through which it had ever passed." Customary, local responses to suffering had proved inadequate. The puritan response of discriminating between the deserving and the undeserving, famously enunciated in Winthrop's "Model of Christian Charity," underlay early Massachusetts social and economic policy. Tough punishments for the idle, the improvident, wastrels, drunkards, scroungers, thieves, and sturdy beggars, plus remedial philanthropy for the unfortunate, formed the basis of the local and national policy in England, the model for colonial "poor relief."[1]

Between 1540 and 1600 a series of experiments and procedures for dealing with "the many headed monster of the poor" had been pioneered by local authorities in places like Norwich, Ipswich, Colchester, and Salisbury, to which paupers flocked in search of work or relief.[2] Norwich's 1570 Census of the Poor listed 2,300 people out of a population of under 20,000. Much smaller Ipswich had 186 destitute in 1597. Wood-pasture regions, like North Essex and High Suffolk, were also a common destination, and many villages by 1630 had streets or hamlets or areas of waste where cottagers squatted in illegal hovels and vagrants camped. Parishes in the forefront of the problem were naturally eager to prevent the settlement of any more marginal people by "warning out" or more brutal methods.[3]

Municipal and parish experiments of poor relief culminated in comprehensive national legislation in 1598, confirmed in 1601. The Elizabethan Poor Law, seventy years in the making, would have been familiar to the settlers of Watertown. It distinguished between three types of poor: the "impotent" (i.e., disabled), the unemployed, and the work-shy. In lieu of family support, the legislation made the home parish responsible for executing the law, through its elected overseers and its compulsory poor rate. It provided relief for the disabled, the mentally ill, and the penniless elderly, as well as training through fostering and apprenticeships for orphans. It made work for the genuinely unemployed through the purchase of raw materials, and it sought to terrorize the rogues and vagabonds by whippings and spells in houses of correction. Begging was forbidden; vagrants were sent back to their parishes of settlement. Since "poverty was rife," by the decade of the Great Migration "the poor rate had become the most regular and familiar form of taxation in England and the administration of the poor law and related problems of settlement were the most consistent concern of parish and local government." The "godly magistracy" of puritan gentry were particularly committed to ensuring the effective running of the system, though even they would be at their wits' ends when crises like those of the 1620s and early 1630s struck.[4]

Few, if any, paupers would have emigrated to Watertown; the cost of the fare, of a year's supply of food, and of livestock would have seen to that. The town records, the main source for social problems, have few welfare entries in the first two decades.[5]

The planters were not immune from misfortune or from self-inflicted calamities, however, and from the late 1640s to 1680 the town had to deal with its share of home-grown problems. These included mental illness, orphans, and families and old people at risk. The detailed case studies examine the challenges posed by a child abuser, a mental patient, and a single parent.[6]

Besides the melancholic Lieutenant Feake, Watertown had two other mental cases to deal with, both involving violent outbursts. Thomas Philpot had to be incarcerated during the 1640s at the town's expense, and during his dotage in the 1670s, his poor neighbor William Price was receiving four shillings per week for providing care.[7]

Much more dangerous was Elizabeth Ball. Genes, deaths of children, and an unhappy marriage to tailor John Ball all probably contributed to her "disturbed mind." In December 1656 the selectmen supervised foster-child arrangements for some of her surviving children. In 1657 and 1659 she was presented to the Middlesex County Court (usually a last resort) for "several disorderly carriages against both her husband and her neighbours." She pleaded "hard usage from her neighbours" and complained that "her husband neglects her in suffering her to want necessary supplies and also did kick her." She had scratched and punched her father's face; when a man witnessing this attack was asked why he had not intervened, he said "because he was loath to be struck himself." Elizabeth and three older children went to the Pearce grandparents, while an infant went to Aunt Esther (Ball) Morse.[8]

John the tailor remained paternally responsible for their welfare. As for Elizabeth, "if she be brought to be comfortably enjoyed as a wife fit to live [with], she is to return to her husband again." Meanwhile she had to earn her keep, "and if she refuse she must expect to be sent to the house of correction," just like the sturdy rogues in her birthplace of Norwich. She died in the early 1660s, and John remarried in 1665. His new life in the frontier town of Lancaster was cruelly cut off in 1676 during King Phillip's War.[9]

In a family-centered society, orphans would normally be brought up by relatives. In May 1656, however, the General Court decreed that "the child born in prison should be provided for by the town of Watertown including time past." It permitted them to recover any "property of Mary Davis or her husband's or of the fathers [sic] of the child."[10] Her husband, the ne'er-do-well John Davis, had been sentenced to a severe whipping in 1639 "for gross offences in attempting lewdness with diverse women and to wear the letter U [for unclean] upon his breast upon his uppermost garment." Their first child was Mary, born in March 1642; others followed but died young. The father of the child born in 1656 was reputed to be yet another unruly townsman, James Knapp, aged twenty-seven and married to Elizabeth Warren; their eldest daughter Elizabeth had been born the previous year. Thirty-three-year-old Mary Davis was in prison awaiting trial for the capital crime of adultery and there gave birth to the illegitimate child. Shortly thereafter, she died.[11] Although the town continued to fulfill its obligation for the child, Ben Davis, it refused to consider him an inhabitant and he was warned out in 1692. The selectmen no doubt thought that Watertown had more than paid its debt to Davis.[12]

Some families needed help only during crises, but others proved to be chronic problems. Among the former were the Braybrooks. In the winter of 1651–52 their house was destroyed by fire, and for a while they had to live under borrowed canvas. The town voted the large sum of £30 for their relief, and two selectmen were nominated "to take care that it be laid out for the best advantage of John Braybrook." After John's death in 1654 the town oversaw the affairs of his widow, Elizabeth, leasing family land and cattle in return for provisions and services, apprenticing older children, and spending small sums of town money on essential work. In 1663 she was sent back from Woburn "in distress." The returning of indigents to their place of settlement was a frequent feature of English town and parish life, codified in the Act of Settlement of 1662, and was becoming increasingly noticeable in New England. Subsequent Watertown expenditures up to her death in 1667 were defrayed by posthumous sale of the Braybrook estate.[13]

Similar occasional assistance was needed by the Parsonses between 1660 and

1664 and by the Thomas Whitneys in 1664 and 1678–79, when the family was struck down by smallpox. The town spent £1.10.0 on William Goddard for attending Thomas Whitney, fifteen shillings on a rug, nine on a bedstead and cider, four on firewood and milk. In all £5.4.5 was expended. All seem to have survived.[14]

The Beeches and the Sanderses were longer-term problems. From 1653 to 1675 there are twenty-three entries concerning Richard Beech and his family. Most are for payments by the town—the first is for £5 for a cow, the last for carting wood and muck. The selectmen also provided clothing, agricultural services, and medical treatment (by Dr. John Alcock of Roxbury and Boston in 1660). In 1656 Selectman Joseph Tainter monitored Beech's "improvement of the time of the family" on a weekly basis for three months. Four years later the Beeches were one of four families named after a survey of educational standards ordered by the General Court; with four young children, they were in need of relief because of their negligence and carelessness. For the last five years of Richard Beech's life, 1669–74, the town had to provide steady assistance. The Beech family was probably in abject poverty for such concern to be shown.[15]

The Sanderses were deemed at risk by the selectmen in 1661. With six young children they needed doles between 1661 and 1664 and again between 1669 and 1671. Two children were "put into some honest families" to try to prevent the demoralizing effects of long-term "welfare dependency." A "cycle of deprivation" could encumber the next generation of townsmen with further burdens. The selectmen's chain of reasoning and response echoed identical reactions among parish overseers of the poor in early-modern England; the spirit of the English Poor Law had traveled well.[16]

Many Watertown residents lived to great ages, as we saw, and in most cases were cared for in their declining years by their children. There were, however, four cases of old men unsupported or alone in the world, for whom the selectmen had to supervise alternative arrangements.[17]

"Old [William] Knapp," once reviled as a "bast thievish knave" and a "dog's-prick slave" and patriarch of a brood of helions, "came on the town" in December 1655 after his children refused "to provide such necessities for their father and [step]mother as is convenient." The selectmen took control of his £130 estate, but the rent failed to cover the £20 for two years' relief.[18]

On 16 January 1661 the bachelor Henry Bright Sr., aged eighty, made an agreement with his neighbor. He sold off all his small assets for £30, to be paid in ten annual doles of "corn, pease, wheat and Indian." He was allowed to keep his house and barn and two acres of planting ground. When the decade and the annuity ended, Old Bright was still alive, and the selectmen had to take over responsibility. For three years Widow Hannah Bartlett undertook "to carry in his diet or send it for his necessary supply." Then, as she herself aged, John Sawin took over. John Biscoe agreed with the board to supply wood, and Martin Townsend, a young weaver, "to make his fire and cut his wood and help him up and to bed as he needeth." He slept on a mattress stuffed not with feathers but with chaff and straw. Occasionally the town supplied Old Bright with shirts, stockings, a waistcoat, a rug (paid for out of the seven selectmen's pockets), and other services. Old Father Bright died in 1674, "above an hundred years old." His inventory, a meager £2.9.6, included "a little pot" that the town gave to John Applin's wife, Bathshua, Widow Bartlett's daughter.[19]

Henry Thorpe, widower, whose children and stepchildren had moved elsewhere, "fell to the town to look after him" from 1668 to his death in 1672, and the selectmen "treated . . . upon as good terms as they can" with the needy Goodman Whittaker, who could farm Thorpe's land. Anything Old Thorpe earned was to be abated from the £9 annual allowance.[20]

"Father [Edmund] Blois" lost his son in 1665 and then ten years later, his wife of some sixty years. The town already paid him as meetinghouse verger, and now he was married to rape-victim Ruth Parsons. She was about thirty-two; her husband was eighty-eight. She may have been considered unmarriageable by her peers. She also suffered from an "infirmity," during which she was liable to hurt herself. From November 1679 the deacons had to "arrange suitable supply" for them until his death two years later at the age of ninety-four.[21]

Toughness and tenderness mingled in the selectmen's treatment of these ancient neighbors. The town took its responsibilities seriously, sending senior selectmen to discover what was needed and how best it could be supplied. At the same time, they did not want their hard-earned tax money squandered, and so they used family money wherever possible to offset expenses.[22]

These were the main welfare problems that the Watertown selectmen had to deal with in the first fifty years of settlement. The infrequency of recorded welfare cases in the first twenty years is partly because the town accounts are undetailed and also because certain types of challenge, like unsupported old people, did not yet exist. The 1650s and 1660s were the worst decades for coping with long-term dependents, with the period 1668–73 producing the most intense pressure on scarce resources, as two elderly men joined two problem families, a single parent, and a mental patient on the town appropriations. The constables on 16 October 1671 mention "the poor" generically in their long reckoning: "cloth for the poor," "work for the poor," as well as individual beneficiaries. In all, Watertown spent a minimum of £36 that year, £10 more than the whole "country rate" toward colony expenditure, and over a third of the whole year's outgoings. Toward the end of the 1670s the disbursements eased, which, given the huge colony demands to finance King Phillip's War, must have been a profound relief. Often throughout the period 1645–75, as one problem was solved, another reared its head.[23]

In confronting these problems, the selectmen—sometimes called with good reason "the prudential men"—used several strategies. Wherever possible, they would expect and require the relatives of sufferers to help. Only where families or individuals had no supporting kin or financial reserves would the board feel obliged to intervene. The initial, emergency response was to provide necessities: food, clothing, heating, and shelter. Such requirements would cost at least £12 per year for a family. Bearing in mind their annual £120 or £140 payment to the pastor and £30 to the schoolmaster, a country rate that was usually over £50 and could rise to £100, and special calls for bridge repairs, building or extending the meetinghouse, renovating Harvard College, supplying the militia, or expenditure on the fish weir, three families on poor relief could be burdensome to the town's budget. Poor families were likely to be at their most vulnerable in late winter after bad harvests—just the time when their neighbors had least to spare themselves. Nonetheless, compared to the demands on English taxpayers, this was a modest obligation.[24]

A second remedial strategy was to monitor and encourage household performance. Several families were led by careless, improvident, and inadequate adults. Lacking any birth control and with a marked decline in infant mortality in New England, problems multiplied alarmingly for these parents. The townsmen deputed to oversee vulnerable households were primitive work-study analysts trying to galvanize their overwhelmed subjects into self-sufficiency. They also acted as advisers and auditors where money was involved—in land sales, rentals, and wage settlements. The terms of detailed contracts they recorded demonstrate that they were intent on safeguarding the gullible from being fobbed off by their sharper neighbors with substandard corn, undervaluations, or shoddy services.[25]

A frequent response to long-term family welfare problems was placing children in other families. This move reduced the drain of hungry mouths on scarce provisions. Older offspring could earn wages or work on the family land. One rationale for this strategy was undoubtedly the saving of money. The selectmen were preempting by a few years a system of "putting out" adolescents that was common practice in old England. Apart from the transfer from over- to underpopulated households, an exchange involving board and lodging in return for the use of brawny arms or busy fingers, there was also a genuine reformist motive here, as with household monitoring. Impressionable children were removed from hopeless, ignorant, unlettered, and irreligious surroundings and placed in more encouraging situations. Thus might the depressing generational replication be broken. Had Mary Davis Jr. or William Knapp Jr.

had more positive and constructive upbringings in foster homes, they might have grown into more adequate, more capable adulthood. This was the hope.[26]

The selectmen were accountable to their fellow townsmen. They had to be seen to be minimizing their neighbors' civic expenditures. Two final initiatives were therefore frequently used. Income from land or other assets of beneficiaries offset town spending where possible. Only the destitute could expect their neighbors to contribute to their livelihoods. Wherever possible, those who "fell upon the town" were encouraged and expected to work, even if it was only spinning or other simple repetitive labor, even if the recipient, like Old Thorpe, was in his midseventies. Not only did this expectation emphasize the ethic of self-sufficiency, but it also inculcated in young paupers the dignity of labor.[27]

As elected guardians of the town's resources, the selectmen, like English churchwardens or overseers of the poor, took certain precautions in order "to save the town harmless." Encouraged by the General Court and the colonial clergy, they inspected families in the town regularly in order to identify any potential problems and try to nip them in the bud. Such a survey in 1661 listed the Sanderses and the Beeches as households at risk. Two others, Charles Stearns's and George Adams's, never appeared on the poor rolls. Young men living on their own or in groups without the discipline of a household patriarch or a regular master received short shrift from the board: get a master and produce a contract by such and such a time, or we will get them for you. For a young person to live alone was forbidden by colonial ordinance. If major breadwinners were going to be away for any length of time, the townsmen wanted guarantees that their families would be provided for. When Daniel Metup and Jonathan Whitney proposed to go to Cape Fear, the seven men insisted that enough assets be lodged with neighbors to keep their dependents from want. They got court sanction for this requirement and, killing two birds with one stone, arranged for a cow to be left with the ill-nourished Beeches. Finally, future welfare responsibilities were prevented by two strategies: encouraging emigration of the deprived to new settlements like Groton in 1660, and "warning out" unauthorized visitors—"strangers" or "foreigners"—who lacked settlement rights in the town. Sometimes they bade individuals or families to pack their bags. Thus on 21 July 1671 they "warned Mary Ball to depart the town forthwith." They had already had enough trouble with the Ball family, and the last thing they wanted in that demanding year was a heavily pregnant single woman "to fall upon the town." At other times warning out safeguarded Watertown from future responsibility for the welfare of incomers and visitors. All of this ordering people about makes the selectmen seem authoritarian and illiberal, but they were simply obeying "the will of the town" (and of all the other towns and parishes in the anglophone world).[28]

The lack of individual freedom, privacy, and self-fulfillment was a side of community living often forgotten by its present-day apologists. The welfare arrangements of Watertown do, however, reveal a more positive side of town life: neighborliness, active involvement, and face-to-face kindliness to the unfortunate. Some of Watertown's poor came from disreputable, scrounging, and probably scorned families: Mary Spring Davis, William Knapp, Edward Sanders, the haltered child-abuser, Hugh Parsons, possible wizard, or Elizabeth Ball, violent wife. We may suspect that little sympathy was wasted on them. Others, however, were the hapless victims of providential disasters—poor distracted Lieutenant Feake, the homeless Braybrooks living under canvas in midwinter, the Whitneys smitten by smallpox, Old Thorpe, a respectable citizen succumbing to dotage, or Father Blois and his wife, whose house burned down in 1673. Such calamities could happen to anyone.

The selectmen were often the richer members of the community, but by no means always. There was nonetheless a relatively small gap between the rich and the poor, and misfortune lurked everywhere. The pauper's death for Robert Feake, a London goldsmith's son, warned everyone that riches could come to rags, as did distinguished East Anglian names like Knapp, Blois, or Spring borne by welfare recipients. Even among brothers, like the Whitney boys, there could be considerable variations of wealth. John was comfortably off; Thomas was near the breadline. No one in seventeenth-century Watertown was secure.[29]

Certain people in the town were regularly recorded as overseers of the poor and the unfortunate under the general supervision of the deacons. Other townspeople acted as long-term caregivers. These primary caregivers were often themselves near the breadline, as "young beginners" or as chronically low earners or as widows. Appointing them fulfilled the dual function of providing income for the needy and nursing for the weak. An impressive number of other people, however, were paid for helping their less fortunate neighbours. In 1670, for instance, ten are listed for major tasks, like digging a well, providing twenty-odd yards of cloth, cutting and carting three loads of wood, delivering seven loads, or feeding for a year. Other small acts were performed out of kindness, like the selectmen each chipping in two shillings for a new rug for Henry Bright Sr., or Jeremiah Norcross's gift of two ewes, whose offspring could form capital for a fund for "poor members of Jesus Christ in Watertown."[30]

We should never forget that the main responsibility rested with the relatives. "Family values" in seventeenth-century Watertown meant that individual kin had personally to care for needy family members. Even a relatively poor parent like Lewis Jones recognized this obligation when he made his will in 1684. From his very modest estate of £62, he made special provisions for his youngest son, Shubael, "a poor decrepit person . . . in a weak and helpless condition."

There are many more allusions to illness, "craziness," decrepitude, infirmity, weakness, and disablement in the records, but sufferers were usually tended at home. The family was all there was. The people described in this chapter were the exceptions. Even they were not handled by government agencies or confined to institutions. They were genuinely "in the community" in the sense that everyone in the community recognized a responsibility toward them. We need not sentimentalize such cooperative values. The people of Watertown did everything they could to minimize their burdens. They used the poor to support the poor. They drove out pregnant women and parentless girls, happily bade farewell to penniless widows, and threatened a mentally ill woman with prison if she failed to work. They treated some neighbors a great deal better than others, distinguishing between the deserving and undeserving poor just as they had on the Stour. Jeremiah Norcross's philanthropy was reserved for unfortunate church members. The townspeople gave the violent and disruptive Elizabeth Ball "hard usage," even though she was a church "sister." The Knapps got the shortest shrift. When in 1679 the young and childless Mary (Bigelow) and Michael Fleg sought to take in a second foster child from Cambridge, the selectmen reported to the court: "Sundry of our inhabitants are dissatisfied that the child might become a charge. We have poor enough in our town already. Michael Fleg has little enough to begin the world withal . . . He hath no great matter of prudence." Tangible dissatisfaction no doubt extended to other improvident and imprudent neighbors. They would have to face general disapproval and hostility. Powerful social pressure was exerted to prevent the shame of "going on the town."[31]

Nonetheless, when they could not escape, they *all* assumed at least financial obligation and often expenditure of time and energy as well. This "good neighborliness" was the foundation of the concept of a "moral community" in England and New England. It accepted certain "minimal standards below which a neighbour fell at the risk of losing local goodwill (peaceableness, a recognition of customary obligations, avoidance of placing unreasonable burdens on the neighbourhood) and positive standards (recognition of obligation to render aid and support, a willingness to accept the neighbours as a reference group in matters of behaviour)." The strategies the prudential men adopted to enforce or elicit good neighborliness would have been immediately recognizable by their cousins back home in Boxted or Nayland, Colchester or Bury. The only difference was that the great millstone of English poverty had become a mere boulder in the brave new world.[32]

10

The Rising Generation

The people who settled Watertown believed in "eternal time." Life on earth was so chancy, so inexplicable, that it could not add up to all of existence. Hence the obsessive concern with the eternal life after death and the sense of being part of an ongoing process, a link in an endless chain of ancestors, kin, and posterity. The living must provide for generations to come. As we saw, land was the essence of this family continuity. Wills spoke of property "to stay within the family for ever."[1]

Such a mind-set loaded encumbering responsibilities on the shoulders of "the rising generation." In colonial, as well as western European, societies, further frustrations arose from the delay of marriage and economic independence for years after puberty. Enforced dependence of the physically mature was bound to raise a head of steam and produce an up-rising generation.[2]

Seventeenth-century Massachusetts Bay was a society in flux. Its population was exploding at unprecedented, un-European rates. New towns were formed at a dizzying rate. By the mid-1650s the second generation was achieving adulthood, marrying, and breeding. Rising generation here meant rising population.[3]

In this chapter I explore how Watertown coped with rising population and its rising generation, how this second generation fended for itself, and how these young people were fitted and prepared for full adulthood. I seek to measure intergenerational conflict and to examine how effectively the lid was kept on the pressure cooker of adolescent restlessness and willfulness.

There was no census of Watertown during its first fifty years. The best counts available occur in lists prepared for other purposes, which do not enumerate women and children:

1636 120 "townsmen" mentioned, 540 estimated total
1637 (February) 106 townsmen, 477 est.
1637 (June) 113 townsmen, 509 est.
1642 104 townsmen, 468 est.
1651 160 families, 720 est.
1658 153 polls, 689 est.
1664 154 heads, 693 est.
1669 192 heads, 864 est.
1678 176 persons, 792 est.
1690 151 militiamen (census), 800 est.[4]

The estimates above of total inhabitants for the various years are based on multiplying the figures given by a factor of 4.5 (5.3 for militiamen). These totals err on the low side, but their population increase for Watertown of nearly 50 percent from 1636 to 1678 correlates with figures for comparable towns.[5] Watertown's natural increase, however, was a good deal greater than the listings convey. If it conformed to the rest of the colony and to regional rates, its population by 1680 would probably have approached 1,700.[6]

All town records point to such dynamic growth rates. Lockridge's vital records graph shows raw totals from 1637 to 1680 of 960 conceptions to 257 recorded deaths, a gross increase of 603. Corrected estimates suggest a Watertown birth rate averaging 44 per 1,000 population, double the death rate of 22 for the period. The most conservative count shows an average of 4.1 surviving children from the town's founding families, a doubling of the town's population each generation, to 900 by the 1660s and 1,800 by the 1690s. All the Watertown and regional evidence argues for a population explosion more than quadrupling that which had so traumatized old England.[7]

How did Watertown cope with such numbers, with "the perpetual encounter between the belly and the womb"? The first response was the severe restriction on immigration and proprietorship after 1635. Subsequently, considerable quantities of inhabitants were "disposed of" by outmigration.[8]

Watertown was the "rich hive" for several outswarms, each approaching a dozen families: to Wethersfield, Dedham, and Sudbury in the 1630s; to Lancaster, Stamford, and Hampton in 1640s and 1650s; and to Groton in the 1660s. However, the types of migrant changed markedly over the decades. During the 1630s many were well-established and well-endowed community leaders, who could eventually have expected liberal allotments in Watertown's allocations, but they needed instant access to grazing and fodder, not merely lines on a plat.[9]

Young families and single men had joined these early outswarms, but with the founding of Lancaster (originally Nashaway) in the mid-1640s, migrant groups changed markedly. Now the recently married, the landless or uncapitalized, people making a new start, and single men "on the make" predominated. Typical of this safety-valve migration were the Watertown founders of Lancaster. For instance, Thomas King, "of little capital [but] great ambition," was interested both in fur trading and in the iron ore and graphite or black lead in the Nashaway grant. Winthrop's account of Lancaster's slow start describes the founders as "many of Watertown . . . no members of any churches . . . most of them poor men, some of them corrupt in judgement and others profane."[10] Stamford's Watertown contingent in the mid-1640s included families low in the town pecking order, in trouble with the law, and/or with few acres to feed increasing numbers of offspring.[11]

The settlement of Groton in the 1660s and the 1670s saw the new generation moving west in a concerted group. In this new "company," along with siblings or newly married neighbors, like minister's daughter Abigail (Sherman) Willard, went paupers, troublemakers, orphans, and family misfits. Twenty-eight out of the original fifty-one grantees of land there had Watertown connections. The list of witnesses in a Groton fornication case in 1672 reads like a roll call of names from the old town, a "New Watertown."[12]

A major reason behind this exodus is vividly brought out in Thomas Parke's deposition of 20 December 1670. He supported his sister-in-law's opposition to risking frontier life at Groton, where her fiancé Abraham Brown had land. They went to Brown's mother in Ipswich and persuaded her to pass on her life interest in the Brown farm in Watertown, neglected and "damnified" by trespassers.[13] Shortage of land motivated young Abraham's westward ambitions; once a farm was found closer to the Bay, Groton dreams evaporated. Not everyone had such well-endowed families. Groton's founders described themselves as "being something straitened for that whereby subsistence in an ordinary way of God's providence is to be had."[14]

To settle a frontier plantation required capital, and several of the young men who settled Groton had worked in the score of thriving sawmills and lumber camps along the Piscataqua River or had even ventured further east into the Kennebec area for furs, a trade they hoped to repeat in Groton.[15] Outmigration was a major means of preventing the generational doubling of Watertown's numbers from placing intolerable pressures on the available resources.

Despite these periodic purges, however, the counts of inhabitants continued to rise during the 1650s and 1660s and were well over the eight hundred mark by the start of the 1670s. In these years the town selectmen had to expand relief measures. Concurrently, better-endowed families gradually transferred assets to the next generation in the form of dowries for marriageable daughters, craft training, or land for sons before the last will and testament allocated what remained. Thus was posterity nurtured and protected.[16]

Outswarming and reallocation of estates occurred in young adulthood. Before that stage the children and adolescents of the rising generation must be taught the culture of discipline and prepared for membership of church and community.

By the 1670s it had become a truism that the first planters had "eternal time" and posterity very much in mind: "Why came you into this land? Was it not mainly in respect to the rising generation? . . . You came hither for your children, sons and daughters, and for your grandchildren to be under the ordinances of God."[17] There were negative and positive aspects to this parental mission: discipline and control on the punitive side, education and protection on the nurturing.

In the first decade of settlement the youth of the colony did not appear as a special cause for concern. Worries about the rising generation emerged in the late 1640s and oscillated for the rest of our period, depending on perceptions of the Almighty's attitude toward his chosen people. His anger, evidenced by the visitation of disease, war, famine, or some other disaster, prompted panicky reforms. Thus in the late 1640s, in the wake of the political, economic, and religious crisis of mid-decade, legislation was enacted against disobedient, unlettered, and indolent youth.[18]

During the 1650s youthful corruption, profanity, extravagance, sexual promiscuity, drunkenness, assertiveness, and indiscipline were targeted. A whole series of colony-wide measures was taken to control the willfulness and independence of young people. The 1660s slump, provoked no doubt by "the woeful neglect of instructing and governing the rising generation" and lack of "proper control of youth in families and . . . denial of subjection," led to laws that proscribed the living alone of adolescents (1668) and instituted the English means of establishing putative paternity in bastardy cases (1668). Brothels, gambling, and theft were the focus of the early 1670s, and the divine warning that was King Phillip's War of 1675 and 1676 led to a fresh wave of soul searching, legislative fulminations, and local supervision.[19]

Thus driven, Watertown selectmen exposed some dark corners of the town: the families of John Fiske, George Lawrence, William Price, William Knapp Jr., Edward Sanders, Charles Stearns, George Adams, Richard Beech, Mistress Phillips, and William Barsham all had to be called to account for their offsprings' ignorance, neglect, or indiscipline. The board punished breaches of the dress code, like John Wellington's "delinquence about fashion" in 1664. They were eagle-eyed for idleness. They slapped down insolence. They harried young people living "from under family government" or without masters. After dark, their alertness against adolescent "night-walkers" was complemented by the town watch. On 5 January 1680 Watertown appointed fifteen tithingmen responsible for ten families each, further swelling the mature inspectorate.[20]

Two other town organizations acted as agents of discipline: the church and the militia. "The care and wise management of the lambs of the flock is one third part of the charge of the ministry, and in some respect the difficultest." After the Half-Way Covenant of 1662, the net of church discipline covered the grandchildren of church members, who could now be baptized and later called to account.[21] Between 1654 and 1680 a series of measures was adopted to improve seating and monitor adolescent behavior in the Watertown meetinghouse, involving constables, selectmen, "chief men," deacons, and vergers. Repeated orders suggest that misdemeanors, including cursing, striking, and fighting, persisted.[22]

Military discipline also controlled youthful behavior. From the age of sixteen, able-bodied young men were required to train with the militia. The town had its training ground on the south side of Meetinghouse Green, its drum, its leading staff, and its colors. Training days were held eight times a year, including general trainings of the whole Middlesex County Regiment. Besides arms and foot drill, there were shooting competitions and regular inspections of gunpowder, ammunition, and weapons. Command was in the hands of senior members of the town elite. In this activity, as in others, they kept a watchful eye on the bearing and performance of younger militiamen.[23]

Central and local authorities adopted parallel positive policies to protect and educate vulnerable and inexperienced young people. The early modern world was a very dangerous place, and Watertown had its share of accidents and atrocities. Every household had at least one gun. In 1654 herdsman's son Caleb Johnson was accidentally shot dead by twelve-year-old John Woods out in the forest.[24] The river was especially hazardous. In his journal for 1646 Winthrop recorded the miraculous survival of one of the sons of Thomas Smith: "One Smith of Watertown had a son about five years old, who fell into the river near the mill gate, and was carried by the stream under the wheel, and taken up on the other side, without any harm. One of the boards of the wheel was fallen off, and it seems (by special providence) he was carried through under that gap, for otherwise if an eel pass through, it is cut asunder. The miller perceived his wheel to check on the sudden, which made him look out, and so he found the child sitting up to the waist in the shallow water beneath the mill."[25]

Others were not so lucky. Two boys were drowned in the 1660s, and in 1674 two more were killed, "run over by a load of bricks." When a bough toppled off a cart, just missing a young servant, the driver was chastized: "Po! Po! 'Tis no laughing matter! It might have killed the boy so."[26]

Other young people were the victims of human violence or vice. Nathaniel Biscoe, a young Harvard usher from Watertown, fell victim in 1639 to the drunken sadism of Master Nathaniel Eaton. Two years later Nicholas Gilberd was "cruelly used" by his master, Christopher Grant. Young girls and serving maids were particularly vulnerable. A 1643 jury had "to inquire whether Abner Ardway, late of Watertown . . . did make an assault on the body of Mary Giles, being an infant maid under the age of ten [and] did carnally know and ravish her." "For want of proof," the case was "dismissed, with admonition." Elizabeth Sturgis's employers, family, and neighbors rallied round to protect her from the lecherous Daniel Patrick in 1639. The older generation provided character references for compromised young people and protection against jilting or predatory males.[27] Orphaned minors had to have formally approved guardians. Customarily kinsmen, they took their wardship duties seriously. Similar protection covered apprenticeships, which were reassigned if a master died.[28]

The best protection in puritan eyes for the rising generation lay in education, which also was a family responsibility. The town held family heads, not the schoolmaster or the minister, responsible for shortcomings, as did Goodwife Ives when she accused her son-in-law Lewis Allen of "not taking care of his children which he had by [my] daughter to give them due education and bring them up in some honest employment." The instituting of elementary and grammar schools in 1647 was intended to supplement rather than replace this parental obligation of preventing "that old deluder Satan" from ensnaring gullible, unlearned, unoccupied youth.[29]

Watertown began building its schoolhouse in 1649. Two years later the town entered into agreement with Mr. Richard Norcross (1621–1708) to teach English (i.e., reading and, subsequently, writing), Latin, and "any maidens that desire to learn to write . . . as also such as desire to cast accounts." The salary of this renaissance man was to be £30 a year. By October 1664 there were seventeen Latin and Greek texts in the schoolhouse.[30]

Until 1676 the school proceeded on its course, with occasional graduates going on to Harvard, where town support continued for the needy.[31] The huge financial strains of King Phillip's War led to neglect of the schoolhouse and search for a cheaper schoolmaster. When the 1680 court threatened them with the ignominy of sending their scholars to Cambridge, the inhabitants of Watertown claimed to have been "a very ingenious, candid and free people as to promoting and maintaining . . . schools of learning among them. Their love of betterment . . . was so great . . . to the great encouragement of the poorest inhabitant who now might have a gust or taste of [Latin] grammar learning which otherwise could not so well have had such an advantage." The court challenge forced them to weigh and reassert deep-seated values loosened by the fiscal shocks of war.[32]

All this discipline, protection, and education in a community of family farms and long-lived elders suggest a highly patriarchal society. The founding generation owned the lion's share of the land as well as the labor of their adolescent offspring. A farmer was surprised to hire seventeen-year-old Zechariah Smith "not from his father but of himself."[33]

It was most unusual for the county bench to have to buttress parental authority, as with the "very stubborn and wicked carriages" of Ephraim Gale. More typical was sixty-eight-year-old William Knapp's arrogant claim that "young men [kissing] would only give a touch, but he would give [young Phoebe Page] a cleaving kiss," reflecting a general sense of superiority reinforced by founders' pride in their courageous decision to emigrate.[34]

The long-lived first generation retained the reins of power. Men like Captain Hugh Mason died in the family driver's seat in their seventies or even their eighties. Sons rarely shared office on a board with their fathers. It was not until the 1680s and 1690s that the next generation could succeed to office as old warhorses finally bit the dust: John Sherman, Thomas Hastings, Henry Bright, Samuel Thatcher, Nathaniel Treadway, and Joseph Tainter. These replacements had often had to wait beyond their primes before assuming power, and it is feasible that the repeated assertions of accountability during the 1670s reflected this frustration.[35]

The town records support the impression of persistent patriarchalism. With a few exceptions, the young people of Watertown seem generally well-behaved, kept in their place by assertive elders. It was these very elders, however, who wrote the town records; other sources give a different impression.

According to court records, the younger generation, far from being cowed and biddable, was rising in another sense, that of resisting authority. Young people were involved in a wide range of nefarious, criminal, and rebellious behavior, both as individuals and in groups. Besides revealing certain problem families, court documents also demonstrate that intergenerational conflict was spread across the social scale. Young people were involved in a predictable range of misdemeanors: drunkenness, fornication, stealing, gambling, and "nightwalking."[36]

Stealing was the least common offence. It was usually the preserve of servants, though a few young men gave poverty as their justification.[37] Extramarital sex was both a more frequent and a more serious long-term problem, especially if the couple would not or could not marry. When Ruth Sawtel gave birth in 1671 to Zechariah Smith's baby, he had already been killed by Indians in the Maine woods. In 1674 the "turbulent youth" Zechariah Crisp was left holding the baby when his paramour, Mary Stannard, died in childbirth.[38] The number of fornication cases involving Watertown adolescents rose during the 1670s, reflecting Middlesex County trends. Details of motivation are often sketchy, but this increase may indicate a rise in adolescent assertiveness.[39] In some cases young couples used pregnancy to force reluctant parents to consent to marriage, as did the enraptured Daniel Smith when his mother opposed his union with the disreputable Grant family. Mary Grant's "great belly" ensured that the lovers became yokefellows.[40]

Some adolescents seem to have embraced a counterculture of sexual promiscuity. Phoebe Page had such a reputation. Jane Bowen had had other illegitimate children before David Dunster's. Ruth Sawtel was twice convicted of sexual misdemeanors.[41] Newly married Judith Sawin, aged seventeen, was importuned in 1668 by her kinsman Henry Summers Jr., "that he might lie with her . . . to go to the barn or up to the chamber . . . he threw her on the bed and would have committed folly with her, and told her that he could have the use of Timothy Brooks's wife as often as he wanted and of Hannah Walker, a singlewoman, and therefore she [Judith] might much more who had the cover of a husband . . . [He also said] three times a day he could cause his seed to fly the breadth of the house and he could give her a quart."[42]

Ephraim Bemis tried to inveigle a neighbor's married daughter into prostitution with a visiting client in 1678. Jonathon Phillips was depicted as a sexual stalker and attempted rapist in 1666. This flouting of communal mores sometimes ran in families. Between 1659 and 1679 five of the children of Christopher and Mary Grant "conceived at least six babies out of wedlock." Two sons, Christopher and Joseph, were described by neighbors as arrogant Lotharios full of braggadocio and easy promises to their innocent prey. James and John Knapp, kinsmen of Zechariah Smith, were charged with adultery and fornication.[43]

Sex fascinated many of these adolescents. Weddings were fraught with sexual excitement. On 23 May 1674 teenagers Moses Whitney and Jonathan Smith "about noon, left work to see a wedding that we heard was to pass that way which was between William Shattuck and Goodman Randall's daughter." The bride's brother was later sued "for making and publishing an obscene and scurrilous writing or libel tending to the corruption of youth and defamation of several persons therein named as particularly Phillip and Elizabeth Shattuck and others." The (lost) libel was probably full of sexual innuendo and bawdy suggestions. This was a deprived, but not an innocent, age.[44]

Drink, partying, and riot often went together. In 1666, for instance, a breach of the peace was explained by strong liquor on empty and inexperienced stomachs: "Jonathan Morse, aged twenty-three, deposed that after a fast day in Watertown about sunset he went to Roger Wellington's [house] along with Justinian Holden Jr., Jacob Onge, Ephraim Smith, William Sanders, Sarah, Mary and Jonathan Mason, Benjamin Allen and John Clary. In the space of two hours they together drank a gallon of [hard] cider and a pint of strong waters. Afterwards he was very sick, full of pain and vomitted much."[45] All the members of this riotous gang were in their late teens or early twenties. They were a mixed bag.[46]

Drink was probably the lowerer of inhibitions after a militia training day in Cambridge in 1660. The Watertown ringleaders of this town-gown partying were John Fleming, aged eighteen, and Samuel Stearns, twenty-two. With twenty other young people, they were charged with "suspicion of uncivil carriages and disorderly conduct at Andrew Belcher's ordinary [inn] and at the College." Fleming did "kiss and dally" with a young woman from Boston, Mary Cartland; earlier, "in a very uncivil manner, walking up and down among the company . . . Fleming in the open field [did] salute the said wench by kissing her sundry times the which was matter of great offence." Stearns, somewhat more discreetly, "had Sarah Boatson in his lap and did kiss her at a chamber of one of the scholars [probably Watertown's Bezaleel Sherman's]."[47]

Membership of the militia seems to have been the vital glue that bound these groups and others in Middlesex County together. Militia training days (in the presence of a young female audience) were an opportunity for young people to get together and to let off steam after (and, in Fleming's case, during) parade. In 1663 the General Court inveighed against groups of young militiamen who "vainly expend their time and powder by inordinate shooting in the day and night after their release." Drinking after training was similarly castigated.[48]

Significantly, recorded adolescent unrest in Watertown and throughout New England was not confined to the poorer sections of society. It ranged across the social spectrum, affecting church and nonchurch households. Three pastors' children were presented for misdemeanors, two for fornication, as was the son of a deacon. The children of selectmen were just as likely to fall foul of the law as those on welfare. The gatherings of the young knew no class barriers.[49]

The records suggest a distinct, if embryonic, youth culture in Watertown. Far from the passive, patriarchally overawed adolescents of parental expectation, young people had their own means of circumventing restrictions on their freedom. The emigration of a contingent of uppity members of the second generation to Groton in the 1660s argues a group decision, a cellular division, an age-group's response to frustration. Outmigration was a safety valve in a second, emotional sense. It was a declaration of generational independence. "Rising generation" took on another meaning. Such independence might be interpreted by Jeremiahs in the colony as another sign of declension, but with population exploding and land opening up on the frontier, the needs of the rising generation became increasingly urgent. Like their parents in town meetings, in confrontation with central authority, or like conscientious dissenters from imposed religious orthodoxy, a powerful urge toward individual liberty continued to thrive.[50]

Watertown, by the end of our period, had won a reputation as a leader in this young-adult assertiveness. In 1678, two years after the end of King Phillip's War, some young people of Cambridge were caught holding feasts during the traditional Twelve Days of Christmas. One of the accused defended these gatherings: "It was a sad thing when they had come home from the war but they must be so requited, and he did believe that if *the young men of Watertown* should be dealt with in this manner they would go nigh to burn the town over their ears that should so serve them."[51] They were plainly less biddable than the authorities in their town minutes would have had us believe. Intergenerational conflict was alive and well. For that the posterity of Watertown had reason to be thankful.

11

The Family

The family was the basic unit of society in the seventeenth century. It was expected to fulfill a multitude of roles: production unit, job training, clinic, bank, religious cell, primary education, police force, rehabilitation center, old people's home, and social service. Those people "in the care of the town" were the unusual few for whom family nurture was unavailable. The occasional adolescents disciplined by the authorities were aberrants from normal family control. Watertown's land policy was shaped by considerations of family posterity. The town's economy was the product of cooperation and interaction between generations and among its association of households. Its godly families were expected to pass on their grace-worthiness from generation to generation. Whenever town or colony were faced with disasters, seen as God's wrath vented on them, failures of family government were blamed; reforms sought to reinvigorate, buttress, and improve it. The culture of discipline targeted those who lived "from under family government." "Masterless men" were invitations to anarchy, chaos, and misrule. The family was a major breakwater against the waves of individualism, selfishness, and "merriment" always beating against the shore.[1]

Despite its centrality as a unit, the family was as various and as unique as its individual members. The most obvious difference was one of wealth. Education, appearance, opportunity, calling, horizon, comfort, social attitude, and community status were all reflections of family assets. Other variations depended on the productive specialisms of each family firm, its location within the town, its relationships, matrimonial and intergenerational, as well as neighborly and communal. Age also affected family functions and interactions.

Important though it was as the foundation of communities and nations, the family has proved a frustratingly opaque institution. Its very centrality meant it was taken for granted. A growing preference for family privacy inhibited the airing of domestic problems and discontents. Family life then, however, was less easily defended and hidden than it can be today. Servants peeked and blabbed. Neighbors justified nosiness as a communal obligation of "holy watchfulness." Walls had ears; gossip was pervasive. Everyone knew or wanted to know everyone else's business. For their insufferable inquisitiveness, we must be thankful.[2]

Marriage formed a new household, and for adults over thirty matrimony was a near-universal experience. Age of marriage also proved remarkably uniform in Watertown: men conventionally began housekeeping at twenty-eight, women five or six years younger. Their firstborn usually arrived within a year or so.[3]

First marriages were both unions of two young people and "corporate mergers" of two family firms. Herein lay the first zone of potential conflict. Choices of partner, then as now, depended on a complex range of criteria. For the young, physical and emotional attraction was enormously important. Some courters were totally infatuated with each other. Jane Bowen wrote David Dunster a passionate love letter. Daniel Smith could not keep away from Mary Grant. Mary Davis Jr. was dying to show off her new "sweetheart." Mary Linfield was prostrated when John Whittaker jilted her. Mary Ball was besotted with Michael Bacon, as was John Fleming with Mary Cartland. Sarah Hammond was "entangled" by Richard Smith.[4]

Such madness was emphatically not on the parental agenda. A young couple should grow in love, but elders resisted infatuation with sentiments like "Marry for love, live on love." Their requirements included economic, religious, and status compatability. Serving wenches could not marry ministers' sons, nor soapboilers' daughters deacons'. Children of the church should marry within the godly. Illegitimate births often arose from family resistance to unacceptable matches. The differing priorities of courters and mergers made for friction and emotional storminess.[5]

Both did agree that reputation was crucial. Nonvirgins were considered soiled and had a hard time finding husbands. Notorious Phoebe Page finally became the third wife of the disabled James Cutler when she was thirty-five. Twice-prosecuted Ruth Sawtell had to make do with a poor orphaned weaver from distant Scituate. Susannah Woodward never married. Thirty-two-year-old Ruth Parsons, victim of child sex abuse, became the wife of eighty-eight-year-old Edmund Blois.[6]

Disreputable men also found wives hard to get. Jonathan Phillips, for instance, had to wait until he was forty-seven, and then his bride, Sarah Holland, was young enough to have been his daughter. Samuel Benjamin, married at thirty, John Knapp, thirty-six, Joseph Grant, thirty-eight, and John White, thirty-five, had all been in trouble as adolescents.[7]

Once a young couple had developed a fancy for each other, families, called here friends, got actively involved. By law, young men had to have parental permission before they could begin formally courting a daughter. In 1673 William Parry sued when his youngest daughter, Abiah, was courted by her master, the widower Richard Hassell of Cambridge, "contrary to the mind of Goodman Parry."[8]

After family approval came "how they might be comfortably provided for," or the joint endowment of the new household: dowry for the woman and land for the man. Captain Richard Beers's will, typically, left little to his "daughter Stearns" because she had already received her "portion," as the dowry was significantly called. Similarly, Ellis Barron's will gave title to "the farm my son Ellis now enjoys."[9] Normally, parents united their efforts to give the new household the most helpful start possible. When John White died in 1684 within weeks of his marriage to Rebecca Bemis, his inventory totaled £100. This represents a rare record of a specific capital sum with which a couple began housekeeping.[10]

Sometimes, however, there was greater enthusiasm from one family than the other. In 1654 John Barnard's "strong affection" for Sarah Fleming was approved by her father, but Widow Barnard, egged on by cousin Ensign John Sherman, expressed "some dislike." This resistance was overcome only by Fleming Sr.'s pledge of a £150 dowry, which would "maintain them as well as any Sherman of them all." Occasionally, though, bargaining between families could turn nasty, with unhappy results.[11]

Once the parents were agreed, the parties were, literally, engaged or committed. This obligation was quite clearly spelled out by George Phillips to Richard Smith of Long Island when he tried to escape his 1640 betrothal to Sarah, the daughter of William Hammond of Watertown after publication of the banns. The clincher for Governor Winthrop was in his memorandum to Phillips's account: "Mr. Smith confessed before me and the Treasurer that her father and he did agree upon portion." Smith bowed to the inevitable, and the marriage went ahead. Promises before witnesses and the financial agreements between families clearly marked points of no return.[12]

Second marriages were common in Watertown, as everywhere else in the early-modern period. For women at least, contracting new unions was distinctly different. The widow, unlike the spinster or wife, was a person of rights and property. Widows usually required a premarital contract to safeguard their property in their new relationship. Before Widow Ann Goldstone became Goodwife Ann George in the late 1630s, there was compiled "an inventory of her goods before she [re-]entered into the married state." These items were later safeguarded before the administrators began distributing the deceased John George's estate.[13]

Widows' rights were legally protected. William Knapp had pledged £10 of his modest estate before marrying his second wife, the widow Priscilla Akers, in the early 1650s. After he died, court orders ensured that this precondition was obeyed by his disputatious offspring.[14] When Watertown's schoolmaster Richard Norcross married a widow as his second wife in 1673, he had to enter a £90 bond at the county court before he could use her £45 to bring up her three children "as his own."[15] Though the intention of prenuptial agreements was to protect widows' assets, remarried widows usually handed over management of their estates to their new "masters."[16]

Second marriages were fraught with potential problems. Younger widows or widowers might be desperate for a mate to help with a growing family, but they might come to repent their hurried choice at leisure. They would have to familiarize broods of step-siblings; older children, like Susannah Woodward, might become jealous of new arrivals. If second-marriers were older, they might be seen as financial rivals by adult offspring eager for a share of family assets to start their own households.[17]

The roles of husband and wife were sharply distinguished. He was the producer, she the processor. He the breadwinner, she the bread-maker. He protected; she nurtured. He managed business, land, the farm; she managed the home, the hearth. He begat; she bore their children and nursed, weaned, and taught them as infants.

Men were the primary producers, "the breakers of nature," the acknowledged providers. Provision for one's family, first and foremost, entailed farming, and almost all male inventories contain details of land, livestock, and "utensils of husbandry." Many also list grain and hay stored in barns and garrets, or standing in the fields if death struck between April and September. This irreplaceable role was played upon in the petition of George Adams in the hungry season of early 1653. He was in jail awaiting trial. Meanwhile, deprived of their breadwinner, "his wife and four children are in a perishing condition."[18]

Protection was a male role. This duty meant nightly watching and warding by rotation, as well as membership in the militia. Men were also responsible for the safeguarding of familial persons and reputations. Thus Samuel Stratton defended his wife's reputation against "that slander laid upon her [that] she tendered her body to use to [John] Sears [of Woburn] of her own voluntary will." Fidelity was a wifely virtue that any husband must protect for both their sakes.[19]

The paterfamilias was the manager of the family estate. He would organize any land transactions. True, wives often indicated their agreement to sales, but this was a legal renunciation of their widows' rights, without which title would have been incomplete. Married women were hardly ever legally involved in the *purchase* of land, even when their dowries were contributing to the acquisition, as, for instance, was Margaret Cheney's after her marriage to Thomas Hastings in 1650.[20] For some women this exclusion produced frustration and bitterness, especially when their children's future welfare was at issue or when their husbands were ineffective managers.[21]

Women reigned supreme in domestic life, which centered on the incessant tasks of child-bearing, child-rearing, and cooking. The average interval between births was just over two years. Fertile Watertown women were thus either pregnant or nursing for much of the first twenty years of marriage. They were also expected to practice a wide range of processing skills. Inventories list many of the household utensils women used: spinning wheels, wool cards, cheese presses, dairying bowls, butter churns, preserving tubs, brewing vats, as well as the universal pots, spits, and trammels used for boiling and roasting. They would also have been involved in marketing and bartering their surpluses of cheese and butter, eggs, spun-wool, and baked and preserved goods.[22]

Women's nurturant role was most fully expressed during the delivering of babies and in caring for the sick. For more than three decades Elizabeth Child, Deacon Ephraim's wife, was the main midwife and nurse of the town. In May 1653 Ephraim wrote to John Winthrop Jr., "My wife would entreat you to send her a parcel of your physic divided into portions for young and old. She hath many occasions to make use thereof to the help of many." During the 1670s a number of women gave expert testimony about paternity, prematurity, and sexual abuse.[23] Widows were regularly responsible for caring for old people left alone and the infirm. Many more married women earned part or all of the payments for other welfare services credited to their husbands.[24]

Domestic space centered on women's focus, the hearth. Initially, most households lived in very simple structures, with a cellar for storage, a hall for eating, working, and cooking, and a chamber for sleeping, the only privacy for adults provided by the bed curtains. With rising affluence and population, however, these early buildings were either replaced or extended. Larger chimney stacks allowed expanded fireplaces incorporating built-in ovens. Huge bressumer beams created an inglenook and supported the hooks, trammels, and chains that held pots and spits over the heat. Extra rooms and lean-tos were tacked on to the original.[25]

These improvements produced an increase in privacy for those who could afford it. The parents had the parlor both for sleeping and for display of family treasures. A second story above the parlor would provide chambers for older children. The lean-to often held a kitchen or "fireroom" and a dairy. By 1680 some Watertown families had homes with nine separate rooms; six-room dwellings were not unusual, though for younger or poorer couples the two-room building would still have to suffice. Early domestic "life in a common-room" developed into a more affluent living style conducive to a greater sense of personal individuality or marital discretion, with enormous long-term repercussions.[26]

A second result of rising affluence was "conspicuous consumption." Early domestic settings seem to have been starkly austere. The only furnishing listed for the seriously wealthy Thomas Hammond in 1655, for instance, was a tapestry coverlet. Gradually, however, through the 1660s and 1670s, luxury items became more common: pewter, china, glass (compared with the wooden bowls and trenchers, or platters, used by the poor), silverware, even "gold and silver plate" and some valuable furniture, like clothespresses and great chairs. The looking glass must have revolutionized the way people perceived themselves—a potent encouragement to the "consumer revolution." Most of the nine mirrors listed belonged to the second generation.[27]

Occasionally, wealthier women like Anne Fleming, Hannah Thatcher, or Hannah Hammond acquired impressive and colorful wardrobes and collections of linen. For most farmers and their wives, however, "apparel" was a very minor item in appraisals, much of it well-worn homespun.[28] Soft furnishings were also rare. Richard Beers was unusual in having ten cushions. For most townspeople, spartan bareness was the norm.[29] The one exception to this dour picture (there were no pictures!) was the bed. By 1660 all but poor families had featherbeds, bolsters, pillowcases, sheets, and bed-curtains. Many households owned at least one warming pan. Given the extreme winter cold, short daylight, and inefficient heating, people probably spent a considerable part of their wintertime in bed. It explains why William Hagar and William Parry, both of whom died in January, had beds in their kitchen firerooms.[30]

Most wills and all inventories were compiled by men. The interior of houses was of far less importance to them than land, stock, provisions, or craft goods. Any spare wealth went on land. Only at the end of our period, and only among the town elite, was personal or domestic adornment thought worthy of expenditure.[31]

Even modest increases in display would widen the perceived gulf between haves and have-nots. Though Watertown people accepted hierarchy, were the new self-styled ladies and gentlemen worthy of the privilege accorded a Saltonstall? Town meeting put-downs and individual protests signaled popular resistance to such pretensions. Materialism and possessiveness undercut communal cooperation and equity. Furthermore, a new emphasis on privacy conflicted with older notions of neighborliness. As we shall see, making oneself at home in other people's houses in this new era could lead to intense irritation and anger. Affluence, as the preachers constantly intoned, was at best a mixed blessing.[32]

Economic well-being, with its concomitants of material comfort and physical privacy, could contribute to the emotional stability of family life, though it did not ensure it. Two of Watertown's dysfunctional families, the Pages and the Knapps, had severe financial problems. Other families' difficulties were probably made worse by lack of assets. Yet actual marital breakdown was extremely rare. Persistent loutishness or indolence, alcoholism or sour temper were insufficient causes for the bonds to be broken. Even madness might be cured and relations restored. The only legal grounds for divorce were violence, female infidelity, and desertion.[33]

Only two marriages in early Watertown ended in divorce. Wealthy former Londoners Samuel and Apphia (Quick) Freeman were divorced about 1644; she had earlier been involved with another migrant from London, Mr. William Clark, and Samuel had been absent in London for six years. Mary (Wellington) Mattack had been deserted for thirteen years by her husband, Henry, when their marriage was dissolved in 1679. Two potential deserters were warned to return to their families during the 1660s. Susan Clements, "forced" into marriage and so repelled by her husband, William, that she preferred to sleep with the oxen, spent time in Watertown in the care of the Benjamins during the 1650s. Sarah and Thomas Boylston were granted legal separation in 1652. She may have "dallied" with Mr. Richard Brown in 1643, but Thomas proved a violent railer, a constant tippler, an idler, a curser, and an absentee from church. Unlike in England, divorcées could remarry, and in Watertown they did; others unhappily yoked were rescued by the early death of their mates.[34]

Fidelity, constancy, industry, mutual support, tolerance, gentleness, patience, and cooperation were plainly the qualities missing from these sad relationships, and the predictable result was suffering, deprivation, and emotional and physical injury. Attraction, desire, and love were prerequisites for "yokefellows." Many wills and deeds refer to spouses as "loving" and "dear." It is easy but inaccurate to dismiss such epithets as merely formulaic. The generosity of spirit that often followed suggests that such endearments were heartfelt.[35]

Most marital breakdowns occurred during the first ten years, economically as well as emotionally the most vulnerable period in the marriage cycle. Financial well-being was a factor of age as well as class. Families passed through predictable stages: young, vigorous, reproductive, but often relatively poorly endowed; mature, with grown or growing offspring and financially more comfortable; elderly, retired, declining in independence, but still with some wealth. Thus Richard Stratton died in 1658 as a newlywed of thirty. He and his wife, Susanna, had to rent land and dwelling, sleep on a chaff bed with baby son Samuel, and subsist on the crops from twelve acres. They had only one ox and one cow, a cock and three hens. By contrast, Richard's father, Samuel, who died in 1672 aged seventy-two, left a respectable £258.[36]

Middle-aged men's wills show that they were still working and that the arrangements that they were forced to make with their greater assets were precipitate, conditional, and temporary. John Fleming, for instance, left much incomplete financial business, as did the fifty-five-year-old Edward Dix. Stress was laid on the appointment of responsible male executors and administrators to help the widow, especially one with younger children.[37]

The majority of Watertown men and women of the first generation made their wills at impressive old ages. Several had turned some of their assets into cash or had extended loans to younger kin and neighbors or passed on ownership of land to their heirs. Some lived with children in a part of the home, like the ancient John and Phoebe Page out by Beaver Brook in the 1670s. Retirement allowed the unhurried ordering of affairs. Grandchildren often figured large, especially with some grandmotherly bequests.[38]

Of course, age did not necessarily equal wealth in the Watertown hierarchy. Some ancients died wretchedly poor. The thirty-seven-year-old merchant Thomas Hammond, who had an affluent father and had married a well-endowed wife, left a princely £652.[39] Most of Hammond's assets were in land. Real estate among Watertown's first and second generations (even maltsters, merchants, or tanners) dwarfed all other assets in value. Artisans with little land were among the poorest inhabitants.[40] Despite exceptions, age and affluence did tend to go together, and with them went all the familiar dynamics of need, power, dependence, apprehensiveness, envy, and punishment. Younger married couples could have put to better and more pressing use money that their far less needy elders possessed. Little wonder generational conflict caused such tensions.[41]

Cross-generational relations were not always edgy and antagonistic. In 1678 William Barsham, aged nearly seventy, deeded reversion to land in Watertown to his youngest son, Nathaniel, who was about to marry. This consideration was in exchange for supplies and annual rent until parental death, but "more especially for the natural love I have and bear to my son who has been, is, and like to be the staff of mine and my wife's old age."[42] As aged parents sank into dependence, such retirement "land-for-care" agreements were common. Sickly or elderly widows or widowers were particularly vulnerable. The infirm

Ruth Blois made a specific contract in 1681: in exchange for four acres of land, Henry Godden would "provide a meet and comfortable room in his house in Watertown for my abode (unless I marry) and, when I am afflicted with the infirmity I am afflicted to, Henry Godden and his wife are to care for me to prevent any hurt to myself." Though some arrangements were as loving as William Barsham's, others built in safeguards implying a certain distrust.[43] Formalizing agreements would protect not only parents fearful of abandonment but also caregivers against subsequent claims from their siblings. As the Page, Gale, and Pearce family conflicts demonstrated, these precautions were prudent.[44]

The important rituals associated with death were overseen by women. When, for instance, childless John Loveran was failing in 1638, three neighbor women were in attendance, Elizabeth Child, Elizabeth Pearce, and Margaret Howe, as well as his "sickly" wife. Three days before he died, it was Elizabeth Child who "urged him to make his will." A sudden turn could create a dangerously agitated death room and subsequent conflict among the heirs, as happened with John Fleming, and was just prevented with George Phillips.[45]

Phillips's 1644 funeral was the grandest event in early Watertown. By comparison, Old Thorpe's burial in 1673, where town cider was drunk, was a very meager affair, like Old Knapp's. The only other surviving records of these departures are the gravestones in the Old Burial Ground. The earliest markers are for John and Mary Coolidge, both 1691. The dead family members lie grouped together in the cemetery, an ancestral extended kinship.[46]

The reallocation of the family assets after paternal death followed certain conventions. If the father died young, the convention was to leave all the estate to the widow for life or until she remarried or until all the children had reached majority, at which time she would receive her widow's "thirds" for life. The decedent often also laid down the proportional legacies of the next generation after his widow had eventually died. Custom gave the eldest son a double share, with equal shares to his brothers and sisters. Real estate went to male legatees, and "movables" like stock, household goods, cash, or its equivalent, to female. The great majority of Watertown men made wills, but the courts could divide estates in cases of intestacy.[47]

Where the family might have both adult and dependent children, as with George Woodward, executors had to safeguard the upbringing of the young. In the Woodwards' case, they divided movables among older offspring; the widow retained the real estate for ten years and then reverted to her thirds.[48]

Although heirs would sometimes call in influential neighbors to act as arbitrators,[49] the reorganization of family resources usually went smoothly. Occasionally, though, conflicts and difficulties arose between offspring and widows, or among offspring, over administration and valuation, especially from the disinherited. Sudden deaths left estates in disarray. Not all families were happy families.

Settling the Fleming estate between three older children in England and two younger in Watertown took five years, five court appearances, eight legal instruments, and two civil actions with seventeen witnesses. Some siblings outstripped others, since the Fleming estate only realized £100, far less than its valuation.[50] Administration of the chaotic estate of Thomas and Hannah Hammond took eight years. Contested loans, suits by English creditors, a battle royal over valuation, appraising lands in England, interventions by clan members, and outside arbitration all created an executor's nightmare.[51]

Sibling rivalry and parental favoritism could create major conflicts among heirs. Such a crisis was explained by Anna Pearce, widow of Anthony Pearce, in 1678. "Our youngest son [Benjamin] hath lived at home to the age of thirty, and hath been prudent and diligent in the management of our affairs; a great part, more than £80 hath been added to our estate. Therefore his father possessed him eight years since with the house that was his grandfather's [John Pearce of Watertown] with six acres of land . . . [Benjamin] repaired the roof and fabric &c., building a stone fortification in the time of danger, but now his brothers want this property [valued at £44] included in the inventory."

"His father," claimed the grieving widow, "would rather have lost his right arm than deprive Benjamin of his gift" (in which, it emerged, she hoped to lodge!). The court refused to nullify Anthony Pearce's written will, thus canceling the prior verbal gift and demonstrating the necessity of formal contracts.[52]

Sometimes the older generation displayed their deep disapproval of their children's behavior. For instance, William Parry's first will in 1681 reflected both a lyrical puritan conviction and concern about the family future. His bequest to daughter Sarah was conditional on her preparedness to "live with her mother and give her help and live free from scandalous walking [and not to] grieve her mother." A later codicil cut out his two sons Obadiah and Samuel: "My first immediate seed being not so conscious to bring up children in religion and to read the English tongue, therefore I give to my grandchildren what I gave to Obadiah and Samuel to learn [teach] true religion and learn to read their father's will in their mother tongue."[53]

The wicked stepmother of folk tales more often emerges in Watertown as the victim of intergenerational and intrafamilial conflict. Once widowed, her needs and rights were in competition with the heirs of the first wife. One stepson prevented firewood being cut for his stepmother, whom he saw as an intruding plunderer of family assets; the larger her fires now, the smaller would be his and his eight children's in the future.[54] Another widow's court petition threatened that unless her stepchildren provided her rightful "comfortable maintenance... I shall be forced to roam to the town or else perish for want of relief. I have none else to make my moan to." The allusion to going on welfare quickly did the trick.[55] Bereaved natural parents and in-laws could, by contrast, expect their children's support; in one case sons forwent legacies "considering the desolate estate of our dear mother." All Watertown's intergenerational probate battles were with stepmothers rather than natural mothers.[56]

Probate issues were time consuming and intensely sensitive. As in so many similar areas, the nuclear family relied on the extended clan for practical assistance and emotional support. We have already encountered kinship networking in the defense of adolescents. It was equally important in financial, legal, and welfare concerns.

Kinfolk often gave financial help outside their immediate households. Grandparents endowed grandchildren with land or dowries. Nephews were "possessed of" land belonging to childless uncles or aunts. Family members preferred to sell land to kin rather than to strangers. Probate documents often record loans or gifts between relations; loans became gifts in the dying person's will. One will stipulated that "no stranger is to dwell in my house, but it [must] be let unto kin." Others specified first refusal to family for any land put on the market. Land once acquired for a family should remain "in its hand forever."[57]

Extended families could be summoned in crises. When forty-year-old John Child suddenly succumbed on 14 October 1676, the three men who gathered to take his nuncupative will were his father-in-law, Daniel Warren Sr., his brother Richard, and his cousin William Goddard.[58] Kinsfolk rallied in defense of relatives in trouble with the law.[59] Where business differences threatened family peace, other clan members acted as conciliators. In 1650 Joshua Foote, a London ironmonger, began to lose patience with his Massachusetts agent and cousin Joshua Hewes; who better to arbitrate than another cousin, Ephraim Child of Watertown, who worked out a timetable for repayment of an £800 debt? Child in London in 1647–48 had borrowed money from a Foote kinswoman. She sent yet another kinsman, William Goddard, to recover the £100 from Child's executors. Once in Massachusetts, Goddard witnessed cousin Richard Child's will. Such clan commercial linkages were commonplace in Massachusetts and the wider Atlantic economy.[60]

The extended family provided the first safety net for members who fell from the notoriously wobbly high wire of domestic security. Guardianship of orphans was conventionally sought by uncles and aunts, like Samuel Stearns for his deceased brother's son Isaac, or Thomas Fleg Jr. for his niece Lydia Brown, about whose welfare he petitioned the county court twice. In 1673 Lambert Chenery of Watertown and Dedham made a formal instrument safeguarding his stepgrandson. Chenery had had three wives; the latter two had brought children and grandchildren to their new union.[61] Other Watertown men felt obliged to protect quite distant relatives in other communities. In 1664 John Wetherall expressed concern that "his loving brother[-in-law] Stephen Fosdick (of Charlestown) hath left behind him an aged infirm crazy wife [Grace] being about seventy-five, lame of her feet, going on crutches; [she] had been his wife near forty years [and] was married to him in a single state. Upon her marriage with him [she] had six of his children to take care of." Ellis Barron acted as appraiser of the Ipswich estate of his wife's brother's mother-in-law. Such were the coils of kinship.[62]

The supportive clan, however, could also be intrusive and domineering. It could override attempts at greater personal autonomy and privacy, especially among the rising generation. In a world needing adaptation and innovation, the clan could be a hindrance to young aspirations.[63]

The pervasive influence of this basic unit of society is suggested by the ways in which certain behavior "ran in families." Like the Knapps and Grants, two generations of hard-drinking Hawkinses, lecherous Summers, and infighting Pages replicated delinquency.[64] The loss or inadequacy of fathers had a disastrous effect on the development of immature sons. The wildness and insolence of so many fatherless or ill-fathered young men cannot be pure coincidence. The same phenomenon applied to motherless young women. The inability of Mistress Phillips to control her wayward son or George Woodward's problems with Susannah derived from divisions of gender roles. Mistress Phillips was not an inadequate mother; she just was not a father.[65]

Conversely, leading families reproduced leaders to succeed them: Samuel Phillips went to Harvard and became a minister; Ephraim Child handed on civic authority to his ward William Bond, Simon Stone Sr. to Simon Jr., Isaac to Samuel Stearns, Nathaniel to John Biscoe, and so on. Between the dysfunctional and the town elite, many families were effective little firms glued together by mutual affection, interdependence, and protectiveness. Distrust between the generations centered on steprelatives, invasive cuckoos despoiling the nest.[66]

Watertown, a "company" town, began with rudimentary kinship networks that provided communal coherence and replicated simplified English social forms. As time went by, there was a noticeable thickening of interfamilial bonds as the maturing young intermarried within the town. In nine cases there were multiple unions between families, where two, or even three, members of one clan married two or three members of another. Endogamy similarly flourished, though the pool of potential mates within the town and in neighboring communities was large enough to allow "fancy" to play its part.[67]

English family law and customs also persisted in areas like inheritance and widows' rights. Though divorce was a radical legal innovation, it was extremely rare and had little effect on marriage relationships. Differences in land and labor availability made subtle changes to family dynamics. For instance, several youngest sons remained at the Watertown home until both parents died and then inherited the family house and homestall. This practice resembled "Borough English" in East Anglia. Its popularity there, however, derived from delaying payment of the next generations' entry fines; in Watertown similar procedures were the result of extraordinary first-generation longevity.[68]

While the separation of gender roles in Watertown was another continuation of English practice, the comparative shortage of servants and homogenizing of class distinctions helped erode male exclusivities. Watertown wives were veritable "deputy husbands" and partners in the firm. Labor scarcity enhanced the value and influence of all family members in the productive team. There is little support in Watertown for the idea of heightened New England patriarchalism. Pervasive suspicion of authority and an embryonic youth culture combined with these changes in family relationships to favor the younger generation. Interdependence between generations and awareness that cooperation was mutually beneficial seem to have been the norm. Most parents were much more concerned about being cared for in their old age by their progeny than hanging on to economic power relentlessly until the moment of death.[69]

Patchy early records blur changes in family culture over the whole half-century. Three bitter probate cases in the late 1670s turning on conflicts involving brothers and sisters and the formalizing of land-for-care retirements may signal intensified competition for land, especially after King Phillip's War rendered frontier expansion dangerous. Two disinheritances may also imply increased generational conflict. The gradual rise in fornication convictions during the 1660s and 1670s may point to adolescent attempts to buck family involvement in marriage choices and to greater friction over this potentially contentious decision. Perhaps "declension" involved decline in parental authority.

Some marriages proved far more materially successful than others, because of better endowment, greater ambition, closer cooperation, or sheer luck. The seventeenth century was dangerous for adults as well as children, as the number of early deaths, injuries, and infirmities shows. The faltering colonial economy could also pull down faltering households. Gaps between rich and poor, though minute by English standards, were widening during the 1670s, and with rebuilding, purchase of luxuries, and increasing comfort, they were widening very visibly.[70]

Marriage represented the forming of new households, the bonding of loving yokefellows, the alliance of two clans, the founding of a new firm, the creation of a new unit for welfare, education, discipline, and population growth, as well as the seat of cross-generational interdependence; such a complex and multipurpose institution was bound to feel stresses and strains as it grew and changed. Yet it lost none of its attractiveness in Watertown's first half-century. It continued the near-universal choice of the people of the town, and if one marriage failed or ended, most survivors reentered the wedded state as soon as they could. Someone without a family was like a finger without a hand.[71]

V
REINFORCING CONSENSUS

12

Invisible Indians

"There were no Indians in Watertown. It was virgin land ready for the taking." This would have to be the conclusion of a careful reading of the early town records. The one or two allusions to Native Americans there give no evidence of local residence. The only non-English place-name, Pequusset Common, was soon changed to King's Common.[1] Yet, the assumption of *vacuum domicilium,* or an empty place to settle, so reassuring to puritan tender consciences and subsequent generations of European settlers, is false. Not only were native people present at the very founding of Watertown, but they continued to affect life in the town directly or indirectly for its first fifty years of white settlement—which coincided, roughly, to the period between the 2,600th and 2,650th years of known Indian contacts with the place.[2]

Throughout the first fifty years, white intruders into Pequusset were driven by a bonding undercurrent of racialism, from the first letter home to the assumption in October 1679 that the word of any Englishman must be inherently more trustworthy than that of a Native. This sense of white superiority derived from a mixture of puritan arrogance and assumed divine mission, abhorrence of wild people in a wilderness—cruel, untrustworthy "savages" who "lurked" and "skulked"—and possession of guns and killer germs.[3] All surviving judgments on Indians by townsmen reflect uninhibited and undiscriminating revulsion. There is no evidence of any expression of guilt about white treatment of Amerindians. Shared racialism was a unifying force to white "pioneers," but it also induced a jittery anxiousness, which could erupt into panic and recrimination.

Yet the presence of Indians also divided the community. Whites needed Indians: as initiators in new-world mysteries, as fur trappers in frontier communities, as labor in more settled areas, as allies against other tribes or other Europeans, as hunters of wolves, as guides. These needs meant that, pace Watertown records, there were always Native Americans about. They might show up out of the woods at any time; their wigwams might be spied one morning near a familiar pond, by a brook, in a clearing, or by a highway. By the late 1640s they had become an integral part of the summer harvesting, like modern-day migrant workers. Yet only wealthier townsmen could afford to hire these Indian "servants."[4] Poor men or young beginners could get much needed help only through promising illicit grog. If trouble ensued, others often had to deal with it, as watchmen, constables, or pursuers. If there was violence, others were often the victims. If there was war, some families suffered terrible blows, gnawing anxieties, financial ruin; others dodged, evaded, even profited. Such factors, in a more or less fearful atmosphere, excited conflict and jealousy.

The first Europeans known to have struggled ashore near what became Watertown were an exploring party of the Dorchester contingent, who had arrived in Massachusetts Bay at the end of May 1630, ahead of the main *Arbella* fleet. Roger Clapp recorded their experiences:

> We went up Charles River, until the river grew narrow and shallow, and there we landed our goods with much labour and toil, the bank being steep; and night coming on, we were informed that there were hard by us 300 Indians. One Englishman, that could speak the Indian language, (an old planter), went to them, and advised them not to come near us in the night; and they hearkened to his counsel and came not. I myself was one of the sentinels that night . . . In the morning some of the Indians came and stood at a distance off, looking at us, but came not near. But when they had been a while in view, some of them came and held out a great bass towards us; so we sent a man with a biscuit, and changed the cake for the bass. Afterwards, they supplied us with bass, exchanging a bass for a biscuit cake, and were very friendly unto us . . . Had they come upon us, soon might they have destroyed us! I think we were not above ten in number. But God caused the Indians to help us with fish at very cheap rates. We had not been there many days (although by our diligence we had got up a kind of shelter to save our goods in) but we had an order to come away from that place, which was about Watertown, unto a place called Mattapan, now Dorchester.[5]

Their brief encampment, above Clapp's Landing, continued to be known by their successors as Dorchester Plain. Their ritual exchange became enshrined on the town shield above the motto *In Pace Condita,* "Founded in Peace."

There are three reasons for presuming that this land had been recently occupied by an indigenous band. First, there is archaeological evidence, already described. Second, its openness and lack of woodland up to the edge of the river, as reported by early settlers, argues that it may have been an old Indian field, a village's cleared planting ground for the maize, squash, beans, pumpkin, and tobacco that the women cultivated in their multicropping system.

Third, the gift of bass and the proximity of the falls suggests that Pequusset was a rendezvous to exploit the spring spawning runs of smelts, shad, and alewives, as well as bass. The "dense temporary settlement" would feast on the catch, after the lean late-winter, dry or smoke fish for later consumption, and celebrate the rites of the annual rebirth.[6]

The earliest surviving letter from Watertown, dated 15 March 1631, to William Pond in Edwardstone, Suffolk, from his son, describes, the "eingeines" as "a crafty people, and they will cozen and cheat, and they are a subtle people, and whereas we did expect great store of beaver, here is little or none to be had, and their Sagamore John weigheth it, and many of us truck with them and it layeth us many times eight shillings a pound. They are proper men and clean jointed men, and many of them go naked with a skin about their loins, but some of them get Englishmen's apparel. [Pond asked his father to send out coarse cloth] for here is nothing to be got without we had commodities to go into the east parts amongst the Indians to trade, for here where we live is no beaver."[7] The naming of Watertown's main stream as Beaver Brook, "because the beavers had shorn down great trees there and made divers dams across the brook," suggests their extinction was recent, possible victims of the 1620s boom in fur trading.[8]

The shortage of pelts may also have been due to the shortage of local trappers. Imported European diseases scythed through nonimmunized Amerindians. The "virgin soil epidemic" of plague between 1616 and 1618 is estimated to have killed off between 75 percent and 90 percent of the local Americans. The heaps of bones and skulls, "a new found Golgotha," reported a few miles south was indicative of a scourge running all along the coast from Naumkeag (Salem) to the eastern shore of Narragansett Bay. The Massachusett and Pawtucket peoples around Watertown were struck again in the winter of 1630–31. "Here are but few eingeines," reported Pond, "and a great sort of them died this winter. It was thought it was of the plague." Two years later, the second surviving letter from "Waltur toune," sent by William Hammond to his English patron, Sir Simonds D'Ewes, reiterated that "as for the eingeines, we have but few amongst us. They are quiet." As Jennings commented, "The land was not so much virgin as widowed."[9]

A 1634 map shows two villages within ten miles of Watertown. One, Sagamore John's Pawtucket band, is located on the Mystic River, to the northeast of Fresh Pond, near modern Arlington; the other, Chickataubet's Massachusett village, is on the Neponset River, where Milton now stands. Terms like "village" are misleading, however. The indigenes practiced an extensive and mobile system of sustenance, a semisedentary lifestyle involving the removal of the whole village at certain seasons for hunting or fishing, and dispersal at others for food gathering. This movement brought their temporary encampments much closer to hand, at Nonantum across the Charles, at the Falls, at Sherman's Pond near the town's northern bounds, and at Waban to the west.[10]

Interaction between the cultures raised major problems. The local bands were used to protecting their ripening crops only from wild animals. Excluding English pigs and cattle was a new and gigantic problem. Their whole concept of ownership was different from European ideas of private property. Indian hunters who ranged over many square miles could claim ownership of an animal only after stalking and killing it. Indian mobility and English sedentarism were bound to clash. Hammond reported that if the Indians "do offend, the governor have them fetched before him and admonish them, and if that any of them steal, the sagamore that is over them bring them to the court and there they are punished." Chickataubet and Sagamore John "promised unto the [18 May 1631 General] Court to make satisfaction for whatsoever wrong that any of their men shall do to any of the English, to their cattle or any other way." The former was ordered the following month to pay a skin of beaver "for shooting a swine of Sir Richard Saltonstall's." In 1632 the sagamore promised "against the next year, and so for ever after," to fence in his people's planting land, a huge change in native practice. Misdeeds by the English were also compensated by order of the General Court. When, for instance, Sagamore John and Peter complained to the court held at Watertown on 8 March 1631 that James Woodward, servant to Sir Richard Saltonstall, had burned two wigwams, his master was held liable, as he was eighteen months later when his cattle damaged some of the Indians' maize. White awareness of the Natives' sense of invasion and injustice was stirred by fears of reprisal, as we shall see, but the compensation was pitiful.[11]

In May 1634 two leading settlers were fined £5 for "employing the Indians to shoot with pieces," presumably hunting or fowling. This unprecedented rapping of elite knuckles about native access to guns—the second most powerful force in the European armory of domination, after disease—reflects the panicky jumpiness during the first fifteen years of settlement that could reerupt throughout our period. Puritan distrust of "a crafty . . . subtle people" was inevitable, since it was understood that the "salvages" worshiped devils, had witches for their priests, and were themselves bewitched. The apparent laxity of Indian morality and of household government, enslavement to appetite, female promiscuity, male idleness, and ineffectuality "vividly illustrated the power of the devil . . . Here Satan could be seen at work before their very eyes, and the sight was a repulsive one."[12]

Watertown precipitated the earliest alarm in 1631: "Upon 25 March [1631] one of Watertown, having lost a calf, and about ten o'clock at night hearing the howls of some wolves not far off, raised many of his neighbours out of their beds, that by discharging their muskets near about the place where he heard the wolves, he might so put the wolves to flight and save his calf. The wind serving fit to carry the report of the muskets to Roxbury three miles off at such a time, the inhabitants there took an alarm, beating up their drum, armed themselves and sent in post to Boston to raise us also. So in the morning, the calf being found safe, the wolves affrighted and our danger past, we went merrily to breakfast."[13]

Watertown people had special reason for fears of Indians because several early settlers had been victims of attacks. The first and foremost of these was the explorer and Indian trader Captain John Oldham. In 1633 he led an overland expedition to the Connecticut Valley, where the Dutch and Plymouth traders were already competing for the fur trade. They made contact with the Pyquag Indians around the "wide-stretching lowlands and the gentle ridge" that he and a party of eight townsmen acquired in 1634 and renamed Watertown.[14] After 6 May 1635, when formal permission for removal was granted, Oldham led a second band of fifteen to twenty settlers to the rich grazing of "New Watertown" on the Connecticut. In July 1636, as intertribal and international rivalry surged, Oldham, on a trading trip to Block Island, was assassinated by Ausdah, an Eastern Niantic. Captain William Jennison of Watertown was on the misinformed mission of retaliation that took a Pequot scalp and ravaged Pequot property and pride.[15]

In spring 1637 the pioneers in Watertown on the Connecticut, terrified of retaliation, evicted the Pyquags, who fled to the Pequots. On 27 April 1637 "these salvages went to Watertown, now called Wethersfield, and there fell upon some sawing and slew nine more whereof one was a woman, the other a child, and took two young maids prisoner, killing some of their cattle and driving some away."[16] Among the settlers was the young John Sherman, later Watertown's third minister. The New England forces, including a contingent from Watertown, wrought a terrible vengeance, massacring a whole village of noncombatants in a surprise attack. Warfare had taken on a new genocidal ferocity in the new world.[17]

Massacres might have removed the threat of the Pequots, but tensions with the indigenous peoples continued to mount. At the end of the 1630s rumors spread of a pantribal conspiracy to expel the white invaders, with one chief's exhortation spreading fear: "We are all Indians as the English are, and say brother to one another; so must we be one as they are, otherwise we shall all be gone shortly, for you know our fathers had plenty of deer and skins, our plains were full of deer, as also our woods, and of turkeys, and our coves full of fish and fowl. But these English having gotten our land, they with scythes cut down the grass, and with axes fell the trees; their cows and horses eat the grass, and their hogs spoil our clam banks and we shall all be starved."[18]

Watertown felt these tensions. In 1640, after two years' negotiations, the town was ordered to pay £13.8.6 "that the Indians may have satisfaction for their right" to the weir lands and Nonantum (Newton). Such conciliation might deter local Native Americans from joining any anti-English tribal league. Nonetheless, precautions continued. In February 1641 the meetinghouse belfry was adapted for a lookout post for the nightly watch. In the following year they must have thought that the feared attack had been launched. "The minds of men were filled with fear from these rumours of a great conspiracy, and every noise in the night was alarming. A poor man in a swamp at Watertown [on 19 September 1642] hearing the howling of a kennel of wolves, and expecting to be devoured by them, cried out for help, which occasioned a general alarm through all the towns near Boston." A week later, the town ordered the recovering Pequot War veteran Sgt. Richard Beers to "breed saltpetre" in readiness for an attack. In the summer of 1645 invasion was again feared, and Watertown men were pressed for another campaign. It did not happen. Nonetheless, chronic insecurity and unease remained for the next three decades.[19]

Conversion and anglicization was an alternative defense against savagery, and Watertown was the source of a notable Christianizing mission, the first in New England. In 1642 the son of one of the first-generation leaders of Watertown, Thomas Mayhew Jr., sailed to Martha's Vineyard, settling Great Harbour, now Edgartown, with a group of followers from the town, including John and Peter Folger, John Dogget, John Bland, Thomas Harlock, with their wives and children. His father, Thomas Mayhew Sr., and stepmother joined them by 1647. The Wampanoags on the island proved ready converts after an epidemic, incurable by their own powwows, laid them low in 1645. When an Indian who had scoffed at Mayhew's first convert, Hiacoomes, was struck by lightning, Christianity boomed. By 1652 there were 282 native islanders who had entered the covenant. In 1659 Thomas Mayhew Sr., who had assumed leadership after his son's death by drowning, established the first Indian church on the Vineyard. Unlike the mainland, however, adoption of Christianity did not threaten loss of native identity, land, leadership, or culture. The Indian churches, greatly outnumbering the white in the seventeenth century, retained much of their own autonomy.[20]

In 1649, three years after the General Court decree committing Massachusetts to a policy of Indian conversion, John Eliot, that other great apostle to the Indians, crossed the Charles from Roxbury to preach to the Indians at Watertown. Native minds had already been prepared by such miracles as God's downpour in prompt response to puritan prayers to end the 1633 drought. By 1674 there were an estimated 2,300 "Praying Indians" in New England. Christian Indians from Natick upstream and from Martha's Vineyard and Nantucket regularly hired themselves out at harvest time in Watertown and other Massachusetts towns.[21]

By the late 1640s English labor shortages forced settlers to hire Indian harvest workers, who used their earnings "to get apparel" for the winter. Hence, according to Eliot, "the Indians have frequent recourse to the English towns." Unfortunately for race relations, not all these casual workers or visitors behaved with puritan restraint. After guns, alcohol was the most strictly forbidden commodity for Europeans to pass on to Indians. As with European diseases, the Native Americans had little inbuilt resistance to the effects of alcohol and rapidly succumbed to drunkenness. Behind puritan abhorrence of excess, however, lay fears of Indian workers reverting to a "savagery" that might well take out its frustrations on white exploiters. For the less scrupulous or the less wealthy, however, there were strong temptations to pay the Indians in cheap liquor or to make an illicit profit by selling them what they thirsted after.[22]

Both gun and drink taboos were broken in the late winter of 1652–53. Five Indians trading furs from "the wigwam at Woburn" were found at twilight by the Watertown watch "in drink." Not only had they had "a bottle of strong waters" in the woods, ten quarts of beer from Watertown tavern, and "five gills of strong waters" from glover George Adams, but he had also bartered three guns and shot for skins. His crimes were referred to the Court of Assistants, which ordered a severe whipping. Watertown's impoverished publican Edmund Blois was replaced by Indian-fighter Richard Beers.[23]

Despite these commotions, Indians continued to frequent the town during the 1650s and 1660s. They bought goods on credit,[24] helped harvest,[25] and got into trouble. Jethro, one of the drunks in 1653, exploded with violence a decade later and "took up a great club to knock old Goodman [Nathaniel] Bowman on the head, had not some prevented." He was remanded on bail to the next Indian court at Nonantum.[26] Employment of Indians was confirmed in 1664, when a native servant of John Biscoe's was accused with another of robbing the Watertown schoolhouse of seventeen Greek and Latin books.[27] In 1668 former Watertown residents who had moved to Groton were alarmed at the murder of an English servant at Pennycook (Concord, N.H.) by Indians crazed by drink. In February 1669 came reports of Indians "travelling up and down in the woods" around Watertown.[28]

Despite such fears and irritations, Watertown farmers came to depend on Indian labor during the summer months. By 1670 "Indians [farmworkers] get so much money from the English" that they were tempted into drunken "fighting and killing one another and the abuse of our inhabitants." In the future, "country pay" (i.e., payment in kind) must be the only currency. The

General Court also decreed that "Indian testimony [about illicit liquor purchases] shall be accounted good testimony against any English accused."[29]

Despite their need for native help, the people of Watertown wanted to be rid of the Indians as soon as their usefulness had passed. A special town meeting summoned on 12 April 1671 aptly summarized these xenophobic feelings: "Upon consideration of the Indians being like to buy the privilege of the weirs and fishing at the river which the town apprehend will be much to the damage of the town, they being like to be bad neighbours, the town voted all as one man that they were altogether against their having the weir or that they should set down so near the town . . . All that were present but four [voted] that they were willing to buy [the weir] for the use of the town." Nathaniel Coolidge, the owner of the weir, had certainly guaranteed himself a good price.[30]

The 1670s opened with a foretaste of violence to come. In April 1671 a young Englishman had been killed on the road near Dedham. Three Indians were suspected. Three months later, a hue and cry went after an Indian in a white coat suspected of knocking out the brains of a young maidservant of John Warren Jr. in her master's house. There were four or five other Natives with him. There was a further assault reported on 30 August: an attempted rape of Mary, wife of Daniel Bacon, by Sam the son of William Indian. In October news came of the death of young Zechariah Smith at the hands of Maine Indians.[31]

Drink continued a problem in the years before the war. A little before sunset on 8 August 1673 six Indian harvesters, three Narragansetts and three Quaboags, were involved in a "very outrageous" drunken brawl near Traine's Farm, where the Narragansetts had pitched their wigwam. Harry Indian, one of the Narragansetts, had bought two quarts of liquor from Thomas Traine, the twenty-year-old son of John Traine. The following April Traine was fined the princely sum of £12 as a signal of official displeasure. After a typically crawling apology, this amount was respited to ten shillings.[32]

There was a rising tide of Indian violence both along the edges of white penetration and closer to home, especially during the summer and fall harvests. Jumpy Watertown whites must have worried about kinsfolk and friends in frontier settlements. To them, as their unity over the weir showed, the only good Indian was a distant Indian.

The equation of goodness with deadness came in June 1675 with the onset of King Phillip's War, which triggered a murderous outburst of popular white frenzy against all Native Americans, friends as well as foes, Christian and heathen, near and far. It included in its vitriolic hatred any white who dared make distinctions. Watertown no doubt shared in this orgy of race hatred, especially as early victims of an Indian raid on Lancaster were former townsman William

Fleg, his wife, and two children, killed on 22 August 1675, the Lord's Day. Eleven Indian suspects from Marlborough passed through Watertown en route for trial in Boston, held in file by neck pinions. On 10 September 1675 another Lancastrian from Watertown, John Ball, was killed.[33]

Watertown also had its share of fear, perils, and suffering in the war. Its first casualty was incurred in the opening days of the campaign at Miles's Bridge, Swansea. In late June of 1675 a Watertown militia contingent joined those of ten other towns in a preventive march from Boston southwest toward Metacom's (King Phillip's) heartland. On 29 June the colonial

> army would have engaged with the enemy, [but] the Indians shot the Pilot [guide] who was directing our soldiers in their way to Phillip's Country, and wounded several of our men and ran into the swamps; rainy weather hindered a further pursuit of the enemy [along with desertion, cowardice, and disobedience]. An awful providence happened at this time: for a soldier (a stout man) who was sent from Watertown, seeing the English guide slain, and hearing many profane oaths among some of our soldiers . . . and considering the unseasonableness of the weather was such that nothing could be done against the enemy, this man was possessed with a strong conceit that God was against the English, whereupon he immediately ran distracted, and so was returned home a lamentable spectacle.

Given the ineptitude of this first feeble thrust, he can hardly be blamed.[34]

Later that summer Watertown soldiers were sent west to the Connecticut Valley to help defend outlying English settlements like Deerfield, Hatfield, and Squakeag (Northfield). On 25 August 1675, under the command of Pequot War veteran Captain Richard Beers, with comrades from Beverley, they fought a bloody skirmish at Hopewell Swamp. According to a contemporary letter, "The English intended to parley with the Indians, but on a sudden the Indians let fly about forty guns at them, and were soon answered with a volley from our men; about forty [of whom] ran down into the swamp after [the Indians] and poured in shot among them . . . after a while our men after the Indian manner got behind trees and watched their opportunities to make shot [upon] them. The fight continued about three hours; we lost six men upon the ground, though one was shot in the back by our own men; a seventh died of his wound coming home, and two died the next night, nine in all of nine different towns . . . Of the Indians . . . there were twenty-six slain."[35]

Worse was to follow. On 3 September 1675 Beers and thirty-six horsemen set out to cover the evacuation of Squakeag. They camped that night four miles short of their destination and next morning set out on foot. According to local historians, Beers

> appears to have kept up on the high plain till he came in sight of the little brook, now known as Sawmill Brook. The ravine was now covered with a rank growth

of grass and ferns and the leaves were thick on the young trees. It was at this place that the Indians had placed their ambuscade. He advanced across the brook by the accustomed fording place, and just at the passage, and when his company was most exposed, was furiously attacked in front and flank, and all were thrown in great confusion, but soon rallied and fought bravely for their lives, but were soon forced back by superior numbers some three-quarters of a mile to a narrow ravine on the south of a hill now known as Beers's Hill. Here a stand was made, and here the little band fought about their leader, with the courage of desperation, till their ammunition was exhausted and the captain with nearly every man had fallen; only a few escaped, joined the guard left behind with the horses and made their way back to Hadley, thirteen in all. An undoubted tradition points out the grave of Captain Beers in the ravine.

When a second, stronger rescue party came into the ravine, they found the heads of some of the victims impaled on poles, others hanging from chains. Of the sixteen dead, five had Watertown connections. Nine other townsmen served under Beers.[36]

The carnage of Squakeag and other disasters hardened race hatred among the colonists. Beers's sergeant was John Shattuck. He survived, and six days later he was back in the Bay (perhaps with news of the disaster). On 13 September, waiting for the ferry to Boston on the porch of the Three Cranes at Charlestown, he shared his sense of outrage that the Indians then on trial in Boston for murdering his contemporary, William Fleg, might be acquitted (just because they were innocent): "For my part [he told a group of people] I have lately been abroad in the country's service, and have ventured my life for them and escaped very narrowly; but if they clear those Indians, they shall hang me by the neck before I ever serve them again." The hangman was spared either grisly task. The Indians were cleared (only to be interned on wind-blasted Deer Island for the winter). Shattuck himself drowned when the ferry he boarded sank fifteen minutes after his challenge.[37]

By December 1675 twenty Watertown men had been drafted to the colors. John Sherman Jr., son of the town's ensign, was killed at the Narragansett Fort fight on 19 December 1675. Some conscripts wheedled their way home, however, like Joseph Tainter Jr., who "never did a day's service in the war." Understandably, draft dodging raised local hackles among neighbors such as "new-married men [sent] from their wives" and families like the Harringtons, who had lost one son and had another disabled in battle.[38]

The war came much closer to home in the late winter of 1676. On February 10 "some hundreds of Indians . . . fell upon Lancaster," burning, killing, and kidnapping. George Harrington died in the recapturing of the ruined town. On 2 March it was Groton's turn. Forty foot-soldiers from Watertown were sent to their relief, but the Indians had fled. Eleven days later, however, the town was again attacked, and its inhabitants, many raised in Watertown, had to abandon their homes. Some refugees ended up sheltering in their birthplace. Others, like John Morse of Lancaster, Watertown-bred, were captured. The high point of the Native American offensive occurred on 20 April 1676, when an estimated five hundred warriors attacked Sudbury, Watertown's immediate neighbor to the west. A relief party of Watertown militia rushed ten miles to the battle and helped drive back the Indians west of the Sudbury River. Then they had to attack again to free some surrounded defenders. Many English were killed in the panic as smoke from fired bushes suffocated them, but Sudbury held. Watertown was in a state of high alert. A week after the Sudbury fight, its miller petitioned for six men to be allowed to help him garrison "so considerable a concern as the mill." On 9 June 1676 there occurred an "alarum . . . by reason that sundry of the enemy were seen at Billerica and (it seemeth) had shot a man there." The same month Indian wigwams were reported on the western shore of Sherman's Pond. These incidents proved the town's last terrors of the war. Thereafter Indian strength, weakened by winter starvation, fearsome casualties, and divided counsels, rapidly waned. On 12 August the great Metacom himself was killed at Mount Hope, and the war named after him was effectively over.[39]

The killing might be over, but its aftereffects lingered. Hatred against those few who had defied race hatred and spoken out in defense of the sometimes heroic friendly Indians persisted.[40] Besides the sufferings of widows like Elizabeth Beers and the other families who had lost loved ones, Watertown felt huge fiscal costs. On 19 July 1675 a double country (i.e., colony) tax demand of £93.14.3 was delivered. Soon after there were "impressed [five] able and sufficient horses for public service, with saddles, bridles and well-shod." This cost was followed on 14 December 1675 by a vast country tax on Watertown of £358.14.5 and ten more extraordinary taxes amounting to £469.18.0 on 18 July 1676. In one horrendous year Watertown had had to find £910.6.8, ten to fifteen times the usual amount. On 9 January 1677 six more "war rates" added to the town tax rate totaled £311.10.4, and a year later the country rate was still about double the prewar average at £120.18.10. Town money was also needed for powder and bullets, firewood for the watchhouse, and "fetching biscuit for the soldiers." This revenue had to be found from a shrinking tax base as war dead were listed in deficit accounts as "rates lost." Little wonder that on 6 November 1676 the selectmen were instructed by the town meeting to find a schoolmaster "as cheap as they can."[41]

The Indians did not go away either. Harvesters were even more desperately needed. In the summer of 1677 a runaway Indian called John Wompas caused a scare, less for "threatening to shoot Mrs. Oliver if he had a gun" than for "endeavouring to work discontent in the Indians toward the English and giving out reports rendering him justly to be suspected of conspiring with the enemy against us." Indians continued to "lurk" and "skulk" in the woods. The town accounts for 1678 laconically note: "To an Indian for killing a wolf in our town, ten shillings."[42]

White need, poverty, and irresponsibility were all spotlighted by an incident in the summer of 1679. On 3 July John Naaskonit had been arrested near Fresh Pond; his squaw "was bloody in her face being scratched," and John had struck at the watchmen and broken their gun. He had a wooden bottle containing a pint of rum mixed with water. Half of this was pay for harvesting William Price's peas, he claimed, and the other half was secured by the pawn of a wampum girdle. Price, brought face-to-face with Naaskonit two days later, utterly denied the allegations about supplying the rum and offered to clear himself by his oath. Daniel Gookin was suspicious, however. Price admitted that he had employed the Indian, unconvincingly denied ownership of the bottle, and evaded questions about John's missing girdle. Although poor and disreputable, Price was a war veteran; his bondsman was William Shattuck, father of another less fortunate veteran. The county bench permitted him to "purge himself by his oath," and he went free. Did they fear renewal of popular hostility if they believed a drunkard Indian over a war veteran? Such discrimination had been a major grievance cited by Phillip as a cause of the war. Defeat destroyed any lingering chance of equity.[43]

The postwar town records of 5 February 1678 reveal yet another result of the trauma of near extinction that the Lord had permitted. Many puritan minds explained the disaster by reasoning similar to Cotton Mather's: "Our Indian Wars are not over yet. We have too far degenerated into Indian vices. The vices of the Indians are these: They are very lying wretches, and they are very lazy wretches: and they are out of measure indulgent to their children; there is no family government among them. We have become shamefully Indianized in all those abominable things. Now the judgements of God have employed Indian hatchets to wound us, no doubt, for these our Indian vices." It was inconceivable that the Native Americans had triumphed so often because of superior tactics and fighting skills. The providences of God determined all events, and the Almighty's profound dissatisfaction with His chosen people promised further wrathful visitations unless they reformed. On 5 February 1678 Watertown selectmen appointed twelve tithingmen; the chairman "shall send a note to each of them to signify to them the several families that are committed to each man's care."[44]

There were only the three official recognitions of the existence of Native Americans in the town during the period 1630 to 1680. Only once was an Indian named, and then with an Anglicized spelling. The original inhabitants were "invisible" people. Yet native people were involved in town life on a day-to-day basis. There was a willful denial of Indian existence on the part of the settlers. Such distancing enhanced the comfortable deceit that the land was empty. It erased a proud people from the newcomer's consideration. It was a mental form of ethnic cleansing to accompany the physical destruction of "Pigsgusset's" ecology and inhabitants. Watertown might claim to have been founded in peace; what it denied was its continued need for cooperation and exchange with the indigenous people.[45]

Yet the persistence of a native presence, either evident at harvest season or sensed in the surrounding forest throughout the rest of the year, had a potent effect on townspeople. Though in specific instances involving labor needs, drunkenness, or illicit guns the Native Americans could divide and disrupt the community, their very existence, with its inherent threat to white security, moral, physical, and spiritual, could bond and unify the normally quarrelsome settlers of Watertown. However different and disagreeable neighboring whites could be, their similarity nonetheless reinforced a sense of "usness" when contrasted with neighboring red men.

13
"Foreigners" and Community

Watertown may have been "founded in peace," but its inhabitants showed a penchant for contention in the succeeding fifty years. Nonetheless, the community survived intact. Two forces counterbalanced persistent internal frictions: unifying opposition to external threats and neighborly conciliation and restraint.

We have seen how Native Americans achieved the near miracle of uniting their white neighbors and also the parochial concept of foreignness or strangeness referring to people from the other side of the regularly beaten bounds of the town. These town lines were an insulator between "us" and "them." No one from "away" could come to live or even lodge in Watertown without the permission of the town. Considerable numbers were ritually warned out.[1]

Relations between townspeople and outsiders were subtly different from interactions within the community. Civil actions for debt or breach of contract between townsmen were almost nonexistent. Suits involving strangers were not uncommon, however, and were often triggered by the absence of informal but binding community conciliation.

In debt cases brought by outsiders, there are several pointers to a less responsible, even evasive attitude on the part of Watertown borrowers. For instance, money owed to English creditors was liable to be long overdue. Edmund Ravens of Wissington, Suffolk, a Stour Valley clothier, wrote in his letter of attorney of 14 August 1654 of interest unpaid by John Coolidge "from many years past." Massachusetts lenders could keep a closer eye on borrowers; to get overdue debts to New England "strangers" paid, however, a writ was often required. Large loans, such as the £52 borrowed by Roger Wellington in 1662, needed outside creditors, usually merchants, who alone could command such amounts of credit or cash.[2]

Lawsuits resulting from the administration of out-of-town estates also often involved indebtedness and unfulfilled contracts, sometimes of hoary antiquity. Thus, Michael Bairstow was sued in 1661 by Samuel Sprague of Malden for possession of a house belonging to the estate of John Crawford, dead for twenty-seven years. Town founder Charles Chadwick testified that "part of the land Michael Bairstow is now possessed of was a lot that Mr. Crawford was possessed of when he was living." In 1655 Sprague had married Rebecca Crawford, heiress of the Crawford home lot. He had sought possession for six years before finally resorting to law. Fortunately the Bairstows were childless, otherwise the house might have been a crucial part of planned inheritance. Nonetheless, news of the repossession must have shocked not only the Bairstows but their neighbors as well.[3]

Another of these exotic claimants was not so lucky. Mr. William Goddard, aged thirty-five, arrived in Watertown from London in 1665. He had power of attorney from his mother-in-law, Elizabeth Foote, a widow, to foreclose a mortgage of £100 advanced in 1647 to Ephraim Child, now deceased. Child had never paid a penny back, and Goddard soon discovered that there was little cash in the Child coffers. He therefore decided to settle on the mortgaged land, summoned his wife, and remained in Watertown for three decades. Having Child kinsmen in Watertown and undoubted title to the land, Goddard was able to convert from outsider to insider. In the minds of his new neighbors, this was a very significant leap.[4]

The thickest-skinned debtors must eventually settle up with local creditors whom they might bump into any day or who might start spreading reports of unreliability, ingratitude, and disrepute. Lenders from afar were a different matter. They could all too easily be shunted to the back of borrowers' minds. When, patience exhausted, the lenders sued, the cornered defendants might hope to share a certain sense of victimization and invasion with their neighbors.

Absentee landlords could be even more threatening and infuriating than absentee creditors. The most ominous threat from an absentee was posed by the Saltonstalls, who after a long battle received £40 compensation from the town—a small fortune in the 1640s, but getting rid of the repeated lawsuits was plainly thought worthwhile.[5] Another nonresident threatening the town's sense of inviolability was Mr. Richard Dummer, a wealthy land speculator from Newbury, who had acquired the five-hundred-acre Oldham Farm in 1648. Three times Dummer had to sue townsmen for illicit mowing and tree felling. In October 1659 he had to fight a town petition in the General Court against his claims. The town was warned against further opposition. In 1661 Dummer sold up, making a handsome killing.[6] Shakier claims from outsiders got much shorter shrift, like that of Sudbury's John Grout to a Watertown farm in 1671. His court action was successfully repelled.[7]

Ownership of the Watertown mill proved yet another bone of contention. Conflicts with nonresidents going back to 1641 culminated in 1676, when Judith, daughter of Hannah (Payne) Appleton, came of age and presented her claim at the entrance to the mill: "I do here demand of you, Caleb Church [miller], herein possession of Mr. Payne's right, £400 given me by my grandfather's will." In the absence of £400, the mill was seized by the county marshal. For four-fifths of our period, the most important mechanical plant in Watertown was owned by outsiders. Three claims for possession by residents had been thwarted in the courts in 1641/44, in 1662, and in 1676. Their opponents were among the wealthiest merchants in the colony. Such uneven confrontations would drive home the comparative powerlessness of mere husbandmen.[8]

Most antisocial behavior and petty crime within Watertown was the work of restless, frustrated, or badly raised adolescents. Some of the worst culprits were servants from out of town who not only pilfered and idled, cursed and fought, but also ran away and got themselves locked up. Their presence was a divisive irritant, but their very foreignness and impermanence eased the trouble they caused.[9]

A few adult members of the town disturbed its peace. Some were overfond of the bottle: Christopher Grant, with four convictions, plus John White, James Knapp, and William Hammond, who was set in the bilboes to cool his head. Booze exacerbated the Boylston's marital problems and helped pull George Dill and Henry Bright Sr. down into pauperism. One or two miscreants were prone to violence of fists or tongue: John Knapp, John Whittaker, Joseph Wellington, and Jacob Bullard. Overofficious constables or hogreeves could also excite angry reactions. On the whole, though, adult inhabitants seem to have respected their neighbors' property and peace.

Certain outsiders, however, felt untouched by such communal obligations. Watertown's "foreign" herdsman in the 1650s betrayed "thievish and unneighbourly ways." Joseph Garfield saw "Solomon Johnson [of Sudbury] go through his [own] orchard to Henry Curtis's orchard with a drove or company of hogs following after him, and he took a pole about ten or twelve feet long and went about the apple trees and throwed down the apples to the hogs." A search revealed stolen stock (a pig, a horse) and goods: shirts, gloves, hay, and firewood. Living out on the borders between the two towns, Johnson was literally a frontiersman who seemed to think himself beyond the law.[10]

When, in the late winter of 1669, the house of recently married Hannah and John Livermore Jr. was "broke ope" and they lost winter clothing, cloth, furnishings, accessories, pewter, spoons, scissors, and a loaf of bread, hobo-peddler William Drake was a prime suspect. Not only was his lifestyle shiftless, but his manner was shifty. Ten eagle-eyed witnesses ensured his (third, and therefore capital) conviction.[11]

Suspicion of outsiders activated millwright Caleb Church in 1680. "Having [had] taken from me a pair of sheets and two shirts and half a bushel of Indian meal, and hearing that there were several men gone up newly to Groton, I got a special warrant, hired a man to go with me, and went after them . . . When we came to 'Grawton' we saw Samuel Church's horse at a man's door . . . and sent in Peleg Lawrence on purpose to discover any bulk about Samuel Church, and then [Caleb Church] went in to call out [accuse] Samuel Church . . . Samuel said he found a bundle as he came by." When Caleb itemized his losses, "Samuel immediately drew them out of his bag along with a woman's cloak. He said he found them wrapped up in that cloak at a slew near Dr. Read's." Despite his attempts at plausibility, Samuel was convicted. He was sentenced to threefold restoration of the goods.[12]

Stealing was rare *within* the Watertown community. It was recognized as doubly harmful in a culture of scarcity: it poisoned trust, and it deprived, even endangered, the victim. Thieves were typically marginal: servants, Indians, disreputable youths, "frontiersmen," and outsiders. Their capture and conviction was an assertion of community vigilance and values, a collaborative restoration of good faith.

Freed from communal inhibitions when they traveled in adjacent towns, Watertown men occasionally let their hair down. In April 1677 Cambridge's constable Peter Towne, enforcing the customary curfew, went "to the ordinary [pub] after nine to close the house; Timothy Hawkins of Watertown and others, then present, were bidden to be gone. They said they would when they had drunk their drink. [They dawdled. Constable Towne] charging them several times to be gone, Timothy Hawkins said he would stay till he had drunk up his drink though all the country come. The constable told him to tarry no longer, but Hawkins in a contemptuous manner took the cup and threw it behind the table and throwing the drink out of the pitcher, he threw it upon the ground and kicked it against the wall. The constable departed to fetch his staff, but when he returned they had gone." Despite a difficult upbringing and some adolescent indiscretions, the thirty-seven-year-old Hawkins had behaved himself acceptably as an adult within Watertown bounds. Just as people in the town felt they must show more goodwill toward their neighbors than to strangers, so cocking a snook at "foreign" authority was more personally excusable.[13]

Reinforcement, or the setting off of outsiders from the body of a community, strengthens the sense of similarities and cohesion of the in-group. Besides Indian scapegoats, blacks and "ethnics" were another set of others. In his will Ellis Barron left his wife "the negro man-servant, and desire her to have a care of him that he may suffer no wrong." Regional differences may have hastened some departures in the 1630s and 1640s. Dislike of Celts crossed the Atlantic undiluted. George Robinson was derided as a "Welsh dog," and Henry Mattack's Welshness may have prompted his desertion. The shadowy and unfortunate Hugh Parsons was another fellow countryman. Scots got short shrift in Watertown, for they were exploited and expelled. Such unfavoring contrasts of outsiders helped the self-righteous process of "gathering-in."[14]

Communal welding held strong in intertown stock disputes. Town witnesses lined up like rival football teams. Elderly deponents had diametrically opposite recollections about historic bounds. Neighbors heroically defended their side's claims about ownership, damage, fencing, value, and responsibility. Breaking the ranks was almost unheard of, particularly in disputes between Watertown and Cambridge. Even Christopher Grant could count on full support from Watertown witnesses against a Cambridge man. The town boards might address each other as "loving brethren and friends," but this was far from the mood on the front line. Cambridge had built a mile-long dry-stone boundary wall, but this failed to prevent flanking engagements.[15]

Reinforcement came into play when Watertowners had to deal with "strangers" and "foreigners." Suspicious parochialism and preference for the devil you knew were cornerstones of group togetherness.

Hanging together did not depend entirely on negative reinforcement. The community also benefited from various active agencies of conciliation and reintegration. Church members were required by the minister and deacons to be at peace with one another, with their "brethren" and "sisters." This was a prerequisite of taking Communion, which "affirmed the collective unity of a [godly] society." There was particular outrage when a member took the opportunity to commit fornication when fellow saints were at the Lord's Supper. Among nonmembers, the selectmen often sought to lower flaring tempers, defuse crises, and find compromises. Captain Hugh Mason wrote a "few lines for caution [since] men's spirits are in such paroxysms." Sometimes, arbiters were appointed to settle controversies. Neighbors acted as go-betweens and conciliators.[16]

Confession or apology leading to reintegration were important strategies employed within the church to wipe the slate clean. Though the fulsome penitence of some energetic sinners strains credulity, it nonetheless earned them absolution. Without it, they lost their church privileges, especially the invaluable right of having their children baptized. Expressions of sorrow, the more craven and groveling the better, also accompanied the petitions of nonfreemen for remission of punishments in the courts. For some, this may have been a cynical exercise in damage limitation, but the ritual of apology and forgiving was an important prerequisite to official and communal forgetting. For those convicted of stealing, the triple recompensing of victims had a similar reconciliatory intention for both parties.[17]

The people of Watertown were relentlessly monitored. An impressive or oppressive array of fellow townspeople was always keeping an eye on their neighbors' behavior. Selectmen, deacons, constables, fenceviewers, hogreeves, appraisers, and commissioners for small causes all had formal supervisory responsibilities. Various crises prompted closer inspections of households, first by pairs of selectmen and then, in 1678, by tithingmen. By night the watch patrolled Watertown, and as Phoebe Page found out, they had a way of appearing at just the wrong moment. Informally, neighbors relished the duty of "holy watchfulness." They were in and out of each other's houses, patrolling the lanes and footpaths, eagle-eyed for sin. Compared to modern urban society, it was not easy to commit criminal or antisocial acts, and it was well-nigh impossible to escape detection—a powerful deterrent.[18]

The disastrous suit of Phoebe Page against the slander that she was pregnant suggests the conformist power of gossip and rumor. Phoebe was not pregnant, but she soon discovered the depths of village disapproval at her misbehavior. Libels could also be preventive shots against presumptuous bows. Fear of losing reputation by spread of scandal or ridicule powerfully buttressed resistance to temptation.[19]

In extreme cases there was the ultimate sanction of removing a persistent source of friction. The Whittaker family, magnets for mayhem, sold up and moved to Billerica in 1678. Even such tough-hided and self-righteous troublemakers finally got the town's message. Similar squeezing out was used on others. New settlements like Groton and Lancaster provided valuable safety valves for misfits. No one in authority would have put any hurdles in the way of such departures. Once they were gone, those remaining could not only breathe a collective sigh of relief but also prevent return by warning-out procedures.[20]

Conflict in Watertown was real enough, but it should not be exaggerated. Besides the hostilities, we have also noted acts of touching altruism—care of the sick, poor, and disabled, sons ensuring their widowed mothers' welfare, aged parents' gratitude for children's nurturance, and gifts from elders to endow new households. Some left bequests to poor neighbors or to the church and the ministry. Sellers showed a readiness to lower prices to preempt buyers' feelings of injustice. There was an element of calculation involved in all this kindliness. This was a culture of interdependence and reciprocity. The curse "I'll get even with you" had the positive opposite of "being even" with neighbors, paid up and all square. Giving a little more than necessary when you could afford it would elicit similar generosity when you were in need. "Do as you would be done by" and "Love thy neighbor as thyself" were ancient and effective maxims.[21]

Yet, despite plenty of goodwill and goodness, despite extrusion of the unassimilable, irritants and discords remained in the little island of Watertown. I call the town an island because of the intense local circumscription of life there. Watertown cases in the court records are immediately recognizable from the names of witnesses. It is most unusual to see outside names among them or for Watertown people to be involved in external cases. After the 1640s few townsmen were involved in colony-wide activities, few incomers arrived, and the population turned in on itself. Though the town straddled a major path westward, we read of relatively few passers-by. There was none of the mingling bustle of ports like Boston, Charlestown, and Ipswich, or of the court and college town of Cambridge.[22]

One vital strategy remained in this "isolated" community for securing peace and a unity of purpose: a communal restraint, a collective sublimation, a group counting to ten. Cases reflect a reluctance to pressure neighbors, a painstaking patience, a suppression of irritation. Debts went uncollected for years, as many inventories demonstrate. Witnesses relate accounts of events long past, minor infractions or serious suspicions, which may have been gossiped about but went no further. Speakers employed elaborate circumlocutions: "I could not say but that I might." All this holding back and turning of blind eyes in a settlement surrounded by "wilderness" finds echoes in another, twentieth-century island, as described by David Guterson. The narrator's father, founder-editor of the first local newspaper, had

> been, at best, an anguished editorialist; he was incapable of fully indulging himself when it came to condemnation. For he'd recognized limits and the grayness of the world, which is what endeared him to island life, limited as it was by surrounding waters, which imposed upon islanders certain duties and conditions foreign to mainlanders. An enemy on an island is an enemy forever, he'd been fond of reminding his son. There was no blending into an anonymous background, no neighbouring society to shift toward. Islanders were required, by the very nature of their landscape, to watch their step moment by moment. No one trod easily upon the emotions of another where the sea licked everywhere against the endless shoreline. And this was excellent and poor at the same time—excellent because it meant most people took care, poor because it meant an inbreeding of the spirit, too much held in, regret and silent brooding, a world whose inhabitants walked in trepidation, in fear of opening up. Considered and considerate, formal at every turn, they were shut out and off from the deep interplay of their minds. They could not speak freely because they were cornered: everywhere they turned there was water and more water, a limitless expanse of it

in which to drown. They held their breath and walked with care, and this made them who they were inside, constricted and small, good neighbours.²³

Reserve, control, self-restraint, "brotherly forbearance," "the quiet man," "a bridled tongue," and "a web of silence and collusion" all derive from the necessity of sublimating personal needs to the greater good of a well-ordered community. Allied to fear of potential danger and suspicion of outsiders, such imposed self-denial created a powerful antidote to atomizing conflict.²⁴

CONCLUSION

Continuity and Change, Decline and Discord

In this account, I have ranged over many areas of activity during the first fifty years of Watertown's existence: its peopling and settlement; its multiplying and outmigrations; its political, religious, economic, and domestic conflicts; its relations with the Native Americans, with its neighbors, and with central authority; its lands, crafts, assets, and welfare. In this journey, we have encountered many remarkable characters, rich and poor, young and old, male and female; we have seen them playing many different roles: parent and child, employer and servant, landowner and tenant, debtor and creditor, buyer and seller. For uncovering the intimacies of these people, their relationships and their personal family and community affairs, we have to thank the survival of a remarkable range of records.

Two major themes have run through *Divided We Stand:* the interchanges between continuity and change, and those between conflict and community. Here I draw some general conclusions from particular findings.

Moving from the Stour Valley, the Wiltshire Downs, the Yorkshire Dales, or the teeming streets of London to the north bank of the Charles River in the 1630s was bound to involve traumatic changes, if only of having to cope with widely differing English regional traditions. How could John Warren from Suffolk actually understand the broad Yorkshire accent of Michael Bairstow, the Sussex twang of the Benjamins, or the West-Country burr of Thomas Mayhew, let alone accommodate to their varied ways of doing things? For some, adaptation proved impossible.[1]

Then there was the unprecedented challenge of surviving in what they thought of as a wilderness, among dangerous "savages," in a climate of lethal extremes when they were weakened by weeks at sea preceded by months of anxious packing, selling up, and farewells. Nothing in their English lives could have prepared them for the shock of the new.

In four areas in particular, we have seen revolutionary change. The nature of *landholding* in the new world was unprecedented. In England ownership of land by every householder was restricted to the dreams of utopians. Having as much land to play with as they did in Watertown, enough in many cases for the next two generations, was a total overturning of all they had had to live with in England.

Religion was also revolutionized. From existing as illicit, subversive, suspect cells on the margins of the state church in England, the godly found that they were now the establishment. From its earliest days, the church in Watertown was a microcosm of debates, discussions, hostilities, and ruptures that distracted and disturbed the whole New England region. The two novel issues of exclusive membership and infant baptism rocked the town for its first three decades.[2] Equally novel was the sloughing off of the constricting skin of church hierarchy, tradition, and discipline. The power this ecclesiological revolution conveyed to individual churches was completely unknown in the Church of England. So was the opportunity for purity among the gathered saints and the unfettered imposition of a reformation of manners. All of this was change with a vengeance.[3]

There was a matching change in *politics* too. The adaptation of a company charter to a colonial constitution produced such radical innovations as elected governors and magistrates, widened franchise, and stricter political accountability. The absence of royal court, officials, judges, and an aristocracy, even a greater gentry, meant that leadership carried less "natural" authority than it did in England. Those given power in Massachusetts Bay had been small fry and minnows in the old-country pond, and their fellow settlers knew it.[4]

After Saltonstall's early departure, Watertown did not even have a resident magistrate. This lack made the practice of local politics yet more egalitarian and factional. There was a cadre of town leaders, qualified by experience, expertise, wealth, and popularity, but if popularity waned, they could be quickly replaced. There was no figure in seventeenth-century Watertown like the English squire. Major Gookin might claim that he kept a better man than the Watertown Grants to wipe his shoes, but he soon found himself sued for slander. A sense of hierarchy did persist in Watertown, but the social ladder was far shorter, and deference had to be earned.[5]

The fourth area of innovation lay in the *labor market*. Two black slaves worked in the town in the 1670s, but the names of servants are the most fleeting and untraceable. The only certainty is that there were never enough. Unlike England, with its hordes of day laborers, servants in husbandry, and serving maids, good hands were hard to find in New England. With opportunities for high wages, low rents, or outmigration, few young men or women with any ambition or initiative were likely to spend their lives working for others.

Labor was therefore likely to be supplied by the young—by children (expected to be able "to earn their own livings") or premarital adolescents, either for their own family firm or "put out" by a poor family to a wealthier one needing more hands. Neighbors did chores to repay debts, to help the incapacitated, or to build up some savings. The general shortage of help meant that farms tended to be family businesses with greater equality of holdings than was the case in much of England. There were indeed wealthier and poorer families, but there were no landed magnates in early Watertown, and no permanent day laborers.

These were revolutionary changes enough for any community to come to terms with, without dwelling on the rapid acceleration of population or the presence of a potentially threatening indigenous population or the vast amount of "waste" to be "improved." In their very coping, however, there were all kinds of traditional rituals and procedures that would preserve a balancing sense of continuity and conservation.

English speech patterns, as frequently quoted in preceding chapters, do not appear to have altered noticeably by 1680, and pronunciation—if spelling (fairly phonetic) is anything to go by—seems similarly unchanged. It must have been reassuring to hear Groton still spoken in the old Suffolk way as "Grawton," rather than the clipped "Grotton" of modern New England speech. Cursing retained its old English patterns, and defamations—the well-worn "rogue" and "whore," "cheat" and "thief"—kept to the tried and often untrue. Though literacy increased and the quality of handwriting and spelling improved enormously during the 1660s, there is little evidence that these advances had the revolutionary or radical effects on consciousness sometimes ascribed to them.[6]

Many English customs and folk beliefs were imported into the new settlement. The annual beating of the bounds—particularly important where boundaries were so new and liable to overgrowth or dispute—was one such communal act, of territoriality and claiming. Old-world beliefs in witchcraft, magic, and prediction throve in the new. English shaming punishments were performed for similar offenses (often sexual) in the meetinghouse in Watertown. Calling of ministers, exclusive church membership, reformation of manners, and church and town covenants were all foreshadowed in puritan experiments along the Stour Valley.[7]

Though for many saints attendance at the Thursday lecture and two long services on "the first day" reflected their English zeal and Sabbatarianism, and the suppression of "pagan" festivals like Christmas signaled long-sought purification, less fanatical spirits continued the traditional cult of "merriment," feasting, and drinking. The alehouse's aura did not vanish in the new world, nor did sociable drinking at funerals and at work.[8]

Village gossip was a time-honored weapon for ordinary people to enforce communal morals. Nor was a talent for discord a New England invention. East Anglia was notorious for its obstinacy, and ritual riotousness was commonplace in Jacobean London. To be a puritan entailed a discordant urge for social criticism, moral aggressiveness, and religious obduracy. Even a three-thousand-mile voyage does not seem to have permanently broadened most Watertown people's horizons from the intense localism and xenophobia of English village life. There is evidence of outside contacts for a few townsmen, far-flung for a handful. By and large, though, the bounds they helped to beat each year were the bounds of most of their lives.[9]

All kinds of familiar English economic and employment practices were also instituted. The townsman responsible for standard weights and measures was called the clerk of the market, as in Norwich or Colchester. Quality control was maintained by the traditional "sealers of leather." Complaints about workmanship prompted the customary solution of an exclusive "company" of coopers or shoemakers. The nurturing of home industries followed well-worn lines: banning the export of unfinished materials and bounties for new products. Agrarian customs emigrated: the impounding of stray cattle, the practices of commoners' rights, and determining grazing stints for cattle. Proprietorship in Watertown's land was not dissimilar from English town or manorial membership. Training craftspeople, preventing oversupply, and maintaining standards were achieved in the time-honored way by apprenticeships. Despite inevitable adaptations to new materials and ecologies, habitual ways of doing things on the farm, the workshop, and the kitchen, building, processing, and preserving, were used wherever possible. The agricultural environment was inexorably anglicized, especially through the adoption of English grasses, grains, and fruits.[10]

Parish institutions and procedures were often transplanted. The Watertown constable, complete with his staff, had a range of law-enforcement and tax-collecting duties, many of which originated in the English Middle Ages. Imported group responsibilities included the hue and cry, watch and ward, and work on the "highways." The founding and funding of the school was a natural continuity from the most literate and educationally blessed areas of the old country. Watertown deacons could have swapped experiences with English parish overseers of the poor, like differentiating between genuine sufferers and indolent rogues. Similarly, the system of "settlement," of "warning out," and of preventing local liability for welfare were all familiar procedures from home, as were the floggings of miscreants from parish to parish employed against the Quaker missionaries in the late 1650s and early 1660s.[11]

The whole militia organization with its training days, hierarchy, colors and drum, and responsibility for personal arms and service and for local ammunition was the direct descendant of the English trained bands. The 1640s saw colonial moves to found elite companies modeled on the London Honourable Artillery Company. In times of threat or war, Watertown experienced English-style drafting or the impressment of horses, carts, or forage by the military authorities.[12]

Although attempts were made at radical innovations in the law, like the introduction of biblical penalties for certain crimes and the discouragement of lawyers, many such efforts failed to "take" after initial enthusiasm waned. The procedures of the courts and legal practice settled back into a predominantly English pattern. The grand and petty jurymen nominated by towns performed identical functions as at quarter sessions; Middlesex magistrates could have easily transferred their expertise back to old Suffolk or Essex. Worshipful members of the bench were accorded traditional respect for office. Writs, attachments, recognizances, deeds, leases, mortgages, and many other legal documents were based on English models. The county courts took over much of the business of the archdeacons' courts in England, but they also retained the plethora of administrative duties heaped on them during the last century back home. One such transfer was oversight of probate business. Here centuries-old conventions like the widow's thirds and the double portion for the eldest son were observed. Testamentary customs like borough-English, where the youngest son cared for aged parents in exchange for the family homelot and dwelling, were continued too, as were land-for-care agreements between parents and children.[13]

Perhaps the strongest force for continuity and conservation was the sheer longevity of so many early settlers. Two-thirds of the 1630s planters who survived the decade and did not move lived in Watertown for at least twenty years; one-third were still around in the 1670s. This residential stability represented a living bridge back to the old world. Many leading families remained in the town over many generations into the nineteenth century.[14]

It is impossible and unrewarding to compute a balance between transatlantic continuity and new-world change. While emigration entailed some radical alterations in people's lives, there were significant retentions and imperceptible adaptations of old ways and beliefs to prevent a sense of total revolution. Their world had turned, but it had not turned upside down.

Watertown was a constantly developing culture throughout our period. Cultural conservatism could not mask the fact that this was a *new* creation. It was bound to suffer from social simplification in its unfamiliar environment, with its absences of association of place and its comparatively thin networks of kin and neighbors. The reassuring power of authentic local custom would take time to regenerate. The precipitous soaring and plunging of the frontier economy, unnerving even to people who had experienced England's instability, quickly destroyed expectations of a static social order envisaged by Winthrop's "Model of Christian Charity." The gradual realization of radical differences from old-world conditions produced long-term ripple effects. For example, extensive land ownership would tend to decelerate agricultural innovation and experiment necessary in intensive regimes. The fact that the minister was entirely beholden to the town rather than a patron, that he depended for ordination on a church's call rather than a bishop's bestowal, and that he lacked the tenure of a parson's freehold would all affect relations with the laity. Such unintended outcomes had to be painfully incorporated into new ways of thinking.[15]

A significant number of cultural developments can be grouped under the heading of growing individualism: greater emphasis on privacy and on display and consumption, the dispersal of aggregated farms, unregulated bargaining and exchange, involvement in the land market, and familial herding arrangements. Some traditional institutions did not "take" in the new world. After the 1640s we hear little of guilds (or companies), fairs, clerks of the market, or searchers and sealers of leather. None of these erosions amounts to a "market revolution," but they were essential prerequisites. The rising incidence of youthful sociability and recorded sexual misdemeanors during the 1660s and 1670s may represent adolescent striving for greater personal independence and an ebbing of parental control. Plummeting freemanship during the 1660s and 1670s could reflect withdrawal from church and community involvement. These developments were slow and barely perceptible, a modest reduction rather than a breakdown of community values.[16]

The most striking change in Watertown is the move from its early importance and aspiration to the settled state of the 1650s and beyond. At its foundation Watertown was on a par with Boston and Charlestown in the numbers and wealth of its population, the presence of a leading investor and assistant, the size and leadership of its church, and the diversity of skills and origins of its settlers. Particularly promising for the future was the presence of several merchants with capital to invest, a young minister with excellent credentials along with a ruling elder experienced in voluntary gathered churches, and what appeared to be a fine location just below the first falls on the Charles with a vast expanse of well-watered, varied land astride a major westward trail. In the first valuations for colonial levies, Watertown's contribution was equal to Boston's and greater than any other town's. Bond, somewhat boosterishly, claims that "for the first four years Watertown was the most populous town in the colony, and it is not improbable that it continued so for fifteen or twenty years." He quotes Edward Johnson's 1651 description of Watertown as "this great town." Yet, even by 1645 Watertown's rating had slipped to seventh place, behind Boston, Cambridge, Charlestown, Salem, Ipswich, and Dorchester. By October 1675 its £45 war tax was barely a seventh of Boston's £300; three years later Watertown's contribution to the brick building at Harvard College was the same fraction of Charlestown's.[17]

Whereas several of Watertown's early leaders like Saltonstall, Mayhew, Jennison, Feake, Oldham, Brown, and Pendleton were active in commercial enterprise and colony affairs and well known beyond the town bounds during the 1630s, by the 1670s only Mason, Sherman, and Beers appear in the *Massachusetts Bay Records,* the last two mainly as surveyors.

The townsmen of the 1670s appear parochial and petty, engaged in quarrels about the town bull or herding arrangements. Though the citizens lived in greater comfort, the average appraised value of probate inventories showed a decline from the 1650s and 1660s, reflecting economic stagnation. The town's ministers never seemed to realize their potential; good pastors maybe, but not voices to be listened to across the colony, not Shepards or Cottons or Mathers. Watertown, frequently in the headlines in the 1630s and 1640s, is barely mentioned in colony records or archives after 1660. Its citizens did not address the General Court on important issues as did those of other towns. Even its religious concerns were deflated from the grand issues of belief and doctrine to seating plans, ministerial pay, and meetinghouse discipline.[18]

What had gone wrong? Why had horizons narrowed, ambitions shrunk? Several factors contributed to Watertown's decline. The town's position did not prove favorable to trade. The oyster banks at Cambridge blocked ocean-going shipping; the falls were too close to the river mouth to offer entrepôt-portage opportunities, as at Hartford or Albany. Boston and Charlestown would become the Charles River ports. The amount of overland traffic on the route westward was insufficient to boost the town; it was, anyway, too close to the end or the start of the trail to act as a staging post. It is doubtful whether there was even a town inn during the last twenty years of our period. Sooner or later, merchants and entrepreneurs moved away. By 1650 Boston had become the major commercial and administrative center. It acted as a magnet to any specialists. Watertown's few Harvard graduates were not tempted to return.[19]

The other economic disappointment in Watertown was its lack of meadow, so vital for forage for overwintering cattle. There were plenty of moistlands in the township where lush grasses could be grown and hay crops mowed, but they came in patches, many of them "remote" at the far western end of the grant and scattered in the woods. It was not long before ambitious spirits began exploration in search of larger, more concentrated tracts. Their finds drained off enterprising planters in the first decade of settlement. As the Watertown herd grew, pressures on pasture and meadowland increased, leading to the herding squabbles of the 1660s and 1670s and to the steady but expensive purchase of additional hay-land in Rocky Meadow within Cambridge bounds.[20]

The loss of its founding magistrate and the low-key parochialism of its ministers helped deprive Watertown of the opportunity of becoming the seat of the college and the press, and later the county town of Middlesex. Its neighbor Newtown, founded two years later, scooped these honors, which gave it the edge as an administrative, intellectual, and religious center. It was to Cambridge that the key colony elections were resited during the antinomian crisis; it was the Cambridge, not the Watertown, Platform that set the course for mature Massachusetts congregationalism; Cambridge was where the Middlesex Regiment held its training days; to Cambridge or Charlestown went a gaggle of officials and citizens with business at the county court or for summary justice before a magistrate. If some colonial crisis necessitated a conference of church elders, it was to Cambridge or Boston that Phillips or Sherman must go.[21]

Watertown thus became, in the oft-quoted words of Edward Johnson, "a plantation for husbandmen principally." It did have its mill and its bridge over the Charles. It became an important center for the leather industry, with three tanners working in the town. It also supported a considerable textile production and boasted a fulling mill after 1662. Its militiamen distinguished themselves during King Phillip's War and paid heavily for their involvement. Their young men thereafter had a reputation for independence and assertiveness. Yet Watertown was essentially a farming community, like so many other New England townships, with most of its households earning a "competency," a few acquiring moderate riches, and a few sinking into penury. The spread of probate valuations held pretty steady from 1660 to 1689, with about three-quarters leaving estates of less than £300, and only a fifth under £100. No one in Watertown enjoyed the kind of wealth accumulated by leading Boston merchants. Not until the 1690s was an inhabitant considered worthy of election to the magistracy. There had never been more than the slightest opportunity that Watertown could maintain a leading position among New England towns. Its failure to rival Cambridge or Charlestown is therefore not all that surprising. One Watertown speciality may have sealed its fate, and that was conflict.[22]

Discord has provided the leitmotif for most of the chapters of this book. The town founders had barely unpacked their sea chests before they fell to arguing about religious issues: the requisite purity of the church, the extent of depravity of Roman Catholicism, the precise organization of congregationalism, and the theology of ordination. Disputes soon spread to other issues, including the allocation of land, the nature of baptism, discrimination against nonchurch members, and the payment of taxes and financial support of the ministry. So intense were these confrontations that wider controversies—over antinomianism, for instance—seem to have passed by Watertown and its embattled pastor. When Cambridge's minister, Thomas Shepard, came to write his preface to George Phillips's nit-picking counterblast to a nit-picking attack, his first words to the reader were: "Satan's Masterpiece and greatest work in the Kingdom of Christ is at this day . . . to divide and sow tares of discord between man and man." Many in Watertown might have said Amen to that, but disputes went on.[23]

There were further storms over land, rumbling on into the 1660s with regular lightning strikes. The causes were various—jealousies between inhabitants and proprietors, resentment at preferential treatment for others, inadequate surveying—but the intensity of feeling was uniformly highly charged. The town leadership was at least three times unceremoniously dumped by irate townsmen. There were other divisions about siting the church, about support for the minister, between craftsmen and farmers about taxes. There were perennial crises about livestock. Support of the school and the schoolmaster prompted a major row at the end of the 1670s.

Throughout Watertown's first fifty years, furthermore, beneath the inevitable stresses and strains of household, communal, and farming life, there throbbed, like the persistent beat of the bass, regular spats between neighbors, often over stock and fences, but also involving personal rivalries and envies, long-nursed grievances, dark suspicions, generational jealousies, and family feuds. Occasionally the townsmen would unite to thwart some external threat, such as Native American weir-seekers, Sudbury graziers, Saltonstall landclaims, or Cambridge cattle-filchers. The general impression conveyed by the surviving records, though, is that, among themselves, most inhabitants followed the old, ornery East Anglian maxim, to "do different."

Three questions arise from this apparent pattern. Did discord hasten decline? Was Watertown unusual? Are conflict and its effects exaggerated?

I have pointed to some damaging effects of discord. Religious disputes did blight the pastorate of George Phillips and may even have helped cause his early death. Several of his major antagonists left Watertown. The most serious loss was of Nathaniel Biscoe, wealthy, influential, a potential town leader. John Prescott, later an effective developer of Lancaster, was also driven out. A suspicious number of people held office much less often than their early elections might have predicted. Some may have proved ineffectual; others may have begrudged the time and energy required. Several, however, were probably victims of town rivalries, which was another sad loss. We cannot plumb the extent to which other townspeople moved away because of enmities or the discordant atmosphere, nor the ill effects of Watertown's reputation for conflict over colony policy. We can safely conclude that being a byword for belligerence did Watertown no good.

But was Watertown alone? Bailyn's examples, quoted in the introduction, make his case forcefully enough, but they are only the tip of the iceberg. The row in Hingham over the election of militia officers became a colonial cause célèbre in the 1640s. The dissidents from Sudbury soon created a Marborough mare's nest. The initial settlements of Groton and Lancaster were both delayed by disputes. Hampton quickly split into two camps centered on its two warring ministers. Early Gloucester and Marblehead were "riven with conflicts." Watertown's pastor was one of a group summoned to pacify the church of Woburn during the 1660s and was consulted about the fearsome standoff in Boston's First Church. Capt. Hugh Mason was nominated conciliator for both Salem and Salisbury in the 1670s, when Newbury church also faced renewed conflict. Malden was a town of equally poisonous antagonisms, which brought its minister, Michael Wigglesworth, close to despair. Islanders on Martha's Vineyard petitioned bitterly against the autocratic usurpation of power by Thomas Mayhew. The 16 May 1670 return of a committee appointed by the General Court to inquire into "the causes of the Lord's anger . . . against us" started its list of provocations with "contentions, unbrotherly distances" and continued with "jealousies, whisperings, back-bitings, slanderings." For much of the 1670s Watertown's deputies represented the town under the dark clouds of a three-way conflict involving the colony's elders, the magistrates, and the deputies. Much legislation was sabotaged by this feud. The report about Mendham on 9 June 1671 might have been written about Watertown and several of its neighbors: "The inhabitants . . . labour under some disquiet in the managing of the prudentials of the place, whereby their welfare is greatly impeded and many other inconveniences do occur inevitably threatening the ruin of the place." Shepard's Satan seemed to be having a field day.[24]

Watertown had no monopoly of discord. Conflict was widespread, though not universal or permanent. Some of Watertown's neighbors were relatively peaceful: Cambridge, Roxbury, Dedham, even bustling Charlestown. Disagreement over one topic need not spill over to disturb others: the Half-Way Covenant controversy did not directly affect nonmembers, for instance, and need not intrude on the economic or civic affairs of a town. In Watertown's case, the impression conveyed by the records is that the heated disputes of the 1630s and 1640s cooled off during the 1650s, especially after the General Court arbitration over land. There were subsequent disagreements, but the anger and aggression seems much reduced, and various procedures for conflict resolution and compromise were effectively employed. Their living "scatteringly" and "not compacted" may have helped reduce friction. It would be a community of angels that did not have disagreements (and even the angels had to be purged of dissident elements!). In an economy so vulnerable, opinions on difficult issues were bound to be strongly held and forcefully voiced. Factional conflict about town policy—the siting of the meetinghouse, for instance, or the future of the school—were of a different order to disputes between neighbors, which were and always have been a fact of life in farming societies.[25]

In living, working communities, disagreements, arguments, differences of opinion, and clashes of interest are inevitable. Indeed, they are signs of genuine communal vitality. In times of stress, of sudden change, in the face of particular individuals or households, these differences may blow up into hostilities, outraged accusations, bitter recriminations, explosions of violence, or longer-running feuds where one household will not acknowledge another. Yet these alarms are not necessarily signs of social dysfunction or communal breakdown. They merely confirm that no group of people in normal circumstances can get along the whole time.[26]

The yardstick of social order and vitality is not the amount or intensity of conflict, which may well reflect the sense of commitment and deep involvement in a community's life and future. The real tests involve the will and the ability of inhabitants to solve these problems, the preparedness to compromise, to conciliate, to arbitrate and show restraint, to recognize a communal "general will" over the selfish and anarchic "will of all." Active, accountable, sensitive, prudential leadership can make the process smoother. Christian altruism and neighborly caring can absorb some social shocks, as can a sense of responsibility to the group and simple acts of sympathy and thoughtfulness. These lubricants rarely enjoy the acknowledgment they deserve, except in wills or gifts of gratitude.

The ultimate tests are whether people stayed together and whether there was an overarching consensus. In genuinely dysfunctional communities, families or groups are so alienated that they withdraw, either physically or emotionally. This happened in Sudbury, in Boston's First Church, and in the founding of Hadley by dissident Hartfordians. There was outmigration from Watertown, but it mainly involved members of the younger generation in search of more land or opportunity, rather than group rejection and division. One of the most striking characteristics of Watertown in its first fifty years—indeed of its first two hundred and fifty years—was its residential stability. Individual family members might leave, but family names persisted. The early kinship networks thickened and strengthened through endogamous marriages. Despite discord, there was underlying consensus. It manifested itself in a pulling together against external threats. It was there in "the mind of the town" or "it is agreed" at town meetings. It was evident in the year-by-year voting of stipends for minister, schoolmaster, and verger. It was there in the readiness of a large range of people to serve the town in myriad capacities. It was there in the organized care of the vulnerable, in group herding, in common fields, in watching and warding, and in militia training days. Three times each week consensus was restated with the shared rituals, the carefully graded precedences, and the self-imposed order of the meetinghouse. Their "accommodation of divergent interests" depended on a Christian and organic philosophy of cooperation and neighborliness cemented by kinship, friendship, and church membership. Over much they quarreled. Deep assumptions they shared. They shared enough to stay. Divided they stood.[27]

APPENDIX A
Case Studies

John Sawin Jr.: Horse Thief (1667)

In 1667 John Sawin was a "young beginner."[1] He needed every penny he could find. He had just married Judith Pearce, who was only seventeen. He had had to have a house built for them. He had to produce the rent for land he leased from Sgt. John Wincoll. People in Watertown and beyond became suspicious, however, when he began offering a colt for sale. When Henry Rice of Sudbury was "riding back from the Bay" (through Watertown, with his wife riding pillion), Sawin accosted him: "Corporal Rice, you asked me a while agone whether I would sell you one of them colts. Now I will sell you one . . . the biggest."[2]

John had a way with horses and was eager for work, which explains why John Clary hired him to go into the woods "looking for horsekind," any stray "jades," but particularly for a missing mare and colt of Clary's. Sawin returned from this mission with a mare and colt and soon began offering the colt for sale. He was a persuasive salesman: the colt was "gentle and handy, of good mettle; he had taught him to drink out of a pail." Prospective buyers naturally wanted to know the colt's provenance, and it was at this point that his stories began raising suspicions. Two contemporaries recounted that "when John Sawin was thrashing corn at Henry Curtis's barn, he told us that he had been in the woods after jades, and he bought a colt from a poor man who wanted corn, a young beginner like himself. He would sell it for forty shillings for he had bought him a good pennyworth." To another he reasserted that he "had bought the colt honestly . . . had shut him up in a hovel or houseyard . . . and the colt had broke out to the woods and fell in company with Goodman Treadway's mare, now Jones's mare." Sawin offered Samuel Church, another possible customer (currently accused of stealing broadcloth), to exchange the colt for a two-year-old heifer and £1 worth of corn. His wife and mother corroborated the fact that John had bought the colt, but their story was that he had bought him off John Clary in exchange for a day's labor and a fat shoat (i.e., young hog). This version was repeated by Sawin to another questioner. He told

Henry Rice and his wife: "He should pay John Brewer what he owed him towards building his house . . . the colt was out of Goodman Wilson's mare that drowned last June [1667]." Sawin asked only £1 of Rice.[3]

Sawin was getting desperate. When the skeptical Rice checked with Goodman Wilson, he discovered that he had been told a pack of lies. There had been no mare, no colt, no drowning. Meanwhile the colt's true owner got wind of the scam. John Child, aged thirty-two, and Daniel Warren, thirty, found Sawin in company with Ephraim Curtis at Henry Curtis's. They were "seeking a roan colt belonging to Sgt. Wincoll," whose affairs Child was managing, since Wincoll had moved to southern Maine. They asked, "Why does John Sawin go about to sell his landlord's colt, Goodman Wincoll's colt, unto Corporal Rice?" Sawin denied that he had ever done such a thing.[4]

Sawin went on denying when first examined by Captain Gookin, the magistrate in Cambridge. The net was tightening, however. Someone, probably Child, sent to Gookin's colleague Thomas Danforth two and a half pages of foolscap entitled "An Information of a suspicious piece of Knavery or suspected theft acted by John Sawin of Watertown," which gathered together damning evidence. Confronted with this document, Sawin confessed. Yet he managed to shuffle off his own responsibility. "God's providence is just, to let this case fall upon me unsought." The fact that "the witnesses do witness as they do" somehow neutralized his own sense of shame, and he simply prayed that "this unexpected blow of His to me" would be sanctified to the benefit of his soul. The words "sin" or "sorry" were conspicuously absent. Though the confession bears all the marks of a far more articulate phrase-maker than Sawin, he appears to have convinced himself that he had been misunderstood and that the various tales he had invented were true. The temptation to raise some much-needed income must have been powerful, especially when his landlord was far away to the east and plausible explanations were available. Unfortunately for Sawin, he did not stick to one story, and in this mistake lay his undoing.

At the April 1668 county court Sawin was found guilty of theft; he was probably required to pay triple damages as well as costs of court.[5] Although this case was not that unusual, it may have been the catalyst for two new laws. In May the General Court enacted the order proscribing promiscuous grazing and mating. Three months later the central authority proscribed "the stealing of horse-kind, and other neat cattle and selling them as their own."[6]

Whittaker (1660–1678)

Though disputes about fences and stray animals were a fact of life in seventeenth-century communities, they were usually brief and contained.[7] Occasionally, however, they escalated, thanks to long-running resentments and the volatile nature of one of the combatants. Such a human firework was John Whittaker.

Born about 1636, Whittaker first hit the headlines in Cambridge. In 1660 he had been courting Mary Linfield, an orphan in domestic service, for some months: "He gave her a silver bodkin and hath sat up with her and kept her company by night and by day [a possible reference to a modest kind of bundling, or "queesting"] sundry times." She loved him to distraction and considered herself betrothed, but his ardor cooled: "His affection for her is less than formerly." He had fallen for someone else, possibly Mary's sister Elizabeth. The Cambridge authorities, worried about Mary's future, hauled Whittaker before the local magistrate. After severe warnings, "he solemnly promises forthwith to take to his wife the said [Mary—the document has "Elizabeth"] and caused the publication of the said marriage to be affixed on the meetinghouse door." Then, on the day, "he refuseth to perform the contract." He disappeared from Cambridge and is next heard of a year later in neighboring Watertown's vital records: in March 1661 the first child of John and Elizabeth Whittaker was born. In April he was sued for breach of contract. Because "he had behaved toward Mary Linfield with much unfaithfulness and fraud," the enormous damages of £50 were awarded.[8]

The Whittakers thus began their turbulent married life in Watertown with suspicious reputations and heavy debts. During the next decade, 1661–71, five more children were born. In 1668 they began four year's paid employment, "dietting Old Thorpe," a neighboring widower. They not only received nearly £10 per year for this service but were also permitted to farm Thorpe's land. This mutually beneficial arrangement was a common means of mitigating the caregivers' extreme poverty: welfare as work. Even so, money was tight. Whittaker was sued for nonpayment of wages to a young laborer in 1670. Unfortunately Old Thorpe died in 1672, and his stepson appeared from Dedham and successfully claimed the farm. The Whittakers could harvest their crop but must then move.[9]

Their new home was part of Eyre's Farm, near the northern boundary of Watertown with Cambridge. They took a three-year lease at £8 per year in 1673 but were quickly embroiled with the former tenants, the Cheneries, who had neglected the land and removed timber. Whittaker was back and forth to court over this dispute, and over the case of the kidnapping of the town bull, normally pastured on the land of his new neighbor, Cpl. John Hammond. He got into a fistfight with a friend of the Cheneries, another scoundrel called William Price. Whittaker emerged from these proceedings with his reputation for fair dealing further sullied. He was plainly vindictive, provocative, inquisitive, acquisitive, and combative. By the end of 1674 the Chenery clan were his sworn enemies, but they, like him, were among the less affluent members of the community.[10]

Within a year, John Whittaker had become embroiled with an altogether more potent enemy: his neighbor and erstwhile supporter Cpl. John Hammond. Elizabeth Whittaker testified in April 1676 that back "in October 1675, Hammond struck her husband on his own land with a big stick, and threw her down and tread on her stomach and then laughed and jeered at her and bid her husband carry her home in a cart." This incident was corroborated by the Whittaker daughter Mary, who saw it happen near the dividing fence after Hammond had come home from Chelmsford. Why this violence? It seems that Hammond was merely responding to Whittaker's earlier challenge. According to Hammond's eighteen-year-old servant Sambo Negro:

> John Whittaker coming to my master to the barn as he was giving the horses meat and as he came he took a cudgel out of the hedge. He asked my master

"How do you do Goodman Hammond?" and my master replied "Never the better for you Goodman Whittaker. Why did you cart over my land without my leave and suffer your boy to drive my sheep from off my own pasture and put them upon my own rye?" To which Whittaker replied "You are a lying rogue and devilish rogue" with many railing expressions and bid him come out of the barn if he dare. My master coming out with hay for his cattle, Goodman Whittaker met him and struck at him with the cudgel and broke it [illegible]. My master said "Go home Goodman Whittaker and do not thus provoke my spirit" and so shuted him before him till he came out of the barn.

Abigail Hammond, also eighteen, added, "My father warded off the blow with his pitchfork staff, [and] as he went away Whittaker said to my father 'You devil you! I'll be revenged of you at one time or another.'"[11]

Fences and stock were at the root of this conflict. In December 1673 the Watertown selectmen had prosecuted Whittaker for "rescuing a parcel of sheep from the town officers." They had probably been pounded for straying on to Hammond's land. Whatever the reason, Capt. Hugh Mason, Watertown's leading citizen, was alarmed at Whittaker's volatility, especially after a March 1676 mortgage signaled his intention to stay at Eyre's Farm. He wrote warning the magistrates of "distempers in the spirits" of the neighbors and of "paroxysms" (whose spelling quite defeated him). He attempted conciliation. He might as well have saved his ink and his breath. Both parties went to law. Whittaker sued Hammond for "malicious striking and wounding." Hammond countersued for damage caused by Whittaker's cattle.[12]

Hammond was victorious in this April 1676 suit, but the feud continued. On 6 July 1677 Hammond and "divers neighbours" complained about Whittaker's insufficient fences and savage dogs. The selectmen trooped out to view the fences, concluded that Whittaker and Hammond were equally at fault, and issued a series of orders four days later. Both were to bring their fences up to town standards, Whittaker was to "forebear hunting other men's cattle and swine [with his dogs] at his peril and . . . forthwith to yoke and ring his hogs." If he failed to obey the fencing order, Hammond was to do the job for him and "have double pay for it" from Whittaker.[13]

All this expenditure meant that by September 1677, Whittaker was "in dire straits for livelihood." He needed to borrow £8 and provisions, and the creditor John Dix extracted vast security before he would lend them. The collateral included four cows, four calves, three young cattle, thirty bushels of Indian corn, all English corn and hay on the farm, about one hundred cord of wood already cut, ten swine, and one bay mare. Dix was not going to take any risks with such a slippery debtor. Three weeks after this agreement, however, on 9 October 1677, Dix complained to the magistrate that two hogs had been removed. The town constable had seized them in settlement of Hammond's suit against Whittaker. Hammond had promptly sold them to Jeremy Morse. To recover his security, Dix sued Morse. Hammond's servants asserted that the two swine awarded to their master were over and above Dix's porcine collateral.[14]

That was not the story from the other side of the fence. Elizabeth Whittaker, then aged thirty-five, "told them [the constable and Corporal Hammond] that the cattle and swine were none of my husband's. They were another man's. Hammond said it was no matter. He would bear the constable harmless; he did nothing but what he did by advice and counsel and he had it from Mr. Danforth [the Cambridge magistrate]." This account was corroborated by the Whittakers' eldest children, who claimed that the stock were those "which our father did sell to John Dix on 20 September 1677." Dix then sued Hammond "for procuring the constable to attach cattle when Hammond knew they were "Dix's security." It began to look as though Morse was an innocent victim, a third piggy in the middle.

Dix took Martin Townsend, the stock reeve, with him on a visit to Morse's. They found him "dressing of a ram. 'Where had you this ram?' asked John Dix. 'I bought it of Corporal Hammond.' 'Hammond is a thief,' said Dix, 'for he hath stole this ram from me and I forewarn you [against] carrying it to market for I will send the constable for it before night.'" Others, including Whittaker, testified to Morse's innocence and Hammond's deviousness. Whittaker went further: Hammond "stole sheep and lambs from Goodman Barron's." When Sarah Hammond defended her husband's honor, Whittaker dismissed her as "a foresworn wretch." Hammond had had enough. He sued Dix and Whittaker for slander and defamation.[15]

To confound the confusion, an incident in late September 1677 exacerbated the Whittaker-Hammond feud. Elizabeth Barron, aged seventeen, and Abigail Hammond, eighteen, deposed:

> My [Abigail's] father came in from abroad and said his sheep was in Whittaker's grounds and my father bid George Robeson to fetch them out. This maid and I did think that Whittaker would quarrel with the boy so we got up on the side of the garrison [this was just after the end of King Phillip's War] next the highway which is feldst up about a man's height from the ground with earth . . . We saw Goodman Whittaker in the highway and George Robeson was going over the highway for the sheep. "Whither are you going?" said Whittaker. "I am going for my master's sheep," said the boy. "You Welsh dog," said Whittaker, "you shall have no sheep here," and fell upon him with a great stick about the bigness of three fingers and struck him several blows inasmuch as we thought he would have killed the boy and we called out and my father and Sambo Negro came and rescued him.[16]

George and Sambo took up the story: "When our master came to the place where John Whittaker was abusing me [George], said my master 'Why have you done so roguishly, Whittaker, as to strike my servant in the highway?' 'Bear witness!' said Whittaker, 'He calls me rogue.' 'No,' said my master, 'I do not call you rogue.' Goodwife Whittaker being there a railing and fighting and throwing of stones. 'Get in,' said Whittaker [to his wife], 'You whore.' Said my master 'Do you call your own wife whore?' 'Bear witness,' said Whittaker, 'He called my wife a whore.' 'No,' saith my master, 'you called her whore yourself, and you know best!'" Hammond sued Whittaker for assaulting his servant. Whittaker countersued for defamation. There were, then, by October 1677, seven actions arising from Dix's original loan to Whittaker and the disputes between Whittaker and Hammond.

As in many witchcraft cases, the insults flung back and forth often had a background of long-standing resentment and popular suspicion. Lost tempers were the catalysts for settling old scores. Whittaker's jilting of Mary Linfield and Elizabeth's role in the breach of promise sixteen years earlier may have branded them rogue and whore in popular opinion. The previous fight, when Hammond was said to have trodden on Elizabeth's stomach and told her husband to carry her home in a cart, suggests that they may have been an ill-matched pair: the wife large, the husband small. In a subsequent case, a provocative woman neighbor described Whittaker as "a pretty little rogue . . . and of a sudden clapped both her hands upon his face and kissed him whether he would or not." His faulty fences and straying cattle were notorious. He had several times broken into the town pound or Hammond's barn and yards to retrieve them. His whole family was suspected of irreligion and ignorance. His eldest son was described as "a very lying boy." The Chenery clan regarded young John as a chip off the old block.[17]

Hammond was not without critics either. He had a long-standing reputation for sharp practice, for taking other men's timber and sheep. He was rich. His probated estate totaled £961, and his was the highest rating assessment in 1690. The family had at least three servants, two white and one black. If some of their wealth was known to be ill-gotten, how much more impropriety might there have been? To Whittaker, forced to rent, borrow, and give crippling security, as well as being an object of neighborly jeering, insults, and mockery, the arrogance of Hammond must have been deeply galling. Getting even, "being revenged," must have been a compulsion for so combative a coxcomb.[18]

Another emotion muddied the waters: youthful pride. Was the sixteen-year-old George Robeson or Robinson going to admit that the puny pauper John Whittaker had beaten him up? According to John Randall: "As I was coming along from work I overtook George Robeson in the highway. I asked him whether Whittaker beat him; he answered 'No! We beat him upon his own dunghill and made him lick in his blood like a dog.'" Joseph Hassell was told that Robeson had "made [Whittaker's] nose bleed and he licked his blood like a dog licks pottage."[19]

It could not have been easy for bench or jury to arrive at the truth. But truth perhaps was not the major aim of the numerous contestants, but rather a periodic bloodletting, a settling of scores, a purging of communal poison. The verdicts on 2 October 1677 were evenhanded and resulted in a weary draw. The Hammonds came out £11 ahead, but at the cost of a large load of dirty washing.[20]

Meanwhile the Watertown authorities expressed concern about Whittaker's children. Deacon Hastings and "Father [John] Coolidge" were sent "to see if his children be taught to read English and their catechism." Another family they visited was Whittaker's erstwhile brawl victim, William Price. The fall brought another inspection. Whittaker, perhaps lacking a barn, had crammed his harvest into his house, combustible hay and straw close to ovens, fires, and chimneys. He refused to move it and greeted a court order with "contemptuous carriages." The magistrates on 20 November 1677 sentenced him to be "fined twenty shillings in money and to be imprisoned ten days."[21]

The feisty Whittakers must have got the message that Watertown was tired of their constant shenanigans. In the summer of 1678 they sold the Eyre's Farm mortgage and moved on to Billerica. Even this curtain call was not without incident. In October 1678 Elizabeth Whittaker had to pay triple damages for defacing the deed of sale.[22] Watertown's gain was Billerica's loss. The Whittakers proceeded to provoke upset and outrage in that frontier community—but that is another story.[23]

Fleming Executors v. Jones, 1658

Death might be the final reckoning for the deceased, but for those appointed executors in the will there was another series of reckonings, with those who were in debt to the estate.[24] Inventories regularly included moneys owed the estate as potential assets. Where much credit had been advanced, some debts were listed as "hopeful," others as "desperate."

The Fleming family suffered double reckoning in 1657. In June the father, John Fleming, Watertown's maltster, died at the age of sixty. Only five months later, his wife, Anna, followed him to the grave. In April 1658 Sgt. John Wincoll, one of Anna Fleming's executors, went to law to recover a debt of £4.8.0 from Lewis Jones.

The Jones family had arrived in Watertown only in 1651, having spent the previous eleven years in Roxbury. Lewis was in his fifties and was one of the poorer townsmen. He had a severely handicapped child to support. The £4.8.0 owed was for malt bought by Jones's wife, another Anna. The calculating of this sum was described by young John Fleming. "Making out of a reckoning betwixt his father and Goody Jones, the debt she owed was £9.14.0. Goody Jones presented a bill of Oswald Smallpeel indebted to her for £4.8.4, [thus reducing] her debt to £5.5.8. His father agreed a debt of £4.8.0 [i.e., discounting 17/8d] and appointed him to give her a note to that effect which accordingly he did."[25]

The issue between the parties: was £4.8.0 a just price? Christopher Grant suggested that Fleming might have further discounted his charges: "John Fleming Sr. abated the prices of his malt and sent a note to Goody Jones by him [Grant] saying 'Goody Jones, I pray make your beer as well as you use to make, you shall be no loser by it, so I rest your Friend, John Fleming, dated 1654.'"

More important, though, was the issue of quality, and here poor executor Wincoll discovered that he had stirred up a hornets' nest of consumer irritation. John Clough Sr., a tailor, had "received forty bushels of malt from Fleming about May 1655, but said malt was very defective . . . not sufficiently dried and besides very much eaten with the weevils . . . Fleming promised satisfaction." Andrew Belcher, Cambridge's licensee, referred to similar problems in 1654: "He went to [Fleming] and complained and carried a sample of old English malt that he was offered great quantity of for 4/6d a bushel; to his thinking one bushel was worth two of Fleming's." Other Watertown heavyweights echoed the judgment of Ensign Sherman (despite his being the other executor) that "good beer could not be made of Fleming's malt, it was so bad." Thomas Hastings, Hugh Mason, Samuel Thatcher, and Charles Chadwick had all had to get their malt elsewhere or make their own. Finally, the Flemings' accounting was suspect, according to Hannah Thatcher. Because of doubts, they had "thought good to set down" what they had bought "as soon as we came home," and they found that the Flemings later "demanded some more" than the Thatchers owed. This eruption of complaint was as though years of frustration were suddenly given full vent.[26]

The case would have a strange legal history. In the county court the jury found for Jones, with costs, but the magistrates dissented from letting the debtor completely off the hook. The issue went therefore to the General Court. Again, there was disagreement. The magistrates judged that Jones should pay the £4.8.0 plus costs to the estate, but the deputies demurred. To them £3.0.0 was quite enough for faulty goods. The magistrates consented. Was the creditor-debtor dichotomy reflected in these divisions?

Standardization is so common nowadays, that it is hard to imagine quite such extreme ranges of quality. Techniques were so primitive, however, that goods could be grossly overvalued because of problems of processing or storage. The wealthier members of the community could afford alternative supplies, but the less affluent, like the Joneses, had to make the best of a bad job, at least until a time of reckoning.

The general shortage of specie after the 1630s created the need to use paper "notes" or "bills" as substitutes. These, duly endorsed, could be used in place of specie or bartered "commodity money." This system depended on considerable faith and local knowledge. The worth of a note depended on the credit worthiness of its signer/marker or endorser. Artisans were expected to extend credit. In farming communities where revenue was seasonal and dependent on capricious weather, such patience, for months or even years, was a necessity. These elaborate systems of exchange required systematic and trustworthy bookkeeping. Where accounting was suspect, it was best to have witnesses standing by.

White v. Bemis, 1679

Actions for debt between neighbors in Watertown were extremely rare.[27] The normal procedure with slow settlers was to ask some other, influential townsmen to lean on the debtor. Such informal pressure almost always worked, which was what Anthony White decided to try on 8 June 1679.[28]

As reported by selectman Samuel Stearns, White "asked him, Ensign [Daniel] Warren and John Stearns to go to Joseph Bemis in order to settle his debt" of £10.16.6, which went back seven years to 1672.[29] Bemis, however, "utterly refused . . . he said they had reckoned formerly. He had tendered his pay two years before." According to White's daughter, Mary Willard, they had indeed "made a general reckoning [on 9 October 1675] from the beginning of the world to that day." Nonetheless, White's bill included subsequent supplies of food and such services as carpentry, fencing, plowing, pasturing, and carting. Witnesses described young John White bringing a load of hay "by order of Joseph Bemis," or carrying four barrels of Bemis's cider to Boston from Robert Harrington's cider mill.[30] There could be no doubt about the indebtedness. Why then the debtor's obduracy?

The conciliators soon discovered when they visited Bemis. He "insisted upon the wrong that he sustained from that family . . . there was differences between them . . . If there were a debt, he reckoned Anthony White owed him fifty shillings for giving information about his sons having cards." On 27 May 1670 the General Court had sadly noted that "the great sin of gambling increases among us . . . to the corrupting of youth." Draconian £5 fines were imposed on possessors of decks of cards or dice. Informers were given a onetime reprieve for their own involvement. This noxious tattling ordinance was one cause of the Bemis-White confrontation.[31]

On 20 November 1677 John White had been fined £2.10.0 for possession of a deck of cards. In the following February and March a string of witnesses had testified about other cardplayers in Watertown. Sarah Hall, aged thirty-three, described how "last winter, Goodman Bemis's sons did frequently resort to our house in the evenings to play at cards though much against my will and desire for often both I and my children were deprived of the use and benefit of the fire and were often constrained to go to bed and they were so bold in it that we knew not how to restrain them." John Wayte, aged forty-eight, had no doubt about the ringleaders: "Living near Anthony White's [I] did see this winter Goodman Bemis's sons often and frequently resort to Anthony White's house and, hearing a rumour of their playing at cards there, caused me to speak of it to Goodman Bemis's sons and reprove them for it, and further, till this winter I never knew nor heard that John White was given or addicted to going out at night or to company-keeping." The court records also contain an abominably spelled and craven letter from John Bemis to Major Gookin, the Cambridge magistrate, bewailing that he had had the effrontery "to take away the cards out of Major Gookin's house . . . rashly to do such a thing not considering of the evil that was in it . . . please to forget and forgive . . . it is a warning to me for overrunning." For this self-condemnation he was let off with an admonition.

White's incrimination of the Bemis boys' cardplaying and their fining by Gookin had plainly enraged their father, but for the Whites it was far less serious than another interfamily outrage of that winter. On 14 March 1678 Joseph Bemis had to try to ingratiate himself with the General Court to seek a reduction for his son Ephraim's fearsome punishment for "trapanning and procuring [a young married woman] by his lying and false information in order to her being abused by one John Oynes [Owens?] under the name of Mr. Woodman . . . to the end that John Oynes might commit adultery with her." The respectable woman thus ensnared was Anthony White's daughter Mary, married in 1677 to Jacob Willard.[32] It is easy to see why White should have decided to call in Bemis's debts.

This was not a confrontation between young hotbloods. Bemis was sixty and White seventy in 1678; both had been in Watertown nearly four decades. The court did not allow White the £10.16.6 he claimed; Bemis must pay £5.0.6 in money, £2.6.d in country pay, and £1.11.8 in costs. It was not fifty shillings less, but a £1.17.4 discount could not but help to calm frayed nerves. Five years later, in 1684, John White married Rebecca Bemis, He was thirty-five, she thirty. They may have had to wait for the feud to subside.[33]

Habitual restraint in neighborly relations was only broken by behavior perceived as betraying communal expectations. Two households previously conforming were thrown into conflict by breaches of trust. The sins of the younger generation were held against the older. It took years rather than months for the sense of injury to abate and normal relations to be restored.

Edward Sanders; Child Abuser, 1654

On 25 October 1654 Watertown's constable arrived in Boston with three elderly women and a teenage boy and girl.[34] They had been summoned to the General Court to repeat evidence that they had already given in the first trial of one of the most chilling cases of the century.[35]

The indictment, which had been found "a true bill" (i.e., plausible) by the Grand Jury on 5 September 1654, read: "Edward Sanders not having the fear of God before his eyes, and being devilishly seduced, on 8 June 1654 abused the body of Ruth Parsons aged eight or nine, which [girl] upon search is found to have been so abused."

The evidence on which their finding was based turned out to be overwhelming. First there was the child's own detailed account:

> Ruth Parsons, aged nine, the daughter of Hugh Parsons of Watertown, complained of Edward Sanders of Watertown for forcing her and abusing her and entering her body with his pissing place (as she called it). He did it four times and she cried out but Sanders sometimes threatened her and whipped her and pinched her on the back, which was sore after, to hinder her crying nor was anyone in or near the house but two or three little children which he put out of doors to the [illegible] common. Sanders pulled her by the coat into his leanto and sitting upon a high stool took her upon his knee and opened her legs and put one on one side and t'other on t'other side of his body and then he danced her (as she saith) and opened her body with both hands and hurt her and then he put in his pissing place and wet her and she was sore afterward every time but durst not speak at first for fear of beating as he threatened her to make her mother whip her &c. She denieth that any other did meddle with her ... he forced her the fifth time in her father [sic] chimly [the chimney-nook of her father's house] and there did her most hurt using her as formerly and did clap her [her mouth with his hand] lest she should cry out. Thus the child declared the business.[36]

Furthermore, testimony accorded with her physical symptoms: "Anne George, aged sixty-four, and Elizabeth Pierce, aged sixty-seven, being requested by Alice Parsons, the mother of Ruth Parsons, to search her daughter Ruth, we found her body abused by carnal copulation, as we verily conceive and Ruth told Alice [sic] George that Edward Sanders had abused her and no other. Sworn in court 26 October 1654."

Third, several witnesses attested to the dreadful remorse displayed by Sanders. The sixty-year-old Grace Wetherall swore that

> On the fourth day (Wednesday) at night, before Edward Sanders was apprehended, he complained that the great sin he had committed came to his mind now, or remembrance, more than ever it did before, and he being looking upon the bible, I asked him what he looked unto, he replied what sin they fell into which had to do with whores. The fifth day [Thursday] in the morning, before he was carried to prison, he bewailed his great sin again before me and Joseph Morse and Hester his wife. Edward Sanders's wife told me and Mary Wetherall my daughter, aged nineteen, that her husband told her soon after he was committed that he had done that if he fell not into the hands of merciful women he was condemned by the laws of God.[37]

Only one question raised any doubts about the legal situation. The Watertown constable, Mr. Jeremy Norcross, testified "that I asked Edward Sanders whether he did it with her will or against her will and no other words." Sanders's answer was witnessed by Goody Wetherall and reported by young Obadiah Parry: "He answered 'With her will,' but I did not understand what he meant by it, being ignorant what the first discourse was [about]."[38]

Despite the child's evidence to the contrary, the court seems to have accepted Sanders's claim that he had not raped Ruth. Had they believed her, the death sentence would have been mandatory. Thus began one of the most extraordinary, hairbreadth escapes from the gallows. By a law passed in 1642 Sanders would still have been liable to execution whether a child had consented or not. However, the Court of Assistants was unsure of the current status of that law:

1. Whether the 1642 law concerning carnal knowledge of any girl under nine either with or without her consent be in force or not . . . because it was not printed in the 1647 Book of Capital Laws, and that Book ordained that "any laws not printed herein are repealed."
2. If repealed, whether our first law of 1642 doth not carry it to the General Court to be judged according to the Word of God.[39]

To the first question, the deputies voted in the negative, that the law *was* repealed, and in the affirmative to the second, referring the case to the General Court. Their judgment was that Sanders was "not guilty of death but justly deserving a high and severe censure." His punishment was a whipping of not more than thirty strokes in Boston, another at some public meeting in Watertown. He was to "wear a rope round his neck openly to be seen hanging down two feet." If he were found more than forty rods (220 yards) from his house without the noose, he was to be whipped again." There must have been times during his painful, eye-catching, and extended disgrace that Sanders would have preferred the scaffold he had so barely escaped.[40]

Lt. Robert Feake

The town accounts for 1651 are only partly legible, but after routine payments for trapping foxes and work with the dry herd, comes the entry "Due to Samuel Thatcher for Mr. Feakes."[41] No sum is legible. This civic disbursement, usually about £8 annually, continued for the next thirteen years. It is the iceberg tip of a tragedy.[42]

Lt. Robert Feake came from an old Norfolk family. His branch had moved to London. He was baptized in 1602 at St. Edward's Church in Lombard Street, the son of a goldsmith and of a wealthy draper's daughter. He had been one of the founders of Watertown in 1630 and a member of Governor Winthrop's exploration party above the falls in January 1632. An eminence had been named Mount Feake in his honor, perhaps because he had joined the governor's clan by marrying Henry Winthrop's young widow, Elizabeth (née Fones). During the 1630s Feake was a leading figure in town affairs. He had probably acquired some military skills in England or Europe. In 1632 he was appointed lieutenant to Capt. Daniel Patrick, muster-master of the towns north of the Charles. From 1636 to 1640 he represented Watertown in the General

Court, where he was often entrusted with important colony business. In 1636 he was appointed associate judge of what became the Middlesex County Court. He received generous land grants in the first four Watertown distributions.[43]

In July 1636 both he and his wife wrote similar letters to their brother-in-law John Winthrop Jr., whose first wife, Martha Fones, Elizabeth's sister, had died in 1634. Winthrop was preparing the settlement of Saybrook near the mouth of the Connecticut River. Feake referred to "distractions we have been in by reason we were altogether unsettled . . . [but] we are resolved again for Connecticut and therefore I have now sent my man to mow grass there for to winter my cattle there . . . I purpose God willing in the spring [of 1637] to come there with my wife and family." Elizabeth specified that their destination would be "Watertown," the original name for Wethersfield, in order to be near Winthrop; otherwise, "we had chosen Concord for to dwell in." God seemed to have other plans, however. The Pequot War broke out in Wethersfield in the spring of 1637, and Robert Feake's only experience of the Connecticut Valley was confined to his service as Patrick's lieutenant in the conflict.[44]

In 1639 Feake's father died in London, and the Boston notary Thomas Lechford made out a letter of attorney to dispose of property on behalf of Lt. Robert Feake of Watertown, Gent.; Judith Palmer, his niece who lived at Yarmouth, Massachusetts; and her brother Tobias Feake, aged seventeen. In 1640, after toying with the idea of moving to Dedham, the Feakes left Massachusetts with Captain Patrick, a former Dutch guardsman, and settled near New Amsterdam at Greenwich, Connecticut. After persistent threats from local Native Americans and assertions of sovereignty by the Dutch governor, the fledgling plantation was forced to pledge allegiance to the Netherlands. Feake opposed submission but was overruled by Patrick and Elizabeth, who signed over Greenwich on 9 April 1642. This breach of fidelity seems to have undermined Feake's reason. He was judged "unfit to dispose a plantation," which his wife took over.[45]

Elizabeth, in turn, seems to have lost her reputation, according to an April 1644 letter of her aunt Lucy Downing. She may have fallen under the unsavory influence of Patrick, a womanizer whose arrogance and untrustworthiness led to his murder in January 1644. This brutal blow dealt another shock to Robert's unhinged mind. In June 1646 there was a recruit to the Feake household: Thomas Lyon, who had married Robert Feake's stepdaughter, Martha Johanna Winthrop. He moved in "because my father [Feake] being distracted I might be a help" to his mother-in-law, who despite Robert's illness was pregnant with her sixth child, Sarah. (Or perhaps it was *because of* Robert's illness?) About this time, there appeared on the scene William Hallett, who soon moved in with Elizabeth and took over the running of the Feake property. In March 1647 Robert suddenly made over his land and half his cash to his wife and Hallett and left Greenwich. On the same day that Elizabeth's child was baptized in New Amsterdam, 14 April 1647, the Feakes were divorced on the grounds of her adultery.[46]

We next hear of Feake in Boston in 1647 bound for London, expressing apprehension about "how God would deal with him in England." In March of 1650 Robert Feake was issued with a pardon by the House of Commons, possibly for his taking an oath of allegiance to what had now become a hostile power. He was back in the new world by September 1650, but by then his mind had completely given way. His neighbors recalled him at this time as a man

> whose God-fearing heart was so absorbed with spiritual and heavenly things, that he little thought of the things of this life and took neither heed nor care of what tended to his external property. We moreover considered him as a man so unsettled and troubled in his understanding and brain, that although he was, at times, better settled than at others, nevertheless in his last years and about the time he agreed with his wife respecting the division of their temporal property, he was not a man of any wisdom or capable of acting understandingly like any other man in a matter regarding his own benefit, profit and advantage. In like manner, we testify that he as yet on all occasions exhibited a more than ordinary respect towards . . . his wife [Elizabeth], and that he in our opinion was easily to be seduced by her to do whatever she wished than what was wise and reasonable in the opinion of a man who was *compos sui,* and as we say his own man.[47]

Thereafter "he became melancholy, and about fourteen days after was seriously ill, headstrong and crazy." While his wife, later romanticized as Anya Seton's *Winthrop Woman,* made a questionable marriage with Hallett, sought refuge in New London, and then settled at Hellgate on Long Island, poor deranged Robert Feake somehow ended up in Watertown. There he was cared for until his death at the age of sixty in February 1663. By early 1660 his distress had become unmanageable, and Capt. Hugh Mason, chairman of the board of selectmen, and Deacon Ephraim Child were deputed to "go to him, and use their discretion in words to the moderating of him in his disorder." He died in the care of Deacon Thatcher, next door to his original lot granted in 1630. The town petitioned the county court on 6 October 1663 for £8 from his estate to defray "entertainment" and £3.14.0 for Feake's funeral. Over the previous thirteen years £90 had been disbursed from town funds. They had not first spent all of Feake's assets because "if something [of his estate] had not been spared such as he might call his own, it would have been further destruction of his mind." The residue of his property consisted of "one suit and cloak and an old jacket, two old coats . . . some other old clothes . . . one Bible, three books . . . valued in all at £9.9.2d."[48]

Susannah Woodward, 1671

Watertown selectmen received an order from the Middlesex County Court on 24 October 1671 "to take care for the disposal of the child of Susannah Woodward, for its maintenance both for quantity, manner and time."[49] This was the climax of a dramatic confrontation in the town. Court Folio 59, dated June to December 1671, contains nineteen depositions and examinations in this fiercely disputed paternity case. One group of witnesses swore that they had seen Susannah in highly compromising situations with Thomas Hastings Jr., her master's son. Another group, including her master's family, rejected the accusations and asserted that the father was John Chadwick. When the nineteen-year-old Susannah was examined in June 1671, six weeks before the child was due, she denied "that ever she had company with any other in that kind" than her master's son. In her confession she listed their frequent lovemaking, including "several times . . . when she was in bed with two children on the outside of the bed and two on the inside." Each suspect "utterly denied it and protested solemnly that he is innocent." Susannah stuck to her story, even when the midwives "in the extremity of her labour require[d] her to confess the truth and declare who was the father." The jury was in a quandary. They found John Chadwick "not legally guilty [of fornication] but find cause to suspect his unseasonable company-keeping with Susannah Woodward." He was acquitted. Though the court found "no legal evidence appearing to convict" her master's son, he was nonetheless ordered "to pay charges necessarily expended for the maintenance and bringing up of the said bastard as the reputed father thereof." Susannah was sentenced to fifteen stripes. Thus the court conformed to the colony paternity law of 1668, which in turn copied the legal practice of England. In September 1671 the selectmen of Watertown indicated their opinion of the true culprit by warning John Chadwick out of town.[50]

The irony of the situation becomes evident as the selectmen made the required arrangements for the child. The engagement to pay the £7 annual maintenance to John Waite was agreed by the board "with Deacon Hastings." He engaged not as a church welfare official but as the father of the reputed father of the child, Thomas Hastings Jr. That year the deacon was himself a selectman, as well as town clerk and moderator of the town meeting. Divisions between adamant groups of witnesses must have reflected wider town opinion. Young Hastings later married Anna Hawkes in 1672 and began a forty-year career as a doctor. He neither married nor practiced in Watertown, however, but 150 miles west in the Connecticut Valley.[51]

Why were Susannah and her child at John Waite's? Why had she not returned to the home of her father, George Woodward? Waite had penned the crucial midwives' deposition, had paid for her delivery, and had orchestrated family witnesses who alleged "so much of unseemly carriage by Thomas Hastings and Susannah Woodward that before long Deacon Hastings would be a grandfather." The answer may supply the vital clue explaining why Susannah either succumbed to Thomas's advances or set her cap at him. John Waite was the husband of Mary (Woodward), Susannah's older sister. They had married six years earlier and had young children. So did Susannah's father. Her mother had died when she was about seven and her father had remarried to a younger second wife, Elizabeth Hammond, from neighboring Cambridge. Between 1660 and 1675 George and Elizabeth Woodward were steadily producing a second Woodward brood. A sense of displacement, rivalry, and alienation may explain why Susannah preferred her sister's home to her stepmother's. Later, her child "lived successively with Deacon John Morse, William Hagar and his son Samuel Hagar up to the age of twenty-one in 1692. The following year he married Sarah Tarbell of Newton where he settled." Deacon Hastings was not reelected to the Board of Selectmen until 1677, a six-year gap unprecedented since 1639.[52]

The Watertown Underworld Falls Out, 1657

A series of livestock and poultry disappearances from Watertown during the 1656–57 fall and winter might plausibly have been blamed on hungry wolves.[53] The first victim was a sheep. Thanks to human rivalries, however, the following spring saw the wolves exculpated and several of the most notorious members of the town's second generation in court. Twenty-five-year-old John Coller[54] described how

> At the beginning of December last by accident I met John Knapp in the latter end of the week. He then asked me if I came to the meeting the next Lord's Day in the forenoon. I answered that I knew nothing to the contrary but that I should. John Knapp replied "Though I say no more to you, come to my house and take a pipe of tobacco;" so that accordingly I did and when I had taken out a pipe of tobacco John Knapp asked me if I would eat a bit of victuals with him. I answered, "I care not if I do." When I had finished eating with him he asked me if I knew what meat it was. I told him I thought that I did. He then said to me, "If you will say nothing, I will tell how I came by it." He said there were for some days a company of sheep about his father's grounds and they came to the barn door to eat the droppings of pease he was threshing and he set his father's dog upon them and the sheep went away and did not mind the dog, and at night he came again and saw the dog eating of a sheep which sheep he took by and laid it into his cart and carried it home and dressed it that night. I asked him why he did not make it known before he carried it home; he answered me because his father was a poor man and, if it should be known, must pay for it because his dog killed it. And then he said he would show it to me if I would say nothing. I then went with him into his chamber where he showed three-quarters of it hanging up and would have had me carry home a quarter of it. I answered him I would not. He answered "Though you will not, I know who will." I asked him who; he answered his brother James and his brother[-in-law] Nick [Cady] and he would [illegible] of it before meeting; and I saw him go to both and speak to them but they went together away from me that I could not make out what they said. About a day or two after, Knapp came to my house and I asked him what he had done with the meat that did hang by his house. He answered me that his brother James and his brother Nick carried home half of it and the skin that sabbath day that I was there. Then I asked him how they carried it and he said they carried it under their coats but he repented that he gave them so much for now he wanted it himself, and further said that [illegible] to curse the wolf that got it and see the devil take him. My wife was present at the discourse by my house.[55]

Somebody, possibly Samuel Benjamin, informed on John Knapp, who on 6 April 1657 made a confession to Captain Gookin but denied giving any "good fat meat" to his brothers. To secure his appearance at the court, he pledged his house and land, "which was formerly mortgaged to Robert Jennison."[56]

Jennison was also a victim of another act of petty larceny. On 11 February 1657 a witness reported hearing Jonathan Phillips, son of Watertown's first pastor, say that he "wished that he had [some] fowls to make merry with . . . Within a week or a fortnight Robert Jennison lost seventeen young fowls." That was not the only thieving Jonathan Phillips was alleged to have committed. The informant continued: "Last summer being at work in the Indian corn . . . and going in Samuel Benjamin's house, Jonathan Phillips brought in a live pig and said he got it in Mr. Whitney's field." Others were implicated: Thomas Pratt, Thomas Fanning, and John Bush.[57]

The informant was none other than John Knapp, "troubled in conscience" after receiving an invitation from the feasters, who threatened that, if he betrayed them, "they would take their oaths that Knapp had [stolen]" the pig and poultry. They also planted evidence, he claimed. "He found a bag in his orchard and there came feathers like hen's feathers out of it." In retaliation, Knapp "had been the occasion of making a search at Benjamin's house for a holland shift [a linen undergarment] stolen from Robert Jennison's." He also sought to revive old animosities by urging Benjamin to plant the stolen shift in the cowhouse or pigsty of John Bush.[58]

Benjamin's reputation in Watertown was little better than Knapp's. He claimed that he was terrified of Knapp's violence. "John Knapp have threatened a mischief . . . once in a boat to Boston, John Knapp knocked me down with a bill because I would not do as he required in trimming and he hath said in the hearing of others that if I had died he would have tied stones to my body and sunk me in the river." Returning from accusing Knapp of stealing the chickens and pig to the magistrate, Benjamin was again challenged: "As we were going home to Watertown meeting with John Knapp, he understanding where we had been, saith 'Well, Benjamin, well, the devil will pick thy bones,' and said Benjamin replied, 'Why this? It is said, John Knapp, whenas a man discover any searches then he will tell it abroad.'"

The weight of evidence told against Knapp. Just to drive another nail in his coffin, Abraham Brown accused Knapp of stealing a pair of gloves. In all Knapp had to pay £7.11.6. Furthermore, he was to be whipped thirty stripes and enter a £10 bond for good behavior. His sureties, brothers-in-law Nicholas Cady and Thomas Smith, saved his back by paying a £10 commutation fine. Other suspects were also punished.[59]

The events of the fall and winter of 1656–57 shed light on several facets of the culture of the rising generation. The feasts that followed the thefts were reenactments of "merriment," or bucolic indulgence that harked back to English popular culture, in this case, possibly the pre-Lenten festivities of Shrove Tuesday. It is particularly ironic to hear the hated word "merry" from the son of Watertown's first pastor. Several ringleaders had matured in fatherless or dysfunctional families. Phillips and Benjamin had both lost fathers when they were children; Knapp's father was a foul-mouthed drunkard despised by his neighbors.

Although there were preexisting enmities, Bush v. Benjamin, Benjamin v. Knapp, this distrustful, whispering, and violent subgroup all shared a culture of poverty and dependency that may have helped select their targets. Was it sheer coincidence that the loser of seventeen hens happened to have been Knapp's creditor? Or that he had had goods seized by the marshal to pay £3.10.0 to Widow Abigail Benjamin, the mother of his main rival? Or that the owner of the fat mutton was one of the richest men in Watertown, John Biscoe? The thefts and the joking about poor wolves getting the blame smack of second-generation have-nots redistributing the goodies of the well-established haves.[60]

Page v. Page, 1678

Rivalry between heirs was the stuff of Jacobean drama.[61] Among ordinary people, such quarrels revealed the vulnerability of families to economic disaster, the underlying causes of family stress, and the polarizing effects of fraternal feuding on the community.

The Page family proved to be unexpectedly dysfunctional. John and Phoebe (Payne) Page, with infant daughter Phoebe and baby John, had arrived in Watertown in 1630 as part of George Phillips's Company. Goodwife Page was well connected; she counted Elizabeth Hammond, Dorothy Eyre, and the successful merchant William Payne as siblings. Forty-four-year-old John was nominated by the General Court as Watertown's first constable. When Page's "lamentable letter" fearing that "unless God stirring some friends to send him some provision he is like to starve" reached Dedham in 1631, the great preacher John Rogers donated a pound toward flour, and the family was saved. A younger son, Samuel, was born in 1633. The new-world future must have looked rosy.

Then, during the 1630s, something went wrong. John never again held town office. The family withdrew themselves from the town center and settled to the northwest on land purchased in the Great Dividend, near Beaver Brook. Page also bought land in Cambridge and may have temporarily moved there in 1639. The family did not share in the 1642 division of farms. By 1640 there were more financial problems. John Page borrowed £30 secured on five and one-third head of cows from Edward Payne of Wapping, London. In 1643 the farm was mortgaged to Thomas Crosby of Cambridge for £130.[62]

Daughter Phoebe filed a defamation suit in 1650 that revealed her hatred of life at home, and especially of her father: "My mother I can love and respect, but my father I cannot love." Advised to return home, she answered, "No, before I will do so I will go into the wilderness as far as I can and lie down and die." These enmities were mutual. The daughter's attempt to defend her reputation had proved a profoundly shaming exposure of Page family life.[63]

By 1662 the "not unblemished" Phoebe, aged thirty-five, became the third wife of the poor, older, and probably crippled James Cutler and moved out to Lexington. Two brothers survived to manhood. The younger, Samuel, was prosecuted on 4 June 1666 for refusing to assist Watertown's constable. Soon after, Samuel married and left town for Concord. When he tried to return to Watertown, he was warned out.[64] The elder brother, John Page, became a housewright, left home in his late teens for the Piscataqua River, and prospered during the early 1650s. After some time back in Watertown, he helped found Groton in the early 1660s. He married Faith, a cousin of Harvard College's first president, Henry Dunster. By the mid-1660s all three Page offspring not only had fled the troubled nest but had put town lines between themselves and their parents and each other.[65]

The older Pages died within a year of each other; John in December 1676, aged about ninety, and Phoebe senior nine months later, in her eighties.[66] Both were intestate, and their deaths unleashed a fraternal feud that had been snarling for years.

On 18 December 1678 Samuel Page and James Cutler petitioned the county court about the failure of executor John Page Jr. to bring his father's "considerable estate" to administration: "We through lameness and other weakness are exposed to much suffering in our families, which cause us to look out for our just right to supply our necessity." They asked the court to approve a committee chosen by the three parties to arrange an equal division, including what had already been distributed. John Page, however, denied that there *was* any estate to divide. Both sides furiously assembled evidence. There were thirty-one different sworn affidavits for the court to consider.[67]

Much of the testimony favoring John Page as saviour and caregiver was written out in the neat hand of Joseph Tainter. Several witnesses corroborated Thomas Goble's recollection of events in 1650 or 1651: "I and John Page being at the eastward about Piscataqua River working there . . . and old Goodman Page sent a letter to his son Page to come down and redeem his house and land that were mortgaged to Mr. Crosby else he should be turned out of doors. John Page, to my knowledge, went down and . . . redeemed it."[68]

Ejection had been a real possibility. Joseph Tainter recounted: "Old Mr. Crosby's agent, Mr. Fowle, was twice very eager to sell John Page Sr.'s house and homestall. It had been mortgaged for £60 for three years, country pay; it was convenient for me &c. Twice I said no, sticking not through the nail, and John Page the younger came down from Piscataqua, redeemed the house and land, and the old man lived there until he died."

The parental home had been saved, but at a price. In order to have the property redeemed, Old Page (according to young John's supporters) had made it over to his son. John Hammond, one of the richest men in Watertown, remembered "about 1670 or 1671, being at my uncle Page's, and aunt was very importunate to give Samuel Page a piece of land. Uncle answered: 'Thou knowest it was mortgaged and son John has redeemed it and it is his.'" Others agreed—Thomas Straite, who "planted in the same field"; Daniel Pearce, whose father, Anthony, bought Page land; and John Bigelow, who worked for the family. James Knapp, one of John Page's most effusive supporters, remembered the father saying, "All will be son John's; he spoke with great rejoicing."

Opinion was bitterly divided, however, and attempts at arbitration between the siblings failed.[69] A supporter of Samuel Page and James Cutler testified: "Old Goody Page came to him and said her two sons were fallen out and she feared would do one another a mischief and prayed him to go to her house and when I came then John Page Jr. brought forth a writing which he said was the agreement betwixt his father and he concerning his father's estate [the gist] whereof to my best remembrance was that he was to take care of his father and mother and take the benefit of the improvement of the estate [in a different hand] so long as they both agree."[70]

Benefit of improvement, or the increase in value, typical of many tenancy agreements, was very different from ownership. An even tougher agreement was reported: the younger Page could have the improvement "Till God in his providence should call John Page Sr. some other way." Then John Page Jr. was to leave his father's estate "as good as he found it."[71] Two younger men had heard Old Page deny that any of the estate had been made over.[72] No written agreement has survived, but John Page had one at the time of his mother's death.

The amount of filial care and money expended on the old couple was hotly disputed. Some saw the younger John's enterprise as the salvation of the family fortunes; two carpenters had been "employed and put to work by John Page Jr. while he was a bachelor, in the ten years between his being in Piscataqua and Groton . . . he managed the whole business . . . he paid us our wages [of] £60 or £100 [and] that time managed his father's whole estate . . . old Goodman Page said: 'All the lands north of Beaver Brook and Chester Meadow were to be his son John's; he took possession of them twenty-six or twenty-seven years since [i.e., 1651/52].'"[73]

John presented accounts to show that he had expended more than the full value of the estate when he had looked after his parents in the 1650s and during their dotage ("so crazy a condition") in the 1670s, when he and Faith had moved down to Watertown from Groton. Hannah Barron, aged sixty-three, told how her gossip, or intimate friend, "Phoebe Page [Sr.] did weep and lamented very much to me if John Page Jr. did not take care of them, they must fall into the hands of strangers and come to the town [go on welfare]. She desired me to go to John Page Jr. and offer him all the estate. He said it would offend his brother Samuel. Later Phoebe Page did bless God for providing so well for them and was much content in son John and daughter [Faith] both."

Before returning to Watertown, the younger John had promised, "If father and mother pleased to come up to Groton they should never want while he had anything. He sent supply several times."[74] A witness observed that "John Page Sr. thanked his son John with tears in his eyes."

To his critics, however, John was a money-grubbing opportunist. Phillip Shattuck, a physician, wrote asking him to come to help his parents "but there came no answer. The father said: 'If he [the father] had any more lands for him to sell or come to receive then he would soon come for he had almost undone him by selling his lands already. He had one cow that son Page carried to Groton and promised him pay but would not pay him anything for it and now he would not come near him.'"

During the 1650s, said others, the younger John had enriched himself through building houses, constructing frames for at least five fellow townsmen.[75] It was Samuel who "was employed about his father's business the greatest part of the time, who took care of the cattle," whereas "John was nowise obliged to his father . . . and followed his own occasions."[76] Four leading citizens of Watertown, however, asserted that the parents had specifically asked for John and Faith and rejected Samuel. The four judged that John and Faith had nursed the old couple well.[77]

Other doubters contested John's accounts, which greatly undervalued his parents' estate and inflated his expenses. Martha Ives, aged seventy-eight, "was at the house of old Goody Page the night before she died and she told me she was chargeable to her son for nothing but household diet and one waistcoat cloth." Nonetheless, the verdict was unanimous: John Page Jr. had proved to the court's satisfaction that his parents' estate was wholly his; his siblings received nothing.[78]

The case polarized the town. Each side mustered all available evidence. John attracted an older and wealthier group of community leaders. Phoebe and Samuel Page and some of their supporters had had brushes with the law, and this fact must have told with the court. What emerges with tragic force is the deep anger and mutual jealousy seated at the heart of the Page family. Family fights dominate the testimony: father against son, mother against father, son against son, demanding, challenging, arguing, arguing, arguing. Distance alone stilled the dispute.

Gale v. Gale, 1679

The complex mechanics of matchmaking, of reconciling emotional and material needs, is vividly demonstrated by retrospective testimony about negotiations for a Gale-Spring family merger.[79] On 16 December 1679 Henry and Mehitabel Spring testified that about five years before,

> Richard Gale came to our house to ask our goodwill touching a match [between] our daughter [Elizabeth, aged seventeen] and John Gale [aged about twenty-five]. We inquired what he would give with his son. Richard Gale replied that when he died half the farm would go to John and his heirs and the other half to [eldest son] Abraham. If John should die, our daughter should enjoy the farm as a widow and it would go to her heirs. We gave our consent that the match should go on and gave with our daughter a cow and some sheep and some other things and promised to own her as a child . . . We did shake hands and Richard Gale said his word should be as good as his bond and what he had promised he would perform.[80]

John's eldest sister, Sarah Garfield, recollected that "she had often heard her mother Gale say that John should have the house her mother lived in and her father often said that John had always been a true and faithful servant to him and he [father] had done more for Abraham than all the children he had and the farm should be equally divided between them and that there were those that strained to root John out, but they should never do it and Joseph Garfield testifies that one half of the farm is worth £7 a yard."[81]

Despite all this assurance about intentions, the Springs wanted the agreement in writing. Selectman William Bond deposed that "in the summer of 1677 Richard Gale and Henry Spring came to him for a writing confirming half the farm to John Gale, being at that time a goodwiller unto the daughter of Henry Spring, but during the writing words passed between Richard Gale and Henry Spring, so the writing was not signed nor subscribed to by Richard Gale. He said he would never sign to that writing . . . he would not be engaged as long as he lived but would keep his estate free for the comfort and maintenance of himself and wife."

What had annulled the handshake and the promise? The Springs may have tried to stampede Gale into making over the farmland straightaway. He expressed alarm about risking old-age comfort. Nevertheless, shortly after this parental withdrawal from the merger and Elizabeth's eighteenth birthday, the marriage went ahead.[82] Eighteen months later Richard Gale began to fail and made an unusually detailed will. After his wife's death, half the farm should indeed go to John, but only for life. It should then revert to Abraham, the eldest son, and his heirs. If John and Elizabeth had a male heir, he would receive only £20.[83]

On 8 December 1679 John sued Abraham, the executor, "for withholding half the farm which Richard Gale purchased from Mr. Dummer and promised the half to his son John upon marriage to Elizabeth Spring." Alas, the verbal undertakings of 1677 could not counterbalance the written and witnessed will of 1679. Since their mother survived, the court found for Abraham, with costs of 9/8d.[84]

We can only speculate about the souring of trust that led to *Gale v. Gale.* Perhaps the modestly endowed Gale found the dowry inadequate. Perhaps he had come to disapprove of the Spring family's sullied reputation, though his own son Ephraim was an unstable handful. Perhaps the urge to keep the farm together overcame equity. Perhaps his mind was poisoned against John and Elizabeth. There can be no doubt of the pervasive mistrust: the Springs doubted verbal promises; Gale suspected Spring of greed; daughter Sarah thought Abraham spoiled and scheming. Despite this pall of misgiving, young Elizabeth somehow extracted her parents' consent. Perhaps, for once, love conquered all.[85]

APPENDIX B

Lists of Residents

List 1: Long-Term, First Generation

Criteria for Inclusion: Arrival by 1640; residence for seven-year minimum, usually grantee of town land (proprietor), adult on arrival, usually male head of household.

Thomas ARNOLD, John BARNARD, Ellis BARRON, William BARSHAM, Thomas BARTLETT, Richard BEECH, Richard BEERS, Joseph BEMIS, John BIGELOW, Nathaniel BISCOE, Edmund BLOIS, Nathaniel BOWMAN, Thomas BOYLSTON, William BRIDGES, Henry BRIGHT Sr., Henry BRIGHT Jr., Abraham BROWN, Richard BROWN, George BULLARD, Nicholas BUSBY, Charles CHADWICK, Ephraim CHILD, Garrett CHURCH, John CLOUGH, John COOLIDGE, Benjamin CRISP, James CUTLER, Robert DANIEL, Edward DIX, John DOGGETT, John EDDY, John ELLET, Simon EYRE, Robert FEAKE, John FIRMAN, David FISKE, Thomas FLEG, John FLEMING, Samuel FREEMAN, Richard GALE, Edward GARFIELD, John GOSSE, Christopher GRANT, William GUTTRIDGE, Nicholas GUY, William HAMMOND, Thomas HASTINGS, Timothy HAWKINS, Justinian HOLDEN, Richard HOLDEN, Samuel HOSIER, Edward HOWE, Miles IVES, Robert JENNISON, William JENNISON, Henry KEMBALL, Nicholas KNAPP, William KNAPP, John KNOWLES, Edward LAMB, John LAWRENCE, Edmund LEWIS, Robert LOCKWOOD, Hugh MASON, Thomas MAYHEW, Isaac MIXER, Joseph MORSE Jr., Jeremiah NORCROSS, Frances ONGE, John PAGE, Anthony PEARCE, John PEARCE, William PERRY, George PHILLIPS, Esther PICKRAM, Roger PORTER, John ROGERS, Samuel SALTONSTALL, Richard SAWTELL, John SHERMAN, John SMITH, John SPRING, Isaac STEARNS, Simon STONE, John STOWERS, Gregory TAYLOR, John TRAINE, Martin UNDERWOOD, Richard WAITE, John WARREN, Lawrence WATERS, Roger WELLINGTON, John WHITNEY, Thomas WINCOLL, John WINTER, Richard WOODWARD.

List 2: Short-Term, First Generation

Criteria: Unless they died, five or six years of residence, usually continuous.

John BENJAMIN, Richard BENJAMIN, John BROWN, Robert BULLARD, Richard CARVER, William CLARK, John CLOYSE, John CROSS, Henry DENGAINE, Henry DOW, Daniel FINCH, John FINCH, John FOLGER, John GEORGE, Henry GOLDSTONE, Edmund JAMES, Robert KEYES, John KNIGHT, John LOVERAN, John MARION, George MUNNINGS, Miles NUDD, John OLDHAM, George PARKHURST, Daniel PATRICK, William PAYNE, Brian PENDLETON, William POTTER, George RICHARDSON, Thomas ROGERS, William SANDERS, Robert SEELY, John SIMPSON, Charles STEARNS, Phillip TABER, Thomas TARBELL, Thomas TAYLOR, John THOMPSON, Henry THORPE, Robert VEASEY, Jonas WEED, Barnaby WINDES, John WOOLCOTT.

List 3: "Perchers," First Generation

Criteria: Under five years, mostly 1630s arrivals, hold land or connected in other documentary evidence.

Robert ABBOT, John BACHELOR, George BAIRSTOW, William BAIRSTOW, Nathaniel BAKER, William BAKER, Robert BETTS, John BORDEN, Thomas BOYDEN, Thomas BROOKS, John BRUNDISH, Thomas CAKEBREAD, Oliver CALLOW, Thomas CARTER, John CHAPMAN, Lambert CHENERY, Leonard CHESTER, William CLARK, William CLARK [unrelated], Isaac CUMMINGS, John CUTTING, Henry CUTTRIS, Philemon DALTON, Richard DIFFY, John DWIGHT, John EATON, Thomas FILBRICK, John GAY, William GODFREY, Edward GOFFE, Henry GREEN, John GRIGGS, John HAYWARD, Matthew HITCHCOCK, Nicholas JACOB, Richard KEMBALL, John KINGSBURY, John KNIGHTS, Thomas LINCOLN, Edmund LOCKWOOD, John MASTERS, Daniel MORSE, John NICHOLS, Abner ORDWAY, William PALMER, Daniel PEARCE, William PELHAM, John PRESCOTT, John REYNOLDS, John ROSE, Richard SALTONSTALL, Abraham SHAW, Edmund SHERMAN, John STRICKLAND, Phillip SWADDON, William SWAIN, William SWIFT, Nicholas THEALE, Robert TUCKER, John VAUGHAN, Andrew WARD, John WATERBURY, Emmanuel WHITE, James WOODWARD.

List 4: Latecomers, First Generation

Criteria: Arrival in Watertown after 1640, born before 1620, resident for decade or more.

George ADAMS, Walter ALLEN, Michael BAIRSTOW, John BALL, John BRAYBROOK, John CLARY, John FISKE, Nathan FISKE, William HAGAR, Lewis JONES, John LIVERMORE, Thomas LOVERAN, William PAGE, Hugh PARSONS, Thomas PHILPOT, Thomas PRATT, Edward SANDERS, Robert SANDERSON, William SHATTUCK, John SHERMAN, Daniel SMITH, Samuel STRATTON, Joshua STUBBS, Joseph TAINTER, Samuel THATCHER, Nathaniel TREADWAY, Joseph UNDERWOOD, Thomas UNDERWOOD, John WETHERALL, Anthony WHITE, William WILLIAMS, Thomas WILSON.

List 5: Incomers, Second Generation

Criteria: Born after 1620, arrived from elsewhere in Watertown after 1640.

John APPLIN, Nicholas CADY, John CHADWICK, Thomas CHADWICK, John CHENERY, Caleb CHURCH, Gregory COOK, Thomas FANNING, William GODDARD, Henry GODDEN, Robert HARRINGTON, Nathaniel HOLLAND, Daniel HUDSON, Thomas LOVERUN, Henry MATTACK, Daniel METUP, John NEVINSON, William PRICE, John RANDALL, Stephen RANDALL, Richard SANGER, John SAWIN, Thomas STRAIT, Martin TOWNSEND, Thomas WILSON.

List 6: Long-Term, Second Generation

Criteria: Born between 1620 and 1650, lived ten adult years in Watertown before 1680 (except for early death), offspring of first or occasionally of second generation resident.

John BALL, Benjamin, James, and John BARNARD, Ellis BARRON, Joshua and Nathaniel BARSHAM, Eleazar and Elnathan BEERS, John BENJAMIN, John BISCOE, Richard BLOIS, William BOND, Francis BOWMAN, John and Nathaniel BRIGHT, Abraham, John, and Jonathan BROWN, Jacob and Jonathan BULLARD, John and Richard CHILD, Samuel CHURCH, John, Nathaniel, Simon, and Stephen COOLIDGE, Richard CUTTING, Samuel DANIEL, John DIX, John EDDY, John and Nathaniel FISKE, John and Thomas FLEG, Henry FREEMAN, Abraham and John GALE, Benjamin, Joseph, and Samuel GARFIELD, Caleb and Joseph GRANT, Samuel HAGAR, John and Thomas HAMMOND, Timothy HAWKINS, Samuel JENNISON, Josiah JONES, John KEMBALL, John and William KNAPP, John and Samuel LIVERMORE, John and Joseph MASON, Isaac MIXER, John and Joseph MORSE, Richard NORCROSS, John PARKHURST, Benjamin and Joseph PEARCE, Jonathan and Theophilus PHILLIPS, John SAWIN, John and Phillip SHATTUCK, John and Joseph SHERMAN, Daniel, Ephraim, John, and Joseph SMITH, Henry and John SPRING, Samuel STEARNS, John and Simon STONE, John STRATTON, Joseph TAINTER, Samuel THATCHER, James and Josiah TREADWAY, John and Thomas WAITE, Daniel and John WARREN, Benjamin, Joseph, and Oliver WELLINGTON, John WHITE, John, Jonathan, Richard, and Thomas WHITNEY, John WINCOLL, George and John WOODWARD.

List 7: Officeholders, 1630–1680

This table contains all offices held by Watertown men at town, county, and colony level.

In their complete form, each of these lists contains details of vital records, callings, estates, origins, movements, offices, kin, miscellaneous data, and sources. They are obtainable from the author on request.

ABBREVIATIONS

AgHE   Joan Thirsk, ed., *The Agrarian History of England,* vol. 4 (Cambridge: Cambridge University Press, 1967)
Allen   David Grayson Allen, "In English Ways: Movement of Societies and Transferral of English Local Law and Custom to Massachusetts Bay, 1630–1690" (Ph.D. diss., University of Wisconsin, 1974)
Anderson   Robert Charles Anderson, *The Great Migration Begins,* 3 vols. (Boston: NEHGS, 1995) pagination continuous
Aspinwall   "Aspinwall Notarial Records, 1644–1651," *Reports of the Record Commissioners of the City of Boston* 32 (1903)
Assistants   John Noble and John T. Cronin, eds., *Records of the Court of Assistants,* 3 vols. (Boston: County of Suffolk, 1901–28)
Bond   Henry Bond, *Genealogies and History of Watertown* (Boston: NEHGS, 1860)
CSMP   *Colonial Society of Massachusetts Publications* (Boston: The Society, 1895–)
CSPD   *Calendar of State Papers, Domestic Series,* edited variously by reign (London: Longman, Her Majesty's Stationery Office, 1856–93)
DAB   Allen Johnson and Dumas Malone, eds., *Dictionary of American Biography,* 20 vols. (New York: Scribners, 1928–36)
DNB   Leslie Stephen and Sidney Lee, eds., *Dictionary of National Biography,* 64 vols. (Oxford: Oxford University Press, 1921)
Dunn   Richard S. Dunn, James Savage, and Laetitia Yeandle, eds., *The Journal of John Winthrop* (Cambridge: Harvard University Press, Belknap Press, 1996)
Emerson   Everett Emerson, *Letters from New England* (Amherst: University of Massachusetts Press, 1976)
Fairbanks and Trent   Jonathan Fairbanks and Robert Trent, eds., *New England Begins: The Seventeenth Century,* 3 vols. (Boston: Museum of Fine Art, 1976) pagination continuous
Francis   Convers Francis, *An Historical Sketch of Watertown* (Cambridge: Metcalf, 1830)

Hunt   William Hunt, *The Puritan Moment: The Coming of Revolution in an English County* (Cambridge: Harvard University Press, 1983)

Johnson   Edward Johnson, *Wonder-Working Providence of Sions Saviour,* ed. J. F. Jameson (New York: Scribners, 1910)

Lechford   Edward Everett Hale, ed., "Thomas Lechford, Notarial Records, 1638–41," *American Antiquarian Society Transactions* 7 (1885)

MA   Massachusetts Archives, Columbia Point, Boston

Mass Archives   MHS photostats of Massachusetts Archives and other documents, arranged chronologically, 1508–

MHS   Massachusetts Historical Society

MHSC   MHS Collections, preceded by decadal series number

MR   Nathaniel B. Shurtleff, ed., *Records of the Governor and Company of Massachusetts Bay, 1628–86,* 6 vols. (Boston: White, 1853–54)

MxCC DB   Middlesex County Court, Docket Books 1, 3, transcribed by David Pulsifer, MA

MxCC D&O   Middlesex County Court, Folios of Depositions and Orders, microfilm reels 1–4, MA

Mx Deeds   Middlesex Registry of Deeds, vols. 1–7, County Courthouse, East Cambridge

Mx PR   Middlesex Probate Registers, vols. 1–5, MA; vols. 6–9 on microfilm at Middlesex Probate Registry, East Cambridge

Mx Wills   Microfilm of Middlesex Wills, Inventories etc., series 1, 1648–1871, MA

NEHGS   New England Historic Genealogical Society

NEQ   *New England Quarterly*

NYGBR   *New York Genealogical and Biographical Record*

OED   James A. H. Murray, ed., *Oxford English Dictionary,* 11 vols (Oxford: Clarendon, 1933)

Pope   Charles Pope, *Pioneers of Massachusetts* (Baltimore: Genealogical Publishing, 1965)

Powell   Summer Chilton Powell, *Puritan Village* (New York: Doubleday, 1965)

p.p.   privately printed

R   *New England Historic Genealogical Register*

Savage   James Savage, *Genealogical Dictionary of the First Settlers of New England,* 4 vols. (Baltimore: Genealogical Publishing, 1965) pagination continuous

Smith and Sanborn   Dean Crawford Smith and Melinde Lutz Sanborn, *The Ancestry of Eva Belle Kempton* (Boston: NEHGS, 1996)

Suffolk Deeds   John T. Hassam, ed., *Suffolk Deeds,* book 1 (Boston: Rockwell & Churchill, 1880)

Suffolk Wills   Judith McGhan, indexer, *Suffolk County Wills* (Baltimore: Genealogical Publishing, 1984)

TAG   *The American Genealogist*

test.   testimony of

WBOP   Watertown Book of Possessions, part 2 of *WR*

WJ   John Winthrop, *Journal: "History of New England,"* ed. James K. Hosmer, 2 vols. (New York: Scribners, 1908)

WMQ *William and Mary Quarterly*
WP Allyn Forbes and Francis J. Bremer, eds., *Winthrop Papers,* 6 vols. (Boston: MHS, 1925–92)
WR *Watertown Town Records,* vol. 1 (Watertown: Watertown Historical Society, 1894)
Wyman Thomas P. Wyman, MSS summary of MxCC D&O, 1649–1674, 2 vols., NEHGS

NOTES

Introduction

1. *Mobility and Migration: East Anglian Founders of New England, 1629–1640* (Amherst: University of Massachusetts Press, 1994).

2. *London Review of Books*, 10 November 1994, 21–22. See also Gerald M. Sider and Gavin A. Smith, eds., *Between History and Historians* (Toronto: University of Toronto Press, 1997), 13: "The fractures, tensions and contradictions (not inner coherence) of any society are central for an understanding of its historical dynamic."

3. According to the marker erected by Watertown Historical Society in 1948 near the foot of the Eliot Bridge in Cambridge, "Here Reverend George Phillips' protest in 1632 against taxation without representation struck the first note of Civil Liberty heard in this wilderness."

4. Andrew Delbanco, *The Puritan Ordeal* (Cambridge, Mass.: Harvard University Press, 1989).

5. Unfortunately, for much research on the English background of the founders, Bond relied on a professional genealogist in England, Horatio G. Somerby, some of whose elaborate pedigrees have since been invalidated. The contemporary accolade for Bond's accuracy was awarded by the great James Savage, whose *Genealogical Dictionary* followed *The Genealogies and History of Watertown* closely. Hodges's work was edited by Sigrid R. Reddy, with epilogue by Charles T. Burke (Watertown: Free Public Library, 1980).

6. Darrett B. Rutman and Anita H. Rutman, *Small Worlds, Large Questions* (Charlottesville: University of Virginia Press, 1994), 34; Kenneth Lockridge, "The Population of Dedham, 1636–1736," *Economic History Review*, 2d ser., 19 (1966): 318–44; Kenneth Lockridge and Alan Kreider, "The Evolution of Massachusetts Town Government, 1640–1740," *WMQ* 23 (1966): 549–74; Robert E. Wall, *Massachusetts Bay: The Crucial Decade, 1640–1650* (New Haven: Yale University Press, 1972), 21–40; David G. Allen, *In English Ways: Movement of Societies and Transferral of English Local Law and Custom to Massachusetts Bay, 1600–1690* (Chapel Hill: University of North Carolina Press, 1981), chaps. 10, 11. See also Powell, chap. 5; on local histories generally, John J. Waters, "From Democracy to Demography: Recent Historiography on the New England Town," in *Perspectives on Early American History: Essays in Honour of Richard B. Morris*, ed. Alden T. Vaughan and George A. Billias (New York: Harper & Row, 1973), 222–49. I am especially grateful that much of the quantitative analysis has already been done by others far more qualified than I.

7. Andrew Hinde, review of *Microhistories* (Cambridge: Cambridge University Press, 1996), by Barry Reay, Reviews in History, ihr@sas.ac.uk, 2, 3, 7–8, 9, 10; Jacques Revel, "Microanaly-

sis and the Construction of the Social," in *Histories: French Constructions of the Past*, ed. Jacques Revel and Lynn Hunt (New York: New Press, 1995), 497, 499; Margaret Spufford, *From Chippenham to the World: Microcosm to Macrocosm* (London: Roehampton Institute, 1995), 18.

8. Reay, *Microhistories*, conclusion and response to Hinde, 12, 13; Gerald M. Sider, *Culture and Class in Anthropology and History* (New York: Cambridge University Press, 1986), 6, 10; Pat Hudson, "In Defence of Microhistory" (paper given at Centre of East Anglian Studies, 5 March 1999). Carlo Ginsberg, *The Cheese and the Worms* (London: Routledge, 1980), reveals its apparent crazy miller to have been representative of many aspects of sixteenth-century Italian peasant culture. On international impact, see chapter 8.

9. Rutman and Rutman, *Small Worlds, Large Questions*, 17; Spufford, *From Chippenham to the World*, 4.

10. Both Boston: NEHGS, 1996.

11. Rutman and Rutman, *Small Worlds, Large Questions*, xii.

12. On the concepts of social drama and thick description, see Alan Macfarlane, *Reconstructing Historical Communities* (New York: Cambridge University Press, 1977), 17.

1. The Lie of the Land

1. I was unable to gain access to either the Putnam School tower or the Tufts Medical Plan tower, even better vantage points.

2. This spot was known as Gerry's Landing in the nineteenth century. Hodges, *Crossroads on the Charles*, 9. The granite Watertown/Cambridge boundary marker on the sidewalk beside Mount Auburn Cemetery represents the 1754 redrawing of town lines.

3. USGS 1:25000 map, North Boston.

4. On Native American occupation, see below in this chapter. These tools were found at the third site mentioned.

5. Barnard, Bartlett, Bemis, Bigelow, Boylston, Chester, Coolidge, Garfield, Grant, Harrington, Howe, Hudson, Kemball, Mason, Morse, Prescott, Priest, Shattuck, Stearns, and Warren.

6. This statement is founded on apologetic or inaccurate responses to requests for directions during many visits! I was, however, also given highly knowledgeable help from other informants, listed in the acknowledgments.

7. See chapter 5.

8. See Appendix A, "Lt. Robert Feake." For features, see map 4.

9. See Bond for an excellent map (at the end of his work).

10. *MR*, 1:291; Rutman and Rutman, *Small Worlds, Large Questions*, 62; MxCC D&O, 4, folio 91, 21 December 1680.

11. The sketch map is reproduced in both Bond and *WR*.

12. Max Hall, *The Charles: The People's River* (Boston: Godine, 1986); Hodges, *Crossroads*, 9.

13. The best map of these features is that drawn by Edmund L. Sanderson, *Waltham as a Precinct of Watertown and as a Town, 1630–1884* (Waltham: Waltham Historical Society, 1936), frontispiece. W. J. Latimer and M. O. Lanphear, *Soil Survey of Middlesex County, MA* (Washington D.C.: U.S. Dept. of Agriculture, 1924).

14. This section relies on Dena F. Dincauze, "Prehistoric Occupation of the Charles River Estuary," *Archeological Society of Connecticut Bulletin* 38 (1973): 25–39; idem, "Ceramic Shards from the Charles River Basin," ibid. 39 (1975): 5–15; idem, "Cremation Cemeteries of Eastern Massachusetts," *Peabody Museum Papers* 59 (1968): 1–103.

15. Maize was grown elsewhere from ca. A.D. 800, but little or no dental caries, a sign of maize consumption, has been found in the eastern Massachusetts human remains. Kathleen J. Bragdon, *Native People of Southeast New England, 1500–1650* (Norman: University of Oklahoma Press, 1996), 62.

16. Only three sites in Massachusetts Bay are reported as containing evidence of maize. Ibid., 81,

17. The population of Massachusetts, including Narragansetts, is estimated at about 37,500

in the early seventeenth century. After the first European-borne epidemic in 1615, it fell to around 5,000. Dean R. Snow, *The Archeology of New England* (New York: Academic Press, 1980), 34. On evidence of recent cultivation, see chapter 12.

2. The Peopling of Early Watertown

1. This event forms the centerpiece of the town crest and its somewhat misleading motto, *In Pace Condita* (Founded in peace).

2. The first encounter is described in detail in chapter 12. Newbury and Windsor were other predominantly West-Country towns.

3. Robert E. Moody, ed., *The Saltonstall Papers, 1607–1815* (Boston: MHS, 1971) 1, 3–23, 46; see frontispiece for Saltonstall's portrait, on which the statue is based; the original, painted in the Netherlands in the early 1640s, is in the Peabody Museum, Salem. Anderson. As the only knight to emigrate, and as a man of wealth, Saltonstall was socially among the highest ranking emigrants. It is intriguing to speculate why he was not the first governor of Massachusetts, though no obvious reason is evident. Biographical, genealogical, and bibliographic data on individuals will be found in the lists of settlers, available from the author (see Appendix B).

4. Founders named on the memorial are asterisked in the lists of settlers available from the author. Subsequent research suggests minor amendments: Hugh should be William Clarke; John Eliot should be Ellett; John should be David Fiske; William Gager, John Stimson, and Timothy Wheeler, if resident at all in Watertown, were only "perchers" (i.e., never settling).

5. See chapter 10.

6. Protests: Nayland, 1629: John Warren, John Firmin, and Gregory Stone; Norwich, 1633: John Pearce. See chapter 6. Letters, ?John Pond, John Masters, and William Hammond, see Emerson, 64–66, 83–85, 110–12.

7. 184–204. For similar West-Country group migration, see Robert Lord Goodman, "Newbury, MA, 1635–85: The Social Foundations of Harmony and Conflict" (Ph. D. diss., Michigan State University, 1974), 28–36; Frank Thistlethwaite, *Dorset Pilgrims* (London: Barrie & Jenkins, 1989).

8. In 1631 Masters wrote a letter to Joan, Lady Barrington, of Hatfield Broad Oak near the Essex-Hertfordshire border, Emerson, 83–85. Masters Brook in Watertown was named after him by Winthrop in 1632. The family moved the short distance into Newtown in 1633. See chapter 6.

9. Nicholas Knapp was convicted in 1631 of selling a useless concoction as a cure for scurvy. His fine was paid by Pelham and Lockwood. *MR*, 1:83, 99. Nicholas and William Knapp's exact relationship is not clear, but they are bracketed in WBOP. Pelham probably returned with Saltonstall in 1631. His family connection with Bures was through marriage with the Waldegraves. The Benjamin family from Sussex may have been clients of the Pelham family.

10. Diffy, insolence, *MR,* 1:81; Woodward, burned wigwams, ibid., 1:84.

11. Bright was related to Thomas Bright, a leading godly reformer of manners in Jacobean Bury. John S. Craig, "The Bury Stirs Revisited," *Proceedings of the Suffolk Institute of Archeology and History* 37 (1991): 208–24. Our Henry was called Junior because there was an obscure older man of the same name in Watertown. See chapter 9.

12. *DNB;* Thompson, *Mobility and Migration,* 185–86, amended by Anderson, 245–46, and Smith and Sanborn, 180.

13. See map 4.

14. See chapter 6.

15. E.g., Child-Bond-Warren-Goddard links, or Doggett-Eddy-Benjamin-Firmin, or Page-Hammond; see Anderson, and Thompson, *Mobility and Migration,* 190–96.

16. On the longevity of the first generation and on officeholders, see chapter 4.

17. Richard and Abraham Brown received neighboring homestalls in the first allocation. Bond, "Map of the Original Allotments of Land." See chapters 4 and 6.

18. Dunn, 119, 121, 123–24.

19. Watertown settlers on the *Elizabeth:* John Barnard, John Firmin, Henry Goldstone,

Thomas Hastings, Henry Kemball, Richard Kemball, Edmund Lewis, Isaac Mixer, Joseph Morse Jr., George Munnings, [Capt.] John Sherman, [Rev.] John Sherman, John Spring, Martin Underwood, and Richard Woodward; on the *Francis:* Edmund Blois, Thomas Boyden, William Hammond, Justinian Holden, Richard Holden, John Livermore, and Hugh Mason.

20. Anderson, 675, 853; Firmin had been a Nayland religious resister in 1629; he brought letters, including one from Rev. Henry Jacie, to John Winthrop Jr., *WP,* 3:142, dated 17 December 1633.

21. Richard and Henry Kemball, Thurston Rayner. Dedham: two John Shermans, John Livermore, John Barnard, Joseph Morse, and Edmund Lewis. Michael J. Wood has unraveled the Dedham connections in *TAG* 62 (1987) and 64 (1989). The Holden brothers were also aboard the *Francis.*

22. Colchester: Dedhamites, Mixers, Jennisons, Underwoods; Bury: Kemballs, Munning, Holdens; Framlingham: Stowers, Blois, Goldstones; Upper Stour: Livermores, Springs. John Spring's fare was subsidized by his distant cousin Sir William. G. B. Roberts, *TAG* 55 (1979): 64–72; *WP* 2:204, 3:294. Puritanism: Emerson, 224; *DNB,* s.n. Barnardiston, Powell, 77–85.

23. Kemball-Lockwood, Bright-Goldstone-Underwood, Stearns-Munning, and Page-Hammond; Livermore-Spring-Taylor. Sources for these linkages are in Anderson.

24. *WJ,* 1:152.

25. Payne-Eyre-Hammond-Page, Stone-Stone-Cutting-Kemball, and Parish-Warren. Simon Stone and Edward Howe had been joint witnesses to a Boxted will in 1627.

26. Eddy-Windes-Benjamin-Foster, Lechford, 377, 29 July 1639; Filbrick-Knapp-Warren, *R* 92 (1938): 382; Anderson, 1135; Barnard-Nudd-Arnold-Wincoll-Gosse-Dix, Anderson, 551–52; Underwood-Fiske-Folger-Lawrence-Bigelow, Thompson, *Mobility and Migration,* 191–92, 198.

27. Miles Ives, probably from Nayland, 1639; George Parkhurst, Ipswich, 1639; on Knowles, see chapter 6; on Treadway, a kinsman of Howe, see Smith and Sanborn, 450–61, and chapter 4. He lived initially in Sudbury.

28. Richard Carver, aged sixty of Scratby by Yarmouth, soon died; his widow married Michael Bairstow. Pearce, of St. Edmund's Parish, Norwich, had been cited before the church courts in 1633; his vicar, Thomas Allen, "a notable and dangerous refractory," fled to Massachusetts in 1638. The numerous Norfolk immigrants in the late 1630s usually opted for newer settlements like Hingham, Dedham, or Hampton or for the hinterland of Salem.

29. L. A. Morrison, *History of the Kemball Family* (Boston: p.p., 1890), 1–34; *R* 52 (1898): 280; 56 (1902): 335; 57 (1903): 331–32; 79 (1925): 115; Smith and Sanborn, 256–85. Marriages: Coolidge-Mixer, Rogers-Coolidge, Rogers-Warren, Salter-Hammond, Stone-Lumpkin. Abuttals: Child-Warren-Firmin, Knapp-Knapp, Brown-Brown, Stearns-Warren. See Barbara MacAllan's brilliant work on Hampton settlement patterns, "Custom, Contrast, or Compromise" (Ph. D. diss., University of East Anglia, 1999). I have been unable to unearth kinship connections for Hugh Mason, from Maldon, and Suffolk man Thomas Hastings, both leading townsmen of Watertown who arrived in 1634.

30. Ephraim Child, deacon and land speculator, Edward Howe, elder and mill investor, John Masters, puristic canal-builder, and Robert Feake, intensely religious meadow-seeker, spring immediately to mind. See chapters 8 and 9.

31. Feake, St. Edmund's, Lombard Street; Whitney, St. Mary Aldermanbury and Bow Lane; Saltonstall, Swan Alley and St. Stephen's, Coleman Street; Norcross, St. Dunstan's in the East, Fleet Street; Freeman, Blackfriars; Pendleton, St. Sepulchre's Without Newgate; Brown, St. Olave's, Southwark; Clarke, "London"; Boylston, Fenchurch Street; Wincoll, London Stone; Jennison, Holborn. They were quite unlike the St. Stephen's, Coleman St. conventicle, which founded New Haven in 1638. Francis J. Bremer, *Congregational Communion* (Boston: Northeastern University Press, 1994), 89–91.

32. West Country: Guy, Tainter, Mayhew, Ball. Bairstow: Matthew Wood, "English Origins . . . Bairstow," *NYGBR* 121 (1990): 97–101.

33. Besides William Knapp, carpenter, there was Christopher Grant, glazier, Daniel Patrick, professional soldier, Benjamin Crisp, mason, and Thomas Wincoll, stockman.

3. The View from the Stour

1. St. Peter's church guide records the installation of dormers in 1604. For the Stour Valley, see map 4. Alan Everitt, "Suffolk in the Great Rebellion," *Suffolk Record Society* 3 (1960): 120; Hunt, 174; Felix Hull, "Agriculture and Rural Society in Essex, 1560–1640" (Ph. D. diss., London University, 1950), 185, 216.

2. See map 4. The population of Ipswich in 1640 was between seven and eight thousand. Everitt, "Suffolk," 17; on roads, Brian W. Quintrell, "The Government of Essex, 1603–42" (Ph. D. diss., London University, 1965), 229.

3. Everitt, "Suffolk," 17; Hunt, 3–11; Lord Francis Hervey, ed., *Suffolk in the Seventeenth Century: The Breviary of Robert Ryece, 1618* (London: Murray, 1902), 38–42; building ranged from magnificent mansions like Audley End, through handsome halls like Erwarton or Rivers Hall in Boxted, to substantial farmhouses and townhouses, W. G. Hoskins, "The Rebuilding of Rural England, 1570–1640," *Past and Present* 4 (1953): 44–59.

4. Hervey, *Suffolk,* 41; Richard Collyer, "Sudbury Flood-Meadows," *Colne-Stour Countryside Newsletter,* April 1997, 4–5; *CSPD*, 1591–94, 153, refers to eight hundred acres of common grazing belonging to Colchester; Joan Thirsk, "Agricultural Regions of England," *AgHE*, 54–55; Hull, "Agriculture and Rural Society," 13, 50, 53, 73, 99, 105; John Walter, *Understanding Popular Violence in the English Revolution: The Colchester Plunderers* (Cambridge: Cambridge University Press, 1999), 77–78.

5. "Flemish" inhabitants of Colchester numbered 1,297 in 1586, Hunt, 10, 25; G. Rendell, *Dedham* (Colchester: p.p., 1939), 42; *Dedham Town Guide* (Dedham: Countryside Centre, n.d.), 5, 6, 7, 12–13. Langham, between Boxted and Dedham, had to provide a second victualing house in 1604 for increased numbers of weavers and spinners to buy their food.

6. James R. Davis, "Colchester, 1600–1660: Politics, Religion, and Office-holding in an English Provincial Town" (Ph. D. diss, Brandeis University, 1980), 20; Norman C. P. Tyack, "Migration of East Anglians to New England before 1660" (Ph. D. diss., London University, 1951), 189.

7. The wealthy: Thomas Spring, the Baynings, William Cardinal of East Bergholt, the Guyons of Colchester, and Thomas Wincoll "the Rich" of Little Waldingfield, Hunt, 11; Hull, "Agriculture and Rural Society," 282, 286. Processes included cleaning, combing, carding, spinning, weaving, dyeing, fulling, tentering, shearing, and calendaring.

8. Hunt, 19, 167; Walter, *Understanding Popular Violence,* 244, 252.

9. Hunt, 17–19, 31, 32; Tyack, "Migration," 96, 110; Dunn, 731; Keith Wrightson and David Levine, *Poverty and Piety in an English Village: Terling, 1525–1700* (New York: Academic Press, 1979), 40–41, 175; Hull, "Agriculture and Rural Society," 73, 77, 315, 460.

10. Davis, "Colchester," 20, 29–43, estimates that between a third and a half of the population of Colchester were incomers, including about 1,300 of Netherlandish origin. In 1632 one resident claimed that Colchester's population had trebled in three decades; another (still exaggerating) thought it had doubled. Hunt, 19, 78–80; Tyack, "Migration," 10, 236.

11. Literacy levels: Suffolk, 55 percent of the males signed the Protestation Returns, 1641–44; Essex, 35–39 percent. These percentages were among the highest outside London. David Cressy, *Literacy and the Social Order* (Cambridge: Cambridge University Press, 1980), 73.

12. See chapters 8 and 9.

13. John Ball, the leader in 1381, had been a preacher in Colchester. In 1526 Hadleigh, Lavenham, and other Suffolk wool towns resisted Cardinal Wolsey's irregular commissioners to raise taxes with such violence that the attempted levy had had to be abandoned. Boxted: Francis W. Steer, "A Manorial Dispute of the Sixteenth Century," *East Anglian Magazine* 11 (1948): 156–59; boroughs: Maldon, Colchester, Sudbury, Harwich, and Ipswich, Tyack, "Migration," 370–71, 388; Quintrell, "Government of Essex," 82, 330; Everitt, "Suffolk," 16, includes Sir William Spring and Sir Robert Crane of Sudbury, Sir Nathaniel Barnardiston of Kedington, and Edward Alford and Harbottle Grimston of Colchester as leading opposers; Hunt, 212–13, 282, 313; Hervey, *Suffolk,* 266; Hull, "Agriculture and Rural Society," 460.

14. During the 1630s those thorns in the flesh of Personal Rule—Prynne, Burton, and Bastwick—were either welcome visitors to Colchester or celebrators of its libertarianism. A local gentleman, Bastwick's brother-in-law, Thomas Cotton of East Bergholt, was condemned by central authority as "a great depraver of government." Quintrell, "Government of Essex," 6, 89, 340; Paul S. Seaver, *The Puritan Lectureships* (Stanford, Calif.: Stanford University Press, 1970), 111; Tyack, "Migration," 258, 390; Hunt, 153, 187, 205, 209, 261–63, 272, 282; Everitt, "Suffolk," 11. On popular participation and on awareness and assertion of rights and liberties, see David Underdown, "Popular Politics in pre-Civil-War England," in *From Reformation to Revolution*, ed. Margo Todd (London: Routledge, 1995), 208–31; Richard Cust, "News and Politics in Seventeenth-Century England," in ibid., 231–51; Ann Hughes, "Local History and Origins of the Civil War," in ibid., 258; the classic account of the riots of 1642 is Walter, *Understanding Popular Violence*; on rights, see esp. 74–83, 143; on Colchester's stridency, 162–66; on anti-Catholicism, 318–22.

15. Hunt, 189, 209; Tyack, "Migration," 376; Hull, "Agriculture and Rural Society," 200–202; William J. Petchey, "The Borough of Maldon, Essex, 1500–1688" (Ph. D. diss., Leicester University, 1972), 155–57.

16. There were twenty-two Essex martyrs. There were burnings in Ipswich and Hadleigh as well as Colchester. W. A. B. Jones, *Hadleigh through the Ages* (Ipswich: p.p., 1977), 41–45. Stories circulated in Colchester in 1640 that "Irish saboteurs were planning to fire the town . . . an army of papists was said to be assembling with great stores of armour" at Berechurch, just to the south, the seat of the recusant Audleys, Hunt, 87.

17. Arminian reemphasis of free will, church sacraments and ceremony, "the beauty of holiness," and obedience to the hierarchy was a series of red rags to choleric Calvinists. Nicholas Tyacke, *The Anti-Calvinists* (Oxford: Clarendon, 1983); Hunt, 191. "At Bures, a local gentleman asked by the churchwardens whether they should obey the order to rail in the communion table, answered 'It's no matter, it's but a dance before Popery. The king hath a wife, and he loves her well, and she is a papist and we must all be of her religion, and that's the thing the bishops aim at.'" Walter, *Understanding Popular Violence*, 214.

18. Norman C. P. Tyack, "The Humbler Puritans of East Anglia," *R* 138 (1984): 100–101; Hunt, 284; A. R. Pennie, "Evolution of Puritan Mentality in . . . Dedham" (Ph. D. diss, Sheffield, 1989), 114, 168.

19. Hunt, xii, 79, 91–93, 145–46; Patrick Collinson, *The Religion of Protestants* (Oxford: Oxford University Press, 1982) has much Suffolk material throughout; Tom Webster, *Godly Clergy in Early Stuart England: The Caroline Puritan Movement, c.1620–43* (Cambridge: Cambridge University Press, 1997) concentrates on Essex.

20. Henry Wilder Foote, "George Phillips, First Minister of Watertown," MHS *Proceedings* 63 (1930): 193–227, esp. 194. Davis, "Colchester," 84, 96, 102, 178–80, 187–90; Gifford preached, wrote, and agitated in Maldon from 1583 to 1620, Petchey, "Maldon," 214–18, 223, 225; Hunt, 87.

21. Patrick Collinson, *The Elizabeth Puritan Movement* (London: Cape, 1967), chap. 6; in 1590 the conformist Boxted wardens presented their own vicar, Philip Gilgatt: "He hath procured Mr. [Thomas] Farrer, parson of Langham [and sometime member of the Dedham Classis], to preach three times within this fortnight, contrary to Her Majesty's commandment and my Lord Archbishop of Canterbury and my Lord Bishop of London, without licence or authority. Also he hath baptized Agnes Northen without using [the sign of] the cross or wearing surplice and saith he will not make the sign of the cross for none of us." Rowland G. Usher, ed., "The Presbyterian Movement, 1582–89," *Transactions of the Royal Historical Society*, 3d ser., 8 (1905): xlix, 7, 19, 29, 32, 33, 37, 38, 46, 52, 53, 54, 55, 57, 59, 70, 71, 72, 74; Frederick G. Emmison, *Elizabeth Life: Morals and the Church* (Chelmsford: Essex Record Office, 1973), 202; Hunt, 100.

22. John Rogers's cousin Ezekiel (later minister of Rowley, Mass.) was domestic chaplain to Sir Francis Barrington, premier baronet of Essex. Nathaniel's patron was Winthrop's friend Brampton Gurdon. Two of Gurdon's sons emigrated to Massachusetts during the 1630s, Thompson, *Mobility and Migration*, 32; Kenneth W. Shipps, "Lay Patronage of East Anglian

Clerics in Pre-revolutionary England" (Ph. D. diss., Yale University, 1971), 46; M. M. Knappen, *Two Elizabethan Puritan Diaries* (Gloucester, Mass.: Peter Smith, 1966), 23–24; Webster, *Godly Clergy*, 171–74, 191–94, 269, 278–79; Edmund S. Morgan, *The Puritan Family* (New York: Harper, 1966), chap. 7.

23. Tyack, "Migration," 359; Webster, *Godly Clergy*, chap. 5.

24. Collinson, *Religion of Protestants*, 244; Hunt, 113, 119, 196; Webster, *Godly Clergy*, 22.

25. Tyack, "Humbler Puritans," 103; Hunt, 176; Walter, *Understanding Popular Violence*, 74–76, 164, 206; Webster, *Godly Clergy*, 315. Parish cures, or incumbencies, were usually in the gift of a patron.

26. Seaver, *Puritan Lectureships*, 111, 144; Shipps, "Lay Patronage," 243–65; Ward "preached against a set form of prayer [and] the Book of Common Prayer . . . and said they were more fit for popish times . . . against bowing and other reverend gestures in the church saying that a man might teach a jackanapes or a baboon to do it, [against] the discipline of the Church of England [and] against His Majesty's Declaration concerning Recreations to be permitted on Sundays [the hated Book of Sports]." Tyack, "Migration," 276, 295–96, 307–8. Gifford also advocated popular "calling" of ministers. Petchey, "Maldon," 236. Archbishop Laud inveighed against the election of ministers in his 1635 Articles.

27. There was a famous and long-standing Combination Lecture given by a series of divines every Monday at Bury St. Edmunds, the other source of emigration to Watertown. It was patronized by gentlemen like Sir Simonds D'Ewes, Sir William Spring, and Sir Nathaniel Barnardiston, as well as local townsmen and villagers. Hunt, 119; Tyack, "Migration," 338, 358; Collinson, *Religion of Protestants*, 119, 170, 258; Seaver, *Puritan Lectureships*, 323; Shipps, "Lay Patronage," chap. 2; Quintrell, "Government of Essex," 294. Although Groton's Henry Leigh was a strict puritan, Adam Winthrop nonetheless went "gadding" to the Waldingfields, Kersey, Hadleigh, Dedham, and Wethersfield; Francis J. Bremer, "John Winthrop's Heritage: Religion along the Stour Valley, 1548–1630," *NEQ* 70 (1997): 532.

28. George H. Williams, Norman Pettit, Winfried Herget, and Sergeant Bush, eds., *Thomas Hooker: Writings in England and Holland, 1626–1633* (Cambridge, Mass.: Harvard University Press, 1975), 191–220; Shipps, "Lay Patronage," 133–34, 313–17; *CSPD*, 1637, 417; Tyack, "Humbler Puritans," 103; Tyack, "Migration," 338; Seaver, *Puritan Lectureships*, 84–85; Collinson, *Religion of Protestants*, 136–37, 157; *WP*, 1:155–56; Bremer, "John Winthrop's Heritage," 533.

29. Hunt, 110; *Seven Treatises*, originally published in 1603, had gone into its seventh edition by 1630; it was also excerpted in *The Garden of Spiritual Flowers*. Bremer, "John Winthrop's Heritage," 537, also associates Winthrop's "social gospel" aspirations with the proposals of leading Suffolk divine John Knewstubs.

30. Hunt, 120–21; Williams et al., *Hooker*, 4–6; Webster, *Godly Clergy*, 52–54, 129.

31. On puritan introversion and psychology: Knappen, *Two Elizabethan Puritan Diaries*, 35; Michael McGiffert, ed., *God's Plot: The Autobiography and Journal of Thomas Shepard* (Amherst: University of Massachusetts Press, 1972); Charles L. Cohen, *God's Caress: The Psychology of Puritan Religious Experience* (New York: Oxford University Press, 1986); Charles E. Hambrick-Stowe, *The Practice of Piety: Puritan Devotional Disciplines* (Chapel Hill: University of North Carolina Press, 1982); George Selement and Bruce C. Woolley, eds., *Thomas Shepard's Confessions* (Boston: Colonial Society of Massachusetts, 1981); Patricia Caldwell, *The Puritan Conversion Narrative* (Cambridge: Cambridge University Press, 1983).

32. Hunt, 79–84, 140–55, 166, 179; Keith Wrightson, "The Puritan Reformation of Manners" (Ph. D. diss., Cambridge University, 1973).

33. Usher, "Presbyterian Movement," 99–101; the schoolmaster of Dedham, Arthur Gale, was a member of the classis, ibid., 73; Joan R. Kent, *The English Village Constable, 1580–1642* (Oxford: Clarendon, 1986), 20–24, 283, 292. The manorial court might continue regulation of fences, control of livestock, including the services of the town bull, and other agricultural matters. Steve Hindle, *The State and Social Change* (London: Macmillan, 2000), chap. 8, and "Political Culture of the Middling Sort in English Rural Communities, c.1550–1700," to appear in *Politics of the Excluded*, ed. Tim Harris (forthcoming), argues that the early Stuart decay of the

manor and onset of closed vestries has been exaggerated and that the closed vestry was a predominantly Restoration phenomenon. I am most grateful to Steve Hindle for help on issues of English local government.

34. Hunt, 136–37, 143, 154; see also Wrightson and Levine, *Poverty and Piety,* 179; Craig, "Bury Stirs Revisited," 220–24; Walter, *Understanding Popular Violence,* 192–94, 206; for the Poor Laws, see chapter 9. In 1629 Thomas Hooker celebrated the success of the experiment in "The Faithful Covenanter: A Sermon preached at the Lecture at Dedham in Essex," in *Hooker,* ed. Williams et al., 203, 217: "To pray little and do little in good duties, the Lord will not take this of a Dedham Christian; that is for those that have but small encouragements, and a sermon now and then (and that but weak neither) . . . A Dedham man, God will not have him have a stomach only to a good duty and now and then to pray, or to read, or to confer; but He requires great debts from him. A Dedham drunkard, or hypocrite, careless carnal gospeller, or covetous one, the devils will rejoice for him when he comes to hell. They will make bonfires, and make a holiday for him, stand upon their tiptoes to look on him."

35. Emmison, *Early Essex Town Meetings* (Chichester: Phillimore, 1970), v, vi; Wrightson and Levine, *Poverty and Piety,* chap. 6; Collinson, *Religion of Protestants,* 119; Shipps, "Lay Patronage," 63–82, 152, 301–4; for other closed vestries: Harry Clive, *Beyond Living Memory* (Little Waldingfield: p.p., 1979), 25–28; Petchey, "Borough of Maldon," 161, 167–68, 245, 259.

36. For others examples of popular participation: Hindle, *State and Social Change,* 109–10, 212–13, 224–25, 228–29; Walter, *Understanding Popular Violence,* 74–77, 287, 299, 331, 351. Executive functions included warning out nonresidents; apprenticing poor children; hounding the idle, masterless, drunk, and disorderly; helping the sick and dependent; and reporting the incorrigible to the local justice, Emmison, *Early Essex,* xii–xiv, 107–36; for Boxted, see Tyack, "Humbler Puritans," 100–101.

37. There were over eight hundred alehouses in prerevolutionary Essex. Some keepers offered pawn to paupers whose relief had been paid in kind. Quintrell, "Government of Essex," 226–27.

38. A cowl was a water butt hung on a staff carried by two men; a caliver was a small handgun. A cowl staff was used for shaming punishments in Maldon, Petchey, "Borough of Maldon," 222; Collinson, *Elizabeth Puritan Movement,* 226; Usher, "Presbyterian Movement," 63.

39. Usher, "Presbyterian Movement," 70.

40. Anderson, 1934; Tyack, "Humbler Puritans," 101; Hunt, 146, 148, 154, 155; Quintrell, "Government of Essex," 297; Webster, *Godly Clergy,* 98–99.

41. Usher, "Presbyterian Movement," xxi, 77–82; Knappen, *Two Elizabethan Puritan Diaries,* 33; Thomas Hooker consulted with leading London professors like John Davenport of St. Stephen's Coleman Street before emigrating to New England in 1633. Williams et al., *Hooker,* 30; Collinson, *Religion of Protestants,* 50, 324; Quintrell, "Government of Essex," 296; Hunt, 261–62; Walter, *Understanding Popular Violence,* 108, 288; see chapters 2 and 6.

42. Tyack, "Migration," chaps. 5, 6; Hunt, 168–92, 244–45. Exports of Old Drapery cloths through London: in 1606: 14,507; in 1622: 9,003; in 1633: 6,396; through Ipswich: in 1613: 4,154; in 1621: 1,801; in 1635: 1,856. Tyack, "Migration," 203, 474. The grain average index for the 1620s was 594; for 1630: 880; for 1631: 602; for 1632: 698; for 1633: 711; for 1634: 824; for 1638: 969. Hunt, 244–45.

43. There was also "terrible corn scarcity" in the West Country and serious riots among weavers there in the autumn of 1622. Hunt, 172–73.

44. Tyack, "Migration," 102, 160; Hunt, 173, 181–82, 184; Quintrell, "Government of Essex," 73; Emmison, *Early Essex,* xi–xii.

45. Hunt, 239, 241–42; Tyack, "Migration," 104; Quintrell, "Government of Essex," 193; Walter, *Understanding Popular Violence,* 252.

46. *WP,* 2:97; Tyack, "Migration," 18, 72, 133, 164, 215, 219–22; *DNB,* "John Rogers."

47. Anderson, 851; Hunt, 208, 244, 256; Tyack, "Migration," 133, 219.

48. Tyack, "Migration," 215, 222, 236; Hunt, 250; *WP,* 2:57, 91, 130.

4. Government

1. Peter N. Carroll, *Puritanism and the Wilderness* (New York: Columbia University Press, 1969), 70; Hunt, 22, 67, 82–83, 143; see chapter 3.

2. Kenneth A. Lockridge, *A New England Town: The First Hundred Years* (New York: Norton, 1970), 38–42, 48; Lockridge and Kreider, "Evolution of Massachusetts Town Government"; Allen, 343–73; Powell, 74–79; John J. Waters, "Hingham, Massachusetts, 1631–1661: An East Anglian Oligarchy in the New World," *Journal of Social History* 1 (1967–68): 351–370; idem, "From Democracy to Demography," 226; Michael Zuckerman, "The Social Context of Democracy in Massachusetts," *WMQ* 25 (1968): 526–28. A definitive listing of all Watertown officeholders from 1630 to 1680 is available from the author; see Appendix B. See also Bond, 1017–19, 1062–65.

3. These studies by Richard Cust, Richard Tuck, Anne Hughes, Margo Todd, and Quentin Skinner, building on the work of J. G. A. Pocock, are surveyed in *From Reformation to Revolution*, ed. Todd, 208–71, and Skinner, *Liberty before Liberalism* (Cambridge: Cambridge University Press, 1998).

4. What follows is based on *WR*, 54–60.

5. Here meaning householders.

6. *MR*, 1:79, 91, 96.

7. Edmund S. Morgan, ed., *The Founding of Massachusetts: Historians and the Sources* (Indianapolis: Bobbs-Merrill, 1964), 392, 400.

8. *WJ*, 1:78; on resistance in England, Tyack, "Humbler Puritans"; on antiauthoritarianism in England of subsequent Watertown settlers, see chapter 6.

9. Nayland, for instance, "had a monthly meeting which assembled 'by the consent of the inhabitants . . .' and levied a shilling fine for non-attendance." John Warren had been an overseer of the poor there in 1626 and a town feoffee in 1628. Allen, *In English Ways*, 348, 370. On temporal business in parish churches, see Marian C. Donnelly, *The New England Meeting Houses of the Seventeenth Century* (Middletown, Conn.: Wesleyan University Press, 1968), 100. The classic account of the "rise of the parish" is still Sidney Webb and Beatrice Webb, *English Local Government*, vol. 1 (New York: Harper & Row, 1906), part 1, now amplified by Joan R. Kent in her *English Village Constable;* see chapter 3.

10. *WJ*, 1:74–75 recounts the debate and has a useful note by James Savage. *MR*, 1:95. On the desacralizing of the house of worship, see Donnelly, *New England Meeting Houses*, 9–16, 98–103. For a good survey of local government franchise under the first charter, see Timothy H. Breen, "Who Governs? The Town Franchise in Seventeenth-Century Massachusetts," *WMQ* 27 (1970): 460–74.

11. Bond, 1062–63, lists the town's representatives from 1634 to 1692.

12. Ibid., 1065–66, for selectmen.

13. Beneficiaries penalized in 1639 and subsequent years were John Whitney, Edward Garfield, Edmund Lewis, Ephraim Child, John Stowers, John Firmin, and Edmund James. Daniel Patrick left town soon after. See chapter 5.

14. Details of these early leaders are listed alphabetically in Anderson.

15. Died: John Loveran, 1638, Edward Howe, 1644, and Abraham Brown, 1650. Ill: John Eddy, ca. 1639, Robert Feake, ?1639. Scandal: *Assistants*, 2:121. Brown was, however, regularly re-elected deputy to the general court, 1647–55, and was a commissioner for small causes in 1650 and from 1653 to 1656. His name had appeared in town and colony records with much greater frequency before 1643. The Boylston family is discussed in chapter 11.

16. Going to England were William Jennison, in 1648, and Nathaniel Biscoe, and John Knowles, in 1651. Their departures are discussed in detail in chapter 6. Brian Pendleton was in Sudbury 1639–44 and in Maine by 1649. Daniel Patrick and Robert Feake went to Greenwich in 1641, see Appendix A, "Lt. Robert Feake"; Thomas Mayhew went to Martha's Vineyard by 1647, see chapter 12. Payne, Busby, and Eyre went to Boston. On Boston as a growing administrative, commercial, and service center, see Darrett B. Rutman, *Winthrop's Boston: Portrait of a Puritan Town, 1630–1649* (New York: Norton, 1972), 241–73.

17. Jennison's connection with Colchester, Essex, is not documented until 1657. He was, however, appointed agent in Massachusetts in 1646 by the great Essex magnate the earl of Warwick. His 1639 business dealings in London are cited in Anderson.

18. Child, town clerk from 1650 to 1664, was a good scribe, a businesslike accountant, and a methodical record keeper. His predecessor, John Sherman, was also an expert surveyor and builder. He was briefly town schoolmaster in the 1670s. Hastings had financial and arbitration skills and served as moderator of the town meeting. Mason, a tanner by trade, was an execrable speller but a methodical account keeper and respected militiaman. Child and his wife are frequently mentioned by English correspondents of John Winthrop, *WP,* 3:7, 58, 108, 128, 142. An example of Sherman's mapping is reproduced in Fairbanks and Trent, 31. As we shall see, Sherman was out of office in the late 1650s and early 1660s while serving as steward of Harvard College. Hastings became a deacon in 1647, Child in 1648, *WR,* 10, 16. Mason was a leading petitioner for the formation of a "Military Company of Middlesex . . . a Voluntary Company of Gentlemen," which would hold exercises and elect its own officers. It would be an officers' training company and was modeled on the Boston Artillery Company. Mass Archives, 14 May 1645.

19. He and his wife, Elizabeth, are first seen in Watertown in 1637, but he later claimed that he had been in the colony since its foundation. His promotion in 1642 to sergeant of militia and his election to the board coincided with his recovery from Pequot War wounds. He became lieutenant in 1653, started keeping the town "ordinary," or pub, the following year, and in 1659 was one of a party of four who explored what would later become Worcester. He was killed in King Phillip's War. *MR,* 4/2:435; see chapter 12.

20. John Page, first constable, never held office again, see Appendix A, "Page v. Page." John Warren's promising town career was ended by religious disputes, see chapter 6. John Coolidge Sr. was left off the board from 1643 to 1664 but held occasional office in the interim, including constable and deputy. Why he was dropped is not known.

21. See chapters 5 and 6. In 1652 MxCC D&O listed forty Watertown men who took the Oath of Fidelity. Many were younger men; seven subsequently became freemen. No immediate change in the board resulted from this sudden growth of the electorate. *R*3 (1849): 401; Breen, "Who Governs?" 468.

22. Bond (1625–95) was one of the first second-generation leaders. His career is discussed in chapter 10.

23. These events can be followed in *WR,* 73–86.

24. Treadway was fifty-three, Tainter fifty-seven. New: John Biscoe, John Hammond, and John Sawin; returned: John Coolidge and John Sherman. The only regular to retain office was Michael Bairstow. Other explanations for this changeover are that Child and Stone had both died, Hastings had remarried and started a family. These events, however, would not account for the reforms immediately enacted.

25. *WR,* 78; the Triennial Act of 1690.

26. Ibid., 78–80; they discovered that the former appraiser, John Whitney, had seriously miscalculated. War with the Dutch prompted military preparedness.

27. On safeguarding families of absent breadwinners Daniel Metup and Jonathan Whitney, see chapter 9.

28. On laying out the farms in 1662–64, see chapter 5. Conflicts over land policy had led to an exodus from Sudbury to Marlborough in 1657, Powell, 150–77. For membership, see chapter 6. Disunity: Paul R. Lucas, "Colony or Commonwealth? Massachusetts Bay, 1661–1666," *WMQ* 24 (1967): 75–92.

29. *WR,* 91, 92; cf. *MR,* 2/2:173. Artisans: Treadway, Tainter, Coolidge, Biscoe, and Sherman.

30. Dedham had served similar notice on its elite in 1660; Lockridge explains this "upset" as a fit of pique. *New England Town,* 47, 48.

31. *WR,* 90–92.

32. Wyman, 1:51; MxCC D&O, 1, folio 17, 12 July 1667.

33. MxCC D&O, 2, folio 53, 26 June 1669; the General Court finally became involved and supported the selectmen on a legal technicality. *Laws and Liberties of Massachusetts* (Cambridge: Usher, 1672), 148.

34. *WR*, 109, 110.

35. MxCC DB, 3:266; *WR*, 127, 128, 129, 137, 144. See chapter 10.

36. *MR*, 1:276; 2/1:39, 2/2:173, 180, 203–4, 213; 3:358, 376, 396; 4/1:325, 365; 4/2:100, 363, 395, 486; 5:59–62, 155, 240.

37. For instance, Wyman, 1:20, has the grand jury presentment of Watertown for neglect of a bridge. For use of petitions, see chapter 5.

38. In July 1669 his son William, aged fourteen, was drowned. Wyman, 2:92. On the 1671 case involving Thomas Hastings, see Appendix A, "Susannah Woodward."

39. Since 1664 Treadway, along with Haynes in-laws in Sudbury, had been a partner in a scheme to develop a new town (Worcester) beyond Marlborough. Mass Archives, 26 May 1664, 18 October 1665, 10 October 1668, 27 May 1674.

40. *MR*, 1:197; Breen, "Who Governs?" throughout.

41. On the role of the militia in group activities, see Roger Thompson, "Adolescent Culture in Colonial Massachusetts," *Journal of Family History* 9 (1984): 138–39; on church clannishness, Morgan, *Puritan Family*, 161–86.

42. Mason's estate totaled £692, Hastings's £421, Child's £770, and Eyre's £577. Stone's widow also left £577, quickly following her husband to the grave. Estate inventories are entered in Mx PR and Mx Wills, which are indexed. Wall, *Massachusetts Bay*, 28, 344, has tables showing average estates of town officers.

43. Thomas Fleg, who had arrived as a servant and became a regular town official in the 1670s, seems to have had very modest means. So did the older John Whitney, who was an occasional officeholder but frequent appraiser. The rich included John Bigelow, the town blacksmith, who left £627 but was only occasionally given responsibility. Similarly Isaac Stearns, tailor and founder, accumulated an estate of £524, mainly in land, but joined the board only three times in forty years, or Edward Garfield Jr., an equally infrequent selectman, despite being worth £457. Thomas Hammond had an inventory of £652 at his death in 1655. On the "succession" phenomenon, see chapter 10.

44. *WP*, 4:112; see chapter 10.

45. Ola Elizabeth Winslow, *Meetinghouse Hill, 1630–1783* (New York: Norton, 1972), 80.

46. Ibid., 78.

47. Robert M. Bliss, *Revolution and Empire* (Manchester: Manchester University Press, 1990), 80.

48. Winslow, *Meetinghouse Hill*, 51, 65; John Demos, *Entertaining Satan* (New York: Oxford University Press, 1982), 213.

49. David D. Hall, *The Faithful Shepherd* (New York: Norton, 1974), 90.

50. Ibid., 92.

51. See chapter 3, on Nayland, Boxted, and Colchester.

52. *MHS Proceedings* 58 (1924–25): 446–58; *WJ*, 1:74–75, 122–23, 125; Timothy H. Breen, *The Character of a Good Ruler* (New York: Norton, 1974), 66–67, 71–72.

53. On neo-Roman republicanism, see Skinner, *Liberty before Liberalism*, 26–30, 35–36, 37–41, 51–53, 69–70. Davenport election sermon: *CSMP* 10 (1907): 5–6. See Darren Staloff, "High Culture and the Construction of Authority in Early Massachusetts" (paper submitted to World of Winthrop Conference, Millersville, Pa., 1999), 7–17; James F. Cooper Jr., *Tenacious of Their Liberties; Congregationalists in Colonial Massachusetts* (New York: Oxford University Press, 1999), 3, 5–7.

54. Steve Pincus, "Neither Machiavellian Moment nor Possessive Individualism," *American Historical Review* 103 (1998): 705–36, quotes Aristotle's view that these "classical republican" attitudes to self-government and liberty particularly suited "a commonwealth of husbandmen." 711–16, 729–31.

55. See chapter 3.

5. Land

1. *WR,* 2; one child per proprietor could inherit the benefits on parent's death but could not claim them as a birthright when he or she came to majority or married and formed an independent household. Proprietorships could be bought, sold, gifted, and bequeathed. "Freeman" here means church member admitted to freemanship by the General Court. On Watertown land policy, see Robert Charles Anderson, "Early Land Granting in Watertown," *Great Migration Newsletter* 1 (1990): 4–6.

2. Anderson, "Early Land Granting," 4.

3. Book of Possessions, 15–16, *WR;* William Alexander Boyd MacPhail, "Land Hunger and Closed Field Husbandry on the New England Frontier: The First Generation of Settlement in Watertown MA" (Ph. D. diss., Brown University, 1972), 162, 277. *MR,* 1:210. In fact, some post-1635 arrivals did receive land grants after 1635 and up to 1642, though some vetting had taken place. See Lists of Settlers. Alexander Young, ed., *Chronicles of the First Planters of Massachusetts Bay* (Boston: Little, Brown, 1846), 384, has the Charlestown initial allotments of two acres per houselot, with extra two acres for every male "that is able to plant." On the dating and purpose of the three inventories, see Anderson, *R* 144 (1990): 147–50.

4. *WR,* 3; WBOP, 3–5; *MR,* 1:134, 167, confirmed on 3 March 1636 that "Watertown bounds go eight miles into the country within the lines already set out." Rutman, *Winthrop's Boston,* 78–80, describes the allocation of "great lots" to Boston's households, starting in December 1635. Allotments to "the generality" averaged below 30 acres and totaled less than 1,500 acres.

5. Pastor Phillips, forty acres; Sir Richard, thirty; Mr. William Payne, the wealthy merchant from Lavenham, Lieutenant Feake, and Elder Howe, twenty-four acres each. WBOP, 6–8. Anderson routinely estimates Watertown family sizes by the acreage of plowland grants, e.g. 797, 999.

6. WBOP, 8–10. Edward L. Sanderson, *Waltham as a Precinct of Watertown* (Waltham: Waltham Historical Society, 1936), 24.

7. WBOP, 11; MacPhail, "Land Hunger," 205. See "Essay for the Laying Out of Towns," ca. 1635, 5MHSC, 1:474–80, which advocates the nucleation of settlement in Massachusetts. See landholding reconstruction in Bond, endpaper; MacPhail, "Land Hunger," 205. *MR,* 1:172 has the 1636 order that forbade anyone in new towns from living more than half a mile from the meetinghouse. The importance of freemanship is discussed below.

8. *WR,* 4; MacPhail, "Land Hunger," 206.

9. *WR,* 4; *MR,* 1:310. See chapter 4. WBOP, 11–14, 15–16; Mass Archives, 26 [worn]ber 1638, has a list of large farm grants in Watertown that are not in the town records. The "insider" grantees were Sir Richard Saltonstall, Rev. George Phillips, Abraham Brown, Daniel Patrick, Simon Eyre, Edward Howe, Thomas Mayhew, Edward James, John Firmin, John Whitney, Jeremiah Norcross, Edmund Lewis, John Stowers, and Edward Garfield. Firmin and Lewis died before 1642. Firmin's son is listed at the end of the farm grants. My thanks to Robert Charles Anderson for information on this group. See similar insider benefits with farm grants in Cambridge in 1640 and Shawshin in 1648, Lucius R. Paige, *History of Cambridge* (Boston: Houghton, 1877), 40, 57; in Hampton in 1640, MacAllan, "Custom, Contrast, or Compromise." *WR,* 8; WBOP, 11–14; MacPhail, "Land Hunger," 216–20. Allocations range from 287 acres to John Barnard, 270 to John Knights, 259 to Isaac Stearns, and 250 to John Biscoe down to 34 acres to John Winter and 32 to Robert Veasey (two who always seem to bring up the rear). The majority of farm grants were in the 51–149 acre range, which 60 percent received. Three-quarters fell between 51 and 183 acres, including old town leaders like William Jennison (150), Richard Brown (150), and the seven men who would dominate the selectmen's board from the mid-1640s to the late 1670s. Barnard, a weaver, and Stearns, a tailor, both had large households (eleven and twelve respectively). Knights was a maltster, and Biscoe, the twenty-year-old son of a rich tanner, had three siblings. See chapters 2, 4, and 6.

10. Percy Bidwell and John Falconer, *History of Agriculture of the Northern United States, 1620–1860* (Washington, D.C.: Carnegie Institute, 1925), 37–38; *WJ,* 1:143–44, 151–52; Lockridge,

New England Town, 12; Powell 119–20; Philip J. Greven, *Four Generations: Population, Land, and Family in Colonial Andover, Massachusetts* (Ithaca, N.Y.: Cornell University Press, 1970), 41–71; Joseph Dow, *History of the Town of Hampton* (Salem: p.p., 1893), 2:862; see also Goodman, "Newbury MA," 178–79.

11. This is MacPhail's thesis; Johnson, 74. Cf. Paul J. Lindholdt, ed., *John Josselyn, Colonial Traveller* (Hanover: University Press of New England, 1988), 115–16, where Josselyn on his second visit, 1663–71, found "the inhabitants live scatteringly"; he may have used material from Johnson.

12. *WP*, 2:293–95; *MR*, 1:172.

13. Joan Thirsk, "Agriculture in England," in *Seventeenth-Century New England*, ed. David D. Hall and David Grayson Allen (Boston: Colonial Society of Massachusetts, 1984), 39–55; Mark Overton, *The Agricultural Revolution in England: The Transformation of the Agrarian Economy, 1500–1850* (Cambridge: Cambridge University Press, 1996), chap. 1; see chapter 3; Thompson, *Mobility and Migration*, 35, 44–55. On nucleation, see "Essay for the Laying Out of Towns," 5MHSC, 1:474–80.

14. Thompson, *Mobility and Migration*, 230–35; Stephen Innes, *Creating the Commonwealth: The Economic Culture of Puritan New England* (New York: Norton, 1995), 73; see chapter 9.

15. See chapter 2 and 10.

16. *WR*, 6, 35, 37, 71, 87, 105, 135, 138, 147; the rough sketchmap of 1720, drawn when the Second Church was founded, is in *WR*. See chapter 1.

17. James A. Sharpe, *Early Modern England: A Social History, 1550–1760* (London: Arnold, 1987), 198–202; Thompson, *Mobility and Migration*, 101–13. The three linked parishes of Ormesby St. Margaret, Ormesby St. Michael, and Scratby in Norfolk, from which several Watertown residents came, totaled 2,098 acres. MacAllan, "Custom." In about 1630 Winthrop calculated that fifty acres per person would be ample, Dunn, 731.

18. MacPhail, "Land Hunger," 165–66; *MR*, 1:288, 293; 2:59, 80, 89–90, 132, 192, 201; Robert E. Moody, ed., *The Saltonstall Papers* (Boston: MHS, 1972), 1:42. The Saltonstall suit dragged on from May 1640 to October 1647. Despite the General Court's decree on 1 October 1645 that he had "had a full hearing . . . and he ought to rest therein and not trouble the court further," Saltonstall, through his son, Robert, persuaded them to give him one more hearing, and the case was finally settled, with Watertown having to pay £40 and costs. *WP*, 4:112, has a 9 April 1639 letter from Captain Daniel Patrick in Watertown to John Winthrop proposing a new boundary line at Dedham Neck that would add three thousand acres to Watertown's grant without depriving Dedham. His justification was that "Watertown expects something before Dedham as more beneficial through antiquity." *MR*, 1:206 has a 2 September 1637 grant to Watertown of fifteen hundred acres on Concord River, "if it be convenient." There is no record of the town ever obtaining this compensation.

19. Specialists: William Payne, Simon Eyre, and William Nickerson. See chapter 4. For Oldham, see chapter 12. Cakebread, first tempted by Dedham: Anderson; Kemball and Payne: Savage; for the restlessness of the Feakes, see Appendix A, "Lt. Robert Feake"; see also chapter 10.

20. *MR*, 1:201, 222; *WR*, 3; Bernard Bailyn, *The New England Merchants in the Seventeenth Century* (Cambridge, Mass.: Harvard University Press, 1979), 47; *WJ*, 2:17, 31.

21. See chapter 2 and Appendix B. Natural increase in 1634, six births; 1636, eighteen; 1642, thirty-six. Between 1635 and 1642 there were 160 surviving births and forty-seven deaths. See chapter 10.

22. Emerson, 66; Bidwell & Falconer, *History of Agriculture*, 10; William C. Cronon, *Changes in the Land: Indians, Colonists, and the Ecology of New England* (New York: Hill & Wang, 1983), 150; Thomas Hutchinson, *The History of Massachusetts Bay*, ed. Lawrence Shaw Mayo, (Cambridge: Harvard University Press, 1936), 1:402–6.

23. Karen O. Kupperman, "Climate and Mastery of the Wilderness," in *Seventeenth-Century New England*, ed. Hall and Allen, 3–37.

24. Emerson, 71, 92; see chapters 2 and 8.

25. Francis, 23; Emerson, 64–66, 73, 81; Bidwell and Falconer, *History of Agriculture*, 41–2;

WJ, 1:126, 138; *WP,* 3:253 and throughout for letters from England. See also Rutman, *Winthrop's Boston,* 179–80.

26. Lechford, 242–43.

27. By 1638, fully 45 percent of the population of Watertown were nonmembers of the church; see chapter 6.

28. *MR,* 1:161, 172; *WR,* 3, 4. Ralph Crandall and Ralph Coffman, "From Emigrants to Rulers: The Charlestown Oligarchy in the Great Migration," *R* 131 (1977): 13, recount even sharper discrimination against nonfreemen in Charlestown a year earlier than Watertown.

29. *WR,* 4.

30. Ibid.; *MR,* 1:310.

31. See chapter 6. The 1641 *Body of Liberties* gave nonfreemen the right to attend and address town meetings, though not to vote. Breen, "Who Governs?" 462–63.

32. *WR,* 10–11. Biscoe's colleagues were nonmembers Roger Porter and Joseph Bemis, as well as recently admitted freemen John Whitney and William Hammond. Allied officials: Thomas Arnold, Samuel Stratton, and John Warren. On the fallout from the Child Petition, see Wall, *Massachusetts Bay,* 162–209, 228–29. One of the eight deputies voting against the draconian fines levied by the General Court against the Child remonstrants was Brian Pendleton of Watertown. See chapters 4 and 6.

33. *WR,* 10, 17, 18; see chapter 6.

34. Grant's successful suit against the town in 1652 settled "all debts, dues, and demands whatsoever from the town of Watertown from the beginning of the world to this present." His victory may have recommended him to his neighbors, despite his profane lifestyle. *WR,* 30, 42; MxCC DB, 1:20, 27; Roger Thompson, *Sex in Middlesex* (Amherst: University of Massachusetts Press, 1986), 100.

35. *WR,* 37, 39, 60, 74, 78, 89, 92; *MR,* 3:346, 381: MxCC D&O, 1, folios 9, 10, docs. 365–72; 2, folio 52.

36. MxCC D&O, 1, folios 10, 11; *WR,* 60, 71, 74, 78, 79, 92, 105, 135, 138, 147. Mass Archives, 26 June 1655.

37. Robert Charles Anderson, private communication.

38. Watertown's first surveyor, Robert Seely, was dismissed in 1635. His successor, Abraham Brown, died in the late 1640s. *WR,* 2, 10, 26, 39, 60, 92.

39. MxCC D&O, 1, folio 10, doc. 372. See chapters 4 and 11.

40. *WR,* 92; the meeting cited by Curtis is not minuted in *WR;* MxCC D&O, 2, folio 52; *MR,* 4/2:444.

41. 5MHSC, 1:474–80. Six miles square, the grant recommended in the "Essay," contains 23,040 acres, close to Watertown's grant.

42. *WR,* 17, 60, 74, 78; Johnson, 74. On 11 December 1634 Winthrop was affronted when Boston's inhabitants expressed fear "that the richer men would give the poorer sort no great proportion of land" and therefore moved toward wholesale distribution. He was able to dissuade them, in favor of reserving town domain for newcomers and later generations. *WJ,* 1:143–44; Rutman, *Winthrop's Boston,* 68–77.

43. There were similar troubles over land in Sudbury in the 1650s, Powell, 152–57.

6. Religion

1. Excellent studies of these issues are Hall, *Faithful Shepherd,* Stephen Foster, *The Long Argument: English Puritanism and the Shaping of New England Culture, 1570–1700* (Chapel Hill: University of North Carolina Press, 1991), and Delbanco, *Puritan Ordeal.*

2. Bond, 1016–17; Cotton Mather, *Magnalia Christi Americana* (Hartford: Andrus, 1852), 1:79.

3. William Hubbard, *A General History of New England* (Boston: Little, Brown, 1848), 185; Webster, *Godly Clergy,* 286–332.

4. Mather, *Magnalia,* 1:377; Hubbard, *General History,* 186; Foote, "Phillips," 193–227; 1MHSC 3 (1794): 75. Foote's argument that Phillips wrote *The Humble Request* must remain "not proven." On popular election of ministers in East Anglia, see chapter 3.

5. One of the Colchester group emigrated to Plymouth, Smith and Sanborn, 165; Hall, *Faithful Shepherd*, 81–82; Anderson; Edmund S. Morgan, *Visible Saints* (Ithaca: Cornell University Press, 1965), 95; Stephen Brachlow, *Communion of Saints: Radical Puritanism and Separatist Ecclesiology* (Oxford: Oxford University Press, 1988), 56–64.

6. *WJ*, 1:66, 71–72; 2:17. Foote, "Phillips," 213. Ruling elders were responsible for discipline among the godly. On Cotton's early support for Phillips's position on "church administration," see Hubbard, *General History*, 186, and Hall, *Faithful Shepherd*, 82.

7. Hall, *Faithful Shepherd*, 95; *WJ*, 1:95. On the Roman issue, see Peter Lake, "Defining Puritanism," in *Puritan Studies*, ed. Francis J. Bremer (Boston: MHS, 1994), 26–28; Timothy L. Wood, "A Puritan View of Catholicism," *NEQ* 72 (1999): 28–41; and Edmund S. Morgan, *The Puritan Dilemma: The Career of John Winthrop* (Boston: Little, Brown, 1958), 98–100. See also chapter 3.

8. Brachlow, *Communion of Saints*, 12, 118–19, 137–41, 220–25; Hall, *Faithful Shepherd*, 66, 71, 74, 81–85; Thompson, *Mobility and Migration*, 53, 187–89. Laud had become bishop of London, which covered Essex, in 1628.

9. *WJ*, 1:83; Anderson; see chapter 2. On this whole issue, see Foster, *The Long Argument*, 11–13, 26–32, and throughout.

10. Winthrop seems to have been a proponent of this "gathering in of weak Christians." Hubbard, *General History*, 186; Mather, *Magnalia*, 1:79; *MR*, 1:131. Will-worship was defined by Richard Bernard in 1621 as "voluntarily worshipping of God in and by such means as man inventeth." Patrick Collinson, "Evolution of Puritanism," in *Puritan Studies*, ed. Bremer, 150.

11. Brachlow, *Communion of Saints*, 125–37, persuasively questions the requirement of proof of conversion experience for admission to the godly in Henry Jacobs's church in England. Webster, *Godly Clergy*, 291, 298. See also Morgan, *Visible Saints*, 78–80. On Knapp and Grant, see chapters 9 and 5.

12. Hall, *Faithful Shepherd*, 93–94, 117, 119, 127, 152; I am indebted to David Hall for clarifying theological points here and elsewhere. C. G. Schneider, "Roots and Branches," in *Puritan Studies*, ed. Bremer, 182–90; Collinson, "Evolution," 152, 158; idem, "Cohabitation of the Faithful and the Unfaithful," in *From Persecution to Toleration*, ed. O. P. Grell, J. I. Israel, and N. Tyacke (Oxford: Clarendon, 1991), 53, 59, 61–67; David D. Hall, ed., *The Antinomian Controversy, 1636–38* (Middletown, Conn.: Wesleyan University Press, 1995); Rutman, *Winthrop's Boston*, 126–32; Michael G. Ditmore, "Preparation and Confession," *NEQ* 67 (1994): 312; Philip Gura, *A Glimpse of Sion's Glory* (Middletown, Conn.: Wesleyan University Press, 1984), 162–64; see also Cooper, *Tenacious of Their Liberties*, esp. 48–87, which questions the effectiveness of clerical authority and of the "presbyterian challenge."

13. *WJ*, 2:17; Hall, *Faithful Shepherd*, 106. About 1635 Rev. James Noyes had refused an invitation to join Phillips in Watertown in favor of his cousin Rev. Thomas Parker of Newbury. Goodman, "Newbury, MA," 119. In 1649 there was a celebrated protest against the power of the elders by Ezekiel Cheever in New Haven church. Hall, *Faithful Shepherd*, 117.

14. Thomas Hutchinson, *History of Massachusetts Bay*, ed. L. S. Mayo, (Cambridge: Harvard University Press, 1936), 2:373–74.

15. Cakebread subsequently settled in Sudbury, after flirting with the idea of moving to Dedham. *WJ*, 1:224–26, 262; on Feakes and Patrick, see Appendix A, "Lt. Robert Feake"; Anderson. Louise A. Breen, "Religious Radicalism in the Puritan Officer Corps," *NEQ* 68 (1995): 3–43.

16. Robert G. Pope, ed., *The Notebook of Rev. John Fiske* (Boston: Colonial Society of Massachusetts, 1974), 6–7; idem, *The Half-Way Covenant: Church Membership in Puritan New England* (Princeton: Princeton University Press, 1969), 14; see chapter 5. Wall, *Massachusetts Bay*, 39, shows that Watertown's 41 percent compared to 65 percent in Charlestown and Concord, 56 percent in Cambridge, and an average for Middlesex County of 53 percent. Absence of early church records makes it impossible to compute the number of women church members.

17. See chapter 4. According to Biscoe, the fire was an act of man rather than of God. Mass Archives, 1643 petition. He may have been related to puritan divine Rev. John Biscoe (ca. 1606–79), *DNB*.

18. *WJ,* 2:88, 91 *Assistants,* 2:121; Gura, *Glimpse,* 110–11; Mass Archives, ?1638; October 1643. Biscoe claimed to have lost more than £400 through the fire and bad debts. My thanks to Laetitia Yeandle, transcriber of Winthrop's diary, for invaluable help with transcribing his scrawled memorandum of the Sherman-Mason complaint. Mass Archives also contains a letter in Phillips's spidery hand dated 9 October 1643 pleading with the governor and the court to remit Stowers's fine, since he had been sent by the minister to fetch the book. "Though he be not free from human frailties," wrote Phillips, "yet I am persuaded he is free from all Anabaptistical opinions." Stowers's subsequent movements suggest that his pastor was mistaken.

19. Hall, *Faithful Shepherd,* 151; Gura, *Glimpse,* 110; Margaret E. Newell, "Robert Child and the Entrepreneurial Vision," *NEQ* 68 (1995): 247–50; Wall, *Massachusetts Bay,* 48–64; Dunn, 503, 761.

20. William G. McLoughlin, *New England Dissent, 1630–1833: The Baptists and the Separation of Church and State* (Cambridge: Harvard University Press, 1971), 23, 28, 35–37; Gura, *Glimpse,* 110; Carla Gardina Pestana, *Quakers and Baptists in Colonial Massachusetts* (Cambridge: Cambridge University Press, 1991), 4–9. On Prescott, see Samuel Eliot Morison, "Plantation of Nashaway," *Colonial Society of Massachusetts Transactions,* 27 (1927–30): 204–22; Halifax was in Saltonstall and Bairstow country. On Baptists in Colchester, Essex, see Hunt, 90, 277.

21. McLoughlin, *New England Dissent,* chap. 2; Brachlow, *Communion of Saints,* 150–56.

22. Gura, *Glimpse,* 93–94, 113; Ann Hughes, "Religious Polemic," in *Puritan Studies,* ed. Bremer, 213; Johnson, 127; David D. Hall, *Worlds of Wonder, Days of Judgment: Popular Religious Belief in Early New England* (New York: Knopf, 1989) 62–65. The 1644 law against Baptists is in *MR,* 2/1:85; see also 141, 176–78. McLoughlin, *New England Dissent,* 7–9, 23, 28–30, 32; Hall, *Faithful Shepherd,* 127, 145–46; Gura, *Glimpse,* 22. 1646 laws: *MR,* 2/2:176–80; Hall, *Faithful Shepherd,* 93–94, 145–46; Rutman, *Winthrop's Boston,* 132; Roger Williams, Henry Dunster, president of Harvard, Rev. Hanserd Knollys, Lady Deborah Moody and Mrs. Eaton, wife of the governor of New Haven, were all Baptist sympathizers.

23. Biscoe's letter to his Boston son-in-law, Thomas Broughton, 3MHSC, 1:33–35; *WJ,* 2:322; Prescott opened up a trail from the northern side of the Great Pond to Lancaster in 1649, Mass Archives, 12 November 1659; Biscoe's third son, John (1622–90), also a tanner, remained in Watertown and became a leading citizen. On Clark, agent for Rhode Island in its campaign for a colonial charter and author of the anti-Massachusetts *Ill News from New England,* see Richard S. Dunn, *Puritans and Yankees* (New York: Norton, 1971), 134–41.

24. *WR,* 38; MxCC DB, 1:36, 52; Wyman, 1:20, 99, 134; Smith and Sanborn, 470; Anderson; Allen, 348.

25. Wyman, 1:40; Powell, 112; J. O. Austin, *Genealogical Dictionary of Rhode Island* (Albany: p.p., 1887), 240; *R* 48 (1894): 374; 69 (1915): 68; Arnold was regularly elected a deputy in Rhode Island. "Goodman Hammond" was also suspected of sheltering Friends, see Anderson. On Howton, MxCC DB, 1:291; MxCC D&O, 2, folio 34, doc. 2523; Henry J. Cadbury, "Early Quakers in Cambridge," *Cambridge Historical Society Proceedings* 24 (1938): 69–74.

26. 2MHSC, 4:171; Larzer Ziff, *The Career of John Cotton* (Princeton: Princeton University Press, 1962), 239–40.

27. McLoughlin, *New England Dissent,* 27–44; Gura, *Glimpse,* 111; Dunn, 515, 759–60; "To the Reader," G. P., *A Reply to a Confutation* (London: Simmons, 1645), A2v. See also Wood, "Puritan View." For trouble with his son Jonathan, see chapters 10 and 11.

28. *WP,* 3:241; 4:174, 230–31; Anderson; see also Foote, "Phillips," 216–19.

29. Mather, *Magnalia,* 1:376–79; see chapters 2 and 9. Charles Hervey Townshend, "Material from Raynham Records," *R* 52 (1898): 318–20. Caius was favored by Norfolk men. Phillips was seventeen when he matriculated. His contemporary, John Cosin, later bishop of Durham, was the more usual fourteen. *DNB.*

30. Francis, 29–31; 3MHSC, 1:65–66; Mather, *Magnalia,* 2:590–91. *Suffolk Wills,* 2:26; Mass Archives, 5 March 1672, contains a glowing reference for this older "Nonesuch" from Richard Saltonstall Jr. The offer coincided with Charles II's Declaration of Indulgence in England.

31. *WP,* 3:110; Mather, *Magnalia,* 1:511–18; Savage.

32. Savage scorns Mather's hyperbole but nonetheless credits Sherman with thirteen children. Wyman, 1:167; 2:150; *MR,* 4/2:141, 487, 509; MxCC DB, 3:16, 1 December 1671. Mass Archives, 25 November 1673 and 28 May 1679. On his Harvard activities, see Samuel Eliot Morison, *Harvard College in the Seventeenth Century* (Cambridge: Harvard University Press, 1936), 351, 426–28, 440; *Records of Harvard College* (Boston: *CSMP,* 1925), clv, 65, 68, 218, 221, 237, 240, 241, 253, 256.

33. Mass Archives, ?1658, contain "A clear understanding of non-freemen's liberties," laying down procedures whereby the freemen of each town would choose who should be enfranchised. On 25 May 1658, however, the General Court pronounced that provided nonfreemen were English, settled inhabitants, over twenty-four, of honest and good conversation, rated at £20 estate, and sworn to fidelity, they could hold town offices and vote in town meetings. *MR,* 4/1:336; see also Breen, "Who Governs?" 469; Mather, *Magnalia,* 1:516; Hall, *Faithful Shepherd,* 93–94, 119.

34. *WR,* 16, 23, 32, 63, 75.

35. In Dedham, Allin's salary rose from £60 to £80 between 1639 and 1671, but he also received land grants from the town and had a smaller family, Lockridge, *New England Town,* 32; Brown's salary at Sudbury rose from £30 to £60 between 1643 and 1653, but he also received generous land allotments, Powell, 131, 200; Powell quotes J. B. Felt, *Ecclesiastical History of New England,* computing the average in 1643 as £55. Hall, *Faithful Shepherd,* 191–94, quotes second-generation salaries ranging from £45 to £80; Parker at Newbury received £80 per year during the 1650s and 1660s, but he was a bachelor, and his colleague John Woodbridge was paid £60. Goodman, "Newbury, MA," 164. In Essex County, Massachusetts, "typically ministers were voted in the latter decades of the seventeenth century £50–£100 with firewood." David Thomas Konig, *Law and Society in Puritan Massachusetts: Essex County, 1629–1692* (Chapel Hill: University of North Carolina Press, 1979), 98. In Dedham, England, John Rogers had been paid £100 per year.

36. *WR,* 83, 11 October 1664; 77, 29 December 1663. There may also have been resentment at the way the pastor was favored by respiting of fines for livestock offences, when, for instance, the hogreeves found his swine wandering unringed or unyoked, *WR,* 133. Mattack, sometimes Maddock, may have been Welsh, a serious disadvantage in the seventeenth century. On Mattack's subsequent career, see chapter 11.

37. Freemen admitted: 1630s: 115; 1640s: 41; 1650s: 14; 1660s: 16; 1670s: 6, Bond, 1017. See also Wyman, 2:25, 46, Lockridge, *New England Town,* 85–87, Mass Archives, 3 May 1665, for Woburn, Charlestown, and Dedham withholding of church taxes in protest against the Half-Way Covenant. On this colony-wide problem, see Winslow, *Meetinghouse Hill,* chap. 7.

38. *WR,* 94, 113, 119. *MR,* 5:313, 330, 480, 491 minutes arbitration in 1681 and 1685 about part of a one-thousand-acre tract of common land granted to Sherman. Among the causes of the Lord's anger against Massachusetts in 1670 were listed "the stinting of ministers" and "men rising up against their ministers." Mass Archives, 16 May 1670. In 1671 the General Court freed clergy from "all rates" for the future. *MR,* 4/2:485–86. Isolated cases of nonpayment continued. On 5 March 1678, for instance, George Lawrence was reported both because his children were not being taught reading and catechism and because he refused to pay the pastor his tax, *WR,* 128. From 1672 onward, the pastor's salary is quoted in "corn at court price"; in 1677 those who paid in cash were "abated a third part," *WR,* 112, 121, 133. In 1679 the General Court blamed on the low pay of clergy and schoolmasters the fact that "our grammar schools and college are now so low and thin." Mass Archives, 13 October 1679.

39. Mass Archives, 1 June 1671; *MR,* 4/1:490, 493.

40. *WR,* 2, 18, 30; Winslow, *Meetinghouse Hill,* 54; Donnelly, *New England Meeting Houses,* 13, 14, 122. For youthful misbehavior in services, see chapter 10.

41. *WR,* 37–38, 39, 41, 46; Powell, 154–55; Donnelly, *New England Meeting Houses,* 51, 121; Paige, *Cambridge,* 257.

42. *WR,* 58, 47, 59; on "dooming the seats," see Winslow, *Meetinghouse Hill,* 142–49, and R. J. Dinkin. "Seating the Meetinghouse," *NEQ* 43 (1970): 450–64. On 23 May 1665 six long-term

residents were summoned by the board "to answer for not attending their seats in the meeting house appointed to them by the town." *WR,* 85.

43. Winslow, *Meetinghouse Hill,* 121–24. Mass Archives, 8 February 1695, contains a call to Rev. Henry Gibbs from sixty Watertown householders. It opens: "Forasmuch as the inhabitants of Watertown have been destitute of a settled minister in a pastoral office for diverse years past, by reason of some uncomfortable debates referring to the erecting of a new meetinghouse. Notwithstanding . . . [that] we in the east part of the town are very well contented with the present meeting house."

44. Mather, *Magnalia,* 1:518; Fairbanks and Trent, 147; Hall, *Worlds of Wonder,* 58–60; Stephen Innes, *Creating the Commonwealth* (New York: Norton, 1995), 95. Sherman's official role as one of the colony censors may have recommended him; compilers were usually young Harvard master's degree candidates.

45. Alan Macfarlane, *Witchcraft in Tudor and Stuart England* (New York: Harper, 1970), 264–92; Hall, *Worlds of Wonder,* 71–116.

46. David. D. Hall, ed., *Witch-Hunting in Seventeenth-Century New England* (Boston: Northeastern University Press, 1991), 24–25; MxCC D&O, 1, folio 1, 3 November 1649, 24 April 1650; on evil as Satanic force, see Delbanco, *Puritan Ordeal,* 25. It is tempting to identify the nurse with Mary Davis, who died in prison in 1656, aged thirty-three, before she could be tried for adultery with James Knapp. See chapter 9. Hall, *Witch-Hunting,* 197–212, 74–85, and John Putnam Demos, *Entertaining Satan: Witchcraft and the Culture of Early New England* (New York: Oxford University Press, 1982), 90–93, 181, discuss the cases involving members of the Knapp family, none of which occurred in Watertown.

47. Hall, *Witch-Hunting,* 21–23; Demos, *Entertaining Satan,* 92; MxCC D&O, 1, folio 2, undated deposition of Hugh Clark and grand jury presentment 24 April 1650. Hall, *Witch-Hunting,* 134–46; Demos, *Entertaining Satan,* 188–89, 194; Charles Stearns was described as kinsman by Isaac Stearns of Watertown, Anderson. *WR,* 71, has Charles Stearns, with three children, listed on 29 January 1661 as a Watertown family at risk of poverty. On the possible witchcraft connections of Watertown's Hugh Parsons, see chapter 9.

48. *WR,* 121, 128, 137, 144.

49. I have read eighty-five wills and inventories of Watertown decedents from 1654 to 1681. Bowman: Mx PR, 5:155; Hosier: 2:281; Chadwick: 5:228; Beers: 4:202; Norcross: 1:173; Bairstow: 4:183. Mx Wills, 5094, John Coolidge leaves gift of £1 to Pastor Sherman. Bairstow's farm was probably unimproved land worth only a few pounds; Bright: Mass Archives, 25 June 1680. Confessions lodged with the county court show similar providential beliefs and the reality of Satan as a tempter along with remorseful contrition. See, e.g., MxCC D&O, 2, folio 44, test. Daniel and Mary (Grant) Smith, 16 December 1667, Appendix A, "John Sawin Jr., Horse-Thief," chapter 10, and Thompson, *Sex in Middlesex,* 55–57, 196–98.

50. Mx PR, 1:227; 3:72, 60; 4:183, 197; 5:32; Mx Wills, 1332, 1796. On popular publications of piety, see Margaret Spufford, *Small Books and Pleasant Histories* (Athens: University of Georgia Press, 1981), and Hall, *Worlds of Wonder,* 21–70. Foote, "Phillips," 226; *R* 8 (1854): 54.

51. Hall, *World of Wonder,* 138, 139, 140–41, 144–45; at the same time as opposing evil with prayer, the Gibsons believed that Widow Holman might be causing their daughter Rebecca's fits by sympathetic magic when she picked up an oak chip. Explorations of the intermixing of folklore and piety are Hall, *Worlds of Wonder;* Richard Weisman, *Witchcraft, Magic, and Religion in Seventeenth-Century Massachusetts* (Amherst: University of Massachusetts Press, 1984); and Richard Godbeer, *The Devil's Dominion: Magic and Religion in Early New England* (Cambridge: Cambridge University Press, 1992). MxCC D&O, 4, folio 82, 18 September 1678; Mass Archives, 3 May 1665. As well as titles already cited, Hambrick-Stowe, *Practice of Piety,* Cohen, *God's Caress,* are searching explorations of popular piety.

52. *WJ,* 1:83–84.

53. Ibid., 83. The exceptional "insider" was John Warren.

54. My colleague Simon Middleton has been most helpful in discussing issues involved in this paragraph.

7. Living with Livestock

1. John Winthrop Jr., 12 April 1645, *WP,* 5:19–20. See also Daniel Vickers, *Farmers and Fishermen* (Chapel Hill: University of North Carolina Press, 1994), 45. Even in the 1690s a "young beginner" could manage to break only two acres of wilderness in a year. Greven, *Four Generations,* 67.

2. Pond: Emerson, 64–66, 15 March 1631. Brunts: Emerson, 92. See chapter 5.

3. *WJ,* 1:53, 54.

4. *WP,* 3:73.

5. Biscoe: *WJ,* 2:88, Mass Archives, October 1643; see also *WJ,* 1:49, 53 (Phillips), 63, 90.

6. Emerson, 111; 1635 winter fencing order, never repeated, *WR,* 1; corn shortage: *WJ,* 1:86; 2:348, describes another pigeon visitation in 1648, when "it was ordinary for one man to kill eight or ten dozen in half a day, yea five or six dozen at one shoot, and some seven and eight." The previous year they had stripped the cereal harvest. Robert R. Walcott, "Husbandry in Colonial New England," *NEQ* 9 (1936): 234–35. On wolves, see chapter 12. Weather: Kupperman, "Climate."

7. Walcott, "Husbandry," 229–31; Robert Blair St. George, "Domesticating the Yeomanry in Seventeenth-Century New England," in Fairbanks and Trent, 175, and in Quimby, *Craftsman,* 102. It is unclear whether maize was grown by the local Native Americans, but it was certainly cultivated in Plymouth. See chapter 1. Tools: *MR,* 1:86, 3 May 1631.

8. The work ethic applied even to the young. A sickly child was described as "not being able to earn its own living as other children may." MxCC D&O, 3, folio 71, administration of estate of George Woodward, 19 December 1676; Innes, *Creating the Commonwealth,* 107–59. See also St. George, "Domesticating the Yeomanry" 175; Overton, *Agricultural Revolution,* 38. On town support for the culture of discipline and punishment of backsliders, *WR,* 17, 31, 47, 51, 52, 66, 76, 92, 113, 122. An excellent recent economic study is Margaret Ellen Newell, *From Dependency to Independence: Economic Revolution in Colonial New England* (Ithaca: Cornell University Press, 1998).

9. Mx Deeds, 2:177. Virginia de John Anderson, "King Philip's Herds: Indians, Colonists, and the Problems of Livestock in Early New England," *WMQ* 51 (1994): 601–24. Prices: In 1633 William Hammond wrote to his patron, Sir Simonds D'Ewes, "Bullocks . . . are wonderful dear here. There are none to be gotten but at a great price. A cow is worth here twenty-five pounds," as compared to £3–£5 in Lavenham. Emerson, 64, 73, 110–12. See chapters 5 and 8. During the 1630s Plymouth Plantation also sold cattle to its needy neighbors and thereby helped pay off its debts to London creditors. John J. Waters, "Patterns of Community: British," in *Encyclopedia of North American Colonies,* ed. Jacob E. Cooke (New York: Scribners, 1993), 2:418.

10. Bidwell and Falconer, *History of Agriculture,* 10, 19, 25, 26; Cronon, *Changes in the Land,* 139–47, 150; Kupperman, "Climate," 3–37; *MR,* 1:146, 210; *WJ,* 1:140, 160. See chapters 5 and 12.

11. Originally four men were appointed, but by 1647 this number was reduced to two. *WR,* 9. On mixed farming in East Anglia, see Hunt, 8; Thompson, *Mobility and Migration,* 15–17; Overton, *Agricultural Revolution,* 11, 54–55.

12. *WR,* 3. See also Konig, *Law and Society,* 118.

13. *WR,* 5, 6–7, 9, 12, 14, 17, 45, 62. The precise boundaries of Howe's Field are spelled out in the records, 14. For examples of these common fencing problems: *WR,* 15, 30, 35, 61, 147, 148, 139, 135, and below.

14. *WR,* 35–36.

15. E.g., *WR,* 146–48. Age did not necessarily curb contention. Between 19 March 1678 and 28 June 1680 there were suit and countersuit between "Father" [Robert] Bullard, aged about eighty, and Miles Ives, about eighty-six, who had filed a previous complaint in 1661; ibid., 61. On the decrease of communal fields, see chapter 5.

16. E.g., Widow Barnard's complaints: *WR,* 11 [30 September 1647], 87, 88, 118 [19 December 1673].

17. *WR,* 88. A rod measures five and a half yards. E.g., Benjamin v. Child action, Mx CC DB,

1:20; Mx CC D&O, 1, folio 1, doc. 54, dated 5 April 1652. The disagreement with Child involved the "sufficiency" of the fence, its maintenance and worth. Benjamin later had a protracted battle with the selectmen about fence lines, Bond, 27. Jonathan Brown was another long-term fence warrior, *WR*, 60, 107, 118, 119, 125, 128, 129, 134, 136. Anderson; Smith and Sanborn. See chapter 10 and Appendix A, "Whittaker." See also Thompson, *Sex in Middlesex*, 174–75; Mx Deeds, 4:449.

18. Innes, *Creating the Commonwealth*, 280. Thirty-eight of sixty-six Watertown inventories listed a total of 255 hogs. Eleven estates had between 10 and 19 hogs, twelve had between 5 and 9, and fifteen had between 1 and 4. On inventories, see chapters 6 and 11.

19. *MR*, 1:149–51; Mx Wills, 20338; *WR*, 6, 15, 17, 32, 41, 45, 52, 65, 66, 76, 80, 81, 88, 101, 114, 122, 141; Mass Archives, 24 May 1658; see also William Price shooting Justinian Holden's stray hog in 1676, chapter 13.

20. The fine per offence was sixpence. 1657 fines, £8.11.6, 1663 fines totaled £8.13.4; 1678's total was £8.3.1. *WR*, 53–54, 79, 137.

21. E.g., Treadway accusation in 1660 against Jonathan Brown, formally minuted in Book of Proceedings; large fines in 1655 for abusive Williams clan; Chenery charges and countercharges in 1663 by and against various neighbours. *WR*, 66, 45, 76. See chapter 13.

22. *WR*, 9. For every ten acres owned (excepting the farms), a commoner could graze one cow or working ox; for every five acres, a calf.

23. T. J. Wertenbaker, *The Puritan Oligarchy* (New York: Scribners, 1947), 56. Konig, *Law and Society*, 118.

24. *WR*, 7, 18, 21, 22, 24, 67, 69. Solomon Johnson was dismissed in 1660; see chapter 13. His successor was Henry Curtis. *WR*, 62, 73.

25. *WR*, 81–82, 84, 86, 88, 89, 94, 98–99, 101, 104–5, 107, 111, 137. See chapter 4. John Livermore, potter, bought Cowpen Farm, but not until 31 March 1669, probably because of herdsman Curtis's contract. Mx Deeds, 3:361.

26. *WR*, 68. See also Douglas R. McManis, *Colonial New England: A Historical Geography* (New York: Oxford University Press, 1975), 94.

27. Forty-eight inventories from Mx PR, 1–6, 1655–86; eighteen from Mx Wills, 1653–1708. A total of 256 cows are listed in sixty-six inventories, an average of just under 4 cows per estate. Only four inventories contained more than 10 cows, and thirteen had only 1. Fairbanks and Trent, 325–26.

28. The importance of water is demonstrated in a grant on 29 February 1648. John Knight may have some wasteland, "provided he make without the fence a sufficient watering for man and beast."

29. *WR*, 39, 52; rams would be put with the ewes in late October, and lambing would take place in protective winter folds in the spring as the new grass began to sprout. Susan M. Ouellette, "Divine Providence and Collective Endeavour: Sheep Production in Early Massachusetts," *NEQ* 69 (1996): 355–80, esp. 366, 375–76; Robert R. Walcott, "Husbandry in Colonial New England," *NEQ* 9 (1936): 246–47.

30. *WR*, 99, 146–47. The 1670 order forbade taking in sheep from other towns for fattening. In 1680 the town agreed that five hundred sheep should be the maximum in Watertown, each owner's flock dependent on acreage; their grazing grounds were bounded by a line from Kings Common to the mill in the east and Beaver Brook in the west. The selectmen appointed two shepherds, Old Goodman Jones and Richard Child, on 10 April 1680.

31. Walcott, "Husbandry in Colonial New England," 246–47.

32. *MR*, 4/2:355–56; Ouellette, "Divine Providence," 357, 360.

33. Ouellette, "Divine Providence," 365–66, 369–70. Twenty-four inventories list a total of 340 sheep; twelve estates had at least 10 head, five more than 20.

34. *WR*, 8, 9, 95–96, 107. In 1635 a Dutch ship brought a cargo of Flanders stallions and mares to New England, which temporarily improved the size and hardiness of the colonial stock. Fairbanks and Trent, 198.

35. MxCC D&O, 2, folios 27, 34; Wyman, 1:113; Mass Archives, 22 May 1651 and 27 August

1668. See also Grant v. Gookin, chapter 13. Fairbanks and Trent, 325–26, reproduces extracts from the Newbury book of stock earmarks, 1640–1880, another means of establishing ownership. Free-ranging: Darrett Rutman, "Governor Winthrop's Garden Crop: The Significance of Agriculture in the Early Commerce of Massachusetts Bay," *WMQ* 20 (1963): 414–15; Innes, *Creating the Commonwealth*, 301; Mass Archives, 11 May 1668. Thirty-eight Watertown inventories recorded ownership of eighty-two horses. Half the estates had only one horse, however, and only seven had four or more.

36. MxCC D&O, 4, folio 91; DB, 3:325; *WR*, 148. Bullard had a previous conviction: MxCC D&O, 2, folio 33, 6 September 1663; he had, however, also recently served in King Phillip's War; see chapter 10.

37. MxCC DB, 3:20; MxCC D&O, 2, folio 60; 3, folio 79. Ibid., 2, folio 33, 1672. Thomas Fleg had married Rebecca, daughter of Edward Dix, in 1668. The credit he advanced his elder brother may even have come from Rebecca Dix's dowry. In 1670 Thomas Fleg Jr. had been sued on behalf of Mary (Dix) Brown for taking crops off her land and cutting and carting her wood. He had had to pay £3 costs. On Gershom Fleg, see chapter 8.

38. Overton, *Agricultural Revolution*, 50–62.

8. Livelihood

1. See R. B. St. George, "Woodworking Artisans in Southeast New England," in *The Craftsman in Early America*, ed. Ian M. G. Quimby (New York: Norton, 1984), 102, n. 19. Rev. Edward Taylor betrayed his farming pursuits in his meditation: " . . . My tumbril / Unload of all its dung and make it clean, / And load it with thy wealthiest grace until / Its wheels do crack, or Axletree complain. / I fain would have it cart thy harvest in / Before its loosed from its axlepin." Quoted in St. George, "Domestication," 160.

2. *WJ*, 1:128. See chapter 5, Housing: Emerson, 84. For carpenters, see below.

3. Wood, *New England's Prospect*, 60; *WJ*, 1:76, 86–87. See chapter 12. The weir was bought by the town from Nathaniel Coolidge on 12 April 1671. *WR*, 106. See also chapter 7. By the 1650s farmers seem to have reverted to English preference for manure. The 5 December 1660 agreement with dry herdsman Henry Curtis about the cowpen stipulated: "He shall not carry off the premises any compost, muck or manure."

4. *WP*, 3:169, 22 June 1634; Mass Archives, 1634; *WR*, 5. In June 1634 Winthrop wrote to Thomas Graves, "Bring me [from England] a pair of mill stones, peak stones, seven foot broad and of thickness answerable." Emerson, 118. On 10 October 1641 the General Court was asked to rule on ownership of Watertown mill. It judged that Thomas Dudley rather than Edward Howe was the owner because he had redeemed the mortgage to build the mill advanced by Matthew Craddock, London merchant and former governor of the Massachusetts Bay Company, for whom Thomas Mayhew acted as agent. *MR*, 1:344. Dudley paid £560 for half the mill at the height of the 1630s boom, Mass Archives, 7 March 1644. On later ownership of the mill, see chapter 13.

5. *WR*, 144, 5 January 1680. It was tax-free for twenty years. On 18 January 1653 the old mill, likewise tax-free for twenty years, was assessed to the church tax at the sum of £140 estate; a similar town taxation was agreed on 22 November 1653. *WR*, 31, 33.

6. See map 1. The exception was east-west Back Lane, connecting Cambridge to modern Belmont.

7. *WR*, 3, 7, 82, 115. *MR*, 1:247, 4 December 1638, records Watertown's Isaac Stearns and John Page fined five shillings for diverting a road in the town. See chapter 7.

8. An alternative route to Concord was mutually laid out in 1672, and to Sudbury in 1679. Joseph Tainter was often Watertown's representative. *WR*, 5, 66, 115, 116, 145. A minute of 27 November 1639 declares the town's right-of-way to the highway that leads from Dorchester Field to the flats and so through the river. This road comprises Bank and Mill Streets. Ferry, bridge: *MR*, 1:110, 346; see also 2/1:51. Mx Deeds, 3:264.

9. *MR*, 2/2:194, 236–37; *WR*, 11, 16. The town records from 1643 to 8 November 1647 have

not survived, so we have no explanation for the slow response to the General Court's order of 26 May.

10. Rutman, "Governor Winthrop's Garden Crop," 408; *WR*, 19.

11. Kupperman, "Climate," 23; *WR*, 89, 90, 91. Later bridge repair references: MxCC D&O, 3, folios 69, 73. *WR*, 131, 141. MxCC DB, 3:303; D&O, 4, folio 91. Other foot- and cartbridges across streams and wetlands are mentioned in the *Watertown Records*, along with gateways and stiles. *WR*, 17, Sawtell trees for footbridge; 31, footpaths and stiles; 144–45, cartbridge over Beaver Brook.

12. Bailyn, *New England Merchants*, 46–47.

13. *CSMP* 7 (1905): 74–75. In 1640 Ephraim Child mortgaged his house and lands in Watertown to purchase two cows; Thomas Mayhew mortgaged his five-hundred-acre farm and buildings for six cows, *Suffolk Deeds*, 15.

14. *MR*, 1:201, 221. See chapter 5. On 16 February 1638 the body of Watertown freemen empowered the eleven selectmen to "divide all the town land undivided." *WR*, 3. On 6 September 1638 two of those who left, Brian Pendleton and Edmund Brown, with Peter Noyes, were given General Court permission "to go on in their plantation" at Sudbury. *MR*, 1:238.

15. *WJ*, 1:112; 2:6; Johnson, 209; Bailyn, *New England Merchants*, 32, 45–49; *WR*, 5; Hunt, 9–10; Overton, *Agricultural Revolution*, 21.

16. *WJ*, 2:17; see also 6, 19, 31; Johnson, 209; Bailyn, *New England Merchants*, 47.

17. *WJ*, 2:82; Rutman, "Governor Winthrop's Garden Crop," 399; *MR*, 1:307.

18. *WR*, 6, 8, 9. Appendix A, "Page v. Page." *Suffolk Deeds*, 24, 27, 39; on volatility, ibid., 13–58. Mass Archives, October 1643, 7 May 1644. See part 2 above.

19. Innes, *Creating the Commonwealth*, 193; Bailyn, *New England Merchants*, 61; Rutman, "Governor Winthrop's Garden Crop," 400–401.

20. *MR*, 1:294, 303, 322. Richard Saltonstall Jr. had mentioned the "great store of hemp growing naturally" in a letter from Watertown in early February 1632, Emerson, 93. *WJ*, 2:88 records that "divers houses were burnt this year [1642], by drying flax." The next sentence describes a barn fire in Watertown, suggesting that townsmen were engaging in linen weaving.

21. *MR*, 1:316; 2/1:51. Busby, a worsted weaver, had been apprenticed to William Ward in Norwich and had become a freeman in 1620. In 1630 he was a city jurat, responsible for checking quality of cloths. In 1631 he had three journeymen working for him. He moved to Boston about 1646 and combined his craft with dry-goods importing. His inventory, totaling £1,066, included four hundred yards of fabric, haberdashery, and six pounds of cloth in his two looms. His son Abraham was a linen weaver. James W. Hawes, *Genealogy of Nicholas Busby* (Provincetown, Mass.: Library of Cape Cod History and Genealogy, 1912); Anna C. Kingsbury, *Historical Sketch of Nicholas Busby* (P.p., 1924). On Underwood, a weaver-clothier, with north Suffolk linen and northeast Essex textile connections, see Savage; G. A. Moriarty, "Fiske Genealogy," *R* 88 (1934): 270; ibid. 38 (1884) 400–402; 4MHSC, 2:183; L. M. Underwood, *Underwood Families of America* (Lancaster: p.p., 1913). A kinsman who came to Boston about 1660 was a wool draper. Others: Miles Nudd, John Whitney, Henry Kemball (a wheelwright), and John Witheridge or Wetherall, who figures in the Watertown records as a champion fox trapper. Some known Watertown weavers, like John Pearce or John Ball, did not avail themselves of the bounty.

22. Mass Archives, 3 May 1656; *MR*, 3:396, 399; 4/1:256; Bailyn, *New England Merchants*, 71–73. Twenty processes requiring skill and experience were needed to turn flax into linen. Fairbanks and Trent, 260; Adrienne Hood, "The Material World of Cloth," *WMQ* 53 (1996): 43–66. Spain declared war on England in October 1655.

23. *WR*, 50. On the Ball family, see chapter 9. Her son John had recently been apprenticed to his grandfather, worsted weaver John Pearce. At the age of twenty-one, young Ball would be fully trained and, besides "double apparel," would receive "a loom fitted to fall to work." Fulling: Mx Deeds, 3:52; 4:125. Inventories: see chapter 11, which also lists spinning wheels.

24. *WR*, 62; £200 estate was the threshold for genteel dress.

25. Ibid., 84. See chapter 10.

26. E. N. Hartley, *Ironworks on the Saugus* (Norman: University of Oklahoma Press, 1957),

254–61; *TAG* 71 (1996): 149–50; Bailyn, *New England Merchants,* 62–71; Innes, *Creating the Commonwealth,* 237–70. On Child, see chapter 11. Salt: *WP,* 5:374, Mass Archives, July 1654.

27. Rutman, "Governor Winthrop's Garden Crop," 401–11; Innes, *Creating the Commonwealth,* 280–307; Bailyn, *New England Merchants,* 45–74; Daniel Vickers, "Work and Life on the Fishing Periphery of Essex County, Massachusetts, 1630–1675," in *Seventeenth-Century New England,* ed. Hall and Allen, 83–117; Mx PR, 2:81; Dunn, 764. Margaret Newell, "Robert Child and Entrepreneurial Vision," *NEQ* 60 (1995): 254; Johnson, 211; fulling: Mx Deeds, 3:52; 4:125; retailing: Mx Wills, 2390, 3168, 6296; Groton: see chapter 10.

28. Turnips: Mx PR, 4:202; 6:186, 277; Mx Wills, 2190. Cider: ibid., 1796, 1719; MxCC D&O, 3, folio, 74, test. Thomas Loverun; *WR,* 116, 141. See chapter 7 and Appendix A, "Whittaker." Haying season: *WR,* 123. Information on acreages, crops, and values is based on analysis of twenty-four inventories: Mx PR, 1:46, 76, 159, 227, 231; 2:79, 281; 3:72, 168, 291, 374, 389, 406; 4:28, 142, 202, 269; 5:32, 351, 498; 6:136, 154, 186, 277. See also the confession of John Knapp, 6 April 1657, when he describes being in the barn "threshing pease." MxCC D&O, 1, folio 18.

29. Johnson, 71. See also Vickers, *Farmers and Fishermen,* 47.

30. *MR,* 3:44.

31. See chapter 7; MxCC D&O, 1, folio 22, 28 December 1658. Mx PR, 3:291, 389, 406; 5:351; 6:186.

32. John Cherry, "Leather," in *English Medieval Industries,* ed. John Blair and Nigel Ramsey (London: Hambledon, 1991), 295–311, describes the processes of transforming hides to leather. See also Fairbanks and Trent, 175. Tanners in England were often associated with religious and political dissent, Spufford, *World of Rural Dissenters,* 62.

33. Biscoe lost £200 worth of property by fire in 1642; Mason's estate was valued at £661 in 1678, the second highest of first-generation Watertown decedents. Mx Deeds, 6:184. John Winter was also a tanner but on a smaller scale. Gershom Fleg, son of Thomas, left Watertown for Woburn ca. 1668 and built the first tannery in what became "Tan City" in the nineteenth century. See chapters 4–6.

34. This combination of trades continued English practice; Heather Swanson, *Medieval Artisans* (Oxford: Blackwell, 1989), 55–56. On the huge amounts of water used in the process, see Phillip Roth, *American Pastoral* (London: Cape, 1997), 11–12, 33, 123, 224–25. There were many crooked ways of hastening the process, which produced inferior, short-lived leather. They needed an expert eye to spot them. Ironically, Munnings had lost an eye in the Block Island fight! See chapter 12.

35. Anderson, 240, citing Mx Deeds, 4:370 and 6:184–87. It is impossible to locate this parcel with certainty, though Mason and Bright abutted south of Water Street, just east of Mount Auburn. They also abutted to the east of Hill Street. Bark: MxCC D&O, 2, folio 40, 9 April 1666.

36. Now on the Watertown-Waltham line.

37. M. E. Mason, *The Family of Hugh Mason* (P.p., 1930), 35; Savage.

38. Mass Archives, 7 April 1677; such was the shortage of circulating specie, it was ordered that cash payers received 50 percent discounts, ibid., 27 October 1680.

39. E.g., 4 March 1651 agreement with John Bigelow to set up a smith's forge; 17 September 1678 request for a smith's shop from one of Robert Harrington's sons; building specifications for town structures; October 1653 permission for brickmaker Daniel Hudson to dig for clay on King's Common; 1652 cooper Richard Waite to hoop town's gunpowder. *WR,* 10, 19, 20, 22, 28, 32, 97, 101, 108, 117, 136. Various craftsmen are identified in the lists (see Appendix B). Watertown had to buy in certain skills from neighboring towns. There was no resident doctor, for instance, and occasionally the town accounts record expenditure on behalf of dependents to Dr. John Alcock of Roxbury, *WR,* 65, or Dr. John Chickering of Charlestown, 124. At a less exalted level, they had to go outside for a meetinghouse bell, 112, as well as for locks, 73, and for lime, shingle, and lath for the meetinghouse, 124. Before emigration, Winthrop had listed the skilled tradesmen needed in establishing the colony: carpenters, masons, smiths, coopers, turners, brickburners, potters, husbandmen, and fowlers. *WP,* 2:107. Wood, *New England's Prospect,* 72–73, has a similar list.

40. Innes, *Creating the Commonwealth*, 98; Thompson, *Mobility and Migration*, 80–100; Overton, *Agricultural Revolution*, 61.

41. Abbott Lowell Cummings, "Massachusetts and Its First Period Houses," *CSMP* 51 (1979): 113–221; idem, *The Framed Houses of Massachusetts Bay, 1625–1725* (Cambridge: Harvard University Press, 1979); Catherine W. Pierce, "Browns of Watertown," *Old Time New England* 98 (1939): 67; Society for the Preservation of New England Antiquities, Boston: files on the Brown House. My thanks to Lorna Condon, curator of library and archives. On other craft continuities: Ian M. G. Quimby, ed., *The Craftsman in Early America* (New York: Norton, 1984); Fairbanks and Trent, 159–360, 501–50; L. F. Salzman, *English Industries in the Middle Ages* (Oxford: Clarendon, 1923); Blair and Ramsey, *English Medieval Industries*.

42. Valuations: *WR*, 82, 135; probate: see chapter 11. Extensive farming: Vickers, *Farmers and Fishermen*, 8.

43. On 21 May 1662, because of "shortage of breadcorn," the General Court forbade "export of wheat or wheat grain on penalty of confiscation, unless it be for the provisioning of ships." In 1668 it bewailed "the poverty of the country and the great difficulty of raising money." Two years later the court was wringing its hands about "the blasting their principal grain and abating their increase in other corns and slowness of the market and exceeding low price for what the husbandman can raise." Mass Archives, 21 May 1662, 19 May 1668, 16 and 17 May 1670; *WR*, 60, 93, 101.

44. Wheat and barley were worth five shillings a bushel, rye and peas four, and Indian corn three. *WR*, 16, 8 November 1648. When the new meetinghouse was approved, the town determined that the workmen should receive one-third payment in wheat and the rest in rye, peas, maize, or "cattle" (a generic term that included swine). *WR*, 38, 52.

45. Newell, *From Dependency*, 97–99; Vickers, *Farmers and Fishermen*, 52, 61–62, 64. By midcentury the going rate for labor was two shillings (24 pence) per day, or about £30 per year. Greven, *Four Generations*, 70. Bailyn, *New England Merchants*, 55; Barry Levy, "Child Labor" (paper presented at conference in honor of Richard S. Dunn, San Francisco, 1996).

46. Barnard v. Brown, MxCC D&O, 2, folio 27, 2 October 1662; Biscoe: *WJ*, 2:421. Discounts: Mass Archives, 19 May 1680. Inventories listing cash: Bunker, Mx PR, 1:238–39; William Hammond, 2:19; Stone, 2:113; Stone, 2:286; Thatcher, 3:291; Bairstow, 4:183; Shattuck, 5:28; Mason, 5:351; Pearce, 5:393; Shattuck, 5:475; Thatcher, 6:6; Woodward, 6:109; Perry, 6:154; Livermore, 6:221; Barsham, 6:265. Cashless rich: Isaac Stearns: £504, Mx PR, 4:142; Richard Beers, £460, 4:202; Edward Garfield, £457, 3:374; Thomas Hammond, £652, 1:76. Discounts: *WR*, 133 (1677); Mass Archives, 27 October 1680.

47. Chadwick: Mx PR, 5:228. The £105 John Traine owed Michael Bairstow in 1676 was for Rebecca Traine's dowry, for which her husband, Michael Bairstow Jr., had to wait until John Traine's death five years later. Traine, in turn, was owed £47. Bairstow: ibid., 4:183; Traine: 5:506. Book debts: chapter 11, and Appendix A, "White v. Bemis"; a 16 November 1664 book debt of £6 owed by Mary Howe to John Ball, the weaver, is lodged in MxCC D&O, 2, folio 41, with Ball's assent given "full lovingly" to the repayment plan. Bills: Lerned, Mx PR, 6:328. Flemings: Appendix A, "Fleming Executors v. Jones." Hammond: MxCC DB, 1:180, and chapter 11. Moneylending: John Bigelow, Mx Wills, 1716; John Biscoe, 1796; Richard Brown, 3168; Caleb Church, 4449; Sarah Stone, Mx PR, 2:113; Hugh Mason, 5:351. See also Newell, *From Dependency to Independence*, "Robert Child," 112–21.

48. Mortgages: Appendix A, "Page v. Page" and "Whittaker"; chapter 11; Biscoe: *Suffolk Deeds*, 15, 83. See also 1630s mortgages for cattle: ibid., 13, 14, 15; Mass Archives, 29 November 1638. Currency: MxCC D&O, 1, folio 16, Hammond and Barron; folio 22, Chadwick and Norcross; folio 26, Tidd and Benjamin; interest: Mx Deeds, 1:99, 118; 5:305; chapter 7, Dix v. Fleg, chapter 11, Wright and Sherman v. Hammond. The lawful interest rate was 8 percent, *General Laws and Liberties of Massachusetts* (Cambridge: Usher, 1672), 153. My thanks to Winifred Rothenberg for help on issues of exchange and other economic questions.

49. Jacob E. Cooke, ed., *Encyclopedia of the North American Colonies* (New York: Macmillan, 1993), 2:657, 743; Hunt, 128.

50. The first register of *Suffolk Deeds* includes 451 deeds, and the first seven registers of Mid-

dlesex Deeds cover all legal transactions recorded for Watertown residents, including letters of attorney, sales of stock, and prenuptial agreements. Incomers: *Suffolk Deeds,* 101, Stearns, 103, Norcross; Mx Deeds, 1:34, Clough, 212, Fanning; 2:270, Underwood; 3:136, Allen; 4:108, Townsend, 380, Woolson, 477, Cooke. Leavers: *Suffolk Deeds,* 62, Theale, 66, Potter, 67, Stone, 74, Philbrick, Ellet; Mx Deeds, 1:1, Pendleton, 37, Parkhurst, 56, Arnold, 59, Gosse; 2:137, Wincoll, Page. Speculation by middlemen: Thomas Straite 1649, Eleazar Barron, 1659, Ensign John Sherman, 1672: *Suffolk Deeds,* 104; Mx Deeds, 2:83; 3:307; 4:378, 380, 382. See chapter 11. Outsiders: *Suffolk Deeds,* 46, Ruck, Bridges, 41 and 53, Dudley, 91, Davison; Mx Deeds, 1:7 and 20, Bowman and Cutler, 54, Goffe; 2:18 and 3:116–17, Davison and Fuller; 4:414, 417, Crosby; 6:224, 404, Payne. Mayhew, Child: *Suffolk Deeds,* 13, 15, 24, 27, 29, 39. Land purchases within Watertown are best traced in WBOP, Inventories 1–3. Child: Anderson, 350–51; Page: *Cambridge Records* (Cambridge: City Council, 1901) 27.

51. See chapter 7; Examples of abuttals: Mx Deeds, 2:40, 101, 139, 166; meadow: 4:89, 106, 189, 347, 382. Complete list available from the author.

52. See Lists and Bond for estates. Family buyers: Stearns: *Suffolk Deeds,* 46; Harrington: Mx Deeds, 3:338; 5:325; Nathaniel Coolidge: ibid., 3:107, 239; 4:386; 6:13; Hastings: *Suffolk Deeds,* 55, 58; Mx Deeds, 2:137–40, 266, 366, 368; 3:26; Garfield: *Suffolk Deeds,* 71; Mx Deeds, 1:30, 67, 69, 186, 187.

53. See chapters 5 and 11–13. Nathaniel Treadway and Richard Beers were involved in speculation in land grants west of colony settlement: *MR,* 4/1:293; 5:359; Mass Archives, 24 May 1664, 18 October 1665, 10 October 1668, 31 May 1671. See also Winifred Rothenberg, "The Market and Massachusetts Farmers," *Journal of Economic History* 4 (1981): 283–314.

54. Richard Saltonstall Jr. to Emmanuel Downing, 4 February 1632, Emerson, 92.

55. *WR,* 47, 52, 92, 113, 122. Mx Deeds, 1:172, 8 May 1645, has the apprenticeship contract of the five-year-old son of Widow Guttridge to Samuel Thatcher until age twenty-two. On poor apprentices, see chapter 9; for masterless men, see chapter 10.

56. For a typical "starter-lease," see MxCC D&O, 2, folio 59, 2 October 1672, Richard Parke seven-year lease to John Bush. Daniel Vickers, "Working the Fields in a Developing Economy: Essex County, Massachusetts, 1630–75," in *Work and Labor in Early America,* ed. Stephen Innes (Chapel Hill: University of North Carolina Press, 1988), 49–69; Appendix A, "John Sawin Jr.: Horse-Thief"; Barry Levy, "Child Labor."

57. Mass Archives, 17 May 1670; Dunn, 761: Winthrop recounted a joke on this theme on 3 July 1644: "A Rowley man [was] forced to sell a part of his oxen to pay his servant his wages, then he told him he could keep him no longer because he knew not how to pay his wages; the servant answered him he would serve him for more of his oxen: 'How should I do,' saith the man, 'when all my oxen are gone?' The servant replied: 'Then you should serve me and you should have them [back] again!'" On problems of labor scarcity and family-farm solutions: Vickers, *Farmers and Fishermen,* 77, 83; tenancy: 77–82.

58. Mass Archives, 7 May 1646 and 17 May 1670. Slaves and servants: John Hammond had Sambo Negro as a servant (as well as the "Welsh Dog" George Robeson). In 1685 Scipio Negro was listed in an estate inventory. Ellis Barron, who died in 1676, left his wife the "male negro servant and desire her to have a care of him that he may suffer no wrong." He was valued at £20. His mistress freed him in her will. Mx PR, 2:2; 3:291; 4:197; 6:26; Anderson, 888–89. See chapter 12.

59. There were four hues and cries after runaway servants in 1668 alone, MxCC D&O, 2, folio 49; see also MxCC DB, 1:83, 2 October 1655: order that Justinian Holden must repay the charges of Watertown's constable for loss of time over servant Jeremiah Guttridge, aged about twenty-two; Mass Archives, 18 October 1659, Petition of Thomas Fanning. See chapters 9 and 10.

60. Maddock: MxCC D&O, 1, folio 6, 5 April 1653. Six months later, Alexander Gordon, a Scottish prisoner of war, told a similarly disillusioned story. John Cloyse, a mariner from Watertown, had met Gordon at the prisoner-of-war camp at Tuthill Fields in London and "moved [him] to go along with him by sea without any agreement for wages, only his promise to be as a father to him." Once in Watertown, Goodwife Cloyse had other ideas, however, and after a

year's "bad usage" Gordon had been sold for £17. Wyman, 1:14, 15, 3 October 1653, 3 November 1653. Grant: *MR*, 1:314; cf. Bratcher, ibid., 79.

61. Benjamin: MxCC D&O, 1, folio 1, 5 April 1651; William Knapp, *WR*, 30; John Knapp: MxCC D&O, 2, folio 35; Mx Deeds, 3:312, chapter 10 and Appendix A, "The Watertown Underworld Falls Out."

62. Mass Archives, 1648, 23, 24 May 1672; see Appendix A, "Fleming Executors v. Jones." Robert Reynolds, another erstwhile Watertown shoemaker, also ended up in Boston. Country shoemakers: Rutman, *Small Worlds*, 68.

9. Welfare

1. Peter Bowden, "Agricultural Prices, Farm Profits, and Rents," *AgHE*, 676–79; see chapter 3; A. L. Beier, "Poverty and Progress in Early Modern England," in *The First Modern Society*, ed. Beier, D. Cannadine, and J. M. Rosenheim (Cambridge: Cambridge University Press, 1989), controverts the recent arguments that the problems of poverty in this period have been exaggerated. *WP*, 2:293–95; Bernard Bailyn, ed. *The Apologia of Robert Keayne* (New York: Harpers, 1964), vii–viii.

2. John Pound, *Poverty and Vagrancy in Tudor England* (London: Longman, 1971), 3–24; Thompson, *Mobility and Migration*, 15–18; J. A. Sharpe, *Early Modern England: A Social History, 1550–1760* (London: Arnold, 1987), 111, 218–20; C. G. A. Clay, *Economic Expansion and Social Change* (Cambridge: Cambridge University Press, 1984), 215–21; Wrightson and Levine, *Poverty and Piety*, 21, 25, 40, 108, 179–83; A. L. Beier, "Vagrants and the Social Order in Elizabethan England," *Past and Present* 64 (1974): 3–18; Keith Wrightson and John Walter, "Dearth and Social Order," ibid. 71 (1976): 22–42.

3. Pound, *Poverty and Vagrancy*, 59, 60–63, 79, 81, 100–101; Clay, *Economic Expansion*, 218–20, 226, 229, 234; Paul Griffiths, "Masterless Young People in Norwich, 1560–1640," in *The Experience of Authority in Early Modern England*, ed. Griffiths, Adam Fox, and Steve Hindle (Basingstoke: Macmillan, 1996), 146–86; Sharpe, *Early Modern England*, 215, 218; Wrightson and Levine, *Poverty and Piety*, 179; John Webb, ed., "Poor Relief in Elizabethan Ipswich," *Suffolk Records Society* 9 (1966): 119–40; Michael Reed, "Ipswich Probate Inventories, 1583–1631," ibid. 22 (1981): 1, estimates Ipswich's population in 1597 as about five thousand. Beier, "Poverty," 215: Hartest in Suffolk's wood pasture between Sudbury and Bury St. Edmunds had by 1608 "forty small and poor copyholders, the best of them not having more than two acres, and most of them cottagers, and thirty-five other poor households that have no habitation of their own, nor cow, nor calf." Cf. Dedham, in chapter 3.

4. Pound, *Poverty and Vagrancy*, 54–58, 75, 81, 84; Sharpe, *Early Modern England*, 216–18; Clay, *Economic Expansion*, 224–25, 229–30, 234–35; Beier, "Vagrants," 17–19; Steve Hindle, "Expelled, Half-Pined, Distressed: Poverty in England, ca. 1588–1649" (paper presented at World of Winthrop Conference, Millersville, Pa., 1999).

5. One exception is the case of an orphan described by Winthrop on 10 September 1636. She was treated in the traditional English way of apprenticeship: "Alice Benfield, an orphan of three years, left upon the charge of the country (her parents dying ere they were settled &c.) was put apprentice to Emmanuel White of Watertown and Katherine his wife for fifteen years and in consideration of £10 paid to him by the Treasurer, and they are to educate her as their own child during her minority, and after, to employ and maintain her as a servant during the rest of the term; if she dies within twelve months, he is to repay the money." The Whites moved to Yarmouth in Plymouth Plantation ca. 1642/43. Dunn, 751.

6. See Appendix A.

7. *MR*, 2/2:200; *WR*, 11, 16, 19, 25, 32, 33, 40, 43, 65, 73, 77, 101, 109, 115, 116, 119, 120, 122, 123, 125, 126, 127, 128, 131, 133, 134, 141. Jonathan Clary bought Philpot's land in 1647 for £8, which went to the town. Mx Deeds, 1:43.

8. Her mother may also have been unstable. Norwich had appointed a "keeper" for her in 1636, when her husband, John Pearce, was away preparing a home for his family in Watertown.

WR, 49, 50, 57; MxCC DB, 1:137, 166; MxCC D&O, 1, folio 16; Savage; Thompson, *Sex in Middlesex,* 117.

9. *WR,* 50, 57; Pound, *Poverty and Vagrancy,* 60–68. Savage. Mx Deeds, 3:81, 6 March 1660. Another casualty of this unhappy family was the daughter Mary Ball. Brought up by her grandparents, the nineteen-year-old became the center of a scandal in 1671. Her father complained to the county court that her married master, Michael Bacon III of Woburn, had made her pregnant, sent her off to Rhode Island to have their baby, and then neglected to provide for her. Bacon was arrested but broke out of Cambridge jail and fled toward Watertown. A hue and cry was ordered. He was caught and presumably punished. In a letter in the Middlesex County Court records, Mary claimed to have fallen head over heels in love with her thirty-one-year-old master. She may have craved affection, which seems to have been in short supply in her own family. MxCC D&O, 3, folio 55; *WR,* 106; Thompson, *Sex in Middlesex,* 26, 38, 57, 163.

10. *WR,* 50; MxCC DB, 1:100, 124, 127. Mass Archives, 27 May 1656. Mary Davis had been born Mary Spring in 1623 in the northwest Essex parish of Great Yeldham. Her father, John, who emigrated to Watertown in 1634, was a member of a cadet branch of one of the greatest East Anglian clothier families. His fourth cousin once removed, Sir William Spring of Pakenham, Suffolk, was a supporter of the Massachusetts Bay Company and a correspondent of John Winthrop. He paid his distant kinsman an allowance but had to apologize to Winthrop for John's "large requests" totaling nearly £20, and by early 1637 he had become so irritated that he stopped further payments. Despite his moneyed connections, John Spring made little impact on Watertown. He never held even minor office. When his wife, Eleanor, died, probably in the 1650s, he remarried. However, his second wife, Lydia Hatch of Scituate in Plymouth Plantation, found life with him so unattractive that she left Watertown in 1655. Four years later the Plymouth court ordered her "to repair to her husband with all convenient speed or give reason why she doth not." Gary Boyd Roberts, "English Origins of the Spring Family," *TAG* 55 (1979): 64–72; *WP,* 2:204; 3:294; Thompson, *Sex in Middlesex,* 226.

11. Bond, 140, 441, 752; James Knapp thereby escaped the adultery charge but was convicted of thieving the following year. In 1660 he and his family left Watertown for a new, and even more sensational, life in the frontier town of Groton. See Appendix A, "The Watertown Underworld," and Thompson, *Sex in Middlesex,* 100, 139.

12. In early 1657 Ben seems to have been with Garrett Church's family. In 1666 Joseph Underwood, in return for £12, took over the fostering until the boy, then aged ten, became twenty-one. When Underwood died, his son continued the mastership. *WR,* 51, 53, 54, 87, 129; *MR,* 3:403. There must have been two Ben Davises, because one died in 1689 and his estate was administered by Henry Spring. The Davis warned out in 1692 had been staying with the widow Underwood, but she refused to enter bond to save the town harmless. One of these may have been the child of Mary Davis Jr. Bond, 753. On the career of Mary Davis Jr. and other members of the Spring family, see Thompson, *Sex in Middlesex,* 77, 216.

13. Wyman, 1:77; Savage; Bond. A John Braybrook is recorded in Hampton land allotments in June 1640, but the name is not listed in 1644. *WR,* 14, 26, 28, 29, 30, 34, 38, 39, 40, 43, 44, 45, 46, 47, 51, 53, 55, 59, 77, 78, 81, 82, 87, 92, 93, 100. *Suffolk Deeds,* 85, 91. My thanks to Jerome Anderson of NEHGS for information on the Glovers of Dedham, England, Elizabeth's family. Mx Wills, 2428; Bond, 92. Wyman 1:123, notes a similar situation of the widow Susannah Dix, aged between sixty and seventy, left with a small estate and a youngest child of only sixteen.

14. Parsons: Mass. Archives, 5 September 1654; *WR,* 53, 54, 64, 77, 79, 80. Hugh Parsons may have been the former Springfield wizard, but a grant of land to him in Watertown in 1649 makes this identification unlikely. Hall, *Witch-Hunting,* 29–60. Whitney, in serious difficulties in 1664, had been appointed scarer of dogs out of the meetinghouse at thirty shillings per year. *WR,* 71, 77, 81, 86, 88, 141, 142; Smith and Sanborn, 534; on the smallpox, see Fairbanks and Trent, 345. On Goddard, see chapter 11.

15. Savage; *WR,* 32, 43, 48, 49, 53, 65, 71, 83, 94, 97, 101, 102, 103, 114, 116, 117, 120, 124. It seems possible that Beech was disabled.

16. *WR,* 102, 103, 104, 105, 107, 117, 120, 124, 127; Bond, 786. Goody Sanders was required to

spin in exchange for doles of maize in 1687. A William Sanders moved to Groton but then deserted his wife, Mary, and married another woman in London. The Court of Assistants granted her a divorce in 1674. *Assistants,* 3:30. See also chapter 10. Robert Sanderson, the silversmith, lived for a decade in Watertown before moving to Boston, but there is no evidence of kinship. Pound, *Poverty and Vagrancy,* 53–57; the summer of 1670 had been "very droughty," Kupperman, "Climate," 23.

17. Benjamin Wadsworth, *A Well-Ordered Family* (New York: Russell, 1972), 99; Mx PR, 3:120. See chapter 11.

18. Anderson; Thompson, *Sex in Middlesex,* 100; *WP,* 4:131, deposition dated 5 August 1649. MxCC DB, 1:6, 119, 238; 3:204; MxCC D&O, 1, folios 10, 16, 17; *MR,* 1:133, 143, 199, 318; *Assistants,* 2:137, 139; Wyman, 1:57, 59, 65–67, 95, 118. *WR,* 17, 28, 49, 53, 54, 55, 56, 104, 107, 127, 134, 141, 144; Mx PR, 1:227; 5:32.

19. *WR,* 100, 101, 102, 103, 104, 108, 110, 111, 112, 116, 117, 120, 122, 123, 124; Bond, 1087; Mx Deeds, 2:140; Mx Wills, 2721; Hannah Bartlett died on 11 July 1676. MxCC DB, 3:167. Bright had been convicted of swearing in 1634 and put in the bilboes, *MR,* 1:133.

20. *WR,* 93, 97, 98, 101, 102, 108, 110, 111, 112, 116, 117; Thorpe's wife was Ann, widow of Robert Bullard. E. J. Bullard, *Other Bullards* (P.p., 1928), 11; J. Plummer, "Wives of the Bullards," *R* 146 (1992): 279–80; Smith and Sanborn, 198–99; Increase Mather, *Two Discourses* (Boston: Green, 1716), 134.

21. *WR,* 20, 40, 55, 96, 100, 108, 111, 116, 120, 123, 126, 132, 139, 141, 143; MxCC DB, 1:14, 35, 37; MxCC D&O, 1, folio 6, docs. 196–201; chapter 12; Arthur Searle, *Stuart Essex* (Chelmsford: Essex Record Office, 1974), fig. 17. Mx Deeds, 4:381, 386; Mx Wills, 16956, 16957.

22. Thompson, *Mobility and Migration,* 207, 264–65; Mx PR, 1:80; see also Appendix A, "Page v. Page," Smith and Sanborn, 125; Mx PR, 5:389. See chapter 2.

23. *WR,* 108–9; "charges for the poor" are referred to in December 1642, and a survey of "some poor families" is ordered in January 1661, but the former is a sum under £10, and the latter is centrally ordered by the General Court. *WR,* 9, 70, 71; *MR,* 4/1:365. On 26 December 1656 the selectmen informed the Middlesex County Court that "we have divers families that have fallen into great poverty insomuch [that] the charge of maintaining them will be great." MxCC D&O, 1, folio 16. The two previous winters had been severe. Kupperman, "Climate," 21. In 1668 the General Court bewailed the "poverty of the country in general and the great difficulty of raising money." Mass Archives, 19 May 1668.

24. See chapters 6, 8, and 12. On English tax levels, Pound, *Poverty and Vagrancy,* 75, 81, 84; Sharpe, *Early Modern England,* 215–18; Hunt, 41, 42, 68, 235–36.

25. See chapter 10.

26. Morgan, *Puritan Family,* 68–78, 109–32; Thompson, *Mobility and Migration,* 114–25, 254; Levy, "Child Labor"; chapter 10.

27. The Norwich Municipal Poor Relief System of the 1570s had been among the first to outlaw begging, either licensed or unlicensed, and to require pauper labor and training. Pound, *Poverty and Vagrancy,* 60–68.

28. Emigration: see chapter 10. In 1643 the Watertown constable received a tart warrant demanding that the girl who had been brought to Boston must be taken back. Any delay would increase Watertown's expenses; Mass Archives, 25 September 1643; surveys: *WR,* 71, 93–94, 104, 114, 128, 135; living alone: *WR,* 33, 48, 49, 52, 92, 113; absence: *WR,* 83. On occasion, host households were required to enter bond before being allowed to entertain guests. Warning out and visitors' bonds: *WR,* 58, 81, 92, 106, 107, 109, 113, 144, 148. Once the selectmen tried to send an infant back to its birthplace in Cambridge, only to discover that the county court had ordered a Watertown family to care for the child. The Cambridge infant's foster parent was nonetheless required to enter bond to save the town harmless: *WR,* 137, 138. See also Wyman, 1:135; 2:117, 119, 123, 182; MxCC DB, 3:255. On the Stearnses' involvement in the Holman witchcraft case, see chapter 6. On Cape Fear: Goodman, "Newbury, MA," 182, records the 1664 voyage of Daniel Pearce Sr. "with a probable cargo of livestock." Adams: see chapter 12. After his arrest for selling guns and grog to the Indians, however, he was remanded in prison for the winter. In May 1653

he was sentenced to a severe whipping. Chapter 11; Mass Archives, 28 May 1653. For English precedents for all these measures, see Hunt, 42, 66, 71–72, 192, 250.

29. "Office-Holders, 1630–80," available from the author (see Appendix B), includes known estates.

30. There was, significantly, no formal office of overseer of the poor; the nearest equivalent was that of deacon. Typical example of group involvement: WR, 100–101; chapter 6.

31. Smith and Sanborn, 348–49; Thompson, *Sex in Middlesex,* 157–68. Flegs: MxCC D&O 4, folio 83; Bond, 220. See also the selectmens' determination to prevent the Smiths from evading their obligations to support Ruth Sawtel's bastard, Smith and Sanborn, 428–29. Illness: MR, 1:233, Busby; MxCC D&O, 1, folio 16, Knapp; 2, folio 38, Holden; folio 46, Sawtel; 3, folio 62, Gale; folio 63, Stratton; folio 71, Woodward; folio 73, Fiske; folio 78, Harrington; folio 80, Pearce; 4, folio 82, Pearce; folio 83, Cutler; MxCC DB, 3:267 Knapp; Mass Archives, October 1643, Biscoe; 18 October 1659, Fanning; 3 October 1678, Hammond; Mx Deeds, 4:240, Guy; 7:387, Blois; *Suffolk Wills,* 2:21, Loveran; Mx PR, 1:7, Fiske; 4:28, Shattuck; 5:480, Smith.

32. Darrett B. Rutman, "Assessing the Little Communities of Early America," *WMQ* 43 (1986): 163–78.

10. The Rising Generation

1. Eamon Duffy, *The Stripping of the Altars* (New Haven: Yale University Press, 1992), 181, 328, 335, 348–54; Roger Thompson, "Reflections on the Early-Modern Family in Old and New England," in *Transatlantic Encounters,* ed. Udo J. Hebel and Karl Ortseifen (Trier: Wissenschaftlicher Verlag, 1995), 63, 73–75; see also Colin Thubron, *Among the Russians* (Harmondsworth: Penguin, 1985), 55, 113, 168.

2. Roger Thompson, "Adolescent Culture in Colonial Massachusetts," *Journal of Family History* 9 (1984): 127–29; Richard Archer, "New England Mosaic: A Demographic Analysis for the Seventeenth Century," *WMQ* 47 (1990): 477–502. Vickers, *Farmers and Fishermen,* 49, computes the ratio of dependents to active producers, which almost doubled from .475 in the 1630s to over .900 at the end of the seventeenth century.

3. Daniel Scott Smith, "Demographic History of Colonial New England," *Journal of Economic History* 1 (1972): 165–83.

4. WBOP, 3–14; Johnson, 74, whose estimate may be boosterishly high; WR, 56, 82, 96, 135; Evarts B. Greene and Virginia D. Harrington, *American Population before the Federal Census of 1790* (Gloucester: Smith, 1966), 19. WR, 144 has a 5 January 1680 order that the selectmen were to procure two hundred copies of the tithingmen's law "for the several inhabitants," which here probably means adult heads of households.

5. Greene and Harrington, *American Population,* 14, 19; Greven, *Four Generations,* 7, 21–25, 103–5; Lockridge, *New England Town,* 65–68; idem, "Population of Dedham," 318–44; idem, "Evolution of New England Society," *Past and Present* 39 (1968): 62–80; Smith, "Demographic History," 165–83.

6. Colony population estimates indicate what this increase might have been. Between 1645 and 1655 Massachusetts inhabitants numbered some 20,000; by 1665 they were computed at about 25,000, by 1675 at 40,000, and by 1690 at 50,000. Regional calculations suggest that New England's population trebled from 22,000 in 1650 to 65,000 in 1680. Very little of this frenzied growth was caused by immigration. Jack P. Greene, *Pursuits of Happiness* (Chapel Hill: University of North Carolina Press, 1988), 56–58; Smith, "Demographic History," 175.

7. Lockridge, "Population of Dedham," 327–43 has detailed figures and graphs for Watertown. Correcting is needed for underrecorded deaths. Offspring count from lists available from author (see Appendix B).

8. See chapter 5. Marvin Harris, *Cultural Materialism* (New York: Free Press, 1979), ix.

9. E.g., Pendleton or Cakebread to Sudbury; or Oldham, Edmund Sherman, and Chesters to Wethersfield; and Feake and Patrick to Greenwich. See chapters 4 and 12 and Appendix A, "Lt. Robert Feake." Rev. George Phillips thought it possible that John Winthrop Jr. might be

persuaded to settle in Wethersfield, *WP,* 3:240–41; Hutchinson, *History of Massachusetts Bay,* 44, 86–87, specifies the "fine piece of meadow" and "tract of intervale land" at Wethersfield. The relatively well-endowed John Stone, Anne Howe, and one of the Coolidges were among the earliest settlers of Framingham, pushing up the Sudbury River in about 1647 to Saxonville Falls; Martha E. Dewar and M. Joan Gilbert, eds., *Framingham: Historical Reflections* (Framingham: Historical Society, 1974), 3, 6, 33.

10. See also John Prescott, a journeyman blacksmith, who had missed out on Watertown's land grants and on establishing a smithy there, and Nathaniel Norcross, whose name headed the 1644 petition to the General Court. He was son of Mr. Jeremiah Norcross of Watertown and brother of the town's schoolmaster. He had graduated from Cambridge (Catharine Hall) in 1637 but had received no call in a Bay area seriously overstocked with potential ministers. Like his contemporary, the young John Sherman, he contemplated a frontier mission, but failure to reach agreement led to his returning to England. King: *WJ,* 2:164, dated March 1644; Samuel Eliot Morison, "The Plantation of Nashaway," *Colonial Society of Massachusetts Transactions* 27 (1927–30): 204–22. It was entirely in keeping with this new-style emigration out of Watertown that John Ball should make a new start there in the 1670s with his second wife and family. On Ball's unhappy first marriage, see chapter 9, and on Prescott, see chapter 6. Entrepreneurs like Robert Child, John Winthrop Jr., and Henry Symonds of Boston might be prepared to invest (insufficiently) in the venture, but there was never any prospect of them moving there. Newell, "Robert Child," 243–45.

11. Nicholas Knapp, Robert Lockwood, Gregory Taylor, John Finch, and John Ellet. In Stamford they met other rolling stones like James Weed and Daniel Finch, who had left Watertown earlier for Wethersfield but then moved on again. Anderson, 633; on the outmigration to Martha's Vineyard, see chapters 4 and 6.

12. Siblings: Morses, Lawrences, and Holdens; paupers: Sawtel, Sanders, Onge, and Price. Newly married: Barrons, Fiskes, Claries, Pearces, Tarbells, Whitneys, and Crisps; troublemakers: Benjamin Allen and James Knapp. On Allen, *WP,* 4:97–98; on Price, MCC DB, 3:179; on other youthful lawbreakers who later emigrated to Groton, see below; Samuel A. Green, ed., *Early Records of Groton, 1662–1707* (Groton, Mass.: p.p., 1880), 6–20, 55, 56; Caleb Butler, *History of Groton* (Boston: Marvin, 1848), 15–17, 28, 29; *MR,* 4/2:414. For 1672 case, see Wyman, 2:153. On similar group exoduses from Andover, see Greven, *Four Generations,* 159–70.

13. Smith and Sanborn, 184. Parke had married Abigail Dix, sister of Mary (Dix) Brown, in 1653; Lydia ——— had married Abraham Brown Sr. as his second wife ca. 1629 and then, after his death in the late 1640s, had married Andrew Hodges of Ipswich in 1659. Abraham Brown Jr. died in 1667, aged thirty-seven.

14. Samuel A. Green, "Two Chapters in the Early History of Groton," *Groton Historical Series* (Groton: p.p., 1887), 2.

15. Picataqua: John Page Jr., James Knapp, and Zechariah Smith. Kennebec: George Adams and Joshua Grant. On Simon Willard's interest in the Groton fur trade, see Bailyn, *New England Merchants,* 55–56. Anderson, 1368; Smith and Sanborn, 427; MxCC DB, 3:183; chapter 12; Charles E. Clark, *The Eastern Frontier* (Hanover, N.H.: University Press of New England, 1983), 55, 112–16. MxCC D&O, 2, folio 33.

16. See chapters 9 and 11.

17. Eleazar Mather, *A Serious Exhortation* (1671); John Wilson, *A Seasonable Watchword* (1677), quoted in Winslow, *Meetinghouse Hill,* 104–5.

18. Hall, *Faithful Shepherd,* 168–69; Pope, *Half-Way Covenant,* 3–11. Early adolescent offenders: John Vaughan and Timothy Hawkins, drunk and disorderly in 1634, with Vaughan convicted of fornication in 1639, Anderson; Richard Williams, drunk in 1634, Anderson; Thomas Bigelow, marrying without consent, 1640, *MR,* 1:299; Bridget Barnard, stealing material from William Knapp in 1644, *Assistants,* 2:137. See also chapter 2.

19. Overcompliant publicans were threatened with loss of licenses (1651). Sumptuary legislation forbade flashy or seductive dressing (1658). The first of many orders about misbehavior in meetinghouses was passed on 17 October 1654. Magistrates were empowered to order whippings

or, in serious cases, to commit the incorrigible to houses of correction (1654), as happened to the mentally disturbed Ephraim Gale in 1671. *MR,* 1:328; 2/1:6, 38, 176, 180, 203–4; 3:71, 242, 316, 355, 358; 4/2:43, 100, 393–96, 532; 5:4, 59, 60, 155, 211, 240; for the Gale case, see MxCC DB, 3:6. Mass Archives, 16 May 1670, 27 May 1670, ?1672; see Appendix A, "White v. Bemis."

20. Masterless: Thomas Chadwick, Jonathan Bullard, and Arthur Henbury in 1668. *WR,* 52, 58, 60, 71, 86, 92, 102, 106, 122, 128, 133, 135, 145. See chapters 8 and 9. Watch: MxCC DB, 1:6.

21. Quotation from John Eliot, Foster, *The Long Argument,* 102; Pope, *Half-Way Covenant,* 237–38; Hall, *Faithful Shepherd,* 201–7; Thompson, *Sex in Middlesex,* 55–57.

22. *WR,* 37, 86, 98, 115, 144–45; *MR,* 3:358; 4/2:100; Fighting: Gleison: MxCC DB, 1:166. Cursing: Fanning, see chapter 8. Mass Archives, 8 July 1653, has a report about "sundry abuses and misdemeanours committed on the Lord's Day by children and youths." See chapter 6.

23. Thompson, *Sex in Middlesex,* 94–95; see chapter 12. *WR,* 38, has a 1654 order of the militia company that two pounds of powder shall be used for making fireworks at the general training day at Cambridge, and one pound be given to "John Spring upon a training day for a prize for laying his bullet nearest the mark."

24. MxCC D&O, 1, folio 11.

25. *WJ,* 2:276.

26. 1660s: Robert Bartlett and William Hastings; 1674: John Lawrence and James Smith, Wyman., 1:170; 2:92, 191. Driver: MxCC D&O, 3, folio 63, test. Oliver Wellington et al., 6 October 1674. On other work-related injuries, see chapter 9.

27. Biscoe, Gilberd: *MR,* 1:275, 314; Ardway: *Assistants,* 3:135; Mass Archives, ?1654; protection: Sarah Hammond, Mary Castle, Elizabeth Sturgis, and Mary Davis Jr: *WP,* 4:230–32, 286, 300–303; MxCC D&O, 2, folios 40, 42, 7, 3, September 1666; Mary Willard: Smith and Sanborn, 476–77, citing Suffolk Files no. 1694; the reference was signed by Daniel Warren Sr., Isaac Mixer, John Page, and Benjamin Garfield. See Appendix A, "White v. Bemis."

28. Minors: MxCC DB, 1:16 and throughout; *WR,* 109, MxCC D&O, 2, folio 38, see chapter 11. Apprenticeships and protection of "freedom dues": MxCC DB, 1:51, 147, 148, see chapter 8.

29. *WR,* 93–94, 102, 105, 122, 128, 135. After 1640 the median age in Watertown would have been sixteen; households were overwhelmed by the sheer numbers of offspring to be educated and trained. Bernard Bailyn, *Education in the Forming of American Society* (Chapel Hill: University of North Carolina Press, 1960), 3–49; *MR,* 2/1:203–4; Lockridge, "Population of Dedham," 334–44; Smith, "Demographic History," 165.

30. *WR,* 21–22, 26; Wyman, 2:10, summarizes the charge against some Indians of stealing seventeen books from the schoolhouse.

31. *WR,* 33, 48, 49, 52, 60, 62, 87, 88, 122, 127, 129; MxCC D&O, 4, folio 83; Watertown's Harvard graduates were Samuel Phillips (1650), John Barsham (1658), Bezaleel Sherman (1661), and Daniel Mason (1666). In 1650 and 1651 a bushel of apples and a lamb were sent to the college by Watertown to help finance the education of Samuel Phillips, the son of the deceased pastor. John Langdon Sibley, *Harvard Graduates,* vol. 1 (Cambridge: Sever, 1873), 222.

32. In 1676 William Goddard was appointed teacher, replaced by Lieutenant Sherman in 1677. Norcross returned in 1678. *WR,* 137, 138. MxCC DB, 3:266, 333; D&O, 3, folios 73, 80; 4, folios 83, 91. Mx Deeds, 7:358, 459, record Norcross having to sell land in 1678. See chapter 12.

33. William Parker, "Agriculture," in *American Economic Growth,* ed. Lance Davis and Richard Easterlin (New York: Oxford University Press, 1972), 395; Vickers, "Working the Fields," 68; see also Levy, "Child Labor"; Greven, *Four Generations,* 73–77, 96–99, 137–38. See chapter 2. Labor: Smith: Smith and Sanborn, 427; see also Sherman: MxCC D&O, 1, folio 18, 24 April 1657; after age twenty-one, young people could customarily "work at their own account." Vickers, *Farmers and Fishermen,* 67; Chenery: Wyman, 2:172.

34. MxCC DB, 1:6; 3:6; see also Thompson, *Sex in Middlesex,* 94. Of the ten cases of direct discipline by the selectmen, eight were of fatherless adolescents, *WR,* 48, 52, 84, 92, 106.

35. Bond, 1065. Earlier second-generation successors were William Bond, selectman from 1657; Samuel Stearns, from 1673; John Whitney Jr., from 1673; Simon Stone Jr., from 1672; and Thomas Fleg, from 1671. Second-generation frustration may be echoed in a Dedham petition

of 1665 that describes many younger men as "dissatisfied with and disaffected to this present government as . . . not well-willers to our peace and privileges." Mass Archives, 3 May 1665. Succession rather than co-option was also the custom in Essex, England. Quintrell, "Government of Essex," 40. Frustration: chapter 4.

36. On gambling: MxCC DB, 3:228, John, son of Anthony White, aged about twenty-seven. See Appendix A, "White v. Bemis."

37. Sawin: Appendix A, "John Sawin Jr.: Horse-Thief," MxCC D&O, 2, folio 44, 22 November 1667; Wellington servant: Dunn, 752; Hannah Winter: MxCC D&O, 3, folio 66; see also Wyman, 1:62, 65 (Knapps and Cady); 135 (John Chadwick); see Appendix A, "The Watertown Underworld Falls Out," and chapter 2.

38. Smith and Sanborn, 426–28; Wyman, 2:188. See chapter 9.

39. There were seven convictions between 1671 and 1678, two of which were premarital conceptions, as compared with one adultery and one fornication between 1649 and 1663, and four cases between 1664 and 1670. The missing docket book for 1663–70 may result in underrecording. Thompson, *Sex in Middlesex*, 12–13, 65–70, suggests some tentative causes.

40. MxCC D&O, 2, folio 44; see also chapter 8.

41. Page: MxCC DB, 1:5–7; Bowen: 1:220, 260, 261, 268, 269. For her love letter, see Thompson, *Sex in Middlesex*, 24, 38; Sawtel: Smith and Sanborn, 427; Thompson, *Sex in Middlesex*, 20, 44, 101–2. Two cases are devoid of details: Jonathan Bigelow and ?Esther Jenks, Wyman, 2:75, August 1668; Bigelow later married Rebecca Shepard in 1671. Sarah Warren, aged twenty-one and daughter of Daniel Warren, was presented for fornication in 1679; Richard Cutting and his wife were witnesses. MxCC D&O, 4, folio 88. See also premarital fornication cases: Wetherall: MxCC DB, 3:58; Mary Jr. and Walter Davis: 3:107, 109; D&O, 3, folio 66, test. Christopher Grant, 7 October 1674.

42. MCC D&O, 2, folio 47, 23 March 1668; Summers, a tailor, agreed to make Sawin's sister a waistcoat if "she would let him lie with her. She replied it was a sin against God. He answered her that she might first commit the act and then repent after . . . [she reported that] if he found her alone in the house, he would pull out his privities and spill his seed." Ibid., 23 June 1668. Brooks, in turn, had been convicted of wanton dalliance with Goodwife Elizabeth Glazier in 1662, three years after his marriage. Thompson, *Sex in Middlesex*, 75, 77.

43. Bemis: Smith and Sanborn, 476–77; *Assistants*, 3:116; Mass Archives, 14 March 1678. See Appendix A, "White v. Bemis." Phillips: chapter 9. Grants: Melinde Lutz Sanborn, "Great Migration Diary," *Nexus* 16 (1999): 74; Knapps: Thompson, *Sex in Middlesex*, 100.

44. MxCC D&O, 3, folios 67, 70; Thompson, *Sex in Middlesex*, 90–93, 180–82, 185–86.

45. Thompson, "Adolescent Culture," 132. Seventeen-year-old Thomas Waite "could neither stand nor go . . . and did smell very much of drink" after Election Day 1659, MxCC D&O, 1, folio 22.

46. The Masons were the children of the militia captain and leading selectman, Hugh Mason. Jonathon Mason and John Morse had both already been presented in 1664 for "nightwalking." The Holdens were well-heeled artisans; Jacob Onge's father had died almost immediately after arriving in Watertown from Lavenham, Suffolk, in 1630. Smith, Allen, and Sanders came from disreputable and dependent families. Smith was a brother-in-law of Knapps and a brother of Zachariah, begetter of Ruth Sawtel's bastard. It was claimed that the parent Walter Allen had fled from Bury St. Edmunds in Suffolk to escape paying maintenance on two bastards he had fathered there. Benjamin's brother, John Allen, had been accused of fornication in Salisbury, Massachusetts, during the 1650s. Sanders's pauper father, Edward, had been convicted of attempted rape in 1654; William moved out to Groton in 1674; his neighbors in the new settlement would be most of his drinking companions: Allen, Onge, Holden, and Morse, not to mention James Knapp, a former Watertown thief, adulterer, and hooligan. Mason/Morse: MCC D&O, 2, folio 38, 8 October 1664; Allens: *WP*, 4:97–98, Goodman, "Newbury," 55; Smith: Smith and Sanborn, 425, 436; Sanders: chapter 9, Greene, *Early Records of Groton*, throughout.

47. Wyman, 1:121–22; Thompson, *Women in Stuart England and America: A Comparative Study* (London: Routledge & Kegan Paul, 1974), 244. Others summoned from Watertown were

John Page Jr. (ca. 30, unmarried), Nathaniel Bowman (19), Timothy Hawkins Jr. (21), John Winter Jr. (26), Bezaleel Sherman (ca. 16), Hannah Bright (17), James Barnard (20), Mary Beers (17), Mary Barnard (20), Martha Sherman (19), Mary Sherman (17), Hannah Tainter (16), Joanna Bowman (18), Elizabeth Stearns (ca. 20), and Sarah Barron (20). Stearns and Winter were in trouble again two years later. Along with Samuel Manning and others, they were suspected of "disorderly shooting in the way of an alarm upon the 17th [of July] about the hours of ten or eleven o'clock in the night and about the town of Cambridge to the disturbance of the inhabitants." When summoned by the magistrate, they "carried it very contemptuously and refused to answer . . . if they had been in that company that shot off three guns." Stearns "required me to bring testimony of what he was charged with . . . and refused to answer if he was in company with Samuel Manning at the ordinary in Cambridge after the [curfew] bell rang nine o'clock [or] if he was at Mrs. Manning's about ten o'clock. His carriage with me was very high and with much pride and contempt." Once again drink was the trigger for this alarming outburst, but the overexcitement of courtship may also have been a factor, as Stearns married Hannah Manning six months later. Paige, *Cambridge*, 223–24, 228–29.

48. *MR*, 4/1:97.

49. Thompson, "Adolescent Culture," 137. In 1677 twenty-year-old Mary Sherman, daughter of Rev. John, was convicted of fornication with the married Samuel Church, MxCC DB, 3:190.

50. See chapters 4 and 6.

51. Thompson, "Adolescent Culture," 133, my emphasis. On intergenerational interdependence, however, see chapter 11 and Vickers, *Farmers and Fishermen*, 64–77.

11. The Family

1. Thompson, *Sex in Middlesex*, 83, 89, 149, 166, chap. 10; Wyman, 2:76; for recent citations on this vast topic, Mary Beth Norton, *Founding Mothers and Fathers* (New York: Knopf, 1996). Helena M. Wall, *Fierce Communion* (Cambridge: Harvard University Press, 1990) has an excellent bibliography of primary sources on the early colonial family. The classic response to God's "Controversy with New England" can be seen in the frenzy of reform measures passed by the General Court in 1678–79.

2. Roger Thompson, "'Holy Watchfulness' and Community Conformism," *NEQ* 56 (1983): 504–22; the classic analysis is David H. Flaherty, *Privacy in Colonial New England* (Charlottesville: University of Virginia Press, 1972); see also Stephanie Coontz, *The Social Origins of Private Life* (London: Verso, 1988).

3. Analysis of recoverable ages of 134 marriages recorded in Anderson for Watertown people are as follows:

1620s.	Males:	n = 10, average age, 28.2
1630s.	M:	12, avg. 26.7
	Females:	3, avg. 21.0
1640s.	M:	4, avg. 28.0
	F:	8, avg. 23.0
1650s.	M:	10, avg. 26.6
	F:	27, avg. 21.3
1660s.	M:	21, avg. 28.2
	F:	21, avg. 22.4
1670s.	M:	9, avg. 32.1
	F:	9, avg. 25.4

Alas, even for so learned and painstaking a genealogist as Anderson, the majority of these figures are based on intelligent estimates, which may make the averages several months higher than they should be. The 1670s age rise may have been due to war.

4. Attraction: test. Susan Clements, 1656, MxCC D&O, 1, folio 12; Mass Archives, 14, 15 May

1656; Bowen: Thompson, *Sex in Middlesex*, 32, "My Love, I remember my love to you hoping your welfare and I hope to embrace thee... A letter from you [on] July 1 makes me love you the more because of your expression therein. If you can love me, bestow me word or tell me so. Farewell My Love and dear Esau." Smith, Davis, Fleming: chapter 10; Fleming was subsequently sent to sea to cool his ardor, MxCC DB, 1:217–18; Ball: chapter 9; Hammond: see below in this chapter. See also J. A. Sharpe, "Plebeian Marriage in Stuart England," *Transactions of the Royal Historical Society*, 5th ser., 36 (1986): 69–90.

5. Allegations of forced marriage: see Clements divorce, below. Shepard considered marriage as a possible "sentence" for extramarital pregnancy in a MS in Mass Archives, 1642; "enjoining to marriage" was incorporated in *The Book of General Laws and Liberties* of 1648 but never insisted on as a sentence, see Thompson, *Sex in Middlesex*, 8. On Bowen and Dunster, ibid., 24, 38, 101, 106, 166, and chapter 10. On Woodward and Hastings illegitimacies, see Appendix A, "Susannah Woodward." On godly marriages, see Morgan, *Puritan Family*, 55–56, 80, 84–86, 181–82. For English precedents for town involvement in preventing unwelcome matches, see Steve Hindle, "The Problem of Pauper Marriage," *Transactions of the Royal Historical Society*, 5th ser., 48 (1998): 71–89.

6. Anderson, 918–22, 1366–69; Smith and Sanborn, 427–32; Thompson, *Sex in Middlesex*, 20, 101; see chapter 9 and Appendix A, "Page v. Page" and "Edward Sanders, Child Abuser." After Edmund's death Ruth Blois lived thirty years as a childless widow.

7. Anderson, 163, 1449–50; Savage. See Appendix A, "White v. Bemis" and "The Watertown Underground Falls Out." Rebecca Bemis White was herself thirty when she married; perhaps the match was delayed by family hostilities. Her husband was promptly killed by a bull.

8. The following year Abiah married the altogether more suitable William Bull, Wyman, 2:172; "friends," MxCC D&O, 1, folio 23. Ann Pearce alluded to the proper interfamilial preparations: "Captain Hugh Mason, whose granddaughter my son Benjamin hath a fancy unto and having liberty from all parties to gain his desire... " Pearce Petition, ibid., 4, folio 82, 1 October 1678. Cf. English precedents: Keith Wrightson, "Politics of the Parish in Early Modern England," in *Experience of Authority*, ed. Griffiths, Fox, and Hindle, 17.

9. Beers: Mx PR, 4:197; see also Straite, 4:202; Barron: 5:159. See also Mx PR, 1:117, where Jeremy Norcross, about to embark for England, omitted his daughter Sarah Macey from the beneficiaries of his will because she "has already had her share as her dowry." Thomas Hammond's will of 25 October 1655 left "the Ipswich farm called 'Crosses' to my wife Hannah [née Cross] which I had with her" as dowry. Mx PR, 1:74. The borrowing of £52 in 1662 by Roger Wellington was probably connected with the forthcoming marriage of his eldest son, John. Mx Deeds, 3:48. On gifts of land or capital before death, see chapter 10.

10. White and Bemis were somewhat older when they married. See also Appendix A, "Gale v. Gale," and the Pearce-Mason/Brooks negotiations, MxCC D&O, 4, folio 88 and below. Hannah Brooks, eldest daughter of Joshua and Hannah (Mason) Brooks of Concord, married Benjamin Pearce in 1678. White: Mx PR, 6:286.

11. John Barnard Jr. was twenty-two years old. His father had been a selectman in 1644 but died in 1646, aged forty-two. His widow, Phoebe, never remarried. The handsome endowment promised by the Flemings included the house and homestall called Tarbells, cattle, and movables. Fleming undertook to "add an end unto that house, build a stack of brick chimney, and, if he could, purchase the lot of one Arnold and add unto it and give his daughter, and to furnish the house for them." Possible grounds for opposition to the match were the Flemings' nongodly status or their retailing of inferior malt. See Appendix A, "Fleming Executors v. Jones." Depositions concerning the marriage agreement are in MxCC D&O, 1, folio 16, 29, 30 December 1658. Bargaining: Appendix A, "Gale v. Gale."

12. *WP*, 4:230–32; *New York Genealogical and Biographical Register* 121 (1990): 19–22. Only mutual withdrawal after engagement ("He could not leave unless she were willing") would let Smith off the hook, which was not forthcoming: William Payne (Sarah's uncle) to John Winthrop, 21 April 1640, *WP*, 4:230. On John Whittaker's expensive breach of promise, see Appendix A, "Whittaker." See also Thompson, *Sex in Middlesex*, 59–64.

13. Wills reflected prenuptial commitments. The seriously rich Sarah (Lumpkin) Stone decreed in 1663 that "my covenant made with Simon Stone may be made good to him and also £30 abated from what he owes me." Alas, poor Simon followed her quickly to the grave. At least thirty-nine of the ninety-six long-term first-generation male residents married at least twice. Eleven widows are known to have remarried; twenty-three of the males remarried widows. See below for statistics. George will: *Suffolk Wills,* 1:95, 118; Stone: Mx PR, 2:113; Sarah Stone's estate was valued at £576. See also Barron: Mx PR, 4:197; Underwood, ibid., 6:27.

14. The agreement, whose date is blotted, but probably of 1651 or 1652, is in MxCC D&O, 1, folio 22; Knapp's will is filed at folio 16; various administrators' accounts submitted by Richard Beers and Ephraim Child in April 1659, including Priscilla Knapp's receipt for £11.5.0, are in folio 23. Thomas Akers, Priscilla's former husband, died in about 1651. His inventory was £118.11.8 and was required as documentation in a further Knapp estate dispute in 1674. MxCC D&O, 3, folio 66. See also Anderson, 1143–46. The court appointed Charles Chadwick as the widow's "friend in trust."

15. If she predeceased him, unless she specifically bequeathed the £45 to her new husband, Norcross must return it to his stepchildren. Suggestively, in all this protective legal insurance, the name of the bride does not appear. Bond dated 8 April 1674; MxCC D&O, 3, folio 67; MxCC DB, 3:95. See also Woodward-Gates prenuptial indenture, Mx Deeds, 2:364, 18 April 1663.

16. See also the Garfield case: Joan Garfield petitioned the General Court in 1671: "Through want of understanding or good advice, she unadvisedly signed and sealed to the use of her son Joseph Buckminster, now dead, the deed of sale of houses and lands of her late dear husband Thomas Buckminster, left to her for life, [in exchange for Joseph's] annual payment of rent for her income. He paid some of the £10 rent but not all, and lately hath paid none so that she and her other children, especially her son Jabesh, suffer and are cut off. Neither can myself use any legal course being a woman under covert, and my present husband [Edward Garfield] entered into a bond not to meddle with that estate." Mass Archives, 31 May 1671. For male management, e.g., *Suffolk Deeds,* 55, where Sarah Gosse's second husband, Robert Nicholls, acknowledges prior sale of Gosse land and then proceeds, with his wife's approval, to sell some more. Gosse's inventory, taken on 14 May 1644, totaled £85.

17. Woodward: chapter 9. Financial rivalry: chapter 11. On second marriages: Darrett B. Rutman and Anita H. Rutman, "Now-Wives and Sons-in-Law," in *The Chesapeake in the Seventeenth Century,* ed. Thad W. Tate and David L. Ammerman (New York: Norton, 1979), 153–82.

18. Standing crops: Richard Stratton, Mx PR, 1:159; other provisions: apples: William Knapp, 1:227; turnips: Richard Beers, 4:202, William Hagar, 6:186; tobacco: John Child, 4:246, Nathaniel Fiske, 4:269, Miles Ives, 6:277; onions: Richard Brown, Mx Wills, 3168; honey: William Page, Mx PR, 2:207, John Livermore, 6:221, Samuel Thatcher, 3:291. Adams: Mass Archives, 28 April 1653; see also Metup and Whitney: *WR,* 83, 1 November 1664, and chapter 9.

19. Stratton: MxCC D&O, 1, folio 1, doc. 60, 22 April 1649; Goody Stratton was cleared after medical examination; see deposition of Elizabeth Brown, Anna George, Jane Tidd, and Ellen Pemberton. See also Knapp: MxCC D&O, 1, folio 5, doc. 245, 4 April 1649; Appendix A, "Whittaker."

20. Mx Deeds, 2:137, 138, 140. See chapter 8.

21. Some women proved excellent managers: Mary Dix Brown Rice, Hannah Bartlett, Ann Fleming, and Sarah Lumpkin Stone. Brown: MxCC D&O, 4, folios 84, 87, 89. Bartlett: Anderson, 121, 122; MxCC DB, 3:149, 3 October 1676. Fleming: Mx Wills, 7802, 7803; Stone: Mx PR, 2:113. However, men usually took charge of family assets: e.g., Stearns: MxCC D&O, 3, folio 75, 17 June 1677; MxCC DB, 3:167. See also MxCC D&O, 3, folio 67, and MxCC DB, 3:97, 214: John Coolidge and Henry Bright of Watertown, feoffees in trust of Anna Woods, widow, battled with her husband's estate administrators for eight years, 1670–78, on her behalf. Men controlled this procedure throughout. Frustration: see Appendix A, "Page v. Page" and "Gale v. Gale"; Pearce case, below in this chapter.

22. On birth intervals, an analysis of Watertown births in Anderson produces the following

average intervals: Barsham (first six births), 26 months; Bartlett, 41; Benjamin, 38; Bowman, 30; Bridges, 24; Bright, 24; A. Brown, 31; Chester, 36; Church, 26; Crisp, 22; Dix, 19; Eddy, 31; Feake, 42; Hammond, 32; Hawkins, 27; Keyes, 24; Knapp, 23; Knopp, 24; Mayhew, 29; Onge, 25; Page, 24; Phillips, 22; Saltonstall, 31; Stearns, 35; Warren 29. Overall average interval: 28.6. These figures do not take into account stillbirths and miscarriages. Intervals often increased after the birth of the first four children. Brewing equipment was listed in seven inventories, spinning wheels in thirty-three, dairy utensils in twenty, and salting in eight. Spinning: Ball, *WR*, 50, and chapter 9. Fleming and others on brewing, see Appendix A, "Fleming Executors v. Jones." On marketing: Adrienne Hood, "The Material World of Cloth," *WMQ* 53 (1996): 43–66, esp. 63; St. George, "Domesticating the Yeomanry," 302.

23. *WP*, 5:119, 293; other experts: Susannah Harrington, MxCC D&O, 3, folio 59; three other women assisted her: Abigail Benjamin, seventy-one, Abigail Woodward, forty-seven, and Sarah Cutting, forty-six. Five Hastings prematurity witnesses: Margaret Hastings, Hepzibah ?Wood, Elizabeth Nevinson, Elizabeth Lawrence, and Judith Livermore, MxCC D&O, 4, folio 89. Grace Livermore: Bond, 1074. Anne George, Elizabeth Pearce: Mass Archives, 6 September 1654.

24. See chapter 9. *WR*, 122.

25. John Pearce's inventory of 2 July 1661 refers to "the new chamber." Edward Garfield's will of 30 December 1668 mentions "the new bed-chamber." Mx PR, 2:1; 3:374. On household changes, see St. George, "Domesticating the Yeomanry," 300–308. On house building, see chapter 8.

26. Nine-room dwellings: Richard Beers, Mx PR, 4:202, John Sherman, Mx Wills, 20338; eight rooms: William Shattuck, Mx PR, 4:28; Samuel Thatcher, Mx PR, 3:393, Ephraim Child, Mx Wills, 4401; six rooms: John Traine, Mx PR, 5:506, Anthony Pearce, 5:393, Charles Chadwick, 5:228, Samuel Stratton, 4:15, John Witherall, 3:389, Thomas Underwood, 3:72, John Fleming, Mx Wills, 7803, John Bigelow, 1716. The Society for the Preservation of New England Antiquities in Boston has considerable documentation on Watertown's Brown House of the 1690s. See chapter 8. On family "domestication" and privacy, see Lawrence Stone, *Family, Sex, and Marriage in England, 1500–1800* (New York: Harper, 1977), part 3; Konig, *Law and Society*, 129–33; and Flaherty, *Privacy*.

27. Hammonds: Mx PR, 1:76, 110. Silver: John Cutting, Mx Wills, 5678, John Fleming, 7803, Nicholas Guy, 9999, William Bond, 2190, Captain John Sherman, 20338, Margaret (Howe) Bunker, Mx PR, 1:239, Hannah Hammond, 1:110, Samuel Hosier, 2:281, Simon Stone, 2:285, John Warren, 3:60, William Shattuck, 4:28, Charles Chadwick, 5:228, Daniel Smith Jr., 5:480, John Livermore, 6:221, Ephraim Child, 2:440, Thomas Underwood, 6:27, William Barsham, 6:265. Pewter: Nathaniel Fiske, Mx PR, 2:7, Edward Garfield, 2:374, Michael Bairstow, 4:183, Richard Beers, 4:202, John Whitney, 4:99, Hugh Mason, 5:351, Anthony Pearce, 5:393, Magdalen Underwood, 6:27, Richard Blois, Mx Wills, 2108, John Biscoe, 1796, Joseph Bemis, 1541, John Bigelow, 1716, Ellis Barron, 2110, Edward Braybrook, 2428, Charles Chadwick, 4099, Ephraim Child, 4401, Edward Dix, 6296, Ann Fleming, 7802. Glass or china: Samuel Thatcher, Mx PR, 3:291, John Whitney, 4:99, John Shattuck, 5:575, Samuel Hosier, 2:281, William Shattuck, 4:28, Daniel Smith Jr., 5:480, Thomas Underwood, 6:27, Jonathan Brown, Mx Wills, 3164, Charles Chadwick, 4099. On delftware, see Fairbanks and Trent, 2:274–79; 3:394–96. Woodware: Blois, Mx Wills, 2110; furniture: Sherman (press), Mx Wills, 20338, Bond (press), 2190, Barsham (two chairs), Mx PR, 6:265, Hammond (desk), 1:76, Chenery (desk-box), 4:246, Livermore (livery cupboard), 6:221, Child (settle), Mx Wills, 4401, Hosier (glass case), Mx PR, 2:281, Bairstow (chest), 4:183, Whitney (chest), 4:99, Wetherall (chest), 3:389. Looking glasses: Samuel Thatcher, John and William Shattuck, Charles Chadwick, ut sup., Elizabeth Pearce, Mx PR, 2:325, John Chenery, 4:246, Isaac Stearns Jr., 5:498, William Bond, Mx Wills, 2190, Caleb Church, 4449.

28. Even the twenty-five-year-old Susannah Woodward, a single mother, owned a silk scarf and two silk hoods in her tiny estate of £5.14.8. Fleming: Mx Wills, 7802; Thatcher: Mx PR, 6:1; Hammond: Mx PR, 1:2; Woodward: Mx PR, 6:109. See also Stone, Mx PR, 2:113; Howe, *Suffolk Wills*, 1:31; Child, Mx PR, 3:406; Pearce, Mx PR, 2:325.

29. Ann Fleming had four cushions but also listed a rug and a carpet, as did Michael Bairstow. Edward Garfield left a rug and blanket to his daughter Abigail in 1668, along with a bed and some pewter. Samuel Thatcher boasted a bearskin that his widow kept in the parlor for the thirteen years she survived him. Isaac Stearns had a mooseskin. Beers, Mx PR, 4:202, Fleming, Mx Wills, 7803, Bairstow, 1332 ("napery"), Garfield, Mx PR 2:374, Thatcher, 3:291, Stearns, 4:142.

30. Mx PR, 6:154, 186.

31. E.g., William Bond, Mx Wills, 2190, Captain John Sherman, 20338, Jonathon Brown, 3164, John Biscoe, 1796, Thomas Underwood, Mx PR, 6:27.

32. Privacy: Mary Holden expressed affront when two young men invaded "one evening when her husband was at family duties; they stayed some while in the room where her husband and she kept [the parlor] and after, they went into the kitchen." Richard Holden threatened to fetch the constable in order to get rid of them. Grant v. Gookin, test. Holdens, MxCC D&O, 3, folio 71; Thompson, *Sex in Middlesex*, 144.

33. See chapter 9, Appendix A, "Page v. Page," Mattacks, Cookes, and Agurs below. Thompson, *Women*, 169–81.

34. Willis Freeman, "The Ancestry of Samuel Freeman of Watertown," *TAG* 11 (1934): 73–80, 171–79; Anderson; *MR*, 1:81; on William Quick, see *WP*, 3:321, and chapter 12; Ella F. Elliot, "The Divorce of the Watertown Freemans," *R* 97 (1943): 393. Clarke helped John Winthrop Jr. found Ipswich in 1633 and returned to London in 1639. Boylston: MxCC DB, 1:31, 46, 110; D&O, 1, folio 6; 2, folio 57. Mx Wills, 2390. *Suffolk Deeds*, 67, 247–48. WBOP, 121 lists his town land holdings. Aspinwall, 172, 183, 199, 200. Clements: Mass Archives, 3 May 1656; MxCC D&O, 1, folio 12, docs. 644, 645. Thompson, *Sex in Middlesex*, 115–16, where Susan is incorrectly named Martha. She had been prevented from marrying Richard Willis but still hankered after him. Like Elizabeth Ball (see chapter 9), she lacked "natural abilities to guide herself." Two other Watertown women were mentally disturbed: the wife of William Knapp Jr., see above, and Rebecca (Gibson) Stearns, see chapter 6. Cf. St. George, "Domesticating the Yeomanry," 168–70: three times as many women as men suffered from mental or emotional disorders in the seventeenth century. Preventing desertion: Thomas Agur of Watertown was presented on 6 September 1663 and Gregory Cooke warned on 11 March 1667, the former for "living about a year in the country without his wife," presumably abandoned in England, the latter "for his living from his wife," who may have remained in neighboring Cambridge. MxCC D&O, 2, folios 35, 44. Mattack: *MR*, 5:188. See chapters 6 and 10. Remarriage: Freeman, Mattack; rescue: Ball, Clements, Boylston.

35. E.g., Ellis Barron, Mx PR, 4:197, Samuel Stratton, 4:15, William Shattuck, 4:28, Isaac Stearns, 4:142, William Parry, 6:154, Lewis Jones, 6:260, Joseph Bemis, 6:284.

36. Mx PR, 1:159, 4:15. Samuel Stratton had a six-room house and another house. His land was worth £182, and his stock £58. Cf. John Shattuck, a recently married tailor, who drowned in September 1675 and left £41. He had a one-acre homestall and a small house, the tools of his trade, two horses and a cow, a heifer and five hogs, and (a sign of the attractions of consumer culture to the younger generation) five pieces of chinaware, five glass bottles, and a looking glass. Mx PR, 5:475. On Shattuck, see chapter 12.

37. E.g., William Shattuck, Mx PR, 4:28, estate £425; children: John Randall: Mx PR, 5:429; Susan, Sarah, and Mary were in their early twenties or late teens; Stephen, Samuel, and Eleazar ranged from late teens down to only eight. Cf. Thomas Straite, 5:159, Daniel Smith Jr., 5:480, Isaac Mixer, 1:42–46, Daniel Smith Sr., 1:231, William Page, 2:207, Abraham Brown Jr., 3:168, John Child, 4:246, John Chenery, 4:250, Henry Freeman, 4:148, Richard Blois, Mx Wills, 2108, John Cutting, 5678, Edward Dix, 6296, John Fleming, 7803. See section below on widows.

38. See chapter 10 and Appendix A, "Page v. Page." Estates with cash: Michael Bairstow, Mx PR, 4:183, John Bigelow, Mx Wills, 1716, William Bond, 2190, Richard Brown, 3168; loans: Bairstow, Charles Chadwick, Mx PR, 5:228, Hugh Mason, 5:351, John Livermore, 6:221, Nathaniel Treadway, 7:38. Women: Stone: Mx PR, 2:113; Howe, *Suffolk Wills*, 1:31; Fleming: Mx Wills, 7802; Thatcher, Mx PR, 6:1; Child, 3:406; Pearce, 2:325. Cf. Vickers, *Farmers and Fishermen*, 72–75.

39. E.g., Old Father Blois, aged ninety-four, long-time verger, with his pathetic £25 inventory, which included "a hovel and a barn," or the near-centenarian Old Bright, owner of a straw bed and chaff pillows, a pewter platter, pair of porridge pots, an old sheet, three blankets, a chamber pot, tongs, two chairs, two old chests, a pair of sheep shears, a knife, an old axe, and a candlestick. Blois: Mx Wills, 2110; Bright, 2721; cf. Lewis Jones, aged eighty-four, whose estate totaled £62.2.0, Mx PR, 6:260. Hammond: Mx PR, 1:74–76, William Hammond, 2:79, £468.

40. At least £440 of Hammond's wealth was in land; £368 worth of Samuel Stearns's £481 estate was in land. Mx PR, 6:136. Cf. Fleming's inventory, Mx Wills, 7803; Samuel Livermore: Mx PR, 7:305. Analysis of forty-one inventories in Mx PR, vols. 1–5, shows an average of 35 percent of estates in movables and 65 percent in land. Over-seventies are very similar to these averages, Mx PR, 1, 25 percent, 5, 34 percent. Poor craftsmen: John Rogers, Mx PR, 4:178, William Knapp Jr., 5:32, George Woodward, 3:250, David Fiske, 2:7.

41. See chapter 10 and Appendix A, "Page v. Page" and "Gale v. Gale."

42. Barsham: Mx Deeds, 6:375, 18 November 1678. Annabel Barsham, the mother, died by 1683, and William in July 1684. See also Jane Guy: Mx Deeds, 4:240, Mass Archives, October 1651; Nathaniel Fiske: MxCC D&O, 3, folio 73, 3 October 1676; John and Phoebe Page, see Appendix A, "Page v. Page."

43. E.g., Whitney: Mx Deeds, 3:451–52, 4:344, 9 March 1670; Bairstow: Mx Deeds, 4:183. Blois: Mx Deeds, 7:381, 12 June 1681. Safeguards: Spring, Mx Deeds, 6:220; Chadwick: 7:359, 5 January 1680. See also Walter Allen's conditional disposal of his Watertown lands to his two sons, Daniel and Joseph, reserving living space and a little land for himself and wife, when he was seventy-two. Mx Deeds, 7:142–43, 1 October 1673. On the gradually shifting interdependencies between aging fathers and sons: Vickers, *Farmers and Fishermen*, 67–73.

44. Konig, *Law and Society*, 112–16, 137, 154.

45. Loverun: *Suffolk Wills*, 1:21. George Phillips's second wife was with the pastor as he put his affairs in order before his early death. "Presently his wife putting him in mind of the bond in Elder Howe's hand, he called Samuel . . . [and he told him to] let the bond alone and give it in to your mother when you come off. You shall have nothing if you take the bond." Present with surgeon Simon Eyre were Elizabeth Child and Apphia Freeman, ibid., 1:20, 1 July 1644; Fleming: MxCC D&O, 1, folio 16, doc. 813.

46. Phillips: Dunn, 759–60. Thorpe: *WR*, 116; Knapp: McCC D&O, 1, folio 23, 3 April 1660, list of estate debts includes £1.1.0 for "funeral charge."

47. Conventions: Knapp: Mx Deeds, 2:201, 215, 217. Priscilla Akers Knapp got £11.5.0 and half the movables, MxCC DB, 1:180. Fleming: Ann Fleming got £100 over and above her thirds, ibid., 179. See Appendix A, "Fleming Executors v. Jones." Intestacy: MxCC D&O, 3, folio 43, test. Martha Underwood, 1676. Isaac Mixter left a daughter a quarter-share in a ship. Mx PR, 1:42–46.

48. MxCC D&O, 3, folio 71; MxCC DB, 3:160, 19 December 1676.

49. This was done in 1677 by the five children of the widower Joseph Underwood. The award gave double portion to Joseph Underwood Jr. and extra to Hannah, the youngest and only unmarried sibling. This favoring of the kid sister had been proposed by the elder offspring and presumably included her dowry as well. MxCC D&O, 3, folio 73, 29 March 1677.

50. MxCC D&O, 1, folios 16, 17, 22; MxCC DB, 1:138, 146, 147, 148, 150, 163, 180; Mx Wills, 7802, 7803; Mx Deeds, 2:4, 356–57. The buyer was recently arrived Roger Nevinson. John Fleming Jr. eventually became a minister in England. Savage. See Appendix A, "Fleming Executors v. Jones."

51. Wyman, 1:103; MxCC D&O, 1, folios 17, 20, 21, 34; MxCC DB, 1:169, 180, 282, 283, 291; Mx Deeds, 1:82, 83; Anderson, 852. Rev. John Sherman sued the estate on behalf of an English creditor in Dedham, Essex. Eighty-four-year-old William Hammond contested the low valuation of movables, which would require land sales to redeem his son's debts.

52. MxCC DB, 3:243; MxCC D&O, 3, folios 80, 82. See also the complex legal arrangements of leases and mortgages for transferring Loverun land in 1670, *Suffolk Wills*, 1:21; MxCC D&O, 1, folio 6; Mx Deeds, 6:300, 305.

53. Mx PR, 6:154, 4 January 1681; see chapters 6 and 10. See also the Iveses' disinheritance of neglectful son-in-law Lewis Allen, Mx PR, 6:277, 29 December 1683. *WR*, 135.

54. Sarah Parks v. Thomas Parks, 2 December 1671, MxCC D&O, 2, folio 57. Anderson. See also the arbitration between the widow and executors of Edward Dix, 1660, MxCC DB, 1:216, 218, 226. Anderson 551–52, and Grace Porter v. John Sherman, executor of Roger Porter, 9 October 1654, 28 November 1654, MxCC DB, 1:66, 68, where the county court had to appoint external arbitrators to divide Porter's estate.

55. Petition of Margaret Stratton, 4 April 1673: MxCC D&O, 3, folio 63; Margaret, as Widow Parker, had married the widower Samuel Stratton in 1658. Executor John Stratton had a poor orphaned nephew to worry about. Samuel Stratton's estate was £258. Mx PR, 1:159; 4:15. Cf. Knapps: MxCC DB, 1:165, 28 December 1658. Woods: MxCC D&O, 3, folio 67, 30 July 1670.

56. Waite: Mx PR, 3:120, see chapter 10. See also Hodges: MxCC D&O, 2, folio 46; Wyman, 2:109, 142, 28 July 1667, 13 October 1670; Blois: MxCC D&O, 2, folio 41, 2 March 1666, 3 April 1666; Wyman 2:27; Stearns: MxCC D&O, 3, folio 75; MxCC DB, 3:167, MxCC D&O, 4, folio 80, 26 March 1678; Green: MxCC DB, 3:336.

57. Endowment: George Munnings: Mx Deeds, 2:357, 5 April 1653; see also Stubbs: 6:58, 16 July 1677. Nephews: 6:187, Richard Child, 12 May 1677. Family preference: *Suffolk Deeds*, 51, Benjamin to Wines; 97, Parkhurst to Arnold. Chadwick: Mx PR, 5:228. Childless couples: Michael Bairstow, 4:183, Charles Chadwick: 5:228, John Livermore, 6:221, Martin Underwood, 4:48. Childless couples were not that uncommon in Watertown: the Martin Underwoods, John Wetheralls, Thomas Underwoods, John Loverans, Ephraim Childs, Edward Howes, Michael Bairstows, Charles Chadwicks, Samuel Hosiers, John Wincolls, and Thomas Loverans had no recorded children. Perpetuity: Stratton, Mx PR, 4:15, 19 December 1672. Gifts and loans to kin: Hannah Bartlett, Mx PR, 4:206, David Fiske, 2:7, Simon Stone, 2:285, Edward Garfield, 3:374, Ellis Barron, 4:197, Nathaniel Fiske, 4:269, see chapter 10.

58. Child will: Mx PR, 4:246.

59. See the Hastingses, the Woodwards, the Barnards, the Flegs, and the ancient Grants in chapter 10. See also Pearce relatives defending the pregnant Mary Ball against Michael Bacon, the child's begetter, Wyman, 2:125–27, 3–27 April 1671.

60. *Suffolk Deeds*, 167; MxCC D&O, 2, folio 39. Myrtle Stevens Hyde and P. L. Child, "Child-Foote-Goddard Connections," *TAG* 63 (1988): 17–28, and see chapter 2. See also Thompson, "Reflections on the Early-Modern Extended Family," 62–79.

61. See Page extended family care for the ailing John and Phoebe, which included Hammonds, Barrons, and Hawkinses as well as son and daughter, John and Faith. See Appendix A, "Page v. Page" and Smith and Sanborn, 120. Stearns: MxCC D&O, 4, folio 83, 1679, Mass Archives, 12 March 1664. Fleg: MxCC D&O, 4, folios 83, 87, 89. See also Thomas Smith as guardian for his Knapp niece, *WR*, 109; Randall: Mx PR, 5:429; Chenery: MxCC DB, 3:60; D&O, 3, folio 63, 30 March 1673.

62. Wetherall: Wyman, 2:7; Barron: Smith and Sanborn, 128.

63. See, e.g., Sherman involvement in Barnard-Fleming marriage negotiations, above.

64. Hawkins: Anderson, 889; Summers: chapter 10; Page: Appendix A, "Page v. Page" and chapter 10. See also chapter 9.

65. Young men: from Jonathon Phillips, pastor's son, through Samuel Benjamin, John Fleming, James Barnard, Jonathon Brown, down to the Chadwick brothers, Timothy Hawkins, Jacob Onge, and various Knapps and Grants; Glenn Wallach, *Obedient Sons: The Discourse of Youth and Generations* (Amherst: University of Massachusetts Press, 1997), 2–13. Young women: Susannah Woodward, Mary Davis Jr., and Mary Ball.

66. On transmission of authority, see chapter 4.

67. One hundred thirty-three identifiable offspring of the first-generation long-term residents married fellow Watertown residents. Ninety-three married spouses from other towns, but twenty-three of these married Cambridge people and six Sudburians. There were ninety-nine recorded endogamous marriages among the second generation. Data for those included in first and second generation taken from Anderson, Savage, and Smith and Sanborn; those who

moved out of Watertown and then married have been excluded. Multiple marriages: Widow Hannah Hawkins and her daughter Hannah married Ellis Barron Sr. and Jr. in a joint ceremony on 14 December 1653. Brothers John and Joseph Wellington married sisters Susannah (ca. 1677) and Elizabeth Straite (1684). Mary Coolidge, the granddaughter of Roger Wellington, married Daniel Livermore (ca. 1698), and Oliver Wellington married Ann (Bridge) Livermore, widow of Samuel (ca. 1691). Rebecca and Samuel Bemis were married to Thomas (1686) and Mary Harrington (ca. 1680). A triple alliance was that of Joshua, Samuel, and Mary Bigelow with Elizabeth (1676), Mary (1674), and Michael Fleg (1673). Nathaniel and Peleg Lawrence married Sarah (1660) and Elizabeth Morse (1669). Joseph and John Morse in turn married sisters Susannah (1661) and Abigail Shattuck (1666). A brother and sister Samuel and Elizabeth Stearns married a sister and brother Hannah (1663) and Samuel (1664) Manning.

68. E.g., Mx Deeds, 6:375, 428; on East Anglia: Barbara MacAllan, "Inheritance and Manorial Custom in the Hundred of Fleg, Norfolk," in *Counties and Communities: Essays in East Anglian History Presented to Hassell Smith,* ed. Carole Rawcliffe, Roger Virgoe, and Richard Wilson (Norwich: Centre of East Anglian Studies, 1996), 189–201.

69. Deputy husbands: Laurel Thatcher Ulrich, *Good Wives* (New York: Oxford University Press, 1983), 35–50. See also Vickers, "Working the Fields in Essex County," 51–66; Greven, *Four Generations,* chaps. 4, 6.

70. See chapter 9.

71. The average period for seven widows remarrying, as recorded in Smith and Sanborn, was 12.6 months; for ten widowers, 15.6 months.

12. Invisible Indians

1. William Wood, *New England's Prospect,* ed. Alden T. Vaughan (Amherst: University of Massachusetts Press, 1977), 124, has "Pigsgusset" as the native name for Watertown.

2. See chapter 1.

3. There were a few exceptions—an Eliot, a Mayhew, a Gookin, a Danforth—but none influential in Watertown.

4. Beers, Biscoe, Bowman, Hammond, and Whitney families are recorded as employing Indians; see below.

5. "Memoirs of Captain Roger Clap," in *Chronicles of the First Planters of Massachusetts Bay,* ed. Alexander Young (Boston: Little & Brown, 1846), 350.

6. Cronon, *Changes in the Land,* 42–46; Emerson, 110; see chapter 1, WR, 106; Wood, *New England's Prospect,* 55; Lindholdt, *John Josselyn,* 115–16. According to Thomas Morton, "At the spring, when the fish comes in plentifully, [the Indians] have meetings from several places, where they exercise themselves in gaming and playing of juggling tricks and all manner of revels, which they are delighted in, [so] that it is admirable to behold what pastime they use of several kinds." *New English Canaan* (London: Green, 1632), 20.

7. Emerson, 64. Cf. Wood's promotional depiction, *New England's Prospect,* 88–93, stressing Indian affability, courtesy, generosity, mutuality, "trustiness," helpfulness, hospitality, and general good humor.

8. *WJ,* 1:73. There are no native accounts of their perspective on the English invasion of Pequusset. This chapter must therefore reluctantly rely only on colonial sources.

9. Emerson, 111; however, we should not forget Clap's estimate of three hundred natives at the first landing, nor the report of Increase Nowell, "The Charlestown Records," in *Chronicles,* ed. Young, 366: "At this time [1633] began a most grievous and terrible sickness amongst the Indians who were exceedingly numerous about us (called the Aberginians). Their disease was generally the smallpox . . . [which] in a few months swept away multitudes of them young and old . . . insomuch as there was scarce any of them left." Pond's "plague" was the start of the smallpox pandemic. See Fairbanks and Trent, 66–69. Francis Jennings, *The Invasion of America* (Chapel Hill: University of North Carolina Press, 1975), 15.

10. Wood, *New England's Prospect,* 16; Neal Salisbury, *Manitou and Providence: Indians,*

Europeans, and the Making of New England, 1500–1643 (New York: Oxford, 1982), 183–84; Nelson, *Waltham,* 59–60, cites Josselyn's description of an Indian sagamore, Cutstomack, and some of his tribe living in 1632 on the western shore of Mead's, or Sherman's, Pond.

11. Woodward was probably trying to copy Indian methods of clearing land by fire. Morgan, *Founding of Massachusetts,* 402, 404, 407, 408, 423; *MR,* 1:293–94; see also Philip Vincent, *True Relation of the Battle in New England* (London: Butters & Bellamie, 1637), 12b2v: "The Saybrook lieutenant and ten men armed went out to fire the meadows to fit them for mowing." Virginia deJohn Anderson, "King Philip's Herds . . . Problems with Livestock," *WMQ* 51 (1994): 601–24. Emerson, 81. These are the first references to Indian maize in Watertown, but it does strengthen the argument for local, prewhite cultivation. Cf. Hubbard, *Narrative,* 82: "Indian summer fruits, [as] beans and squashes (besides their corn)." On 3 June 1634 Watertown leader Thomas Mayhew valued the damage done by Charlestown's swine that had got into Indian barns of grain. It is not improbable that conflicts about shared land-use continued, but the records of cases, transferred in 1640 to local small causes courts or selectmen's boards, have not survived.

12. Settlers: Thomas Mayhew and William Pynchon; the Court of Assistants was also fined for permitting them. The 1630 blanket ban on gun sales to any Indians was waived for friendly Indians in 1642. On 21 October 1663 the General Court permitted licensed fur traders, like Simon Willard, to sell powder, shot, and guns to Indians. Two rationales were offered. The Dutch and other colonies were already in the arms trade; wolves, "the destroyers and devourers of our cattle of all sorts," needed to be eliminated. *MR,* 1:76, 100, 127, 196; 2:16, 27, 57; 4/2:365; 5:44, 87, 304. Mass Archives, 27 May 1661, 16 May 1662, 21 October 1663, 27 October 1663. Wood, *New England's Prospect,* 79; Peter N. Carroll, *Puritanism and the Wilderness: The Intellectual Significance of the New England Frontier, 1629–1700* (New York: Columbia University Press, 1969); William S. Simmons, "Cultural Bias in New England Perceptions of Indians," *WMQ* 38 (1981): 56–72, esp. 58; Carole Shammas, "Anglo-American Household Government," ibid. 52 (1995): 104–44, esp. 111–13. Few Massachusetts ministers were involved in missionizing, and little money was raised in the colony, William Kellaway, *The New England Company* (London: Longman, 1961), 83. Mass Archives, 23 October 1651, has a petition from Eliot requesting the General Court to encourage towns like Watertown to compensate Dedham for town land lost to Natick "Praying Indians," but nothing was given.

13. Thomas Dudley to Countess of Lincoln, Emerson, 82–83.

14. New Watertown was soon renamed Wethersfield. Oldham is noticed in both *DNB* and *DAB;* Charles M. Andrews, *The River Towns of Connecticut* (Baltimore: Johns Hopkins, 1889), 8–15. Observers in the 1620s found Oldham passionate, impatient, unruly, and two-faced. Morton, *New English Canaan,* 81, described him as a "Mad Jack." Cf. William Bradford, *Of Plimouth Plantation,* ed. Samuel Eliot Morison (New York: Knopf, 1951), 151, 165. On the convoluted diplomacy behind trade and settlement in Connecticut, see Alfred A. Cave, "Who killed John Stone? A Note on the Origins of the Pequot War," *WMQ* 49 (1992): 509–21. The May 1634 General Court had given Newtown (later Cambridge) permission to seek alternative quarters, and the Oldham party may have been jumping the gun on rivals in the hunt for more spacious grazing.

15. John Underhill, *Newes from America,* in *Puritans, Indians, and Manifest Destiny,* ed. Charles M. Segal and David C. Stineback (New York: Putnam, 1977), 113–14; Alden T. Vaughan, "Pequots and Puritans: Causes of the War of 1637," *WMQ* 21 (1964): 256–69; Salisbury, *Manitou and Providence,* 209–39; Simmons, "Cultural Bias," 67; Michael Freeman, "Puritans and Pequots: The Question of Genocide," *NEQ* 68 (1995): 278–93, records that the Narragansetts bought puritan restraint by returning Oldham's two sons and his goods. William Hammond Jr. of Watertown was also killed by a "giant-like Indian towards the Dutch" in 1636 when he was shipwrecked on Long Island. *WP,* 3:270–71, 276, 284–85. Cf. Charles Orr, *History of the Pequot War* (Cleveland: Helman Taylor, 1897), 146.

16. Vincent, *True Relation of the Battle,* B2. The two girls were the daughters of William Swayne. They were spared and eventually ransomed by the Dutch. *WJ,* 2:29.

17. Known Watertown war participants, along with Jennison, were Daniel Patrick, Robert

Seeley, Richard Beers, and John Stubbin. In all, 160 militiamen from Massachusetts arrived in Hartford, under Patrick's command, on the eve of the Mystic Fort massacre. Thanks to intercolonial rivalries, the massacre took place before they could join the Connecticut contingent. Mason described Patrick as high-handed, obstructive, and choleric and plainly loathed him. Orr, *Pequot War*, 33; Segal and Stineback, *Puritans*, 132; Jennings, *Invasion of America*, 202–27. *WR*, 2; *MR*, 4/2:140; Lechford, 242–43. John E. Ferling, *A Wilderness of Miseries: War and Warriors in Early America* (Westport, Conn.: Greenwood, 1980), chap. 2.

18. Miantonomo, leader of the Narragansetts, speaking to the Montauks of eastern Long Island, was reputed an English ally! He was captured, tried, and executed by the English in 1643. Salisbury, *Manitou and Providence*, 13, 227.

19. 1640: Bond, 1045; 1641–43: Morgan, *Founding*, 404; *WR*, 6; *MR*, 2:30; Thomas Hutchinson, *History of Massachusetts Bay*, ed. Lawrence Shaw Mayo (Cambridge: Harvard University Press, 1936), 1:99; Salisbury, *Manitou and Providence*, 227; *WJ*, 2:131–32, 134–36; Carroll, *Puritanism*. 1645: Mass Archives, July, August 1645. In 1653, during the First Dutch War, the General Court expressed alarm at a Dutch-Indian alliance against them, ibid. Ironically, the Indians had been more effective in controlling wolves by destroying their young, 5MHSC 1 (1871): 480.

20. Segal and Stineback, *Puritans*, 144–45; James P. Ronda, "Generations of Faith: Christian Indians on Martha's Vineyard," *WMQ* 38 (1981): 369–94; Charles E. Banks, *History of Martha's Vineyard* (Boston: Dean, 1911), 81–234; L. C. M. Hare, *Thomas Mayhew Sr., Puritan Patriarch* (New York: Appleton, 1932). Two English memorials were the naming of two towns, Tisbury and West Tisbury, after Mayhew Sr.'s birthplace in Wiltshire, and Assassamoogh, an Indian convert of neighboring Nantucket, taking the name of James Gibbs, John Folger's wife's maiden name. Gibbs Pond on Nantucket is named after James, ibid., 196.

21. Hutchinson, 1:140; Daniel Gookin, "Historical Collections of the Indians in New England," 1MHSC 1 (1792): 141–227, esp. 181; Kupperman, "Climate," 27–28.

22. *MR*, 1:106; 2:85, 258; 3:425; 4/1:201, 289; 4/2:297, 564; Wood, *New England's Prospect*, 79; James Axtell, "Power of Print in the Eastern Woodlands," *WMQ* 44 (1987): 300–309, esp. 301.

23. MxCC D&O, 1, folio 6, docs. 196–201, 329; MxCC DB, 1:14, 35, 37. The Indians named in the depositions were Roger, Jethro, Josias, William, and Netus. Mass Archives, 28 April 1653. In 1639 Adams had bought two hundred acres of land within Lancaster bounds from the local Indian sagamore. He had spent some time as a fur trader "towards the Eastward" on the Kennebec River in Maine and also referred to "when he was up the Lake," possibly Winnepesaukee in New Hampshire. In 1670 he petitioned the General Court, *in forma pauperis*, because Lancaster had granted his land to other planters. Mass Archives, 13 May 1670.

24. Complaint of John Fleming in 1653, and Thomas Hammond's 1659 inventory, Wyman, 1:35, 103.

25. Andrew Pittyme, "about Lt. Beers," 9 August 1661, MxCC D&O, 1, folio 26.

26. By 1663 Jethro had fathered two illegitimate children. MxCC D&O, 2, folio 34, 7 December 1663; Mass Archives, 19, 22 May 1651. In the late 1640s Jethro had injured a mare and colt belonging to sometime Watertown resident Herman Garrett. Exorbitant damages of £16.6.8 and £4 costs had been awarded against Jethro, who had had to mortgage one thousand acres of his lands on the Assabash River beyond Sudbury. In May 1651 the General Court awarded Garrett foreclosure of the mortgage. One thousand acres in recompense for a mare and colt must have seemed like highway robbery to the Indian.

27. The thieves were John Nunnunipe and Richard Pittimore. Nearly a year later the jailer presented his list of charges for holding Andrew Pittyme and five Mohawk Indians. These two entries may have been connected; what use the classics would be to Native Americans is anyone's guess. See n. 25 above, Wyman, 2:10, 18, 3 September 1665. Pittyme's squaw was probably one of the four Indian women murdered by whites at Hurtleberry Hill during King Phillip's War. *MR*, 5:117, awards him and Swagton Indian (see n. 45) £5 compensation each, 11 October 1676. Jenny Hale Pulsipher, "Massacre at Hurtleberry Hill," *WMQ* 53 (1996): 459–86, esp. 463, 468.

28. MxCC D&O, 2, folio 51, test. Joseph Noyes; see chapter 13.

29. Mass Archives, 18 October 1670.

Notes to Pages 150–155　　249

30. *WR*, 106.

31. Mass Archives, 26 April 1671; MxCC D&O, 2, folio 59, 15 July 1671; Smith and Sanborn, 536 (Bacon), 427–28 (Smith).

32. MxCC DB, 3:90; D&O, 3, folio 68, 9 October 1673.

33. Douglas E. Leach, *Flintlock and Tomahawk: New England in King Philip's War* (New York: Norton, 1966), 148; Bond, 762; Hubbard, *Present State*, 30; see chapter 9. On the war as a defining moment in race relations, see Jill Lepore, *The Name of War* (New York: Viking, 1999), 166–67.

34. Increase Mather, "Brief History of the War with the Indians," in *So Dreadfull a Judgement: Puritan Responses to King Philip's War*, ed. Richard Slotkin and James K. Folsom (Middletown, Conn.: Wesleyan University Press, 1978), 89. There is no clue in *WR* as to the identity of this stout man.

35. Hopewell Swamp was just south of Sugarloaf Hill, between Hatfield and Deerfield. Solomon Stoddart in Northampton to Increase Mather in Boston, 15 September 1675, quoted in George M. Bodge, *Soldiers in King Philip's War* (Leominster, MA: p.p, 1896), 127; Leach, *Flintlock and Tomahawk*, 45, 86–87.

36. Bodge, *Soldiers*, 130–31. Dead: Beers, John Chenery, Ephraim Child, Benjamin Crackbone, and William Clough Jr. Served: John Shattuck, Ephraim Beers, Nathaniel Bright, Nathaniel Sanger, John Parkes, John Harrington, Nathaniel Pearce, Benjamin Tainter, and Thomas Hastings, ibid., 133.

37. Shattuck had testified against a Waboquee Indian as a "lewd and abusive" conspirator against the English, responsible for ambushes at Brookfield and Hadley. Daniel Gookin, "Historical Account of the Doings and Sufferings of the Christian Indians in New England . . . 1675, 1676, and 1677," *Archaeologica Americana* 2 (1836): 467. Shattuck had been involved with Mary Davis Jr. in 1666; his incrimination of Jonathan Phillips was allegedly in revenge for "some words spoken" by Phillips. See chapter 10.

38. Drafted: Michael Fleg, William's brother; John and Moses Whitney, a couple of the town's ne'er-do-wells; plus George Dill and William Price, Daniel Warren Sr., John Bigelow Sr., Nathaniel Healey, George Harrington, William Hagar Jr., John Parkhurst, Jacob Bullard, Isaac Learned, Joseph Waite, Nathaniel Sanger, Joseph Smith, Matthew Barsham, John Barnard, and ?John Winter, Nelson, *Waltham*, 62; Mason letter about Tainter: John B. Threlfall, *Twenty-Six Great Migration Colonists* (Madison, Wisc.: p.p., 1993), s.n. Mason; Harrington: MxCC D&O, 3, folio 78, 2 October 1677, petition about wounds.

39. Leach, *Flintlock and Tomahawk*, 210–38; Nelson, *Waltham*, 61; Hubbard, *General History*, 60–61, 72–76; Mather, "Brief History," 115. Mill: Mass Archives, 28 April 1676. Ibid., 19 June 1676, 1 January 1677, has Watertown testimony about the Sudbury fight.

40. There can be little doubt that an outburst in 1676 by Major Daniel Gookin against the insignificant Caleb Grant was exacerbated by the despair that Gookin, the superintendent of the Indians, must have been feeling at his rejection by the electorate and attempts on his life. See chapter 13.

41. *WR*, 123–28; horses from Richard Norcross, John Woodward, John Livermore, Charles Chadwick, and Daniel Andrews, Mass Archives, 2 August 1675. See chapter 10.

42. MxCC DB, 3:194, 2 October 1677; Wompas, alias John White, captured by a hue and cry, was remanded to the Court of Assistants in the altogether sturdier Boston jail, but the outcome of his trial is unknown. He died in England on 5 September 1679. His will was proved at the Prerogative Court of Canterbury and provoked a petition about his land to the General Court in 1684. Mass Archives, 7 May 1684. *WR*, 132.

43. MxCC DB, 3:290; D&O, 4, folio 85. See chapters 9 and 10. Grievance: John Easton, "Relation of the Indian War," in *Narratives of the Indian Wars, 1675–1699*, ed. C. H. Lincoln (New York: Scribners, 1913), 11.

44. *Magnalia Christi Americana* (New York: Russell & Russell, 1967), 2:663; *WR*, 133.

45. *WR*, 106 (weir), 120 (30 October 1674, "To Swagton the Indian for killing a wolf 10/-"), 132 (wolf).

13. "Foreigners" and Community

1. On importance of borders: Ursula Hegi, *Stones from the River* (New York: Scribners, 1995), 180–81. On persistent localism: Flora Thompson, *Larkrise to Candleford* (London: Oxford University Press, 1945), 57.

2. Ravens: Mx Deeds, 1:99, 118. £10.10.0 had been advanced, and any profit was to be shared. On 4 July 1655 arbiters on the amount of "improvement" on a bill of £9.10.0 awarded 14/6d to Ravens. Isaac Walker, a Boston merchant, lent the often impecunious John Spring £50 in 1652 to acquire more land for his sons and his own retirement, Mx Deeds, 1:57. Spring mortgaged his land in Watertown and repaid Walker by 2 August 1655, ibid., 223; ibid., 220, for 25 March 1656 "conditional legacy" to son Henry Spring. On prior Spring borrowing, see chapter 2. Cambridge innkeeper Edmund Angier had to bring suit in 1660 for the relatively insignificant £2.10.0 in wheat, peas, and bills owed by Roger Wellington, MxCC D&O, 1, folio 22; £52 debt: Mx Deeds, 3:48, 15 April 1662. In 1659 Wellington had acquired property from Abraham Williams in Watertown for £100. Mx Deeds, 4:58, 4 April 1659. Thomas Smith of Watertown owed the considerable sum of £16 to Charlestown merchant Richard Russell, who sued for its return in 1664. Thomas's namesake son had married on 19 January 1663, with which the loan may have been connected, MxCC D&O, 2, folio 34; Smith and Sanborn, 426–27. See also Hammond debts to Dedham clothiers, MxCC D&O, 2, folio 34, and Hannah Cross claims on Hammond estate, MxCC DB, 1:282, 287, and chapter 11.

3. Winthrop recorded Crawford's death just off Watertown on 12 August 1634: "About midnight one Crawford (who came this summer) with his brother and servant, having put much goods in a small boat in Charles River over against Richard Brown's house, overset the boat with the weight of some hogshead (as was supposed) so as they were all three drowned, yet one of them could swim well and though the neighbours came running forth instantly upon their cry yet none could be saved." Dunn, 124; *MR*, 1:132. The extreme heat of the summer of 1634 may have explained the night move. Sprague suit: MxCC D&O, 1, folio 26, 18 December 1661. Rebecca's whereabouts before 1655 are unknown. Cf. *WR*, III, 17 July 1672, when Benjamin Bullard of Dedham presented a demand to the Watertown selectmen for "his estate that was his father-in-law [stepfather] Thorpe's land." Bullard was armed with a deed and a bond, as well as kinsmen in Watertown, and the selectmen conceded.

4. MxCC D&O, 2, folio 39; *Suffolk Deeds*, 41; the mortgage is not mentioned in Child's will or inventory (£702) in Mx Wills, 4401; on Goddard's career in Watertown, see chapter 11; *WR*, 141; on kinship: Anderson, 352–53; *TAG* 63 (1988): 17–28; 71 (1996): 149–50; 72 (1997): 53–55.

5. See chapters 4 and 5.

6. Mx Deeds, 2:234, 21 March 1648; the Oldham Farm had been acquired from Thomas Mayhew in 1648 by foreclosure of a mortgage. *WR*, 50. *MR*, 2:70; 4/1:408. MxCC DB, 1:94; MxCC D&O, 1, folio 22. The defendants were Mr. Richard Brown, Widow Mixer, Simon Stone, and Richard Blois, all considerable citizens. Anderson, 588–95. In 1661 Richard Gale paid £100 for the nearer half of the Oldham Farm, valued at £35 in 1659. See also Thomas Fleg Jr., sued for cropping and logging unworked land belonging to a wealthy widow in Ipswich, chapter 11. On similar problems with absentee landlords in Essex County, see Konig, *Law and Society*, 68.

7. His demand was "in the behalf of Ensign Thomas Cakebread, [The selectmen] returned him this answer: that we had with seriousness considered his demand and had also sought the town book [of possessions] and by all we could find in the town book we do not find any ground to answer his demand and therefore left him at his liberty [to sue]." Grout (1619–97) had married Cakebread's heiress, but the miller had moved to Sudbury before farms were granted. MxCC D&O, 2, folio 57; Mx Deeds, 2:175; 4:189. Lotting out of farmland may have continued as late as 1671; see chapter 5.

8. *Suffolk Deeds*, 13, 15, 21, 24, 29, 73; Mx Deeds, 2:383; 3:51; 5:275; 6:465; 7:283. Mass Archives, 7 March 1644. *MR*, 2:60; 3:70. MxCC D&O, 3, folio 74. See chapter 8. The 1662 claim was by the heirs of Edward Howe: Nathaniel Treadway and John Stone, Anderson, 1016. Church retained a sixth part of the mill, which he sold in 1680.

9. Indigenous youth were by no means faultless; see chapters 8 and 10.

10. MxCC D&O, 2, folios 49, 50; *WR*, 67, 80; chapter 7.

11. Drake "had spent this winter in travelling up and down in the woods, sometimes with the Indians and other times lodging in barns and outhouses, also sometimes making fires some thirty miles from any house. His food had been much upon clams and oysters." He traveled "with a white bag at his back . . . last winter he sold linen and a set of silver buttons." He told one townsman that "his name was Thomas Skillikens." Another opined: "I never liked his looks, [and] caught him in contradicting speeches . . . he never lodged in town be the weather never so hard, neither came to meeting." MxCC D&O, 2, folio 51; Mass Archives, 21 October 1670. The value of goods taken was £10; Drake was wearing John Livermore's clothes when he was arrested. William Adams recorded in his diary for 27 October 1670: "I was at Boston and saw a thief and an Indian hanged; the Indian turned off singing," as was their custom when confronting death, 4MHSC 1:10.

12. The Churches were not related. Samuel had been convicted of stealing five yards of broadcloth from Mr. Samuel Saltonstall in 1668; he may also have had an adulterous relationship with Mary Sherman in 1677. MxCC D&O, 2, folio 47; MxCC DB, 3:190. 1680: MxCC D&O, 4, folio 88; MxCC DB, 3:311. Dr. Phillip Read practiced in Concord. A slew is a marshy or reedy pool, *OED*. The goods stolen were valued at £1.12.6, with costs of £1.15.0. On 11 September 1674 a Hannah Winter was convicted of theft and sent to the House of Correction, MxCC D&O, 3, folio 66. No details survive, and it is unclear whether she was a member of the Watertown family.

13. MxCC D&O, 3, folio 74. His father, convicted of drinking offences in 1634, had died when Timothy Jr. was eleven. Hawkins had been one of the youths involved in drinking and "lascivious meeting together" in 1660, again in Cambridge, chapter 10. Hawkins, a carpenter, and his brother-in-law Benjamin Garfield shared an interest in Watertown's fulling mill. Mx Deeds, 4:125. Anderson, 888–89.

14. Kai Erikson, *Wayward Puritans: A Study in the Sociology of Deviance* (New York: Wiley, 1966); Hegi, *Stones from the River*, throughout. Barron: Mx PR, 4:197, 26 October 1676. See chapters 8, 9, and 11, and Appendix A, "Whittaker."

15. E.g., Luxford v. Phillips, MxCC D&O, 2, folio 45, 7 April 1668; Barnard v. Brown, ibid., 1, folios 27, 28, 32, 35, 1661–63; Grant v. Holman, ibid., 2, folio 57, 1671–72; Wellington v. Bridge, ibid., 1, folio 22. Wall: Paige, *Cambridge*, 97. The 1635 bounds were hardly unambiguous: "As they are already from Charles River to Fresh Pond, and from the tree marked . . . on the southeast side of the Pond over the Pond to a white poplar tree on the northeast side of the Pond, and from that tree up into the country northwest by north upon a straight line by a meridian compass." Bond, 987–88.

16. Margaret Spufford, ed., *The World of Rural Dissenters* (Cambridge: Cambridge University Press, 1995), 96–97. Outrage: e.g., David Dunster and maidservant Jane Bowen, Thompson, *Sex in Middlesex*, 38. Mason: MxCC D&O, 3, folio 74, 17 April 1676. Conciliation: e.g., George Phillips letter re John Stowers, Mass Archives, 9 October 1643. Neighbors: Nathaniel Coolidge between Widow Smith of the waterless well and its irresponsible digger, John Knapp, or Daniel Warren and the Stearnses between disgusted creditor White and livid debtor Bemis. See chapters 6, 8, 9, and 11, Appendix A, "White v. Bemis," and Thompson, *Sex in Middlesex*, 186–89.

17. Petitions: e.g., Thomas Chadwick, MxCC D&O, 3, folio 74, 3 April 1677, and William Price, ibid., 29 May 1676. Confessions: Thompson, *Sex in Middlesex*, 55–57. Recompense: see Appendix A, "The Watertown Underworld."

18. Page: MxCC DB, 1:6. Detection: e.g., Loveran and Sawtel, MxCC D&O, 3, folio 70, Appendix A, "Whittaker" and "The Watertown Underworld," Mass Archives, 26 October 1654, test. Grace Wetherall in Appendix A, "Edward Sanders." See also Thompson, "Holy Watchfulness."

19. Libels: MxCC D&O, 3, folio 67, 28 September 1674, John Randall Jr. "obscene libel defaming several persons therein named as particularly Phillip and Elizabeth Shattuck"; MxCC D&O, 1, folio 17, October 1658, letter of Hugh Mason to Lieutenant Thatcher about libel by John Fleming Jr., Nathaniel Lawrence, John Slater, Toomes and Braybrook's son. Cf. Stratton

case in chapter 6. The libels may also have been prurient adolescent devilment. Thompson, *Sex in Middlesex*, chap. 11.

20. Appendix A, "Whittaker"; others: Braybrook, Ball, Knapp, and warning out: chapter 9; Arnold, Biscoe, and Prescott: chapter 6; Benjamin, chapter 10; cf. Appendix A, "Page v. Page."

21. See chapters 9–11. Prices: see Appendix A, "Fleming Executors v. Jones." On the pervasiveness of neighborly cooperation, see Carlo Ginsburg, *The Cheese and the Worms* (London: Routledge, 1980), 37–41; see also Rutman and Rutman, *Small Worlds*, 299.

22. After the 1650s only Hugh Mason, Rev. and Ensign John Shermans, Nathaniel Treadway, and Richard Beers had considerable documented outside contacts or business. Watertown families had links with Groton. A "chapman" was mentioned in 1672. Thomas Waite reeled after Election Day in Boston, 1659. One or two deputies regularly attended the General Court there. Leather and other processed goods, like cider, were cited as being carted to the capital. These were the tenuous recorded links with the "mainland." See chapters 7, 8, and 10.

23. Restraint and silence: e.g., Chenery removal of wood, Hammond attempted avoidance of violence, Appendix A, "Whittaker"; Johnson thefts, above; Summers's sexual predations, chapter 10; months of arbitration, chapter 7; long dissatisfaction with malt, Appendix A, "Fleming Executors v. Jones"; Bemis's disappointed expectations of White, Appendix A, "White v. Bemis"; long suspicion of Fuller sharp practice over Onge land, Mass Archives, 24 October 1679. David Guterson, *Snow Falling on Cedars* (London: Bloomsbury, 1995), 385. See also Thompson, *Larkrise*, 97, 281, 317.

24. Gerald M. Sider, *Culture and Class in Anthropology and History: A Newfoundland Illustration* (Cambridge: Cambridge University Press, 1993), 29, 78–80; Jane Kamensky, *Governing the Tongue* (New York: Oxford University Press, 1997), 22–23, 56; Hegi, *Stones from the River*, 27–29, 71; Rutman and Rutman, *Small Worlds*, 288, 294; cf. Gladys Hasty Carroll, "New England Sees It Through," *Saturday Review of Literature*, 9 November 1935: "Regarding control as the most admirable trait a human being could possess, as the Puritans did . . . "

Conclusion

1. See chapter 4.

2. Membership of voluntary "conventicles," or cells of professors, in England would have been a foreshadowing of exclusivity.

3. Standards of sexual morality, as measured through premarital fornication or bastardy rates, improved markedly between 1630 and 1670, as compared with England's. Thompson, *Sex in Middlesex*, 13.

4. Short of a revolution, it was inconceivable that a senior English magistrate would have to stand in the dock charged by town representatives with exceeding his powers, as happened to John Winthrop in June 1645. Wall, *Massachusetts Bay*, 107–19. On the Essex franchise by 1640, Hunt, 159. See also *MR*, 1:97, 103: in 1633 a Bostonian was punished for saying "in an insolent manner, with his arms on kembow [akimbo], concerning the magistrates, that the best of them was but an attorney."

5. Rev. John Robinson had expressed concern that similarly the Pilgrims were "not furnished with any persons of special eminency among the rest." Bradford, *Of Plimouth Plantation*, 370.

6. David Cressy, *Coming Over: Migration and Communication between England and New England in the Seventeenth Century* (Cambridge: Cambridge University Press, 1987), 98, 217, 220; Adam Fox, "Custom, Memory, and the Authority of Writing," in *Experience of Authority*, ed. Griffiths, Fox, and Hindle, 89–116; see chapters 6 and 10.

7. Bounds: Hunt, 132, 134; reformation: Tyack, "Humbler East Anglians," 86–101.

8. See Appendix A, "The Watertown Underworld," plus chapters 9 and 10.

9. Gossip: see chapters 10 and 13. London: Thompson, "Adolescent Culture," 130–32. Discord: Wrightson and Levine, *Poverty and Piety*, 110; Webster, *Godly Clergy*, 98–99, 116; Walter, *Understanding Popular Violence*, 164. Puritan: chapter 3. Localism: Timothy H. Breen, "Persistent Localism: English Social Change and the Shaping of New World Institutions," *WMQ* 32 (1975): 3–18.

10. Companies: Mass Archives, 27 October 1648. Banning exports: ibid., Mason letter, 7 June 1677. Anglicized environment: Darrett Rutman, *Husbandmen of Plymouth* (Boston: Plymouth Plantation, Beacon: 1967), 34–42.

11. See chapters 6, 8–10. Scott, *English Parish Constable,* throughout. Settlement: MxCC DB, 1:259, 6 October 1663; MxCC D&O, 2, folio 34, 5 April 1664.

12. Mass Archives, 9 May 1662, 8 August 1664, 2 August 1675; *WR,* 18, 25, 28, 39, 80, 123, 126; Hunt, 294–95; Quintrell, "Government of Essex," 231–62.

13. See chapter 11. Thompson, *Sex in Middlesex,* 4–5, 192–93.

14. The old burial ground commemorates these persistent descendants: forty-one original families, whose subsequent generations are buried in the Arlington Street Cemetery. The eighteenth-century records of Watertown's "Western Precinct," which became Waltham in 1738, are dominated by the names of founding families of Watertown. In the 1790 Census forty-three family names in Watertown perpetuate those of our period and forty-four from Waltham. *Heads of Families at the First U.S. Census, 1790* (Baltimore: Genealogical Publishing, 1992), 156, 157. In the 1850 Watertown map based on the survey by S. Dwight Eaton and Elbridge Whitney, thirty-one families who had settled in Watertown by 1650 still held land in the town. List of Arlington Street Cemetery (old burial ground) gravestones kindly supplied by the Watertown Public Works Department; between them, the Coolidge and Stone families have eighty-one headstones there. *Records of the Western Precinct of Watertown, 1720–1738* (Waltham: Aldermanic Board, 1913) contains thirty family names from the first generation of Watertown settlers. MS map in the archives of Watertown Public Library; my thanks to Ann Butler and Forrest Mack.

15. Keith Wrightson, "Politics of the Parish in Early Modern England," in *Experience of Authority,* ed. Griffiths, Fox, and Hindle, 25–27; Jack P. Greene and J. R. Pole, eds., *Colonial British America* (Baltimore: Johns Hopkins University Press, 1984), 14, 95, 216, 371–72; Jon Butler, "Magic, Astrology, and the Early American Religious Heritage," *American Historical Review* 84 (1979): 325; Rutman, *Winthrop's Boston,* 278–79.

16. Privacy: average room listings in inventories: 1650s: 5.0; 1660s: 5.2; 1670s: 5.5; 1680s: 4.7. Sexual misdemeanors: 1649–63: 6 cases; 1664–71: 2; 1672–80: 5, Thompson, *Sex in Middlesex,* 14. Freemanship: 1630s: 115; 1640s: 41; 1650s: 14; 1660s: 16; 1670s: 6, Bond, 1017–18. These figures cannot count women achieving church membership or men members who did not apply for freemanship.

17. Bond, 982–83, 984; *MR,* 5:56; Mass Archives, 27 April 1678. See chapter 8.

18. See chapters 4, 6, and 8. Inventory appraisals are as follows:

1650s.   n = 7, total value £2,177, average value £311
1660s.   20, total £5,205, avg. £260
1670s.   27, total £5,402, avg. £200
1680s.   19, total £3,965, avg. £209.

Other towns: Dedham, Mass Archives, 3 May 1665; Dorchester and Roxbury, *MR,* 2/2:149; Boston and Charlestown, ibid., 4/2:413.

19. See chapters 4 and 10. Cf. Charles Brasch's comments on New Zealand's "drift into a stagnating existence as a dull provincial reflection of the parent society," quoted in Miles Fairbairn, *The Ideal Society and Its Enemies* (Auckland: Auckland University Press, 1989), xiii.

20. See chapters 5, 7, 8, and 10.

21. See chapter 6.

22. See chapter 4. Percentage of estates in various valuations, in hundred-pound categories:

1650s.   n = 7: under £100, 14%; £100–199, 43%; £300–399, 14%; £600 and over, 28%
1660s.   20: under £100, 15%; £100–199, 35%; £200–299, 25%; £300–399, 5%; £400–499, 10%; £600 and over, 10%
1670s.   27: under £100, 33%; £100–199, 26%; £200–299, 22%; £300–399, 4%; £400–499, 7%; £500–599, 4%; £600 and over, 4%
1680s.   19: under £100, 21%; £100–199, 26%; £200–299, 32%; £300–399, 16%; £400–499, 5%

The high percentage of estates under £100 during the 1670s resulted from war deaths among young men.

23. "To the Reader," in Phillips, *A Reply to a Confutation*, sig. A2. Watertown's immunity prompts the question about the overemphasis of an essentially Bostonian antinomian crisis.

24. Marlborough: Mass Archives, 28 May 1674; Groton, Lancaster, see chapters 5 and 10; Hampton: MacAllan, "Custom, Contrast, or Compromise"; Marblehead and Gloucester: Heyrman, *Commerce and Culture*, 30–37; Woburn: Mass Archives, 24 August 1664; Boston: Pope, *Half-Way Covenant*, 159–60; Mason: Mass Archives, 3 September 1677; Newbury: Goodman, "Newbury, MA," 1–16, 91–116, 139–64, 173–85, 237–38; Malden: Thompson, *Sex in Middlesex*, 177–80, 185–86; Martha's Vineyard: Mass Archives, 15 October 1673; Mendham: Mass Archives, 9 June 1671; three-way conflict: see, e.g., Mass Archives, 16 May 1670, 31 May 1671, 1 June 1671, 4 June 1672, 6 June 1672, May 1673 throughout, September 1673, "Report on the Negative Voice." The volume of "Consent Not" votes by magistrates or deputies against proposals from the other house mushroomed.

25. Jean Tappin has enlightened me about similar modern controversies among hill farmers in central Wales. Goodman, "Newbury, MA," 173–80, argues that that town's dispersion lowered the "tight sense of community" by fragmentation.

26. Coontz, *Social Origins*, 78, 86.

27. Powell, chaps. 8, 9; Pope, *Half-Way Covenant*, 160–75; Robert J. Taylor, *Colonial Connecticut: A History* (Millwood: KTO Press, 1979), 113. Accommodation: Goodman, "Newbury, MA," 5–7, contrasts such cooperation with eighteenth-century Enlightenment constitutionalism, checks, and balances.

Appendix A. Case Studies

1. See chapter 7.
2. Sawin was the son of John and Abigail (Munnings) Sawin. His shoemaker father had arrived in Watertown from Boxford, Suffolk, in 1641. The family was poor. The documents in this case are in MxCC D&O, 2, folios 44, 47.
3. Henry Curtis and Henry Rice both lived in Sudbury, so Sawin may have been renting land on John Wincoll's farm near Watertown's line with Sudbury. The 150-acre tract was sold in 1672. The Sawins had had land bought for them by George Munning in 1653, including a farm beyond the Cowpen. T. E. Sawin, *Summary Notes on John Sawin and His Posterity* (P.p., 1866), 3–8; Mx Deeds, 2:357; Bond, 423.
4. Sgt. John Wincoll was probably the son of Thomas Wincoll, who had died after ten years of dotage in 1657, two years after his wife, Beatrice. John had moved about 1662 to Piscataqua and then to Kittery, Maine, where he was appointed a captain. He and his wife, Elizabeth, sold lands in Watertown in 1672. Among the purchasers was Daniel Warren. Bond, 655, 967. Anderson.
5. The docket book for this year has not survived, but triple damages was a common sentence for theft.
6. *MR*, 4/2:373, 384; Mass Archives, 11 May 1668 and 27 August 1668.
7. See chapter 7.
8. This case is discussed more fully in Thompson, *Sex in Middlesex*, 59–60.
9. *Watertown Vital Records*, 24, 25, 26, 28, 31, 35; *WR*, 93, 97, 100, 101, 102, 108, 110, 111, 116; see chapter 9.
10. MxCC D&O, 3, folio 63; MxCC DB, 3:58; *Assistants*, 1:26.
11. For depositions in this and the next paragraph, see MxCC D&O, 3, folio 74.
12. Ibid.
13. *WR*, 130.
14. This complex series of cases is documented in MxCC D&O, 3, folio 76.
15. *Assistants*, 2:108–9.
16. MxCC D&O, 3, folio 77.

17. See Thompson, *Sex in Middlesex*, 144; *WR*, 127, 135; MxCC D&O, 3, folios 77, 78.
18. MxCC D&O, 3, folio 76; Anderson.
19. MxCC D&O, 3, folio 76.
20. MxCC DB, 3:200, 201.
21. *WR*, 128, 5 March 1677; MxCC D&O, 3, folio 80; *WR*, 135.
22. MxCC D&O, 4, folio 82; MxCC DB, 3:238. *WR*, 140, 31 October 1679, records loss of Whittaker's rates because of the family leaving town the previous year.
23. Told in Thompson, *Sex in Middlesex*, 143–44.
24. See chapter 8.
25. The documents for this case are in Mass Archives, 6, 7 April and 24 May 1658.
26. This deposition in Samuel Thatcher's execrable hand is only partially legible.
27. They were usually resorted to only when administrators had to wind up estates in order to share out often urgently needed legacies. See, for instance, "Fleming Executors v. Jones."
28. See chapter 8.
29. The General Court decreed in 1672 that all "book debts" be cleared within three years. Mass Archives, 28 May 1672.
30. The documents in this case are in MxCC D&O, 3, folio 80; 4, folio 84. The hearing of the case was on 17 June 1679, MxCC DB, 3:275.
31. Mass Archives, 27 May 1670. *MR*, 4/2:526.
32. Mass Archives, 14 March 1678. On 5 March 1678 Ephraim had been sentenced to stand on the gallows with a rope round his neck, thirty-nine lashes at the cart-tail (i.e., tied to the back of a cart and drawn through the town), and imprisonment until court fees had been paid. *Assistants*, 1:116.
33. Savage.
34. See chapters 9 and 10.
35. The evidence was filed under the dates given in Mass. Archives. The summons to witnesses was dated 21 October 1654.
36. On both the Parsons and the Sanders families, who were among the poorest in Watertown, see chapter 9.
37. Hosea 4:14: "The men that go aside with whores . . . shall come to ruin." Revelation 21:8: "Fornicators shall go to the lake that burns with fire and brimstone . . . a second death." Leviticus 19:29: "Do not profane your daughter by making her a harlot." The reference to merciful women may allude to the question of whether Ruth had been forced or had consented.
38. The fourteen year-old son of William and Ann Parry.
39. I.e., where there was no specific colony enactment, scriptural law should be followed.
40. *MR*, 3:364; 4/1:212, 1 November 1654. Yet more cruel was the fate of the child, already described in chapter 9. Winthrop described questions of capital punishment arising in court in 1641 over a boy's rape of a seven- or eight-year-old girl. *WJ*, 2:38. He also bewailed the neglect leading to the abuse of two daughters of Mr. John Humphrey by three men. Dunn, 370–74. See also *Assistants*, 3:199, 200, 7 September 1669: Patrick Jennison was found guilty of abusing the body of Grace Roberts, aged less than eight. The capital laws provided only for the rape of a female over ten years of age. On 13 October 1669 the deputies voted that Jennison should be punished with "some grievous punishment." The upper house argued, unsuccessfully, that the sentence should be death. On the same day, however, a bill was introduced that, since "carnal copulation with a woman child of less than ten years [was] more hainous, more inhumane and unnatural and more perilous to the life and wellbeing of a child" than with one over ten, it should henceforward also be a capital crime.
41. See chapter 9.
42. *WR*, 27.
43. Anderson; J. J. Latting, *Genealogical Fragments of the Feake Family* (Chicago: P.p., 1972), 9; Anya Seton, *The Winthrop Woman* (New York: Houghton, Mifflin, 1958), 309, claimed that Feake had a sister, Alice Dixon, living in Germany during the 1630s. The Virginian Cape Feake may have been named after nephew Tobias Feake, who was a trader.

44. *WP,* 3:287–88; Seton, *Winthrop Woman,* 298; chapter 12.
45. Anderson; Latting, *Genealogical Fragments,* 10–13.
46. Anderson, s.n. "Patrick"; *WP,* 5:213–14; Patricia L. Haslam, "Captain Daniel Patrick," *R* 153 (1999): 466–84.
47. Latting, *Genealogical Fragments,* 13–14; Anderson.
48. *WP,* 5:237–39; 6:239; *WR,* 64, 71, 73, 76; Mx PR, 1:89; Wyman, 1:169; MxCC D&O, 2, folio 34, doc. 2287.
49. See chapters 9–11.
50. Anderson, s.n. "Charles Chadwick"; Wyman, 1:135; Thompson, *Sex in Middlesex,* 30, 166; *MR,* 4/2:393–94.
51. Bond, 285; *WR,* 109; MxCC DB, 3:33.
52. Bond, 285–86; Savage; the child's name (John) is never given in the documents. Cf. Lydia Brown, aged fifteen, who preferred her uncle to her stepfather as her guardian in 1678, MxCC DB, 3:220. George Woodward was a soapboiler. His brother John, "reputed to be an atheist until advanced years," had been fined for drunkenness in 1642, aged about twenty-two. *MR,* 2/1:13. Bond.
53. See chapter 10.
54. Coller had been a servant to Thomas Hammond in 1652, when he had taken the Oath of Fidelity. Bond, 163, 743. The depositions are in MxCC D&O, 1, folio 18.
55. John Knapp, a carpenter, was thirty-four in 1657, and still unmarried, unlike his younger brother James and Nicholas Cady, also both carpenters, who were earning good money; see below "Page v. Page." In 1645 John Knapp, aged twenty-one, and Nicholas Cady, about twenty-two, had bought the land granted by Watertown to William Potter, who had moved to New Haven in 1643. *Suffolk Deeds,* 66, 8 December 1645. Cady and John had stood bond for James Knapp when he was charged with adultery in 1656. MxCC DB, 1:97. On 11 March 1656, John Knapp, along with Jonathan Phillips, Joshua Barsham, and Samuel Benjamin, had all been ordered to get masters within a month and give weekly reports of work done to the selectmen. *WR,* 52. The sheep was a wether, or castrated ram.
56. Mx Deeds, 2:14, 30 January 1657.
57. Benjamin was only twenty-one. His father had been addressed as Mr., and his mother, Abigail, was a daughter of a minister. Phillips was twenty-three; he did not marry until 1681, when he was forty-seven.
58. Since Bush seven years before had been ordered by the court to pay Samuel Benjamin ten bushels of Indian corn for some injury, he might reasonably be expected to nurse a grudge. Bond, 733.
59. For "an inordinate course of life and companying with the said Knapp," Samuel Benjamin and John Bush were required to enter £20 bonds for good behavior. Jonathan Phillips was fined 3/- for being "a partaker with John Knapp in killing and eating a pig." MxCC DB, 1:124–25.
60. MxCC DB, 1:122–23; MxCC D&O, 1, folio 18, docs. 989, 1057. Mx Deeds, 2:183, 224. John Bush was in arrears for rent on his orchard. Abigail Benjamin subsequently sold the seized Knapp land to Robert Jennison. Knapp, after masterminding disposal of his father's estate after 1658, also married in 1660. Although he appeared at the county court in 1664, 1666, and 1667, his name is absent from the *Watertown Records* between 1657 and 1670. Samuel Benjamin soon married and headed west to Hartford for a new life. Phillips likewise seemed to quiet down, as far as his appearances in the records are concerned.
61. See chapter 11.
62. *WP,* 2:316; *Suffolk Deeds,* 14, 39; Sanderson, *Waltham,* 7; Anderson. *Cambridge Records,* 1:27.
63. MxCC DB, 1:6; Thompson, *Sex in Middlesex,* 176–77; chapter 10. Her suit was withdrawn, and Phoebe was bound over for six months. Page had to enter bond. It also emerged that Phoebe had sold a "great cleaving kiss" to the sixty-eight-year-old William Knapp for five shillings.

64. MxCC D&O, 2, folio 42. In 1669 he bought twenty-six acres of land from his brother John. Mx Deeds, 6:2; Wyman, 2:119; Bond.

65. Anderson. Watertown's William Page seems unrelated.

66. Bond gives her age as eighty-seven; Anderson estimates it at eighty-three.

67. Documents will be found in MxCC D&O, 3, folios 80, 81.

68. Corroborators: John Biscoe, aged fifty-three, John Bigelow, sixty, and James Knapp, fifty-three.

69. In 1676 Sgt. John Randall was "called by Samuel Page to an argument with John Page Jr. [who] offered him his father's estate if he would give security and take care of his parents and secure him from his engagement."

70. Test. Joseph Bemis.

71. Test. John White (recently Bemis's antagonist, see above, "White v. Bemis").

72. Test. George Lawrence, forty, and Phillip Shattuck, thirty, folio 80.

73. Test. James Knapp, Nicholas Cady, brothers-in-law.

74. Test. Daniel Pearce, thirty-five.

75. George Parkhurst, George Bullard, George Lawrence, Anthony White, and Nathaniel Coolidge.

76. Test. Anthony White, seventy, George Lawrence, fifty, John Parkhurst, thirty-four (a Page lodger), and Isaac Mixter, forty-eight.

77. John Sherman, Thomas Hastings, Henry Bright, and William Bond.

78. MxCC DB, 3:251.

79. See chapter 11.

80. The documents for this case are in MxCC D&O, 4, folio 88. The farm was the northeastern half of the Oldham Farm, sold to Gale by Richard Dummer in 1661. Charles A. Nelson, *Waltham Past and Present* (Cambridge: Ford, 1879), 61, 93.

81. A yard of land was thirty acres. *OED*. On sons as "servants," see chapter 8.

82. 27 September 1677. Bond, 442. On fears of elderly parents about their comfort and maintenance, see chapter 11 and Greven, *Four Generations,* 136–37.

83. At £7 a yard, half the Gale farm would have been worth about £30. John got only a quarter of the family orchard, compared with Abraham's three-quarters.

84. MxCC DB, 3:296.

85. Gale's estate was valued at only £148. A cow was worth £3–5. On Mary Spring Davis and Mary Davis Jr., see chapters 9 and 10. For the incorrigible Ephraim Gale, see chapter 11. He had been returned to Watertown as a vagrant in 1673.

INDEX

accountability, 44–50, 122, 165
Adams, George, 113, 129, 149
adolescents, 46, 76, 77, 96, 112–113, 116–125, 126, 127–128, 136, 137, 138, 158, 159, 166, 169, 171, 190–192, 238–239, 256
adultery, 77, 109, 123, 132, 185, 188
Akers, Priscilla, 129
alarms, 147, 148, 153
Alcock, Dr. John, 110
alehouse, tavern, 29–30, 149, 159, 167, 236
Allen: Benjamin, 123–124; David, xiv; Lewis, 121
Albany, N.Y., 170
almanacs, 76–77
Anderson, Robert, xvi
Andover, Mass., 54
Andrews, William, 17
Antinomian crisis, xiv, 67–68, 80, 171, 172
Appleton, Hannah, 158
Applin: Bathshua, John, 111
apprenticeship, 28, 39, 102–103, 109, 110, 112–113, 119, 166, 167
Arbella fleet (1630), 9, 11, 12, 65, 144
arbitration, conciliation, 46, 156, 160–162, 173, 174
Arlington, Mass., 145
Arnold, Thomas, 11, 18, 71, 79
artisans, craftsmen, 15, 19, 45–46, 52, 67, 92, 98–99, 102, 103–104, 133, 167, 172, 216, 229

Ardway, Abner, 121
Assistants, Court of, 60, 65, 73, 149, 187
astrology, 76–77, 166
Atlantic trade system, 95, 96–97, 136
Ausdah (Niantic Indian), 147

Bacon: Daniel, Mary, 150; Michael, 127
Bailyn, Bernard, xiii, 173
Bairstow, Michael, 19, 44–50, 78, 100, 157, 164
Ball: Elizabeth, 95, 109–110; John, 109–110, 151; Mary, 113, 127, 233
baptism, infant, 70–72, 75, 79, 120, 161, 172
Baptists, 70–72
Barnard: John, 100, 128; Phoebe, 128
Barrington, Joan, Lady, 32
Barron: Elizabeth, 181; Ellis, 78, 128, 137, 160; Ellis Jr., 128; Hannah, 195
Barsham: Nathaniel, 133; William, 119, 133
barter, 100, 149, 161, 169
Bartlett: Hannah, 111; Thomas, 14, 44
bastards, 109, 119, 122–123, 189–190
Beaver Brook, 6, 7, 145, 193
Beaver Plain, 53, 56, 61
Beech, Richard, 110, 113, 119
beef, 97
Beers: Elizabeth, 153; Richard, 19, 44–50, 75, 78, 128 131, 148, 149, 151–152, 170
Belcher, Andrew, 124, 183

259

Belmont, 6
Bemis: Ephraim, 123, 185; Joseph, 184–185; Rebecca, 128, 185
Benjamin: Abigail, 192; John, 132, 164; Samuel, 104, 127–128, 191–192
Bermuda, 43, 58
Beverley, Mass., 151
Bible, 26, 78, 189
Bigelow: James, 90; John, 90–91, 229
Billerica, Mass., 153, 161, 183
birth, 130, 190, 241–242
Biscoe: John, 78, 98, 111, 149, 192; Nathaniel, 43, 60–61, 68–71, 79, 84, 95, 98, 100, 101, 172; Nathaniel Jr., 121
blacksmiths, 98, 229
Bland, John, 148
Block Island, 147
Blois: Edmund, 111, 114, 127, 149; Ruth, 134
Boatson, Sarah, 124
Bond: Henry, xiv, xvi, 169, 207; William, xiv, 44, 137, 196
Book of Martyrs (Foxe), 24
books, 78, 149
borrowing, 99, 100–101, 133, 156–158
Boston, 3, 9, 11, 17, 27, 54, 68, 93, 97, 99, 104, 124, 147, 148, 150, 152, 162, 169, 170, 171, 173, 174
boundaries, 39, 86, 156, 166, 167, 251
Bowen, Jane, 123, 127
Bowman: Nathaniel, 77, 149; Nathaniel Jr., 98
Boxford, Eng., 15, 21, 32
Boxted, Eng., xiii, 15, 20–33, 42, 65, 66, 73, 115
Boylston: Sarah, Thomas, 43, 97, 132, 158
Braintree, Eng., 21, 29, 37
Braybrook: Elizabeth, John, 109, 114
bridge, Watertown (Galen Street), 3, 7, 46, 93–94, 97, 99, 112, 171
Bright: Henry Sr., 14, 110–111, 114, 158; Henry Jr., 14, 44, 78, 98, 122
Brooks, Timothy, 123
Brown: Abraham, 17, 42; Abraham Jr., 118; Capt. Abraham, 99; Jonathon, 100; Lydia, 136; Rev. Edmund, 15, 94; Richard, 17, 41, 42–43, 65–66, 77, 93, 94, 97, 132, 169, 170
Brown House, 5, 99, 101
Browning, Thomas, 103

Bullard, Jacob, 90–91, 158
Bures, Eng., 14, 20, 21
burial ground, Watertown, 5, 134, 253
Bury St. Edmunds, Eng., 14, 15, 18, 29, 115
Busby, Nicholas, 18, 43, 95
Bush, John, 191–192

Cady, Nicholas, 191
Cakebread, Thomas, 57, 68, 92
Calvin, John, 25
Cambridge, Eng., 26, 30, 55, 65, 67, 73, 74
Cambridge, Mass. (Newtown), 3, 5, 6, 7, 14, 41, 51, 53, 56, 59, 65, 71, 76, 77, 85, 93, 97, 102, 115, 121, 124, 125, 128, 159, 160, 162, 170, 172, 173, 178–179, 252
Cambridge Platform, 64, 70, 74, 79, 171
capital, 84, 118, 128, 169
Caribbean Sea (West Indies), 96, 97
carpenters, housewrights, woodworkers, 92, 98, 99, 167, 193
Cartland, Mary, 124, 128
Catholicism, 24–25, 30, 31, 65–66, 171
cattle, 14, 21, 45, 46, 52–53, 54, 56, 58, 59, 83–90, 92, 94, 97, 99, 103, 146, 147, 160, 170, 172, 178–183, 225; dealing, 91; pound, 91, 167
cereals, 83–91, 97, 129, 167, 230
Chadwick: Charles, 44, 78, 100, 157, 183; John, 189
Charles I, 23, 25, 31, 38, 48, 73
Charles II, 45
Charles River, xviii, 3, 5, 6, 8, 9, 41, 46, 88, 92, 93, 99, 120, 144, 164, 170
Charlestown, 5, 1, 93, 99, 137, 152, 162, 169, 170, 173
cheese, 97, 130
Chelmsford, Eng., 21
Chelmsford, Mass., 75
Chenery, Lambert, 136–137, 179
Chester, Leonard, 6
Chester's Brook, 6
Chickataubet, 145, 146
Child: Elizabeth, 130, 134; Ephraim, 15, 43–50, 93, 96, 101, 104, 130, 136, 137, 157, 189; John, 136, 178; Richard, 136
childlessness, 100, 157, 245
children, 58, 76, 80, 102–103, 109, 112–113, 119–125, 130, 133–136, 154, 161, 166, 168, 186–187, 190, 255

Christmas, 166
Church: Caleb, 158, 159; Samuel, 159, 177
Church of England, 25, 65, 66, 165, 169
church, town, 40–42, 64–80, 165, 175; membership, 47–48, 55, 64–71, 78, 114, 124, 126, 127, 160, 165, 166, 169, 175, 221, 252
cider, 97, 110, 124, 134
Civil War, English, 89, 94
Clapp, Roger, 144; landing, 5, 8, 9, 144
Clark: Dr. John, 70–71; William, 41, 43, 132
Clarke, Rev. Thomas, 75
Clary, John, 91, 123–124, 177
Clements: Susan, William, 132
climate, 58, 83–84, 91, 164
Clough, John, 183
Coggeshall, Eng., 21
Colchester, Eng., 1, 17, 18, 21, 23, 24, 25, 27, 31, 32, 33, 65, 70, 73, 107, 115, 167
Coller, John, 190
Colne, River, 21, 27
communion, holy, 28, 30, 66, 73, 160
community, 155, 156–163, 166, 174–175
companies, migrant, 12–19, 56, 64–66, 72, 79, 118
craft, 104, 167
Concord, Mass., 6, 56, 93
Concord, N.H. (Pennycook), 149
confession, 160–161
congregationalism, 65–80, 171
Connecticut Valley, 11, 57, 85, 14, 151–152
constable, 39, 41, 44, 45, 71, 103, 120, 144, 158, 159, 161, 167
consumption, conspicuous, 131–132, 138, 169, 242
contracts, covenants, 112, 134, 135, 136–137, 156–158, 166, 194–195, 196–197; prenuptial, 128–129, 241
Coolidge: John, 5, 15, 134, 156, 182; Mary, 134; Nathaniel, 102, 150
correction, house of, 95, 103, 107–108, 109
Cotton, Rev. John, 55, 73
country pay, in kind, 149
courtship, 127–128
Cowpen Farm, 88
Craddock, Matthew, 43, 91
Crawford: John, Rebecca, 157, 250
credit, 100–101, 133, 135, 136, 149, 156–158, 183–185

Crisp, Zechariah, 122
culture of discipline, 25–26, 28–30, 84, 99, 104, 112–113, 126, 165, 166
Curtis: Ephraim, 61–62, 178; Henry, 97, 158, 177
Cutler, James, 127, 193–195
Cutting: John, 17, 19; Richard, 92

damage, 86–87, 90–91, 160
Danforth, Thomas, 62, 178
Davenport, Rev. John, 50
Davis: Ben, John, Mary, 109, 114; Mary Jr., 112–113, 127
deacons, 39, 43, 46, 48, 87, 120, 124, 161, 167, 235
death, 116, 120, 131, 132, 134–136, 138, 145, 151–153
debt, 23, 32, 38–40, 94–95, 100–101, 136, 156–158, 162, 166, 183–185, 230
declension, 79, 123, 124–125, 138
Dedham, Eng., 15, 20–33, 37, 73, 214; classis, 26, 28–30
Dedham, Mass., 54, 56, 57, 71, 75, 117, 137, 150, 173, 216
deeds, 101, 168, 230–231
Deerfield, Mass., 151–152
Deer Island, Mass., 152
depression, economic, 89, 94–97, 98, 100, 107, 169
deputies, 42, 61, 75, 173
desertion, 132
D'Ewes, Sir Simonds, 15, 17, 23, 84, 94, 145
Dill, George, 158
Diffy, Richard, 14
disease, 83, 87, 100, 110, 111, 114, 119, 143, 145, 146, 148
divine judgment, 77, 119, 126, 154
divine providence, 118, 144, 154
divorce, 132, 138
Dix: Edward, 97, 133; John, 91, 180
Doggett, John, 15, 148
domestic life, 130–132, 167
Dorchester, 11, 144, 170; Company, 83; Plain, 11, 144
dowries, 100, 101, 118, 128, 130, 136, 196–197, 240
Drake, William 159
dress regulations, 45, 46, 96, 119

drinking, 30, 67, 107, 119, 123–124, 132, 144, 149, 154, 158, 159, 167, 236
drowning, 70, 120
Dudley, Thomas, 95
Dummer, Richard, 157–158, 196
Dunster, David, 123, 127
Dutch, 147, 188, 248

East Anglia, 12, 14–19, 20–33, 43–44, 51–56, 84, 89, 90, 138, 167, 172
Eaton, Nathaniel, 121
Eddy, John, 15, 18, 42
education, 23, 28, 38–40, 46, 77, 80, 110, 119–122, 126, 135, 166, 167
Edwardstone, Eng., 21, 32, 145
elder, ruling, 41, 42, 65, 169
Eliot, Rev. John, 148, 149
Elizabeth Tudor, Queen, 24–25
equality, 48–49
"Essay for the Laying out of Towns," 62
Essex, Eng., 12, 14–19, 20–33, 54–56, 64, 77, 84–91, 107, 168
exports, 95, 96–97, 167, 230
Eyre, Simon, 18, 42–43, 178

fair, Watertown, 94, 169
falls, Watertown, 7, 8, 92, 145, 146
family, 126–139, 154, 166; assets, 99, 101–102, 104, 118, 119, 126, 128, 131–136, 138, 165, 169, 170, 193; care, 112, 114–115, 133–134, 136–137, 168, 193–195; crises, 109–110, 132, 134–136, 161, 192–195; size, 54, 74, 112, 137; traits, 137
Fanning, Thomas, 103
farming, mixed, 21, 31, 92, 129, 171
farms, Watertown, 42, 54, 57, 59–60, 61, 62, 88, 95, 158, 165, 169
Feake: Elizabeth, 187–189; Robert, 7, 42–43, 57, 68, 78, 108, 114, 170, 187–189
feasts, 125, 167, 191–192
fencing, 56, 61, 83–91, 146, 160, 172, 178–183; viewers, 85–86, 161
ferry, 93, 152
fertilizer, 83, 90, 91, 92, 227
Filbrick, Thomas, 18
Finch, Daniel, 83
Finchingfield, Eng., 27, 29
fines, 69, 71, 90, 150, 159, 185, 192

fires, firewood, 58, 69, 7, 83, 99, 109, 110, 111, 114, 130, 131, 135, 146, 152–153, 158, 221, 247
Firmin, John, 15, 17, 18, 30, 83
fish, 9, 43, 58, 84, 91, 92, 96, 144–145
Fiske: Ann, 68; David, 18, 92; John, 119
Fleg: Gershom, 91; Mary, 115; Michael, 115; Thomas Jr., 91, 136; William, 151, 152
Fleming: Anne, 100, 131, 135, 183–184; John, 100, 104, 128, 133, 134, 135, 183–184; John Jr., 124, 127, 183–184; Sarah, 128
Folger: John, 148; Peter, 148
folk beliefs, 77–78, 166, 192
Foote: Elizabeth, 157; Joshua, 136
Forced Loan, 23, 31, 49
foreigners, strangers, 156–163, 167
fornication, 118, 122–123, 124, 138, 160, 161, 169, 189–190, 238
Fosdick, Stephen, 69, 137
fostering, 115
Founders' Memorial, xiii, 11, 209
Framlingham, Eng., 18
Francis, Convers, xiv
Freeman: Apphia, Simon, 132
freemen, 47, 53–54, 59–61, 64–71, 75, 79, 165, 169
Fresh Pond, 7, 53, 88, 93, 145, 154
Fuller, Dr. Samuel, 65
funerals, 72, 97, 134
furniture, furnishings, 131–132
furs, fur trade, 96, 118, 143, 145, 146, 147, 149

Gale: Abraham, 196–197; Ephraim, 122; John, 196–197; Richard, 134, 196–197
gambling, 119, 185
Garfield: Joan, 241; Joseph, 62, 158, 196; Sarah, 196
General Court, Massachusetts, 41–42, 47, 55, 56, 57, 59–61, 68, 75, 86, 89, 93, 94, 100, 110, 113, 121, 124, 146, 148, 149, 157–158, 173, 187
generational conflict, 122–125, 133–136, 137, 138, 193–195
George: Ann, 128, 186; John, 129
Gilberd, Nicholas, 103, 121
Giles, Mary, 121

Gloucester, Mass., 173
goats, 56, 85–86
Goddard, William, 110, 136, 157
Godden, Henry, 134
Goldstone, Ann, 128
Gookin, Daniel, 154, 165, 178, 249
gossip, 161, 167, 173
grandparents, grandchildren, 119, 120, 121, 135, 136, 137, 158
Grant: Caleb, 249; Christopher, 60–61, 67, 103, 121, 123, 137, 158, 160, 165; Christopher Jr., 123; John, 128; Joseph, 123; Mary, 123, 127
Great Dividend, 52–53, 57, 62, 88
Great Migration, 11, 12, 94, 108
Great Pond (Waltham), 89
Great Yarmouth, Eng., 18
Greenwich, Conn., 188
Groton, Eng., 21, 27, 32, 166
Groton, Mass., 96, 113, 117–119, 124, 152–153, 159, 161, 166, 173, 195
Grout, John, 158
Gunpowder Plot, 25
guns, 120, 124, 143, 146, 147, 149, 153, 239, 247
Guterson, David, 162–163

Hadleigh, Eng., 21, 33
Hadley, Mass., 151–152, 174
Hagar: Samuel, 190; William, 131, 190
Half-Way Covenant, 45, 68, 75, 79, 80, 120, 173
Halifax, Eng., 12, 70
Hall, Sarah, 185
Hallett, William, 188–189
Hammond: Abigail, 180; Elizabeth, 17; Hannah, 131, 135; John, 97, 100, 179–183; Sarah, 127, 128, 181; Thomas, 48, 131, 133, 135; William, 14, 17, 18, 20, 33, 84, 96, 128, 145, 146, 158
Hampton, N.H., 54, 117
hanging, 77, 152, 159, 187
Harlock, Thomas, 148
Harrington: George, 152; Robert, 46, 102, 152, 184
Harry Indian, 150
Hartford, Conn., 170, 174
Harvard College, University, 3, 5, 73, 74, 112, 121, 124, 162, 170, 237

harvest, 31–32, 57–58, 103, 144, 149–150, 153–154
Harwich, Eng., 20, 2, 24
Hassell: Joseph, 182; Richard, 128
Hastings: Margaret (Cheney), 130; Thomas, 42, 43–50, 122, 130, 182, 183, 189–190; Thomas Jr., 189–190
Hatfield, Mass., 151–152
Hawkins: Timothy Sr., 137; Timothy Jr., 137, 159
hemp, 95, 228
herdsmen, 87–88, 120, 158, 170, 171, 175
Hewes, Joshua, 136
Hiacoomes, 148
hierarchy, 131, 133, 165
Higham, Eng., 21
Hodges, Maud, xiv
hogreeves, 40, 85–86, 91, 158, 161, 181
hogs, 84–87, 97, 146, 147, 158, 180–182, 192
Holden, Justinian Jr., 123–124
Holland, Sarah, 127
Holman: Mary, Winifred, 77, 78
homestall, 51–53, 92
Hooker, Rev. Thomas, 27, 28, 33, 48, 56, 67, 73, 214
Hopewell Swamp, 151
hops, 97
horses, 83–84, 90–91, 97, 147, 153, 158, 168, 177, 226
Hosier, Samuel, 17, 77–78
housing, 130–131, 138, 167, 242. *See also* Brown House
Howe: Edward, 15, 42, 66, 72; Margaret, 134
Howton, Elizabeth, 71
Hubbard, Rev. William, 49, 65
hue and cry, 103, 144, 150, 153, 167
hunger, 57–58, 83–84, 94, 112, 129, 230
hunting, 145–146
husband, 129–130, 138
husbandmen, 23, 54, 158, 171
Hutchinson, Anne, 67–68, 72

illness: mental, 108–109, 111, 115, 151, 188–189, 243; physical, 110, 111, 115, 130, 133–134, 137, 138, 161
Indian corn, maize, 10, 58, 83, 97, 144

inflation, 85, 94, 101, 169, 208, 225
interest, 101, 230
Ipswich, Eng., 17, 20, 22, 26, 27, 32, 107
Ipswich, Mass., 17, 23, 54, 57, 118, 137, 162, 170
Irish, 24
Ives, Martha, 121, 195

Jacobs, Rev. Henry, 65
Jennings, Francis, 145
Jennison: Grace, 77; Robert, 17, 77, 95, 190–192; William, 17, 41, 42–43, 58, 68, 96, 97, 147, 170
Jethro Indian, 149
Johnson: Caleb, 120; Edward, 54, 62, 88, 89, 170, 171; Solomon, 158
Jones: Anna, 183–184; Lewis, 114, 183–184; Margaret, 77; Shubael, 114

Keayne, Robert, 95
Kemball: Henry, 17, 19, 20, 92; Richard, 17, 19, 57
Kendall, Elizabeth, 77
Kennebec River, 118
King, Thomas, 118
King Phillip's War, 112, 125, 138, 150–153, 171
King's Common, 143
kinship, extended family, 11–19, 74, 108, 114–115, 133, 134, 135, 136–137, 157, 168, 174, 175
Kitson, Henry, xiii
Knapp: James, 109,123, 158; John, 104, 123, 128, 158, 190–192; William, 14, 20, 67, 78, 104, 110, 114, 122, 129, 134, 137; William Jr., 112–113, 119
Knowles, Rev. John, 18, 26, 27, 43, 66–74
Kreider, Alan, xiv

labor, 97, 102–103, 122, 138, 143, 149–150, 165–166, 231
Lamb, Thomas, 70
Lancaster, Mass., 70, 96, 109, 117–118, 150–151, 152–153, 161, 172, 173, 236
land in lieu of township, 53, 59–60, 62
landlords, absentee, 157–158
land market, 54–55, 57, 94–95, 101–102, 130, 138, 158, 169, 193

Langham, Eng., 20, 32
Laud, Archbishop William, 18, 25, 30, 31, 33, 38, 50, 64, 66, 67, 73, 212
Lavenham, Eng., 14, 15, 2, 22, 26, 32
Lawrence: George, 119; John, 18; Peleg, 159
leatherworking, 98, 104, 167, 169, 171
lectures, 27, 166
Lexington, 6
libel, 123, 161, 252–252
liberty, 24, 37–50, 113, 217; religious, 60, 68–71
lifespan, 17, 108, 110–111, 121, 133, 138, 168
Lincoln, 6
Lincolnshire, Eng., 14, 55
Lindsey, Eng., 21
Linfield: Elizabeth, Mary, 178–179
Livermore: Hannah, 159; John, 86; John Jr., 159
localism, 162–163, 167, 171
Lockridge, Kenneth, xiv
Lockwood, Edmund, 14, 19
London, 8, 12, 19, 21, 26, 30–31, 33, 55, 60, 64, 70–71, 96, 98, 132, 157, 164, 167, 187
Long Island, N.Y., 96, 128
Long Melford, Eng., 20, 21, 22, 24
Loveran, John, 134

MacPhail, William, xiv
Maddock, Stephen, 103
magistrates, 15, 32–33, 41, 56, 65, 69, 108, 165, 168, 169, 171, 173
Magna Carta, 23
Maidstone, John, 20, 23, 25
Maine, 96, 122, 150
Malden, Mass., 157, 173
Maldon, Eng., 2, 23, 24, 26, 27, 29, 32, 33
malt, 104, 183–184
Manhattan, 96
Manningtree, Eng., 20
Marblehead, Mass., 173
Marlborough, Mass., 151, 173
marriage, 123, 127–130, 133–139, 174, 196–197, 239, 245–246
Martha's Vineyard, 43, 103, 148–149, 173
Mary Tudor, Queen, 24
Mason: Hugh, 42, 43–50, 60, 68–69, 98, 100, 160, 170, 173, 180, 183, 189; Jonathon, Mary, Sarah, 123–124

Massachusett nation, 145
Massachusetts Bay Company, 15, 40–42
Masters, John, 14, 17,42, 66–67
Mather, Rev. Cotton, 66, 72–73, 74, 154, 170
Mattack: Henry, 75, 132, 160; Mary, 132
Mayhew: Rev. Thomas, 148; Thomas, 5, 19, 42–43, 55, 58, 92–93, 95, 101, 148, 164, 170, 173
meadow, 9, 19, 20, 21, 57, 85, 88, 92, 94, 101, 170; Remote, 53, 60, 61–62, 85, 102, 170; Rocky, 102, 171
medicine, 130
Mediterranean Sea, 96
meetinghouse, xviii, 5, 41, 45, 46, 75–76, 80, 93, 112, 148, 166, 170, 172, 174, 175, 224; seating, 76, 170; verger, 38, 111, 120, 174
Meetinghouse Common, Green, 7, 56, 88, 94, 120
Mendham, Mass., 173
merchants, 14, 42–43, 84, 94, 95, 97, 136, 157, 158, 169, 170, 171
merriment, 28–29, 124, 126, 166–167
Metup, Daniel, 113
Middlesex County Court, 46, 90, 108, 168, 171
middling sort, 15, 84, 104
militia, 40, 43, 46, 48, 69, 87, 104, 117, 120, 124, 129, 151–153, 168, 171, 175, 237
mill, water, grist, 6, 57, 68, 84, 92–93, 95, 99, 120, 153, 158, 171, 227; fulling, 22, 96, 171
Milton, Mass., 169
ministry, 25–29, 64–80, 170, 173; salaries, 74–75, 170, 171, 174, 223
missions to Indians, 148–149
Mistley, Eng., 20
"Model of Christian Charity" (Winthrop), 28, 55, 107, 169
money, 94, 98, 100, 184, 243
Morse: Esther, 108, 186; family, 22; Jeremy, 180; John, 153, 190; Joseph, 186
mortgage, 95, 101, 157, 168, 193
Mount Auburn, 3, 7, 9, 51
Mount Bures, Eng., 20, 27
Mount Feake, xviii, 7, 9
Mount Hope, 153

Muddy River, Brookline, 93
Munnings, George, 98, 104
murder, 149, 150, 188
Mystic River, 145

Naaskonit, John, 154
Nantucket, Mass., 149
Narragansett Bay, 145, 152; Fort, 152
Narragansetts, 58, 150
Natick, Mass., 149
Native Americans, 5, 9–10, 85, 93, 102, 103, 122, 143–155, 156, 159, 160, 164, 172, 208
Nayland, Eng., 15, 20, 21, 30, 33, 115
Needham, 6
neighbors, 18, 19, 112, 113, 114–115, 118, 127, 132, 133, 134, 150, 155, 156–163, 166, 169, 172, 174, 175
Neponset River, 145
Nevinson, John, 97
Newfoundland, 97
New Haven, Conn., 74, 96
Newton, 5, 148
Nonantum, Mass., 146, 148, 149
Nonesuch Pond, 7, 62
non-freemen, church members, 59–61, 68–71, 74, 79, 118, 124, 127, 160, 161, 172, 173, 220, 223
Norcross: Jeremiah, 61, 78, 114, 115, 187; Nathaniel, 236; Richard, 121, 129
Norfolk, Eng., 12, 18, 65, 73
Norwich, Eng., 18, 32, 107, 109, 167

old age, 108, 110–111, 121, 122, 130, 133–136, 137, 138, 160, 168, 174, 193–195, 225, 243
Oldham, John, 42, 56, 57, 58, 83, 96, 147, 170; farm, 157–158, 196–197
oligarchy, 37–50, 122, 215
Oliver, Grace, 153
Onge: Jacob, 123–124; Simon, 14
opposition: political, 60–62,131, 172–174; religious, 64–80, 172–174
orchards, 83, 97, 158, 167
ordination, 65–67, 169, 171
orphans, 109, 118, 121, 136–137, 232
Orwell, River, 20
outmigration, 117–119, 124, 166, 172, 174, 193

Page: Faith (Dunster), 193–195; John, 15, 41, 95, 101, 133, 134, 137, 192–195; John Jr., 192–195; Phoebe Jr., 122, 123, 127, 161, 192–195; Phoebe Sr., 133, 192–195; Samuel, 192–195
parents, 123, 124–125, 128, 133–139, 161–162, 168, 169, 192–195
Parish, Thomas, 18
parish government, 28–30, 32, 37–38, 41, 107–108, 113, 167, 213
Parke, Thomas, 118
Parkhurst, Thomas, 96
parliament, 23–24, 31, 49, 71
Parry: Abiah, 128; Obadiah, 135, 187; Samuel, 135; Sarah, 135; William, 128, 131, 135
Parsons: Alice, Hugh, 109–110, 114, 160, 186–187; Ruth, 111, 127, 186–187
paternity suits, 46, 119, 130, 190, 235
patriarchy, 121–125, 130, 138, 154
Patrick, Capt. Daniel, 41, 43, 48, 68, 95, 121, 187–188
Pawtucket nation, 145
Payne: John, 96; William, 18, 43, 57, 96, 158
Pearce: Ann, 78, 134, 135; Anthony, 135; Benjamin, 135; Capt. William, 83; Daniel, 78; Elizabeth, 134, 186; John, 18, 108, 135; Judith, 177
peas, 97, 154
Pelham, William, 14
Pendleton, Brian, 19, 42–43, 55, 57, 77, 96, 170
Pequot War, 58, 147, 247–248
Pequusset, 155; Common, 59, 143
pests, 100
Peters, Rev. Hugh, 73
Petition of Right, 49
petitions, 46, 50, 61, 69, 136, 157–158, 161
Phillips: Elizabeth, 119, 137; Jonathon, 123, 127, 137, 191–192; Rev. George, xiii, 5, 11, 15, 18, 21, 25, 39, 41, 64, 65–74, 84, 97, 128, 134, 137, 169, 171, 172; Samuel, 137
Philpot, Thomas, 108
pigeons, 84, 97
Piscataqua River, 96, 118, 195
plague, 31, 32, 33, 148, 246

Plain Man's Pathway (Dent), 28, 71, 78
Plymouth Plantation, 65, 83, 147
Pond: John, 15, 83; William, 145
Poor Law, Elizabethan, 107–108, 110, 167
population, 8, 22, 28, 39, 57, 68, 76, 84, 116–117, 118, 148, 166, 169, 208, 235
posterity, 63, 116, 119, 126, 136
poverty, 22–23, 28, 32–33, 38–39, 45, 84, 94, 107–115, 118, 122, 132, 135–136, 138, 144, 161, 166, 167, 171, 234
preaching, 26–28, 70, 73
presbytery, 67–68
Prescott, John, 70, 79, 172
Price, William, 108, 119, 154, 179, 182
prices, 94, 150
privacy, 113, 127, 131–132, 137, 169, 243
probate records, wills and inventories, 77–78, 88, 96, 99, 100, 111, 116, 129, 131, 134–135, 136, 138, 162, 168, 170, 171, 174, 193, 196, 226, 253
proprietors, 51–63, 88, 94, 95, 117, 167, 172, 218

Quaboag Indians, 150
Quakers, 71, 167
quality control, 103–104, 167, 183–184

racialism, 143–155, 160
Randall: John, 182; Susanna, 123
rape, 121, 123, 130, 150, 186–187, 255
Ravens, Edmund, 156
Read, Dr. Phillip, 158
religious zeal, 19, 25–31, 64–80, 165, 166, 167
remigration, 83, 94, 172
rent, 22, 32–33, 133, 166
reputation, 123, 127, 129, 161
retailers, 97
Rhode Island, 70–71
Rice, Henry, 177
riots, 32–33, 167
roads, highways, 8, 83, 93, 99, 162, 170, 227; surveyors, 40, 93, 167
Robinson, George, 160, 181
Rogers, Rev. John, 23, 26–29, 32, 65, 68, 74; Thomas, 15
Roxbury, 11, 93, 147, 148, 173
Rutman, Darrett, xv

Sagamore, John, 145, 146
Salem, 11, 17, 18, 68
Salisbury, Eng., 107
salt, 96
Saltonstall: Richard Jr., 14, 57; Robert, 14, 95; Samuel 14; Sir Richard, 5, 11, 12, 14, 17, 19, 24, 41, 53, 57, 66, 71, 73, 84, 131, 146, 157, 172, 209, 219
Sam (son of William Indian), 150
Sambo Negro, 179–180
Sanborn, Melinde, xvi
Sanders: Edward, 78, 110, 113, 114, 119, 186–187; William, 123–124
Satan, 146, 172, 173
Saugus iron works, 96
Sawin: John, 91, 97, 111; Judith, 123
Sawin's Brook, Pond, 5, 9
Sawtell, Ruth, 122, 123, 127
scandal, sexual, 43, 46, 79, 109, 113, 119, 122–123, 129, 135, 161, 166, 169
school, schoolmaster, 38, 39, 40, 46–47, 97, 112, 121, 129, 149, 153, 167, 172, 174
Scituate, Mass., 127
Scots, 103, 160, 231–232
Sears, John, 129
selectmen, 38–50, 71, 87, 89, 95, 110, 111, 112–114, 120, 124, 160, 161, 165
self-sufficiency, economic, 95, 112–113
servants, 14, 58, 84, 102–103, 120, 121, 122, 127, 144, 146, 149, 158, 159, 165, 231
Shattuck: Elizabeth, Phillip, 123, 195; John, 152; William, 86, 123, 154
sheep, 21, 56, 89–90, 190–192, 226
Shepard, Rev. Thomas, 27, 65–66, 72, 73, 170, 172
shepherd, 89–90
Sherman: Bezaleel, 124; Capt. John, 15, 43–50, 60, 61–62, 68, 87, 122, 128, 170; Edmund, 15, 57; family, 22, 29; John Jr., 152; Mary, 74; Rev. John, 27, 64, 73–80, 147, 171; Samuel, 24
Sherman's Pond, 146, 153
Ship Money, 24, 31
ships, 17, 96–97
Shoals, Isles of, 58
slander, 129, 165, 166, 173, 181
slaves, 103, 160, 165
Smith: Ann, 104; Daniel, 123, 127; Dean, xvi; Ephraim, 123–124; Jonathon, 123; Richard, 127, 128; Thomas, 120; Zechariah, 122, 123, 150
soils, 9, 84
Southwark, Eng., 1, 31, 43, 65
speech, dialect, 164, 166
spinning, 109, 115, 130
Sprague, Samuel, 157
Spring: Elizabeth, Henry, Mehitabel, 196–197; family, 114; John, 233, 237
Spufford, Margaret, xv
Squakeag, Northfield, Mass., 151–152
Stamford, Conn., 117–118
Stannard, Mary, 122
stealing, 90, 103, 107, 119, 122, 149, 158–159, 161, 166, 177–178, 191–192
Stearns: Charles, Rebecca, 77, 113, 119; Isaac, 15, 60, 137; Isaac Jr., 136; Samuel, 124, 136, 137, 184
step relatives, 129, 135–136, 137, 190
Stoke-by-Nayland, Eng., 20, 23, 32, 33
Stone, Rev. Samuel, 67; Simon, 15, 18, 19, 20, 30, 44, 103 137
Stony Brook, 7, 93
Stour Valley, 14, 15, 18, 20–33, 65, 79, 156, 164, 166
Stowers, John, 69–70, 79
Strafford, earl of, 30, 50
Stratford, Eng., 2, 21
Stratton: Alice, Samuel, 69, 77, 78, 103, 129, 133; Richard, Susanna, 133
Stubbin, John, 59
Sturgis, Elizabeth, 121
Sudbury, Eng., 20, 21, 22, 27, 29, 31, 33
Sudbury, Mass., 7, 15, 55, 56, 57, 59, 70, 88, 93, 94, 117, 153, 158, 172, 174, 177
Suffolk, Eng., 12, 14–19, 54–56, 64, 77, 94, 107, 156, 164, 168
surveying, land, 50–63, 170, 172
Summers: Henry Jr., 123, 137; Henry Sr., 137
Sussex, Eng., 14, 164
Swansea, Mass., 151
swearing, cursing, 119, 120, 166

Tainter: Joseph, 44–46, 110, 122; Joseph Jr., 152
tanning, 69, 85, 98, 104, 171

taxes, rates, 38–40, 41, 45, 47, 60, 69, 70, 79, 84, 108, 121, 153, 169, 172
Thatcher: Hannah, 131, 183; Samuel, 44, 122, 183 187–189
Thorpe, Henry, 111, 113, 114, 179
timber, 96, 99, 118, 157–158
tithingmen, 77, 120, 154, 161
tobacco, 97, 144
town accounts, 38–40, 44–46, 111, 121, 153, 154
town clerk, 38, 44–45, 216
Towne, Peter, 159
town government, 37–50, 175
town land grants, 45, 51–63, 101, 126, 155, 165, 172, 173, 218
town meeting, 37–50, 57, 86, 89–90, 124–125, 131, 150, 174
town plot, 8, 53, 55, 56, 98
town records, xvi, 44, 47, 52–54, 76, 85, 98, 108, 143–144, 154–155, 173; valuations, 99, 169
Townsend, Martin, 111
Traine: John, Thomas, 150
Treadway, Nathaniel, 18, 44–50, 122, 177
tribalism, puritan, 26
turnips, 97

Underwood: Martin, 95; Thomas, 78

vagrancy, 23, 107–108
violence, 90–91, 103, 108–109, 120, 132, 144, 149–150, 153–154, 158, 159, 174, 178–183, 192
Virginia, 42, 58, 73, 97

Waban, Mass., 146
wages, 94, 102–103, 104, 112, 166
Waldingfield, Great and Little, 21
Walker, Hannah, 123
Wall, Robert, xiv
Waltham, 5, 6, 7, 8
Wampanoag, 148–149
war, 31, 45. *See also* Pequot War; King Phillip's War
Ward: Rev. Nathaniel, 23, 26, 48; Rev. Samuel, 26
warning out, 39, 107, 109, 113, 156, 161, 167, 234

Warren: Daniel, 178, 184; Elizabeth, John, 15, 30, 71, 78, 109; 164
watch, night, 41, 120, 129, 144, 147, 154, 161, 167, 175
water, 88, 98
Waters, Lawrence, 15
Watertown Square, 5, 7
Wayland, 6
Wayte, John, 185, 190
wealth, personal, 48, 55, 99, 104, 130–132, 133, 165–166, 170, 171, 253
weaving, 18, 20, 22–23, 31, 32–33, 85, 89, 95–96, 171, 228
weir, fish, 9, 83, 92, 102, 112, 147, 150, 172
welfare, 38–39, 45, 46, 55, 94, 107–115, 126, 130, 136, 161, 167, 175, 187–189
Wellington: Benjamin, 91; John, 119; Joseph, 158; Roger, 44, 91, 123–124, 156–157
Welsh, 160, 181–182
west country, Eng., 8, 11, 19, 64, 89, 90, 164, 214
Weston, 6, 8
Wetherall, John, 69, 137
Wethersfield, Conn. (New Watertown), 57, 72, 74, 85, 117, 147, 188
Wheeler, G. F. and R. R., xiv
whipping, 41, 71, 107, 149, 167
White: Anthony, 184–185; John, 128, 158, 184–185
Whitney: John, 114; Jonathan, 113; Moses, 123; Thomas Jr., 110, 114
Whitney Hill, xviii, 3, 5, 8
Whittaker: Elizabeth, 178–183; John, 111, 127, 158, 161, 178–183
widows, 100, 109, 115, 128–129, 130, 133, 134–136, 161, 168, 241
wife, 129, 130–132, 138, 144, 241
Wigglesworth, Rev. Michael, 173
Willard: Abigail, 118; Elizabeth, 184–185
Wilson: Rev. John, 27, 65, 79; Robert, 178
Wincoll: John, 177, 183; Thomas, 18, 91
Wine Islands (Malaga, Madeira, Azores, Canaries), 96
winter, 31, 33, 83, 91, 112, 131, 145, 149
Winthrop: Henry, 187; John Jr., 72, 130, 188; John Sr., 14, 15, 18, 22, 26, 27, 32, 33,

41, 48, 55, 60, 63, 68, 69, 72, 73, 74, 78–79, 84, 92, 94, 101, 107, 118, 120, 128, 169
Wissington, Eng., 156
witchcraft, 30, 77–78, 166, 224, 233
Woburn, Mass., 54, 149
wolves, 38–40, 84, 87, 144, 146–147, 148, 154, 190
Wompas, John, 153–154

Woods, John, 120
Woodward: George, 134, 137, 190; James, 14 , 146; Mary, 190; Richard, 11, 92; Susannah, 127, 129, 137, 189–190
Wormingford, Eng., 20
Wren, Bishop Matthew, 18, 26, 32

yeomen, 22, 56
Yorkshire, 8, 12, 19, 44, 56, 64, 164

Roger Thompson retired in 1999 after teaching at Eton College, Newton High School, and the University of East Anglia. He has spent many summers in New England, researching various aspects of the contrasts and continuities between English and New England society and culture in the seventeenth century. He is currently working on a companion volume to *Divided We Stand,* a study of early Cambridge, Massachusetts.

www.ingramcontent.com/pod-product-compliance
Lightning Source LLC
Chambersburg PA
CBHW071242230426
43668CB00011B/1545